Path to Prosperity

Path to Prosperity

Hamilton Project Ideas on Income Security, Education, and Taxes

JASON FURMAN and JASON E. BORDOFF
editors

BROOKINGS INSTITUTION PRESS
Washington, D.C.

Library of Congress Cataloging-in-Publication data
   Path to prosperity : Hamilton project ideas on income security, education, and
taxes / Jason Furman, Jason E. Bordoff, editors.
       p. cm. — (Hamilton project book series)
   Includes bibliographical references and index.
   Summary: "Focuses on three key criteria for fostering broadly shared economic
growth: enhancing economic security, building a highly skilled work force, and
reforming the tax system. Proposals include reforming unemployment insurance,
improving incentives for retirement saving, building quality into each level of education, and simplifying taxation and making it more progressive"—Provided by
publisher.
   ISBN 978-0-8157-3012-5 (cloth : alk. paper) — ISBN 978-0-8157-3013-2
(pbk. : alk. paper)
   1. United States—Economic policy—2001– 2. Taxation—United States. 3.
Education and state—United States. 4. Skilled labor—Government policy—United
States. 5. Economic development—United States. I. Furman, Jason. II. Bordoff,
Jason.
   HC106.83.P38 2008
   330.973—dc22   2008030570

9 8 7 6 5 4 3 2 1

Typeset in Sabon and Frutiger

Composition by Circle Graphics
Columbia, Maryland

Printed by R. R. Donnelley
Harrisonburg, Virginia

Contents

Foreword

The United States of America is at a critical juncture—both because of our unmet long-term challenges and because of the transformational changes taking place in the global economy. From Silicon Valley to the Rust Belt and from Main Street to Wall Street, what we took for granted in the twentieth century is now subject to upheaval in the twenty-first century. Decades of the unrivaled economic dominance of our country have given way to a much more complicated and competitive world.

The challenges we face are increasingly complex and highly consequential, and we are far from where we need to be on most fronts. Too often our political system exhibits understandable reluctance to tackle problems when the solutions to them are hard and impose demands on all of us. Many of the most important issues seem like the electrified third rail of politics.

Greatly contributing to our failure to do what we need to do is the unsatisfying way that economic problems get explained and discussed. There are excellent journalists who provide serious and thoughtful reporting and analysis, but too often public discussion of economics generates more heat than light. The public is terribly underinformed about economic issues. The policy debate is partisan and acrimonious, and problems are too often framed not by evidence but by ideology. Some advocates act as if real human suffering cannot be happening, or if it is, that the marketplace will take care of it all, as long as government gets out of the way. Others would sacrifice everything we know to be objectively true about economics in order to achieve a Panglossian policy result.

The founders of The Hamilton Project—and the contributors to this book—believe that with clear, sound, and proactive thinking, we can find effective approaches to the most pressing problems facing our nation. As explained further in the introductory chapter, the objectives of The Hamilton Project's policy work are threefold: strong and sustained long-term economic growth, wide participation in that growth, and increased economic security for American families and workers. Indeed, we believe each of these reinforces the others rather than being antithetical to them. Furthermore, we believe that markets are the most effective organizing principle for economic activity but that government also has a critical role to play in a successful economy. Based on these principles, we have been working to develop and disseminate an economic strategy and policy ideas consistent with that strategy, all in an effort to inform public policy discussion and formulation.

The origins of The Hamilton Project can be traced back to a congressional hearing on economic issues several years ago. I was sitting next to a well-known conservative economist who said that there was nothing in the academic literature to support the view that budget deficits were economically harmful. I knew that mainstream economists overwhelmingly supported the view that sustained deficits had adverse impacts, and I said so. But I am not an academic economist and could not cite specific research.

After the hearing, I called Peter Orszag, a Ph.D. economist and Brookings Institution scholar who had worked for the National Economic Council and the Council of Economic Advisers during the Clinton administration (and who now serves as director of the Congressional Budget Office). Peter agreed that we needed an objective analysis and fact-based paper laying out the economic evidence on this issue, which he wrote with Bill Gale of Brookings. His paper reached conclusions similar to those of existing research by Bob Cumby at Georgetown University, who was a former official at the U.S. Treasury Department and now serves on The Hamilton Project Advisory Council. But Peter did not stop with the paper. Methodically and with great persistence, he presented the research to journalists, members of Congress and their staffs, and many others who would give the paper salience in the economic policy process. Because it received a great deal of attention and presented the economic evidence in a clear, persuasive, and accessible way, the paper made a real contribution to the public policy debate about budget deficits.

Over the next year or so, Peter and I were engaged in a number of events advocating opposition to a Social Security reform proposal that we felt was fiscally unsound, as well as potentially injurious to retirees. These experiences led Peter and me to begin discussing what it would take to go beyond case-by-case opposition to individual proposals that we viewed as unsound, and instead to set out a serious, systematic strategy to promote growth, broad-based participation in that growth, and increased economic security in our economy. With such a strategy in hand, we could then solicit specific policy proposals, grounded in facts and analysis and evaluated with great academic rigor, that would support that strategy.

We broadened the discussion to include Roger Altman, the former deputy treasury secretary; my successor as treasury secretary, Larry Summers; and Gene Sperling, who was a former director of the White House National Economic Council. We also relied on leaders we knew from the policy, academic, and financial communities for their good judgment and support. And, from the very beginning, Meeghan Prunty, who had been in the White House when I was and later worked with me in New York, was intensely involved both in conceptualizing and in managing the project.

Together, we agreed to proceed with a policy project, and we named this undertaking after Alexander Hamilton, a founding father of our republic who had a vision of a vibrant, dynamic economy and believed that broad opportunity for advancement could drive economic growth. As our nation's first secretary of the treasury, Hamilton advocated federal assumption of the revolutionary debt of the constituent states, which greatly enhanced the credit standing of the new republic in the global credit markets of the day and helped bring the thirteen bickering states together into a single nation. Hamilton also stood for a market-based economy while recognizing the critical role of government in meeting our needs—as he put it, the necessity for "prudent aids and encouragements on the part of government" to enhance and guide market forces.

As visionary and capable as Hamilton was, he would scarcely recognize the global challenges that his country—which he did so much to create—now faces. The U.S. economy is at a critical juncture for the longer term in the context of a transformation in the global economy of historic proportions. That transformation includes profoundly important new technologies; reduced national barriers to trade and investment; a large increase in the range of tradable goods and services; the adoption of effective productivity policies in many emerging market countries; the rise of China and India and other emerging market nations, both as major markets and competitors; intense competition for natural resources and possibly agricultural land; and a massive shift of wealth to the oil-producing countries and to the high-saving countries of Asia.

The United States has great strengths to meet these challenges—our historic embrace of change, our willingness to take risks, our relative openness to trade and immigration, the flexibility of our labor and capital markets, and our sheer size. These strengths create the potential for a bright future. On the other hand, to realize that potential, we must meet highly consequential challenges, and failure to meet those challenges could lead to serious difficulty. Moreover, the imperative for meeting our challenges—with the opportunities great but the risks great as well—is heightened by this transformational change taking place in the global economy. Thus we are truly at a critical juncture. And we are far from the right track on almost all policy fronts for the longer term.

At the same time that our economy is facing growing competitive pressures, workers have experienced increased pressure on wages and job security. During the 1980s middle-income workers' wages fell substantially behind the rate of economic growth. By contrast, the 1990s saw a return to the broadly shared growth that characterized the three decades after World War II. During the 1990s a combination of fiscal discipline, relatively open markets, technological advancement, and public investment in our people contributed greatly to the longest economic expansion in the nation's history and, once the recovery began, to significant wage increases at all income levels and a significant decrease in poverty.

During the current decade, however, median real wages have been stagnant. Moreover, inequality has continued to increase, favoring a very small tier at the top, and job insecurity has risen. The average duration of unemployment is up, as is the likelihood of being reemployed at a lower wage. All these trends are evident in polls of American workers, which consistently show increased economic anxiety.

Under today's conditions the emphasis on widespread income growth and increased economic security must be all the more intense, while recognizing the lesson from the 1990s that the single most important factor in accomplishing these purposes is strong economic growth and tight labor markets. Moreover, the success of the 1990s reminds us of the importance of policy measures designed to contribute not only to growth but also to widespread sharing of growth—for example, more progressive tax policy, long-term investments in science and education, and increased personal saving and retirement security. A critical objective that was not achieved is universal health care coverage, which must be a priority for policymakers concerned with promoting growth and enhancing economic security.

The challenges our country must meet can be broken into several categories. The first is to reestablish sound long-term fiscal conditions, with a multiyear program to reach fiscal balance, while at the same time creating budgetary room for critical public investment. The immediate fiscal deficits are a smaller percentage of the economy than those that drove the deficit reduction program in 1993. But, in other respects, the fiscal dangers today are even more pressing. In part this is because we are now much closer to the time when baby boomer retirements begin and, as a consequence, the major entitlements greatly accelerate their rate of growth. And in part this is because our fiscal imbalances today occur in combination with greatly increased imbalances in other financial areas: a roughly zero personal saving rate, high levels of personal debt, a de minimis national saving rate, and a huge current account deficit partly caused by our fiscal deficits. This combination of financial imbalances is a great threat to our future economic well-being and requires a return to a sound fiscal regime, measures to increase the personal saving rate, and working with other countries to move at a nondisruptive pace to market-based exchange rates.

The second category of challenges is critical shortfalls in the requisites for economic success that markets by their very nature will not meet and that as a consequence can be met only by an effective government. These include quality public education, universal health insurance with effective cost discipline, infrastructure, sound climate and energy policy, robust basic research, help for those dislocated by change, an improved social safety net, measures to equip the poor to enter the economic mainstream, and other factors.

Another category is sound international economic policy, covering trade, immigration, financial crises, global poverty, and other areas. There are other challenges as well of course, such as cost-benefit excesses in our regulatory and litigation regimes, but they have not yet been the subject of focused analysis by The Hamilton Project, so I will not discuss them here.

All of The Hamilton Project's work reflects the view that economic policy issues are inherently complex and uncertain and must be approached on the basis of facts and analysis, not belief and ideology. We also think that much of what needs to be done will be difficult both substantively and politically, and it will require our political system to come together across party lines and across opposing views to find common ground and to make decisions of great political difficulty.

A key strength of The Hamilton Project has been its active advisory committee, which reflects a most unusual gathering of leading policy thinkers, academics from around the country, and highly successful financial experts. One long-experienced participant in the political arena remarked that in all his years he had never seen a process that brought these three groups together in a policy development process the way The Hamilton Project has.

Beyond our advisory council, we have also reached out to leading academics and policy analysts around the country to write many of our policy papers and to participate in events focused on various topics central to achieving our objectives of economic growth, broad-based participation in growth, and enhanced economic security. These discussion papers and events have covered economic topics ranging from education to health care to energy to tax policy to infrastructure. At the outset we made a basic strategic decision to split the Project's efforts fairly evenly between policy development and promulgation of our proposals so that our work would actively contribute to the policy debate. Thus we have held events highlighting our authors' proposals and giving distinguished participants the chance to discuss them, as well as several events responding to pressing current issues, such as the financial market crisis and mortgage policy.

Two years into this project, we felt it was an appropriate time to get the work that has been done under the aegis of The Hamilton Project into book form. In this volume about education, income security, and taxes, as well as in forthcoming Hamilton Project books containing papers we have released on health care and on climate and energy policy, readers can see how the broad economic strategy laid out in the introductory chapter manifests itself in specific policy proposals. All of these policy proposals have been developed by leading academics and policy analysts to address critical policy challenges, and often more than one approach to an issue is put forth. When viewed collectively, these rigorous and evidence-based policy proposals point the way toward a more promising tomorrow of strong and sustained economic growth that benefits all Americans and enhances their economic security.

The Hamilton Project strongly believes that our country can have a bright economic future. The United States has great strengths and a history of great resilience in rising to meet its challenges, from the earliest days of the Republic. And now we must do so once again. We hope that our endeavor can contribute in a small but meaningful way to that end.

ROBERT E. RUBIN
August 2008

Acknowledgments

Over the past several years, many leading policy figures have shared their wisdom, advice, and insights with The Hamilton Project as we developed the economic strategy underlying our work and the specific policy proposals that promote that strategy. Though too many to name, we are grateful to all for their generosity, support, and unwavering insistence on analytical rigor. We are particularly grateful to The Hamilton Project's Advisory Council members, who have sustained and guided our efforts and without whom our policy work would not be possible. The Hamilton Project has been fortunate to attract an exceptionally talented cadre of staff members over the years who have helped bring our policy proposals to fruition, and we thank all of them for their inspired work and dedication to our mission. The Hamilton Project has also benefited enormously from making its home within one of the nation's most respected think tanks, and we are very grateful to the leadership and staff of the Brookings Institution for their continued support and encouragement. Finally, we wish to thank the many leading academics and analysts who shared their innovative ideas for policy reform with us and drew on their vast expertise and empirical research to develop those ideas into Hamilton Project discussion papers and subsequent chapters here.

Path to Prosperity

ROGER C. ALTMAN, JASON E. BORDOFF,
JASON FURMAN, AND ROBERT E. RUBIN

The Hamilton Project has for the past two and a half years put forth an overarching economic strategy, and policy options consistent with that strategy, for promoting strong economic growth, broad-based participation in that growth, and increased economic security. The project's proposals span a wide range of policy areas related to achieving strong economic growth and helping the gains of that prosperity to be more broadly shared—education, health care, income security, science and technology, tax policy, climate change, energy security, workforce training, and poverty reduction, among others. The proposals advanced have come from leading academics, practitioners, and policy analysts from across the nation, taking cutting-edge and evidence-based ideas from economists and others and bringing them to bear on policy debates in a relevant, accessible, and action-able way. Each idea is offered as a potentially innovative step in the right direction to upgrade the country's policies, though they are not collectively a comprehensive "solution" to the nation's challenges. Rather, they are intended to provoke thought and discussion and serve as a portfolio of options from which policymakers may choose. Indeed, at times we have released several different approaches to address the same problem, such as how to achieve universal health coverage (Anderson and Waters 2007; Butler 2008; Emanuel and Fuchs 2007; Gruber 2008).

Americans have long believed that with education and hard work, each generation can do better than the one before and that where one starts in life should not determine where one ends up. This broad-based opportunity for individual advancement has provided an incentive for entrepreneurship, education, and hard work—contributing to the economic growth that the United States has enjoyed. Consistent with this promise, our economic performance should be measured by how well economic growth is raising the living standards of all Americans. While policymakers are fond of reciting John F. Kennedy's famous phrase, a "rising tide lifts all boats," that is not inevitable. It is more an aspiration than an aphorism, and in recent years that aspiration has not been fulfilled (Sperling 2007).

Today, too many Americans are not fully sharing in the nation's prosperity. Between 1947 and 1973, productivity and real median family income both grew by 2.8 percent a year. Since 1973, however, productivity has grown by 1.8 percent a year while real median family income has risen by less than half of that.[1] The disconnect between aggregate economic growth and the income of typical families is accompanied by a large increase in inequality. Since 1979 the share of income going to the top 1 percent has risen by 8 percentage points while the share of income going to the bottom 80 percent has fallen by the same amount. To provide some perspective on the scale of the income shift that has occurred, consider that to fully offset the income shift in 2005 would have required transferring $884 billion from the top 1 percent of households to the bottom 80 percent—the equivalent of nearly $800,000 from every household in the top 1 percent and $10,000 to each household in the bottom 80 percent.[2] No one would suggest this is feasible or even desirable, but it provides a useful benchmark for gauging the magnitude of the public policy interventions that would be necessary to foster broad-based participation in growth.

At the same time that median real wages have stagnated and inequality has gone up, changes in the economy that have brought benefits have also brought new risks and insecurities. Structural changes in the economy have lowered the unemployment rate, but at the same time, the ranks of the long-term unemployed have risen. The increased technological sophistication of

1. Estimates are based on Bureau of Labor Statistics productivity data and U.S. Census Bureau income data.
2. Authors' estimates based on data from the CBO, "Appendix: Detailed Tables for 1979 to 2005" (www.cbo.gov/ftpdocs/88xx/doc8885/Appendix_tables_toc.xls [February 6, 2008]).

medicine has brought longer and healthier lives, but the higher cost has also led to a fraying of the employer-sponsored insurance system. The shift to defined contribution pension plans like 401(k)s gives more workers an opportunity to participate in the growth of the market but has also led to new risks facing workers, particularly the risk that they will fail to enroll in a plan.

In response to the stagnation of incomes and the rise in inequality and insecurity, we need to act now on three fronts. First, our nation must make the right long-term investments to promote economic growth that is both strong and sustainable. Second, it is necessary to put in place economic policies that will better achieve broad-based participation in that growth. Third, for growth to be sustainable, it is necessary to restore sound fiscal policy, moving on a multiyear path to a sustainable fiscal position.

The first part of this introduction elaborates on these two challenges and suggests policy responses to address them. It considers the commonly held view that promoting economic growth, broad-based participation in growth, and economic security may be contradictory policy objectives but finds that these can be mutually reinforcing. It argues that while free markets are the cornerstone of economic growth, there is a necessary role for robust government action to support and supplement market forces and to help share the gains of growth more broadly. The second part provides a more detailed discussion of three issues critically important to achieving growth that is also more broadly based—education, income security, and tax reform—and summarizes the specific policy ideas on these topics that are the subject of this first volume released by The Hamilton Project. The next volume will address health care, with alternative proposals to achieve universal coverage, reduce costs, and improve effectiveness. The third volume will focus on addressing climate change and enhancing energy security.

An Economic Strategy to Achieve More Broadly Shared Growth

Long-Term Economic Growth

Achieving strong economic growth is a key to meeting the economic challenges we face. Increased economic output is necessary if we are to achieve rising living standards and enhance the economic security of American families. Moreover, stronger growth gives us the resources we need to address costly challenges, such as the fiscal challenges associated with an aging population, rising health care costs, and climate change. The importance of growth goes beyond its material dividends. As Harvard economist

Benjamin Friedman argued in his recent book *The Moral Consequences of Economic Growth* (2005), providing for the economic well-being of the vast majority of people encourages social progress outside of strictly economic gains, specifically "greater opportunity, tolerance of diversity, social mobility, commitment to fairness, and dedication to democracy."

Today, America's long-term economic growth is imperiled because we are not making the right long-term investments: a school system that provides students with a world-class education, a health care system that provides all our people with coverage for a sustainable cost, physical and technological infrastructure that can meet the demands of the twenty-first century, support for basic research and innovation, or a national energy policy that mitigates climate change and enhances our national security. To be sure, the economy faces serious short-run challenges from a weakened housing market and credit constraints. But regardless of the immediate challenges and our responses to them, we cannot lose sight of the significant investments we need to make to promote growth going forward.

As we invest in our nation's future, it is critically important that we also restore fiscal responsibility, both to increase economic growth and to make it more sustainable. Large budget deficits are especially problematic given the nation's low private saving rate and large current account deficit (which itself is partly caused by the budget deficit). Over the next ten years, a variety of independent projections suggest the deficit will total more than $5.1 trillion, or approximately 2.8 percent of GDP (Auerbach, Furman, and Gale 2008). Hereafter, as the baby boomers increasingly reach retirement age and claim Social Security and Medicare benefits, government deficits and debt are likely to grow even more sharply.

Mainstream economic analyses of sustained budget deficits underscore the adverse impact of deficits on long-term economic growth (Rubin, Orszag, and Sinai 2004).[3] Under this conventional view, ongoing budget deficits decrease national saving, which reduces domestic investment and increases borrowing from abroad. The external borrowing that helps to finance the budget deficit is reflected in a larger current account deficit. The reduction in domestic investment (which lowers productivity growth) and the increase in the current account deficit (which requires that more of the returns from the domestic capital stock accrue to foreigners) both reduce future national income, with the loss in income steadily growing.

---

3. See also CBO, "The Long-Term Economic Effects of Some Alternative Budget Policies," letter to the Honorable Paul Ryan, Washington, May 19, 2008 (www.cbo.gov/ftpdocs/92xx/doc9216/LongtermBudget_Letter-to-Ryan.pdf).

Under the mainstream view, the costs imposed by sustained deficits tend to build gradually, but in fact they may occur more suddenly than the conventional analysis suggests. Substantial deficits projected far into the future can cause a fundamental shift in market expectations and a related loss of business and consumer confidence both at home and abroad, including a loss of confidence in the economic competence of government. The unfavorable dynamic effects that could ensue are largely, if not entirely, excluded from the conventional analysis of budget deficits. This omission is understandable and appropriate in the context of deficits that are small and temporary; it is increasingly untenable, however, in an environment where deficits are large and permanent. Substantial ongoing deficits may severely and adversely affect expectations and confidence, which in turn can generate a self-reinforcing negative cycle in the fiscal deficit, financial markets, and the real economy.

Broad-Based Participation in Growth

Strong and sustainable growth is a necessary, but not sufficient, condition to increase people's well-being. To date, too many Americans have failed to benefit from our nation's prosperity. This lack of broadly-shared growth is not only inconsistent with the principle that all Americans should have the opportunity to contribute to and benefit from economic growth but also inconsistent with historical experience in this country. As Benjamin Friedman explains:

> Broad-based economic growth in America was not a myth. Nor is it true that the growth Americans enjoyed in the early postwar decades was merely an aberration to which we nonetheless became accustomed. The pace of increase in living standards in those years was little more than what the nation had experienced on average during the previous century and a half. It is instead our own era, dating from the early 1970s, that stands out as exceptional. A rising standard of living for the great majority of our citizens has in fact been the American norm, and it is we, today, who are failing to achieve it (Friedman 2005, pp. 435–36).

Part of the way to promote broader participation in economic growth is to put in place policies that will help prepare people to succeed, for example, by investing in key areas such as education and science. Higher levels of private saving can also better prepare families to avoid economic difficulties because saving and asset accumulation give families a financial cushion when shocks hit.

Another part of the way to achieve broadly shared prosperity is to establish policies that will help people rebound if they do experience economic difficulties by strengthening our social insurance system. For example, universal health insurance would mitigate the risk of financial distress during illness, and wage-loss insurance could be considered in order to soften the blow of job loss for those who are reemployed at a lower wage.

In addition, one direct way to share the gains of growth more broadly is with progressive taxation. Given that progressive taxation is justified by a desire for "equal sacrifice" and by the more fortunate's greater "ability to pay," then to the extent that the share of the nation's income accruing to those at the top increases, their ability to pay should increase as well. Thus rising inequality strengthens the case for progressive taxation.

Economic Growth and Economic Security

Many policymakers and analysts have been trained to believe that the two policy goals discussed above—promoting strong and sustainable economic growth, and securing broad-based participation in that growth—are contradictory objectives. Harvard economist and former chairman of President Reagan's Council of Economic Advisers Martin Feldstein, for example, has said that social insurance programs "have substantial undesirable effects on incentives and therefore on economic performance. Unemployment insurance programs raise unemployment. Retirement pensions induce earlier retirement and depress saving. And health insurance programs increase medical costs" (Feldstein 2005, p. 1).

To be sure, this traditional view offers an important cautionary note, and it is important to be mindful of avoiding what economists call "moral hazard" in the design of public programs. But this traditional view also misses another salient point about the modern economy: while economic growth can clearly increase economic security, economic security can also increase economic growth.

For example, a basic level of security frees people to take the risks—like starting a business, investing in their own education, or trying an unconventional career—that lead to economic growth (Sinn 1995).[4] With inadequate protection against downside risk, people tend to be overcautious, "fearing to venture out into the rapids where real achievement is possible,"

---

4. Empirical evidence also suggests that generous personal bankruptcy laws are associated with higher levels of venture capital; that workers who are highly fearful of losing their jobs invest less in their jobs and job skills than those who are more secure; and that investment in education and job skills is higher when workers have key risk protections. See Armour and Cumming (2004); Osberg (1998); Esteves-Abe, Iverson, and Soskice (1999); Mocetti (2004).

as Robert Shiller of Yale has argued. "Brilliant careers go untried because of the fear of economic setback" (Shiller 2003).

Similarly, if hardship does occur, some degree of assistance can provide the resources to help a family thrive again. Families with access to some form of financial assistance, educational and training opportunities, and basic health care are less likely to be permanently harmed by the temporary setbacks that are an inevitable part of a dynamic economy. For families experiencing short-term difficulties, a safety net can thus be a springboard to a better future.

In addition, increasing economic security is important to help more of America's families and communities share in the benefits of globalization and growth-enhancing policies (Bordoff and Furman 2008). Globalization offers substantial aggregate economic benefits. One study, for example, found a benefit to the U.S. economy of roughly $1 trillion a year (Bradford, Grieco, and Hufbauer 2005). As Nobel Prize–winning economist Paul Samuelson (2005) put it after an academic paper he wrote was misunderstood as supporting protectionism, "Economic history and best economic theory together persuade me that leaving or compromising free trade policies will most likely reduce growth in well being in both the advanced and less productive regions of the world. Protectionism breeds monopoly, crony capitalism, and sloth." Not only is it unwise to turn inward and shut out the forces of globalization, it is also unrealistic given the substantial cross-border connections that already exist. The question is not whether global economic integration will progress rapidly but whether the United States will be part of that process and reap the resulting benefits. Moreover, trade drives economic growth throughout the world, particularly in the developing world, lifting hundreds of millions of people out of poverty (Bhagwati 2007; Dollar and Kraay 2002; Collier 2007).

Despite the aggregate benefits, many workers and communities are hurt by the dislocations and rising income inequality associated with globalization. Many more have lost the confidence that they will be able to succeed in a global economy. Free trade advocates have long argued, correctly, that to increase America's productivity and restore confidence, workers need the tools to succeed through greater investment in education and workforce training. Such policy changes are critically important, but it is increasingly evident that they are inadequate to address the real challenges globalization poses for American families. Globalization is undoubtedly one of the factors responsible for rising inequality and insecurity, together with technological change, which increasingly rewards skilled workers, and institutional changes (Autor, Katz, and Kearney 2008; Levy and Temin

2007; Lawrence 2008). In fact, American workers perceive that globalization is *the* key culprit (Anderson and Gascon 2007). Yale political scientist Kenneth F. Scheve and Dartmouth economist Matthew J. Slaughter, a former member of President Bush's Council of Economic Advisers, recently explained the relationship between income growth and protectionism this way in *Foreign Affairs* (2007): "U.S. policy is becoming more protectionist because the American public is becoming more protectionist, and this shift in attitudes is a result of stagnant or falling incomes. Public support for engagement with the world economy is strongly linked to labor-market performance, and for most workers labor-market performance has been poor."

Supporters of trade must much more forcefully advocate for policy reforms to strengthen the safety net and help make sure that America's prosperity is more broadly shared than has been the case in recent years, both because it is the right thing to do and also because it will have the indirect benefit of helping to sustain support for continued globalization. Universal health insurance, enhanced retirement security, a reformed unemployment insurance system, and possibly wage insurance would all help ease dislocations and cushion income shocks. In addition, more progressive tax policy would be an efficient, immediate, well-targeted, and scalable policy tool to help maximize the number of winners and minimize the number of losers. The American business community may be beginning to recognize, as well, the reality that continued support for trade and globalization, in which business interests have an ever growing stake, is contingent on policies to spread the benefits of global economic integration more broadly.[5]

In short, economic growth will ultimately be stronger and more sustainable if all Americans have the opportunity to contribute to and benefit from it. In political terms, excluding significant parts of the population from the fruits of economic growth also risks a backlash that can threaten prosperity. As former Federal Reserve chairman Alan Greenspan put it, "An increased concentration of income . . . is not the type of thing which a democratic society, a capitalist democratic society can really accept without addressing" (Joint Economic Committee 2005, p. 10).

Effective Government Can Enhance Economic Growth

Markets are the cornerstone of economic growth, but sound public policy and effective government are also critical to a successful economy. Markets themselves cannot function effectively without a government to enforce the

---

5. In fact, a June 2007 bipartisan report commissioned by the Financial Services Forum reached precisely that conclusion (Aldonas, Lawrence, and Slaughter 2007).

rule of law and provide basic regulations. Market forces, while potent, will not by themselves generate adequate investments in education and training. Nor will markets generate sufficient investments in science and infrastructure—such as the type of government-funded "blue sky" research with no immediately apparent commercial viability that led to the Internet's creation—that are crucial to economic growth. Markets also may fail to provide individuals with the tools to manage economic risk, which necessitates social insurance programs like unemployment insurance. Such government programs help individuals to share in our nation's prosperity by better weathering economic storms. Similarly, markets do not sufficiently provide merit goods, like education or health care, which can help people realize the opportunities of a market-based economy.

Given our large fiscal challenges and scarce resources, it is important that government policies be targeted to those most in need and be well-designed, based on evidence and real-world experience about what works. Spending on ineffective programs or in poorly targeted ways not only squanders scarce resources, it also undermines public faith in government efficacy. In some cases, evidence supports larger government investments, such as in early childhood education (Ludwig and Sawhill 2007).[6] In many others, however, government resources can be better targeted than they are today. For example, while college costs have risen sharply, so have the returns on college attendance. Thus it may not be the most effective use of government resources to subsidize the cost of college for the many individuals who will more than recoup their investment. Instead, some have proposed that the government better target its resources to assist those who fall significantly short of those average future earnings by expanding the availability of income-contingent loans (Moss 2007). Although the returns to college education have increased, they are also more varied, so the investment in a college education is a greater risk than it used to be. The use of income-contingent loans allows the government to focus limited resources on those with particularly low incomes in a given year rather than provide less assistance to a larger number of people, for many of whom the investment in higher education pays off handsomely. Similarly, the duplicative and often poorly designed spending and tax programs to subsidize college may be much more effective if they were combined into a single, streamlined program (Dynarski and Scott-Clayton 2007).[7] In the area of climate change, government funds can likewise be better targeted.

6. See also chapter 5 in this volume.
7. See also chapter 8 in this volume.

Indeed, the government could more than double the existing research budget for climate change and energy security just by redirecting funds that are currently used for counterproductive or unnecessary energy programs (Furman and others 2007).

Promoting Broad-Based Growth through Education, Income Security, and Tax Reform

In an effort to advance innovative ideas about how to invest in our nation's future prosperity and to enhance families' economic security, The Hamilton Project has released dozens of discussion papers on a wide variety of topics related to promoting more broad-based growth.

Perhaps the most important topic is health care. In addition to the 47 million uninsured Americans, the typical insured family pays, directly and indirectly, more than one-sixth of its income for health care. And this expensive care is far less effective than it should be. Providing universal, effective, and affordable health insurance is not just a major social objective but also an economic imperative for at least four reasons: first, rapidly rising premiums put a strain on business, wages, and jobs; second, ineffective care results in a less productive workforce; third, the rapid increase in public health spending is a key cause of the serious long-term fiscal challenges we face for Medicare and Medicaid; and fourth, America's patchwork, incomplete system of health insurance is a source of economic insecurity for American families and impedes the flexibility of our economy, for example, through the problem of "job lock" that precludes employees from switching employers for fear of losing their health insurance. The second volume of The Hamilton Project book series will address health care issues specifically, providing alternative approaches for achieving universal coverage along with policy proposals to increase affordability and improve quality.

Addressing climate change and promoting energy security are other critically important issues. Estimates indicate that a doubling of greenhouse gas concentrations would reduce GDP by 1 to 1.5 percent in developed countries, and by much more in agriculture-dependent developing countries. The economy is vulnerable to oil price shocks, which have played a major role in nine of the ten U.S. recessions since World War II. Finally, there are geopolitical concerns with our dependence on oil, which often supports authoritarian governments and contributes to the U.S. military presence in the Middle East.

Our ability to address these challenges in a cost-effective manner will not only determine how much GDP growth is affected by climate policies but also how much individual families are burdened—particularly low-income families, which spend 14 percent of their income on energy (compared to the national average of 3.5 percent).[8] Economists across the political spectrum agree that the most effective policy is the use of a market mechanism to place a price on carbon emissions, which will induce demand reductions and fuel substitution by making energy more expensive. Yet unlike the higher prices we are experiencing today, the increased cost will not accrue to OPEC countries but rather to the U.S. government, which can then return the money to families to offset the bite of higher energy prices. The third volume of The Hamilton Project book series will offer policy proposals to price carbon, through a carbon tax or cap-and-trade system, along with proposals for well-targeted government investments in energy technology and a strategy for engaging the major emitting nations in an international response to climate change.

Health care and energy are just two of many important growth-enhancing investments the nation needs to make in a broad range of areas that The Hamilton Project has addressed to date. This volume, the first in The Hamilton Project book series, lays out the general strategy of the project and contains several such policy reform proposals, written by leading scholars and grounded in real-world evidence about what works, for three other critical areas: improving our educational system, providing greater income security, and reforming and simplifying our tax code.

Building a Highly Skilled Workforce through High-Quality Education

America's extraordinary growth in the twentieth century was underpinned by a huge expansion in education. In 1940 fewer than 25 percent of Americans over twenty-five years of age had a high school diploma; by 2000 more than 80 percent had graduated from high school, and the percentage of Americans over twenty-five with a bachelor's degree rose fivefold during that period (Bauman and Graf 2003, p. 4). The increase in education of the American workforce accounted for nearly one quarter of the total growth in labor productivity from 1915 to 1999 (Goldin and Katz 2001). As one well-known study put it, "Education is both the seed and the flower of economic development" (Harbison and Myers 1965, p. xi.).

In addition, in an era of stagnant median real wages, it is more critical than ever that all Americans have the tools they need to become part of tomorrow's high-skilled workforce and share in our nation's prosperity.

---

8. U.S. Department of Energy, "DOE Provides $96.4 Million to Low-Income Families for Home Weatherization," press release, July 6, 2006 (www.doe.gov/news/3802.htm).

Increasing returns to education are one of the major drivers of increasing inequality (Autor, Katz, and Kearney 2008; Acemoglu 2002). Investing in education can help to offset this rise in inequality. And even workers who do not receive any additional education will benefit indirectly as the reduction in the supply of less-educated workers drives up their wages.

Many education proposals begin with ideas for new investments, and in some cases evidence strongly supports significant new spending, particularly in a child's early years. Helping young children from disadvantaged families get on the right track has the highest potential returns of any education policy. Nobel Prize–winning economist James Heckman observes that "it is a rare public policy initiative that promotes fairness and social justice and at the same time promotes productivity in the economy and in society at large. Investing in disadvantaged young children is such a policy" (Heckman 2006, p. 2). Yet there is relatively little public money for preschool, and fewer than 50 percent of three- and four-year-olds are enrolled in any form of preschool (Census Bureau 2006, p. 16).

In their contribution to this volume, Jens Ludwig and Isabel Sawhill draw on extensive evidence about effective preschool programs to propose one option for expanding preschool and reforming education: a proposal they call Success by Ten. The program is based on the successful Abecedarian project in North Carolina. Compared with a control group, the children who enrolled in Abecedarian—all born to low-income, at-risk women—achieved significantly higher IQ scores (close to the national average), had much lower rates of unemployment as adults, were half as likely to become teen parents, and were 2.5 times more likely to go to college. The total benefits of Abecedarian were estimated to be about twice its costs (Barnett and Masse 2007).

Ludwig and Sawhill's Success by Ten program would give children from low-income families high-quality, full-time education for the first five years of life, and then would use proven effective methods to given them extra help during their elementary school years. Ludwig and Sawhill estimate that, if fully implemented, Success by Ten could increase GDP by up to 0.8 percent, while, on an individual level, bringing the dramatic benefits of Abecedarian—greater employment and college entry, reduced teen pregnancy and crime—to millions of American children.

Even when evidence supports significant new education investments, reform proposals need to be carefully targeted, based on real-world evidence, to address the right sources of the disparities in educational attainment and outcomes. Many education proposals, for example, assume that the skills gap between high- and low-socioeconomic students reflects year-round circumstances and events—whether at school, at home, or in the community. Molly McIntosh and Alan Krueger, by contrast, provide evidence in their chapter that a substantial share of the skills gap between high- and low-socioeconomic students actually emerges during the summer months when school is not in session. They attribute this pattern of summer learning loss to the "faucet theory"—during the school year, the "faucet" of learning is on for all students, while during the summer it remains on only for more advantaged children who continue to participate in some form of educational activity.

Several studies provide evidence that summer school or summer enrichment programs are effective interventions for stanching this summer learning loss. Based on this evidence, McIntosh and Krueger propose Summer Opportunity Scholarships (SOS) so that economically disadvantaged children in kindergarten through fifth grade can participate in a six-week summer school or summer enrichment program of their parents' choosing. As designed by the authors, SOS program providers will be required to use small-group, scientifically based instruction with a strong emphasis on improving basic reading and math skills, which are a particular area of concern for many disadvantaged children. Students and providers participating in SOS will be evaluated annually to assess the program's effectiveness. McIntosh and Krueger propose that financial responsibility for SOS would be shared equally by the federal and state governments, with each responsible for $2 billion a year once SOS is fully phased in. In view of the promising evidence on the effectiveness of summer school, they argue that SOS has the potential to make a lasting contribution toward narrowing the skills gap between advantaged and disadvantaged students.

While evidence suggests that new investments in areas like early education and summer school may have large economic benefits, in many other areas, government resources can be used more effectively and efficiently than they are today. The remaining three chapters on education advance proposals for improving education that use resources more effectively or call for modest new investments.

At the K–12 level, the biggest potential gains will not come from new investments, but from improving the investments we make today. Consider that even the most ambitious proposals for new spending are dwarfed by the roughly $500 billion that federal, state, and local governments already spend annually on K–12 education.[9] Robert Gordon, Thomas Kane, and Douglas Staiger show that the nation can significantly increase student

9. Sources are U.S. Department of Education (2008), tables 26, 28; Office of Management and Budget (2006b).

achievement at relatively little cost by improving the quality of school-teachers. They propose a shift in focus from paper qualifications prior to hiring to teacher performance on the job. Policymakers have traditionally regulated teacher quality by requiring certain credentials for teachers entering the profession. Recent research, though, suggests that such paper qualifications do not help identify effective teachers; people can look good on paper but turn out to be ineffective in the classroom, and those who lack paper qualifications can turn out to be remarkably effective as teachers. Gordon, Kane, and Staiger, for example, studied some 150,000 Los Angeles students in grades three through five from 2000 to 2003 and found no statistically significant achievement differences between students assigned to certified teachers and students assigned to uncertified teachers. They argue that rather than continuing to focus on teacher *credentials*, it would make more sense to increase the focus on teacher *effectiveness* on the job. The result would be that a larger number of teachers would be hired each year, including individuals with and without certification, but a smaller percentage—only those who perform well on the job—would receive tenure.

Higher education is another area in which government resources can be better targeted than they are today. The rising cost of higher education is a concern for American families and policymakers. The average cost of a four-year college degree for a state resident at a public school is about $65,000, with private schools averaging about $130,000 (College Board 2006). Yet while college costs have risen sharply, so have the returns to college attendance; evidence shows that a college degree pays back more than $440,000 in higher wages on average, in present-value terms (Barrow and Rouse 2005; value is deflated to estimated 2007 dollars). For most students college is a good long-term investment. The focus of college affordability policies, therefore, should not be subsidizing the cost of college for the many individuals who will more than recoup their investment. Instead, the key challenge for most families is a liquidity constraint, which government can address by helping students borrow against future earnings. At the same time, rather than redistribute resources to all fortunate enough to attend college, government can better target its resources to assist those who fall significantly short of those average future earnings, which is increasingly likely as the returns to college have grown more varied. This could be done, for example, by expanding the availability of income-contingent loans.

Susan Dynarski and Judith Scott-Clayton argue that another barrier to college attendance is the tremendous complexity and sluggishness of the current system of financial aid, under which students must fill out extremely long, complex forms, only to discover how much aid they are eligible for late in the spring of their senior year. This system creates serious obstacles to college attendance by making it enormously difficult for low- and moderate-income students to assess their eligibility for aid. Dynarski and Scott-Clayton show that the entire financial aid form could be simpli- fied to fit on a postcard and be distributed through schools and the mail so that aid information could be simple, certain, and delivered early. Mean- while, the application process could be as easy as checking a box on the family's regular tax returns. Dynarski and Scott-Clayton estimate that their proposed program would increase enrollment among the grant-eligible population by between 5.6 and 7.4 percentage points. They also estimate that federal student aid would need to rise by roughly $3 billion to pay for this increased college enrollment and for the greater number of aid- eligible students that would apply under the simplified system. In addi- tion, Dynarski and Scott-Clayton recommend increasing federal aid by an additional $2 billion to $3 billion so that no income group would receive less under the new system than it does under the current system.

Postgraduate education is another area where evidence shows that rela- tively low-cost investments can significantly increase the number of stu- dents pursuing higher degrees, particularly in science and engineering, which are critical to developing a high-quality labor force that can prosper in the global information economy. Several studies have found a direct cor- relation between a nation's science and math skills and its rate of economic growth (Barro 2001; Hanushek and Kim 1995). As former Federal Reserve chairman Alan Greenspan explains, "If we are to remain preeminent in transforming knowledge into economic value, the U.S. system of higher education must remain the world's leader in generating scientific and tech- nological breakthroughs and in preparing workers to meet the evolving demands for skilled labor."[10]

A variety of proposals have been put forth to improve science and engi- neering skills, such as dramatic increases in the number and quality of sci- ence and math teachers (Committee on Science, Engineering, and Public Policy 2007; Office of Management and Budget 2006a). Such investments are surely needed, though they involve significant new government resources and would take many years to bear fruit. In chapter 9 Richard Freeman argues that we can increase the number of high-quality U.S. scientists and engineers in the near term at relatively little cost. He proposes increasing

10. Federal Reserve Board, "Remarks by Chairman Alan Greenspan: Structural Change in the New Economy," July 11, 2000 (www.federalreserve.gov/boarddocs/speeches/2000/20000711.htm).

the number of science and engineering graduate students in the United States by increasing both the value and number of National Science Foundation (NSF) graduate research fellowships (GRFs). Freeman builds his proposal on data showing that such an expansion of NSF GRFs can significantly increase the number of students pursuing these fields, with little reduction in the quality of those students. Specifically, he proposes that NSF triple the number of GRFs it awards for science and engineering work, and continue to increase the value of those awards relative to earnings elsewhere in the economy. According to Freeman, tripling the number of NSF awards would roughly restore the ratio of GRFs to undergraduate science and engineering degrees to the ratio in the early 1960s, after the Sputnik challenge. Freeman argues that by making the GRF program more generous, many of the most highly qualified U.S. students will continue on to graduate work in science and engineering rather than pursue other more lucrative fields.

Enhancing Income Security

As the economy has changed, so have the risks facing workers. New institutions and mechanisms are needed to help workers cope with these risks, helping to provide the motivation for them to make the entrepreneurial and potentially risky choices that help drive aggregate economic growth.

The best form of insurance is savings. Higher private saving can also help prepare people before economic difficulties arise by giving them a cushion when income shocks hit. William Gale, Jonathan Gruber, and Peter Orszag argue in their chapter that saving could be significantly increased through relatively simple and budget-neutral changes. They argue that, under the existing approach to 401(k)s and individual retirement accounts (IRAs), busy families who cannot focus adequately on saving decisions wind up not saving, and that tax incentives to save for many middle- and low-income households are weak. In response, they propose, first, that firms be required to automatically enroll their new workers in a traditional defined benefit plan, a 401(k), or an IRA; workers could opt out of the 401(k) or IRA if they chose. Further, they provide for automatic escalation of contributions over time; automatic investment in prudently diversified, low-cost investment vehicles; automatic rollover into a new employer's plan; and automatic annuitization of government matching contributions. (The Pension Protection Act of 2006 permitted firms to offer automatic enrollment and created some incentives for them to do so, but it did not require it nor did it provide for other consumer-friendly defaults related to increases, allocation, or annuitization.)

Second, Gale, Gruber, and Orszag would also replace the existing "upside down" set of tax incentives for retirement saving—incentives that tend to subsidize asset shifting by higher-income households rather than new saving by middle- and lower-income households—with a simple 30 percent match for everyone, thereby strengthening the incentive to save for 80 percent of all households. This approach to asset accumulation has the benefit of not only being budget neutral and continuing to provide people with choice, ownership, and control of their savings but also directs incentives to save where they will have the most "bang for the buck." Current incentives to invest in 401(k)s and IRAs utilize tax deductions for contributions, so that the value of the subsidy depends on the household's tax bracket. A deduction of $1 is worth 35 cents to someone in the 35 percent marginal tax bracket, but only 15 cents to someone in the 15 percent bracket. The current tax deduction for saving, therefore, provides greater benefit to higher income households and, the authors show, largely subsidizes saving that would have occurred anyway rather than encourage new saving. Moreover, fewer than 10 percent of 401(k) participants, and about 5 percent of those eligible to contribute to IRAs, make the maximum contribution allowed by law. Simply increasing the maximum contribution amounts allowed, therefore, would have no effect on the vast majority of families and individuals who currently face no bar against making further contributions.

Although greater saving and education can improve economic security, they are not a panacea. Even those with college degrees still face a three-year job loss rate of about 10 percent (Farber 2005, figure 2). It is therefore critical to also develop effective, market-friendly policies to enhance economic security by helping families cope after economic difficulties arise. Such programs must strike a balance. As noted above, providing too little assistance not only can directly inhibit risk taking and productivity but also can trigger a backlash against policies that are broadly beneficial yet impose concentrated costs on specific firms or industries; at the same time, assistance must be designed to avoid creating harmfully distorting incentives that impair overall growth.

Striking that balance is most critical, and most difficult, for programs that provide crucial insurance but also may have significant incentive effects, such as programs that affect decisions to work and save. An example is the nation's unemployment insurance (UI) system. The innovation, competition, and shifts in business practices that fuel the dynamism of the American economy also create a turbulent labor market with substantial turnover. On an average day in 2005, for example, about 3.7 million people who had lost their jobs through no fault of their own were unemployed and actively looking for work. The current unemployment insurance system helps cushion the shock of job loss and facilitate reemployment by providing limited income support for up to six months to workers who become unemployed through no fault of their own. However, the system has not been significantly updated since it was created seventy years ago, while the labor market has changed dramatically around it.

The authors of two chapters propose the creation of wage insurance and suggest two different approaches to restructuring UI. Jeffrey Kling notes that the current system offers no assistance to workers who become reemployed at a lower wage and face significantly lower lifetime earnings—which happens to about one-third of people who take new jobs after being laid off. Kling proposes a fundamental restructuring of the unemployment insurance system: wage-loss insurance would provide long-term assistance to laid-off workers who are subsequently reemployed at lower salaries; a newly created borrowing mechanism and system of self-funded accounts would assist workers during periods of unemployment. This proposal, Kling argues, would better protect workers against the long-term effects of involuntary unemployment, better target benefits toward those who most need assistance, and encourage reemployment. Kling's budget-neutral reform would provide help to workers coping with the longer-term hardships against which they are least able to protect themselves. If adopted, the new system would cut in half—from 14 percent to 7 percent—the share of laid-off workers who experience very large drops in earnings at their new jobs.

An alternative approach to reforming the unemployment insurance system is described in the chapter by Lori Kletzer and Howard Rosen. Kletzer and Rosen believe that UI should remain focused on providing assistance during short-term periods of unemployment. To make UI more responsive to a labor market that has changed substantially since the program was created in 1935, Kletzer and Rosen propose three broad changes to UI. First, they would establish national standards regarding the level and duration of UI benefits, program eligibility (expanding eligibility to include part-time and seasonal workers and reentrants to the labor force), and program financing (raising the maximum federal taxable wage base). Second, they would allow self-employed workers, and perhaps others, to make a limited amount of tax-favored contributions to newly created personal unemployment accounts. Contributions would be matched by the federal government. Funds could be withdrawn later to cushion severe economic loss or to pay for training or job search. Finally, Kletzer and Rosen propose supplementing UI with a wage-loss insurance program that would offset some of the earnings lost by those who are laid off and then reemployed at lower wages. Together, these changes would cost more than $10 billion a year; financing would come from a combination of payroll taxes and general revenues.

Both papers recognize the need to reform UI and to add a wage insurance component. A significant difference between them, though, is the relative emphasis on long-term protection against reduced wages. Kling believes that this should be the focus of a system to help displaced workers, whereas Kletzer and Rosen hold that short-term income support during the period between termination and reemployment should continue to be the mainstay of a comprehensive unemployment system. In addition, the Kling proposal would be revenue neutral whereas the Kletzer-Rosen proposal would increase funding for UI and related programs.

Creating a Better Tax System

A progressive, simple, and efficient tax system is important not only to raise the funds the government needs to finance investments and priorities but also to help promote productivity growth and broad participation in this growth. In approaching tax reform we should be mindful of several goals. Globalization has posed a twofold challenge to the tax system. Globalization and increased financial sophistication have contributed to rising inequality and thus to the need for a more progressive tax system. At the same time, the process of globalization has strained the ability to tax increasingly mobile capital and business income. These factors, together with policy changes, have made the tax system significantly less progressive over the past several decades. According to estimates by Thomas Piketty and Emanuel Saez (2007), the average federal tax rate—actual taxes paid, including individual, corporate, payroll, and estate taxes, as a share of income—for the top 0.1 percent of households (families making over $1.3 million in 2005) has fallen sharply in the last forty-five years, from 60 percent in 1960 to 34 percent in 2004, while taxes for middle-class families have risen.

More than a third of the reduction in the average tax rate for the top 0.1 percent of households is due to a reduction in estate taxes—and the Piketty-Saez estimates do not include most of the scheduled reduction and eventual repeal of the estate tax enacted as part of the 2001 tax cut. Thus, as Lily Batchelder explains in her chapter in this volume, an important part of the progressive tax system is a robust tax on large bequests and gifts. This tax has several beneficial features: it is highly progressive (affecting less than 1 percent of the population in total); it promotes equality of opportunity by reducing dynastic concentrations of wealth; it may be a relatively efficient way to collect progressive taxes; and it serves as a backstop to the income tax system, bringing back into the system gains that may have escaped taxation for years or decades (Graetz 1983).

Batchelder argues that an inheritance tax would be an even better way to accomplish these goals. She proposes that heirs pay income tax at the usual rates, plus a 15 percentage point surcharge, on any inheritances above a $2.3 million exemption. Batchelder believes that this new system would better reflect a taxpayer's ability to pay, encourage equality of opportunity, and simplify the tax law while raising as much money as the 2009 estate tax. At the same time, the already minuscule number of taxpayers affected by the present estate tax would fall further; indeed, the proposal would reduce the number of heirs burdened by the tax on bequests, from a projected 22,000 in 2009 to 14,000 under her inheritance tax proposal.

Another aspect of the tax code addressed in this volume is the failure of the business income tax system to respond to the challenges of globalization and financialization. The business tax code is enormously complex and unnecessarily inefficient, and often it does not raise the revenue it is meant to raise. The United States has the second-highest statutory corporate tax rate among the thirty countries in the Organization for Economic Cooperation and Development but the fourth-lowest corporate tax revenue as a share of GDP.[11] The sources of this discrepancy include both a wide array of deductions and credits and an increase in sheltering and other opportunities to avoid paying taxes—most notably problems associated with the taxation of international income whereby companies can take deductions on their income as it is earned but defer taxes until the income is repatriated. Moreover, multinational firms can reduce their tax liability by shifting income between their U.S. operations and foreign subsidiaries. For example, if a firm faces a higher corporate income tax rate in the United States than abroad, it can lower the internal (transfer) price that its foreign subsidiary pays to its U.S. operation for goods, services, or intangibles (such as intellectual property).

Kimberly Clausing and Reuven Avi-Yonah provide a dramatic illustration of these problems, pointing out that the top three source countries of overseas profits reported by American multinationals in 2003 were (in descending order) the Netherlands, Ireland, and Bermuda, which together

11. For comparative data on the corporate tax rate, see OECD, "OECD Tax Database" (www.oecd.org/ctp/taxdatabase), table II.1; for data on the corporate tax revenue, see OECD, "Revenue Statistics, 1965–2005," 2006 edition (http://caliban.sourceoecd.org/vl=4034568/cl=17/nw=1/rpsv/~6684/v2006n7/s1/p1l), table 12.

accounted for more than 30 percent of the total. Not coincidentally, these countries have effective corporate tax rates of 5.3 percent, 6.1 percent, and 1.7 percent, respectively, compared with 26.3 percent in the United States. Clausing and Avi-Yonah argue that this allocation of profits reflects tax planning, not genuine economic activity, as evidenced by the fact that none of these three countries is among the top ten locations of U.S. multinational jobs.

In response, Clausing and Avi-Yonah propose an alternative reform to the international tax system known as formulary apportionment, whereby U.S. firms would be taxed on a percentage of their worldwide profits equal to the U.S. share of their total sales. Clausing and Avi-Yonah argue that this reform, which is similar to the way U.S. states tax the income of companies operating across several states, would simplify international taxation while eliminating the opportunity for transfer pricing schemes and other international tax abuses because taxes would be based on market prices and would not require imputing prices on intrafirm transactions. They estimate that their proposal could capture significant additional corporate tax revenue or, alternatively, could allow a sizable reduction in the corporate tax rate. Adopting formulary apportionment unilaterally might be difficult, if not impossible, but Clausing and Avi-Yonah argue that the United States could help prod other countries into taking this step as well.

A third shortcoming of the tax system addressed is the complexity of our present tax system, which is a perennial lament of reformers. Examples abound: in 1940 instructions to the Form 1040 were about 4 pages long; today the instruction booklet fills more than 100 pages, and the form itself is accompanied by more than ten schedules and twenty worksheets (Graetz 2007). Proponents of the recent series of tax cuts justified them, in part, as tax simplification, but according to the IRS it took thirty-four minutes longer to complete Form 1040 in 2004 than in 2000. In total, Americans spend 3.5 billion hours doing their taxes, the equivalent of hiring almost 2 million new IRS employees. Compliance costs $140 billion annually, and about 60 percent of household filers hire a paid preparer rather than try to do it themselves.[12]

Austan Goolsbee proposes simplifying our tax code by offering return-free filing to the nearly 40 percent of tax filers who have relatively simple tax situations. Under Goolsbee's proposed "Simple Return" program, the

12. President's Advisory Panel on Federal Tax Reform, "Simple, Fair, and Pro-Growth: Proposals to Fix America's Tax System," November 2005 (www.taxreformpanel.gov/final-report).

IRS would use information that it already receives from employers and financial institutions to send prefilled tax returns to tax filers with sufficiently simple finances. The program would be voluntary: those who prefer to fill out their own tax forms, or to pay a tax preparer to do it, could just throw the Simple Return away and file their taxes the way they do now. Goolsbee estimates that a return-free filing system would save tax filers up to 225 million hours of tax compliance time and more than $2 billion in tax preparation fees each year. Return-free filing is already used extensively in some European countries and proved popular in a recent California pilot project, where a survey found that 99 percent of participants wanted to continue using the program.

In addition to the loss of progressivity, erosion of the business income tax, and increased complexity, there are numerous other areas in need of reform. For example, our tax system needs to do a better job of raising the money government needs to pay for the level of spending it has chosen to undertake, lest we borrow the money and merely defer the taxes to future generations to pay. Our tax system also needs to do a better job of actually collecting the taxes that are owed and closing the roughly $300 billion "tax gap" between what taxpayers should have paid and what they actually paid each year. Needed steps to close the tax gap include improved service, enhanced enforcement, improved reporting, and simplification. Finally, our system of subsidizing certain socially desirable activities, such as saving and home ownership, through the tax code should be made more effective, equitable, and efficient, for example, by shifting from the use of tax deductions to the use of refundable tax credits (Batchelder, Goldberg, and Orszag 2006). Though much more can be done to improve our tax system, at a minimum the shortcomings addressed by the three proposals in this volume should be considered as part of any major tax reform effort.

Conclusion

Today we are in danger of breaking the quintessential American promise of upward mobility for the next generation, thereby threatening not only America's character but also our future economic progress—at a time when the United States faces growing challenges to its continued economic progress, including rising inequality, the failure to make critical investments, and an unsustainable and economically damaging long-term fiscal position. To meet these challenges, the nation must be willing to make necessary investments now to reap benefits later, and to adopt more robust policies to share the gains of our prosperity more broadly and enhance the economic security of American families. Consistent with The Hamilton Project's commitment to identify smart, pragmatic policy options, grounded in real-world experience and evidence, this first volume offers innovative ideas from leading economic thinkers in three critical areas—education, income security, and tax policy—to create the conditions for continued opportunity, prosperity, and strong, broad-based economic growth. Future volumes will address other critical economic challenges, including the need to achieve universal health insurance coverage while improving the effectiveness of health care, and the importance of addressing climate change and promoting energy security.

References

Acemoglu, Daron. 2002. "Technical Change, Inequality and the Labor Market." *Journal of Economic Literature* 40, no. 4: 7–72.

Aldonas, Grant D., Robert Z. Lawrence, and Matthew J. Slaughter. 2007. "Succeeding in the New Economy: A New Policy Agenda for the American Worker." Policy research report. Washington: Financial Services Forum (June 26).

Anderson, Gerard F., and Hugh R. Waters. 2007. "Achieving Universal Coverage through Medicare Part E(veryone)." Hamilton Project Discussion Paper 2007-10. Brookings (July).

Anderson, Richard G., and Charles S. Gascon. 2007. "The Perils of Globalization: Offshoring and Economic Insecurity of the American Worker." Working Paper 007-004A (Federal Reserve Bank of St. Louis).

Armour, John, and Douglas Cumming. 2004. "The Legal Road to Replicating Silicon Valley." Working Paper 281. Center for Business Research, University of Cambridge.

Auerbach, Alan J., Jason Furman, and William G. Gale. 2008 (forthcoming). "Facing the Music: The Fiscal Outlook at the End of the Bush Administration." *Tax Notes.*

Autor, David H., Lawrence F. Katz, and Melissa S. Kearney. 2008. "Trends in U.S. Wage Inequality: Revising the Revisionists." *Review of Economics and Statistics* 90, no. 2: 300–23.

Barnett, W. Steven, and Leonard N. Masse. 2007. "Comparative Benefit-Cost Analysis of the Abecedarian Program and Its Policy Implications." *Economics of Education Review* 26, no. 1: 113–25.

Barro, Robert J. 2001. "Education and Economic Growth." In *The Contribution of Human and Social Capital to Sustained Economic Growth and Well-Being,* edited by John F. Helliwell. Paris: Organization for Economic Cooperation and Development.

Barrow, Lisa, and Cecilia E. Rouse. 2005. "Does College Still Pay?" *Economists' Voice* 2, no. 4: 5–6.

Batchelder, Lily L., Fred T. Goldberg Jr., and Peter R. Orszag. 2006. "Efficiency and Tax Incentives: The Case for Refundable Tax Credits." *Stanford Law Review* 59, no. 1: 23–76.

Bauman, Kurt J., and Nikki L. Graf. 2003. "Educational Attainment: 2000." Census 2000 Brief. U.S. Census Bureau (August).

Bhagwati, Jagdish. 2007. *In Defense of Globalization.* 2nd ed. Oxford University Press.

Bordoff, Jason, and Jason Furman. 2008. "Progressive Tax Reform in the Era of Globalization." *Harvard Law and Policy Review* 2, no. 2: 327–60.

Bradford, Scott C., Paul L. E. Grieco, and Gary Clyde Hufbauer. 2005. "The Payoff to America from Global Integration." In *The United States and the World Economy: Foreign Economic Policy for the Next Decade,* edited by C. Fred Bergsten, pp. 65–110. Washington: Peterson Institute for International Economics.

College Board. 2006. *Trends in College Pricing.* Washington.

Collier, Paul. 2007. *The Bottom Billion: Why the Poorest Countries Are Failing and What Can Be Done about It.* New York: Oxford University Press.

Committee on Science, Engineering, and Public Policy. 2007. *Rising above the Gathering Storm: Energizing and Employing America for a Brighter Economic Future.* Washington: National Academies Press.

Dollar, David, and Aart Kraay. 2002. "Growth Is Good for the Poor." *Journal of Economic Growth* 7, no. 3: 195–225.

Dynarski, Susan M., and Judith E. Scott-Clayton. 2007. "College Grants on a Postcard: A Proposal for Simple and Predictable Federal Student Aid." Hamilton Project Discussion Paper 2007-01. Brookings (February).

Emanuel, Ezekiel J., and Victor R. Fuchs. 2007. "A Comprehensive Cure: Universal Health Care Vouchers." Hamilton Project Discussion Paper 2007-11. Brookings (July).

Esteves-Abe, Margarita, Torben Iverson, and David Soskice. 1999. "Social Protection and the Formation of Skills: A Reinterpretation of the Welfare State." Paper prepared for the Ninety-Fifth American Political Science Association Meeting, Atlanta, September 2–5.

Farber, Henry S. 2005. "What Do We Know about Job Loss in the United States? Evidence from the Displaced Workers Survey, 1984–2004." Working Paper 498. Princeton University, Industrial Relations Section.

Feldstein, Martin. 2005. "Rethinking Social Insurance." *American Economic Review* 95, no. 1: 1–24.

Friedman, Benjamin M. 2005. *The Moral Consequences of Economic Growth.* New York: Knopf.

Furman, Jason, Lawrence H. Summers, and Jason Bordoff. 2007. "Achieving Progressive Tax Reform in an Increasingly Global Economy." Hamilton Project Strategy Paper. Brookings (June).

Furman, Jason and others. 2007. "An Economic Strategy to Address Climate Change and Promote Energy Security." Hamilton Project Strategy Paper. Brookings (October).

Goldin, Claudia, and Lawrence F. Katz. 2001. "The Legacy of U.S. Educational Leadership: Notes on Distribution and Economic Growth in the Twentieth Century." *American Economic Review* 91, no. 2: 18–23.

Graetz, Michael. 1983. "To Praise the Estate Tax, Not to Bury It." *Yale Law Journal* 93, no. 2: 259–86.

————. 2007. "Tax Reform Unraveling." *Journal of Economic Perspectives* 21, no. 1: 69–90.

Gruber, Jonathan. 2008 (forthcoming). "Taking Massachusetts National: Incremental Universalism for the United States." In *Who's Got the Cure?* edited by Jason Furman. Hamilton Project, Brookings.

Hanushek, Eric A., and Dongwook Kim. 1995. "Schooling, Labor Force Quality, and Economic Growth." Working Paper 5399. Cambridge, Mass.: National Bureau of Economic Research (December).

Harbison, Frederick, and Charles Myers, eds. 1965. *Manpower and Education.* New York: McGraw-Hill.

Heckman, James J. 2006. "Investing in Disadvantaged Young Children Is an Economically Efficient Policy." Paper presented at the Committee for Economic Development forum, "Building the Economic Case for Investments in Preschool," New York, January 10.

Joint Economic Committee. 2005. *The Economic Outlook.* Hearings before the Joint Economic Committee. 109 Cong. 1 sess. Government Printing Office (June 9).

Lawrence, Robert Z. 2008. *Blue-Collar Blues: Is Trade to Blame for Rising U.S. Income Inequality?* Washington: Peterson Institute for International Economics.

Levy, Frank, and Peter Temin. 2007. "Inequality and Institutions in 20th Century America." Working Paper 07-17. Department of Economics, Massachusetts Institute of Technology.

Ludwig, Jens, and Isabel Sawhill. 2007. "Success by Ten: Intervening Early, Often, and Effectively in the Education of Young Children." Hamilton Project Discussion Paper 2007-02. Brookings (February).

Mocetti, Sauro. 2004. "Social Protection and Human Capital: Test of a Hypothesis." Working Paper 425. Department of Economics, University of Siena.

Moss, David A. 2007. "College Access for All: Promoting Investment in Education through Income-Contingent Lending." Paper prepared for the Tobin Project Risk Policy Working Group, Cambridge, Mass., May 6.

Office of Management and Budget. 2006a. *American Competitiveness Initiative: Leading the World in Innovation* (February).

————. 2006b. "Department of Education." In *Budget of the United States Government, Fiscal Year 2007* (www.whitehouse.gov/omb/budget/fy2007/education. html [June 2008]).

Osberg, Lars. 1998. "Economic Insecurity." Discussion Paper 88. Social Policy Research Center, University of New South Wales.

Piketty, Thomas, and Emanuel Saez. 2007. "How Progressive Is the U.S. Federal Tax System? A Historical and International Perspective." *Journal of Economic Perspectives* 21, no. 1: 3–24.

Rubin, Robert E., Peter R. Orszag, and Allen Sinai. 2004. "Sustained Budget Deficits: Longer-Run U.S. Economic Performance and the Risk of Financial and Fiscal Disarray." Paper prepared for "National Economic and Financial Policies for Growth and Stability," Andrew Brimmer Policy Forum, Allied Social Sciences Associations Annual Meeting, San Diego, January 4.

Samuelson, Paul A. 2005. "Response from Paul A. Samuelson." *Journal of Economic Perspectives* 19, no. 3: 241–245.

Scheve, Kenneth F., and Matthew J. Slaughter. 2007. "A New Deal for Globaliza-
    tion." *Foreign Affairs* 86, no. 4: 34–47.
Shiller, Robert. 2003. *The New Financial Order: Risk in the 21st Century.* Princeton
    University Press.
Sinn, Hans-Werner. 1995. "Social Insurance, Incentives, and Risk Taking." Working
    Paper 5335. Cambridge, Mass.: National Bureau of Economic Research.
Sperling, Gene. 2007. "Rising Tide Economics." *Democracy: A Journal of Ideas*
    61, no. 6: 61–73.
U.S. Census Bureau. 2006. "Nursery and Primary School Enrollment of People 3 to
    6 Years Old, by Age, Mother's Labor Force Status and Education, Family
    Income, Race, and Hispanic Origin: October 2005." In *Current Population Sur-
    vey 2005,* table 03-01.
U.S. Department of Education. National Center for Education Statistics. 2008.
    Digest of Education Statistics 2007.

Enhancing Economic Security

Fundamental Restructuring of Unemployment Insurance

Wage-Loss Insurance and Temporary Earnings Replacement Accounts

2

JEFFREY R. KLING

The churning U.S. labor market both creates and destroys jobs as part of a vibrant process through which the economy responds to inventions, changes in production technology, global and domestic competition, and shifts of consumer demand. Employers created 57 million jobs during 2005, and 54 million jobs ended. Of the jobs that ended, 37 percent— 20 million—were involuntary job losses initiated by the employer.[1] On an average day in 2005, 3.7 million people who had involuntarily lost their jobs were actively seeking work, including 2 million who were permanently displaced due to plant closings or adverse business conditions.[2]

Permanent layoffs often cause both immediate income loss and lower wages when the worker is reemployed elsewhere. During the first six months after permanent involuntary displacement from a job, workers

Comments from Silvia Barcellos, Jared Bernstein, Jason Bordoff, Leandro Carvalho, Stephen Coate, Michael Deich, Douglas Elliot, Douglas Elmendorf, Chris Farrell, Kenneth Fortson, Robert Gordon, Jonathan Gruber, Kara Kling, Philip Levine, Jeffrey Liebman, Robert Litan, Erzo Luttmer, Bruce Meyer, James Mitchell, Peter Orszag, Meeghan Prunty-Edelstein, Ellen Seidman, and Timothy Taylor are gratefully acknowledged.

1. U.S. Department of Labor, "Job Openings and Labor Turnover Survey" (http://data.bls.gov/PDQ/outside.jsp?survey=jt).

2. U.S. Department of Labor, "Unemployed Persons by Reason for Unemployment, Sex, and Age" (www.bls.gov/cps/cpsaat27.pdf).

were out of work for an average of fifteen weeks. In those weeks, they lost an average of $11,400 they would have earned at their previous jobs. After returning to work, many had substantially lower wages a year and a half after displacement. One-fourth of these workers had wages that were at least 25 percent lower than on their previous job. For workers with longer tenure, the losses were larger. Among workers with at least three years of tenure on their previous job, one-third had wage losses of 25 percent or more.[3] The average earnings losses five years after job loss among workers with six or more years of tenure have been estimated at 25 percent (Jacobson, LaLonde, and Sullivan 1993), with some individuals experiencing losses much larger than that average.

Involuntary job loss can also have long-term implications for families. Children whose fathers were laid off when their employers' firms closed grow up to have annual earnings about 9 percent lower than similar children whose fathers were not permanently displaced from jobs, with effects about twice as large for families in the lowest quarter of the income distribution (Oreopoulos, Page, and Stevens 2005). Providing assistance to those experiencing such losses while encouraging them to seek work is critical for both fairness and economic growth—in part to avoid a backlash against a dynamic job market that facilitates overall gains in national income.

The principal form of insurance against job loss in the United States is the Federal-State Unemployment Compensation Program, commonly known as unemployment insurance (UI). In 2005, 7.9 million Americans initiated UI receipt, with the average benefit amounts and duration given in table 2-1. UI cushions the shock of job loss by providing to qualifying workers approximately 50 percent of previous weekly earnings for up to six months after involuntary job loss. The payroll tax financing this system, however, is quite regressive. This might be fitting if the UI program were viewed strictly as insurance, because the payroll tax and the associated UI benefits are roughly proportional for all but the lowest wage group of workers (see figure 2-1). As a mechanism to help families cope with the effects of unemployment, however, the UI program is not as well targeted: higher-wage individuals and those with savings or other assets experience much less of a drop in their standard of living in the six months after job loss than do lower-wage individuals and those with less wealth (Browning and Crossley 2001).

---

3. Author's calculations, based on displaced worker survey data for 2002. See Center for Economic and Policy Research, "CPS DWS Data" (www.ceprdata.org/cps/dws_data.php).

Table 2-1. Unemployment Insurance Statistics, Calendar Year 2005

Units as indicated

Covered employment[a]	129,945,209
New beneficiaries[b]	7,917,294
Average weeks of duration[c]	15.3
Average weekly benefits[d]	$258
Benefits paid[e]	$31.2 billion

Source: Author's calculations based on U.S. Department of Labor, "Unemployment Insurance Financial Handbook" (www.ows.doleta.gov/unemploy/hb394/hndbkrpt.asp).

a. Covered employment is the number of employees covered by UI, averaged over twelve months.

b. New beneficiaries are the number of first unemployment insurance checks issued to claimants during their benefit year.

c. Average weeks of duration are the total number of state and federal benefit weeks per number of new beneficiaries.

d. Average weekly benefits are total benefits paid divided by total weeks paid for all federal and state programs.

e. Benefits paid are for all federal and state programs.

This paper outlines a proposal to restructure fundamentally the current UI system in order to redirect existing resources toward helping those who suffer wages losses on reemployment and to increase the system's progressiveness and efficiency. The reform uses a combination of wage-loss insurance and temporary earnings replacement accounts (TERAs).

Wage-loss insurance would provide income support to job losers who are reemployed at lower wages by providing a supplement that increases

Figure 2-1. UI Tax and Benefit Rates by Wage Level[a]

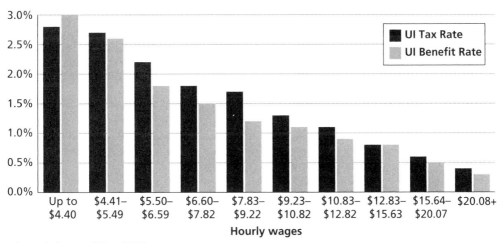

Source: Anderson and Meyer (2006).

a. Tax and benefit rates based on ratios of total taxes and total benefits to total labor income for each wage decile from the 1994 Survey on Income and Program Participation.

the value of each hour worked. Specifically, when an unemployed worker accepts a new job paying a wage lower than the previous one, and lower than $15 an hour, a wage supplement would make up part of the gap. Because these payments would be based on work, they would also encourage shorter unemployment spells.

Through TERAs, cash requirements during unemployment would become partially self-insured. Workers could make voluntary contributions to their TERA via paycheck deductions. In the event of involuntary job loss, an individual could apply for withdrawals from the TERA, with eligibility determination and payment amounts the same as under current UI. Workers who exhaust their TERA balances (or who do not build up savings ahead of time) would be allowed to borrow from their TERA and then repay the loan out of future income, with the repayments collected via paycheck deductions as a percentage of earnings. Any positive balance in a TERA at the end of one's working years could be withdrawn at retirement, with interest. TERAs would carry repayment insurance for those with earnings too low to complete repayment before retirement; such repayment insurance would forgive any outstanding balances at retirement. In addition, individuals with very low wages would not have to repay some or all of their TERA withdrawals. These features would essentially leave the transfer payments of the current UI system in place for those who do not return to work after job loss and those with very low wages before job loss, with greater targeting of these payments to those most in need than exists under the current system.

The proposed system is set up so that government revenue requirements for the wage-loss program, the TERA repayment insurance, and the low-wage coinsurance would be approximately the same as under the current UI system, where each state runs its own UI program under the guidelines of federal law and the details of the programs differ across states (House of Representatives Ways and Means Committee 2004). Figure 2-2 shows the total amount of benefits paid for the years 1980–2005. Benefit expenditures varied substantially with the unemployment rate, ranging from $23 billion in 2000 to $57 billion in 2002, and averaged $43 billion during the 2001–05 period. Revenue is currently raised from UI payroll taxes on firms (where the tax rate varies with the firm's history of layoffs). State payroll taxes are assessed on earnings up to a cap; because the earnings cap in most states is low (in 2005 the earnings cap was $10,000 or less in twenty-seven states), the ratio of taxes to total income is highest for low-wage workers. In this proposal, the revenue needed to support TERAs (equal to one-third of the amounts now collected for UI) would be col-

Figure 2-2. Unemployment Insurance Benefit Expenditures, 1980–2005[a]

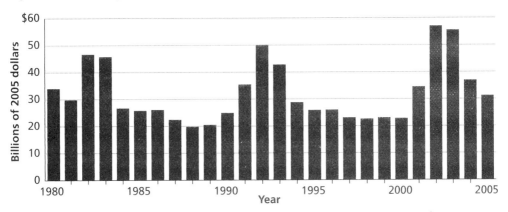

Source: Author's calculations based on U.S. Department of Labor (2006d). U.S. Department of Labor, "Unemployment Insurance Financial Handbook" (www.ows.doleta.gov/unemploy/hb394/hndbkrpt.asp).

a. Sum of all regular and extended state or federal benefits for each calendar year, adjusted to 2005 constant dollars using the GDP chain-linked price index for consumption.

lected from payroll taxes assessed on a broader tax base of taxable income, resulting in much more equal tax rates for low-wage and high-wage workers. The revenue needed to support wage-loss insurance (equal to two-thirds of the amounts now collected for UI) would be collected from firms to pay directly for the insurance claims of that firm's former employees.

The primary goals of the UI program are to help individuals meet necessary expenses as they search for new employment and to reduce significant hardship (Advisory Commission on Unemployment Compensation 1995). Additional goals are to help stabilize the macroeconomy, prevent unemployment, and facilitate reemployment of the unemployed. An interlocking system of wage-loss insurance and TERAs would improve the ability of the unemployment system to achieve several of the original goals of UI. The proposed system would help prevent unemployment by linking employer contributions more directly to job losses than under the current system. Currently, firms have an incentive to generate excess unemployment because they do not face the full cost of subsequent unemployment assistance. Use of withdrawals from TERAs rather than traditional UI would also encourage reemployment by reducing rewards for staying unemployed longer. Moreover, the current UI system offers no protection if the worker's next job, with a new employer or even a new industry, pays lower wages than the previous job. Perhaps most fundamentally, insurance payments in the proposed system, based on hourly wage losses after reemployment, would target resources more directly to reduce significant hardship.

A system of wage-loss insurance and TERAs would function similarly to UI in some ways. Those who qualify for UI under the existing law would receive the same level of cash availability on the same schedule through individual withdrawals from TERAs. Thus the level of support for consumer spending would automatically increase in periods with high rates of job loss, helping to stabilize the macroeconomy in a manner similar to traditional UI. Providing new services without increasing expenditures, however, would entail some difficult trade-offs. For example, those who experience temporary layoffs and subsequently return to their firm and those who have long unemployment spells followed by wage gains would receive smaller government benefits under the proposed system than under the current system.

Many issues associated with UI—including coverage, eligibility, adequacy of benefit amounts, duration and time path of benefits, and reduction of fraud—are not addressed in this proposal but are discussed elsewhere; see O'Leary and Wandner (1997) and Karni (1999) for reviews. This proposal does not suggest altering the level of or eligibility for unemployment benefits, for example. Instead, it focuses on the insurance aspects of the system, and complements other important government activities, such as job search assistance, education, and training.

At a deeper level, this proposal is based on the recognition that private insurance markets are highly unlikely to ever offer widespread insurance against the two main costs of job loss: the short-term cost of being without income for a time and the long-term cost of reduced lifetime earnings as a result of needing to change employers or career paths, or both, and to accept lower wages. When a private insurer seeks to sell insurance against the costs of job loss, it faces the problem that employees know more about whether they are likely to lose their jobs than the insurance company can reasonably discover, and that people who wish to purchase such job-loss insurance would be those who are most at risk for losing their jobs. The firm would have to charge a high premium for selling job-loss insurance to this group, which means that others who are only moderately likely to lose their jobs would find the price of such insurance unattractive. Moreover, private sector banks are not eager to make weekly loans to people who are unemployed and unable to repay the loans until after they are reemployed.

Many individuals can effectively self-insure for short-term income losses with some assistance in saving and borrowing (Stiglitz and Yun 2005). In

1998, 46 percent of UI claimants received benefits for ten weeks or less, with an average total benefit of $1,146.[4] The average age of these claimants was thirty-nine, making the UI benefit a very small fraction of expected income in the future. However, the current UI system only provides funds to cover short-term income losses and no support for long-term wage losses. This proposal would shift resources to focus on the unmet need for insurance against long-term wage losses that are often too large for individuals to absorb. These losses would be most effectively addressed by social insurance that would spread the risk of long-term wage losses across a large pool of individuals. By providing a type of insurance that the private market does not and will not provide, the government can improve the efficiency of the economy while helping those who are in most distress.

How TERAs and Wage-Loss Insurance Would Work

To compare current UI with this proposal in the context of a concrete example, consider an aircraft assembly employee in California who was making $14 an hour and working forty hours a week before her plant closed and she was laid off. If she were to apply for UI under the existing system, the state would check to see that she worked for an employer covered by UI, her earnings in the past year were above a threshold, her employment was terminated involuntarily, and she is available now to work. When verified as eligible, she would receive benefits replacing half her income—in this case, $280 a week. Benefits are financed by a payroll tax on the wages paid to employees at all covered firms, with the firm's tax rate depending in part on the amount of UI benefits paid to former employees of the firm. Payroll taxes from firms are paid to the government, and the government pays UI benefits to eligible individuals.

The workings of the proposal are illustrated by continuing with this example, first from the individual's viewpoint, then that of the firm, and finally that of the government. With the broad outline of the proposal in mind, additional details and system performance simulations are discussed.

Individual's Viewpoint

During the course of her ten years of employment at the firm, the worker voluntarily contributed $2,000 to her TERA. (The default on initial employment was a payroll deduction of 1 percent of pretax earnings

---

4. Author's calculations, including temporary and permanent layoffs, and using 2005 constant dollars, based on Folks, Ihrig, and Needels (2001).

Figure 2-3. Flows of Funds for TERAs

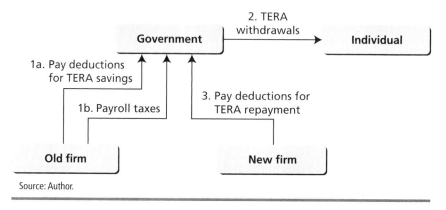

Source: Author.

contributed to her TERA, and she did not opt out of this contribution schedule.) The account was maintained by the government, and her investments were in government bonds. Funds in the account were excluded from asset tests for food stamps, Medicaid, and other government programs, so they did not reduce any potential eligibility for assistance from these programs.

After being laid off from her aircraft assembly job, the worker could apply to receive the same amount of income as under UI—$280 a week, replacing half of her previous earnings. This amount is treated as taxable income, as it would have been under current UI. The eligibility criteria would also be the same as under UI. The difference is that the funds would come from a combination of previously accumulated savings in the TERA and borrowing against future employment income. Say that she remains unemployed for ten weeks, receiving $2,800. She thus draws down the $2,000 in her TERA and borrows an additional $800, leaving her TERA balance at –$800. She then takes a new job that pays $10 an hour. Her new firm deducts 5 percent of her earnings from her paycheck until she has repaid the $800 (plus interest). This flow of funds is illustrated in figure 2-3. In case of personal bankruptcy, the obligation to repay would be treated similarly to student loans and would generally not be dischargeable.

The proposal's other main component involves wage-loss insurance. To be eligible for wage-loss insurance payments, a period of unemployment between the involuntary job loss and the next job would not be required, but all other criteria that apply for initial UI eligibility, such as requirements regarding earnings history and nature of the job loss, would still need to be met. In addition, wage-loss insurance would be available only to those with at least one year of tenure with their previous employer; obviously, individuals would need to have taken a new job with a different employer. The amount of the wage-loss insurance per hour worked on the new job would be based on an insured wage rate—either the wage on the previous job or the fixed amount of $15 an hour, whichever is lower—and calculated as 25 percent of the difference between the insured wage rate and the hourly rate on the new job. The insured wage for each individual would be adjusted each quarter for price inflation, as would the level (initially at $15) of the fixed maximum potential insured wage for future claimants and other parameters of the system based on dollar values.

In this example, the aircraft assembly worker experiences a $4 an hour reduction in wages ($14 an hour at the previous job, $10 an hour at the new one). Assuming no inflation, her wage-loss insurance payments are 25 percent of this $4 reduction—in other words, the wage-loss insurance payment amounts to $1 an hour. These payments are initially deposited directly in her TERA. They would be used first to repay her incurred $800 loan, which would take about fourteen weeks of work at the new job. She would then receive the wage-loss insurance payments for six years, which is a period based on total hours of work in her two years before job loss (three hours of insurance coverage for each hour worked, excluding hours worked in the first year on the job). After her TERA balance reached a maximum threshold ($5,000), additional payments from wage-loss insurance would be sent to her by check. Assuming her wage rate did not change, her income drop would be reduced from 28 percent (based on labor earnings falling from $14 to $10 an hour) to 21 percent (including the $1 an hour insurance payment) over the six years she receives payments. If her wage in the new job did rise or fall, the wage-loss insurance payments would be adjusted as well, so that the wage-loss insurance payments in each calendar quarter would be based on the average hourly wage since job loss through that quarter.

The amounts of transfer payments would vary with individual circumstances. Generally speaking, transfer payments to individuals would be smaller under this proposal than they would be under traditional UI for those experiencing unemployment followed by employment at wages the same or higher than at the time of layoff. Transfer payments would be the same to minimum wage workers and those who never return to work after a period of unemployment, and transfer payments would be larger after permanent job loss for those working at a new job with a lower hourly wage.

Four special conditions that do not apply to our hypothetical aircraft assembly worker are worth noting here. First, those with very low wages on their previous job would receive supplemental assistance if they needed to borrow funds from their TERA. The members of this group are unlikely to benefit much from wage-loss insurance because the wages of their previous jobs were already so low, limiting their potential wage losses at new jobs, given minimum wage laws. The coinsurance rate for this supplemental assistance would run on a sliding scale; therefore someone earning $5.15 an hour (minimum wage in 2005) would not have to repay any borrowing from the TERA—but also would not receive any wage-loss insurance payments. Such a worker would be in exactly the same position under current UI and under the proposed system.

Second, if our hypothetical worker reached retirement age and filed for Social Security benefits, any positive balance remaining in her TERA would be transferred to an individual retirement account (IRA) for her. If her earnings had been too low to repay any loans from her TERA at the point she would begin collecting Social Security, then TERA repayment insurance would pay off the remaining balance.

Third, if she had opted out of making payroll contributions to her TERA, instead of accepting the default option of making such contributions, her withdrawals during unemployment would have been entirely a loan from her TERA, which she would repay with interest through deductions from paychecks at her new job.

Fourth, if she held two or more jobs with separate employers, each job would be separately insured. Withdrawal amounts would be based on earnings at the specific job that was lost, and the insured wage for wage-loss insurance would be based on earnings and hours on the lost job. A new job started a week before being laid off from one's main job and a job started a week after a layoff would be treated the same way for the purposes of wage-loss insurance eligibility and payments, with calculation of the post–job loss hourly wage beginning in the calendar quarter after job loss.

Firm's Viewpoint

The aircraft-manufacturing firm laying off the individual in the example would submit three types of payments to the government over time. Initially, the firm would send payroll deductions for voluntary saving to the TERA; these deductions reflect contributions made by workers who do not opt out of the default saving mechanism for the TERAs (figure 2-3). Taxes based on the firm's payroll (figure 2-3), as under the current UI, would support the administration of the system and finance two types of payments:

Figure 2-4. Flows of Funds for Wage-Loss Insurance

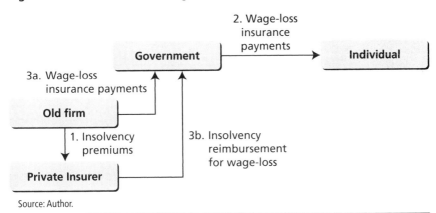

Source: Author.

repayment insurance to pay off loans for individuals who retire but had earnings too low to fully repay their TERA withdrawals, and low-wage coinsurance to reduce potential TERA repayments for those with low hourly wages.

The flow of funds for wage-loss insurance is depicted in figure 2-4. Firms would reimburse the government for wage-loss insurance claims of former employees, and the government would pay the employees. Firms would also be required to purchase insurance on the private market to cover wage-loss insurance claims in the event that the firm became insolvent, and the insurer would then make payments to the government in the event of firm insolvency.

In total, firms would make payments to the government for wage-loss insurance, repayment insurance, assistance on TERA repayments for those with low wages, and other costs of the proposed system that would be approximately the same as the current UI system. In terms of funds currently paid in UI benefits, nearly two-thirds of the money would be reallocated to wage-loss insurance, about 30 percent would go to repayment insurance, and 6 percent would be used for supplemental assistance for TERA withdrawals by those with wages near the minimum wage. Thus revenue from new payments for wage-loss insurance reimbursement would combine with reduced revenue from the payroll tax so that a change to the proposed system would be revenue neutral.

The UI taxable earnings base would be increased from the current caps (for example, twenty-seven states had caps on taxable earnings of

$10,000 or less in 2005) to the Social Security earnings base (which was $90,000 for 2005 and which increases annually with the national wage index). The reduced revenue needs from the UI payroll tax combined with the broader tax base would allow average payroll tax rates to be substantially reduced. UI tax rates would continue to vary by firm as under traditional UI (according to previous use of TERAs by former employees, as opposed to previous payments of UI benefits to former employees). These rates would be more tightly linked to firm layoff histories through the combination of lower average tax rates and a lowering of the minimum rates that states require firms to pay. Since firm-varying rates would be less constrained by the floors and ceilings that characterize the current system, firms that lay off workers would see higher UI payroll taxes in the future.

A firm that hired a previously unemployed worker would carry out mandatory payroll deductions for repayment of loans when that employee's TERA withdrawals had resulted in negative TERA balances. Such deductions would appear on pay stubs as pretax deductions, similar to health insurance, retirement plans, and dependent care expense accounts. This flow of funds from the new firm to the account maintained by the government is shown in figure 2-3.

Government's Viewpoint

Under current law, UI is run by the states under federal government oversight, an arrangement that would remain in place under this proposal. States would continue to be responsible for verifying a person's eligibility for unemployment benefits and would also determine how much each unemployed person could withdraw from his or her TERA per week. States would continue to collect payroll taxes, which would be used for TERA repayment insurance and low-wage coinsurance.

The flows of funds to the government from firms and insurers and from the government to individuals are shown in figures 2-3 and 2-4. Eligible individuals could make TERA withdrawals and receive wage-loss insurance payments. It is sometimes proposed that a minimum size should be set for the level of payments because, for example, very small wage losses could lead to very small payments. However, once an employee has borrowed from a TERA and the wage-loss insurance program has been established, the administrative cost of making these payments would be very low. Once a claim has been approved, benefit amount determination and deposits can essentially be automatic, based on employer reports of earnings and hours for each quarter.

The federal government would manage the TERAs in this system. The government can take advantage of economies of scale to keep costs low, and it can avoid TERA transfers when individuals change employers or move across state lines. The interest rate on government bonds would be the rate of interest required for repayment of borrowed funds.

Funds in the TERAs would be invested and earn a rate of return on positive balances. The automatic default investment would be in government bonds. Such a safe default investment seems appropriate given that job loss is an unpredictable event and thus savings may be needed at any time. For positive TERA balances, workers could opt into a portfolio with a mixture of stocks and bonds, where the portfolio composition would vary according to the retirement age of the individual, similar to the federal Thrift Savings Plan's lifecycle funds. Changes from bonds to lifecycle funds would be allowed once per calendar quarter.

The federal government would also have the power to authorize extending the standard twenty-six-week period in which the unemployed person can make withdrawals from a TERA, just as the federal government now can extend eligibility for unemployment benefits when the economy is in or near a recession. During the extended period, individuals could continue to make withdrawals and borrow from their TERAs. Firms would not have their future payroll tax rates increased because of withdrawals during the extended period. Federal unemployment taxes would contribute to the repayment insurance that would cover borrowed funds that were not repaid.

Simulations of the System

This section uses historical data on wages and amounts of UI receipt to estimate the amounts of savings, borrowing, repayment insurance, low-wage coinsurance, and wage-loss insurance that would have existed from 1984 to 1996 if the proposed system had been in place.

How the Simulation Was Conducted

The data used in this simulation are from the Panel Study of Income Dynamics (PSID), which is based at the University of Michigan. The PSID has been tracking a representative sample of U.S. individuals and families since 1968. Most other sources of government data on unemployment or UI are snapshots of what is happening in a certain month or year. For example, the data tell the number of people unemployed in each year, but they do not reveal whether the same people have been unemployed for several years or what sorts of jobs and wages were gained by those who were formerly unemployed. The PSID, by contrast, tracks family units over time, so it provides data for analyzing how long workers have been unemployed and the patterns of their future employment over time. The variables extracted from the PSID include annual labor earnings, annual hours of work, age, and UI compensation. All dollar variables in this discussion are adjusted for inflation and expressed in terms of 2005 dollars (using the chain-linked GDP price deflator). The sample for this simulation focuses on family heads and their spouses in 1984 that had data available in subsequent and consecutive years. Years of data in the PSID before 1984 are not used in the simulation because separations from previous employers are not clearly identified and not classified as temporary or permanent, and because UI data are not reported for spouses of family heads. The simulation ends with data for 1996 because subsequently data were collected only every other year.

The simulation of TERAs and wage-loss insurance is calibrated to match historical expenditure and revenue levels. The unemployed are assumed to withdraw from TERAs what was actually paid in UI, and firms are assumed to pay the same amount under the proposed plan as they did in taxes to support the current UI system. The duration of the wage-loss insurance payments (in terms of hours compensated) is adjusted so that the total of such payments and unpaid TERA loans at retirement (with proper accounting for appropriate interest payments) equal total UI actually paid. The simulation assumes that people's earnings and the duration of their unemployment are unaffected by the proposal. Possible incentive effects on earnings, duration, and other aspects of individual behavior are discussed later in this chapter.

To simulate the proposal, a number of details needed to be specified. Wage-loss insurance provides payments equal to 25 percent of the difference between the insured wage and the wage on the new job, and the insured wage is the lower of $15 an hour or the wage on the previous job. The coinsurance rate for borrowing from a TERA among earners with very low wages is a sliding scale, going from 0 percent at $7 an hour to 100 percent at $5.15 an hour on the previous job. The loan repayment rate is 5 percent of earnings at the new job. In addition to these programmatic details, some other assumptions are necessary. The participation rate is assumed to be 50 percent in the default option of a 1 percent payroll deduction for savings if the TERA balance is not negative. Interest rates are based on three-month Treasury bills, and all individuals are assumed to keep positive balances in government bonds. Individuals are assumed to retire at age sixty-five.

Table 2-2. TERA and Wage-Loss Insurance Simulation Results[a]

Units as indicated

Proportion with positive ending balance if ever withdrew from TERA	0.63
Proportion of withdrawal dollars from TERAs with positive ending balances	0.37
Ratio of repayment insurance payments to total withdrawals	0.30
Ratio of low-wage coinsurance payments to total withdrawals	0.06
Ratio of total wage-loss insurance payments to total withdrawals	0.64
Wage loss insured hours per hour worked in two years prior to job loss	3.0
Ratio of total paycheck contributions to total withdrawals	1.3

Source: Author's calculations using data from the PSID, 1984–96.
a. See text for simulation assumptions and parameters.

Simulation Results

Simulation results are shown in table 2-2. The simulation was calibrated to work with a balanced budget. The approach was to start with the amount that firms actually paid to the current UI and then figure out how that total amount could be reallocated among three types of insurance described in this proposal: repayment insurance to cover paying off the TERA loans that were not repaid because the worker retired; coinsurance to reduce individual contributions to TERA withdrawals for individuals with extremely low hourly wages (below $7 an hour); and wage-loss insurance. The amount of repayment insurance needed at the end of the simulation was 30 percent of all TERA borrowing over time. An additional 6 percent was used to make coinsurance payments to workers with very low wages. The other 64 percent of the value of traditional UI payments was used for wage-loss insurance. The take-up rate for wage-loss insurance was assumed to be 70 percent, about the same as for traditional UI (Blank and Card 1991). The wage-loss insurance funding provided payments for three hours worked on the new job for every hour worked in the two years before job loss, so someone working full-time before and after a job loss would receive wage-loss insurance payments for six years.

Overall, 18 percent of individuals received UI payments at least once during this thirteen-year historical period. Under the proposal, they would make withdrawals or borrow from TERAs. Despite such withdrawals or borrowing, the majority of these individuals would wind up with a positive TERA balance through a combination of voluntary saving, repayment of borrowed funds, and wage-loss insurance payments. These individuals tended to have withdrawn smaller amounts. Of all

Table 2-3.   Effect of UI versus Wage-Loss Insurance (WL) and TERAs on the
Distribution of Insured Wage Losses during the Ten Years after Separation

Percentage of sample experiencing change

Income change per hour worked	Earnings only	Earnings + UI	Earnings + WL + TERAs[b]
Loss ≥ 50 percent	15	14	7
Loss ≥ 25 percent	42	38	31
Any loss	100	92	91

Source: PSID.

a. The data are from 357 observations with hourly wages below the insured wage after job loss, where the insured wage is the lower of $15 or the wage at the end of the old job, selected from the 70 percent of permanent job losers predicted to file wage-loss insurance claims. Each observation is an individual with one year or more of tenure having a first permanent involuntary separation from an employer in the period from 1984 to 1988 and valid reports of hourly wages before and after separation. Earnings are observed through 1996 for an average of ten years post–job loss.

b. "TERAs" include both repayment insurance for TERA negative end period balances plus TERA low-wage coinsurance. Each row shows the percentage of this sample having a change in income per hour worked.

funds withdrawn from TERAs, 37 percent were from TERAs that had a positive balance in the end.

The last row of table 2-2 shows the ratio of total paycheck deductions to total withdrawals (expressed in present value terms). On average, the values of paycheck contributions and withdrawals are equal when this ratio is 1.0. The estimate shows that the ratio in the simulation is 1.3, indicating that individuals are, on average, saving 30 percent more than they are withdrawing from the TERAs.

Distributional Effects

Among those experiencing a permanent job loss and having one year of tenure with their previous employer, 43 percent received at least some wage-loss insurance payments. Thirty-four percent of all workers had lower hourly wages when averaged over the ten years after job loss, and 29 percent had wages that were both lower than their previous wages and below $15 an hour. The distributional effects of this proposal for those whose wages after job loss were lower than their previous wages and lower than $15 an hour are shown in table 2-3, based on the simulation. For this table, each observation is an individual with at least one year of tenure at a firm having an involuntary separation from that employer during the 1984–88 period. The percentage change between pre- and postseparation hourly income was calculated for labor earnings, labor earnings plus UI (the current system), and labor earnings plus wage-loss insurance plus TERA repayment insurance plus TERA low-wage coinsurance (the proposed system). Income was measured each year for which complete data were available in subsequent years (through 1996) to assess a fairly long-term cumulative impact, for an average of ten years after job loss for this sample. After the initial permanent job loss, individuals may experience subsequent temporary or permanent layoffs, and additional UI and wage-loss insurance payments from these events are included to capture the cumulative effect.

In table 2-3, the first column is based only on hourly income from labor earnings. The first row indicates that 15 percent of all workers with wage losses experienced hourly labor income losses of 50 percent or more. The second column is based on hourly income from labor earnings plus UI payments after separation. The percentage of workers with losses of 50 percent or more was 14 percent, 1 percentage point lower than the scenario without UI. The third column is based on hourly income from labor earnings and the new system proposed in this chapter: wage-loss insurance, repayment insurance for TERAs, and low-wage coinsurance for TERAs. The proportion of workers experiencing losses of 50 percent or more is cut in half to 7 percent.

While the new forms of insurance proposed in this paper are effective at reducing extreme losses, there are inherent limits to the extent that losses can be reduced within this framework. Say, for example, that an individual had an earnings loss of 40 percent relative to her insured wage for ten years after job loss. Wage-loss insurance provides payments that make up 25 percent of this loss, but the loss would still be 30 percent over the ten years. Of course, it is theoretically possible to have insurance cover the entire wage loss, but this would certainly have undesirable effects on the incentives of individuals to seek higher wages at their new jobs. Raising the rate at which losses are replaced would also require financial resources exceeding those currently used for traditional UI. In addition, raising the rate would have to be weighed against the incentive effects of a high replacement rate (as discussed later in this chapter).

Another way to examine how effectively systems target resources to those with wage losses is to examine the proportion of the program dollars received by different groups, as shown in figure 2-5. Among permanent job losers who were eventually reemployed, UI allocated 34 percent of resources to long-term wage losers, while wage-loss insurance and TERAs targeted 61 percent to this group. The proportion of resources devoted to those with long-term wage losses of one-fourth or more was three times higher with wage-loss insurance and TERAs than with UI.

Figure 2-5. Distribution of Program Resources Received by Permanent Job Losers[a]

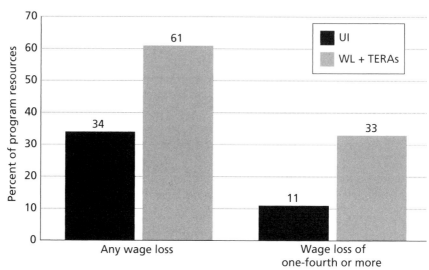

Source: Author's calculations based on data from PSID, 1984–96.

a. Data are from 1,296 observations of individuals with one year or more of tenure who had a first permanent involuntary separation from an employer in the 1984–88 period and valid reports of hourly wages before and after separation. Earnings are observed through 1996 for an average of ten years post–job loss. WL + TERAs includes wage-loss insurance plus repayment insurance for TERA negative end period balances plus TERA low-wage coinsurance.

For those with wage losses of one-fourth or more, wage-loss insurance and TERAs provided benefits over ten years equivalent to an average of 12 percent of the wage level on the preseparation job, whereas UI provided benefits over ten years equivalent to an average of 3.5 percent of the pre-separation wage. For other permanent job losers, both systems provided benefits per hour worked equivalent to an average of 3 percent of the pre-separation wage.

As a budget-neutral proposal, the shifting of resources to support those experiencing long-term hourly wage losses from permanent layoffs implies that transfers are reduced for some other groups. Under this proposal, those who are temporarily laid off and return to the same firm make TERA withdrawals that they later repay, and this group receives smaller net transfers from the proposed system than they do under UI. Individuals who lose their job, experience a long spell of unemployment and TERA

Table 2-4.   Share of Benefits by Income Quartile[a]

Percent

Quartile	UI	WL + TERAs
Lowest	8	8
Third	35	46
Second	37	37
Top	20	9

Source: Author's calculations based on data from PSID, 1984-96.

a. Data include 7,010 PSID household heads and spouses in 1984, ages twenty to sixty-four. Observations used from annual interviews conducted consecutively from 1984 to 1996 through age sixty-four. UI benefits are the present discounted value of UI payments divided by the number of person-years of data observed. WL + TERAs is the present discounted value of wage-loss insurance, repayment insurance for TERA negative end period balances, and TERA low-wage coinsurance divided by the number of person-years of data observed. Income is the present discounted value of annual labor earnings divided by the number of person-years of data observed. Quartiles are based on rank by income, and divide the data into four equal-sized groups incorporating survey weights.

withdrawals, but then find a new job at a higher wage than their previous job also receive smaller net transfers from the proposed system than they do under UI. Younger workers are relatively more likely to experience such an event.

Wage-loss insurance and TERAs also would substantially increase the share of unemployment benefits received by those making less than the median income. Table 2-4 shows that compared to the current UI system, wage-loss insurance and TERAs would reduce the share of program benefits received by those in the top quartile of the income distribution, leave unchanged the share of benefits received by those in the second quartile, and increase (from 43 percent to 54 percent) the share of benefits received by those in the bottom half of the income distribution.

Related Research

In making predictions about how this combination of TERAs and wage-loss insurance would work, we are not operating in a vacuum, fortunately. Over the past fifteen years or so, several bodies of work and experience have built up that are relevant to this proposal. One such body of work is about the operation of earnings insurance. A second is about the operation of accounts designated for various purposes. A third body of work is about programs in which the government seeks to ensure that loans would be repaid out of future income. In addition, the extensive literature on UI and other social insurance programs is informative about incentive effects. The proposal for wage-loss insurance and TERAs draws on these analyses and experiences.

Earnings Insurance

In U.S. policy discussions, insurance for earnings losses after job displacement has received the most attention in the context of free trade—compensating individuals who lose jobs as a result of import competition. See Kletzer (2003) for a summary of these arguments. This discussion contributed to the establishment of a program of earnings insurance called Alternative Trade Adjustment Assistance (ATAA), which was enacted as part of the Trade Adjustment Assistance Act of 2002 (Baicker and Rehavi 2004). ATAA provides earnings insurance for individuals aged fifty or older who are reemployed full time within twenty-six weeks after their separation, with an earnings subsidy equal to 50 percent of the difference between the earnings on the previous and new jobs (as long as the new job pays less than $50,000 a year), up to a total of $10,000 in benefits or until two years have elapsed since reemployment. Firms must have the government certify that their layoffs are caused by trade.

The discussion leading up to the passage of this legislation generated some proposals for extending earnings insurance to all individuals experiencing involuntary job loss, not just those unemployed because of trade (Jacobson, LaLonde, and Sullivan 1993; Baily, Burtless, and Litan 1993; Parsons 2000). For example, Kletzer and Litan (2001) offer a proposal in which employees who suffer involuntary permanent job loss and have at least two years of tenure at that firm would receive earnings insurance for two years, based on the difference in earnings between the previous and the new job. They estimate that the cost of providing earnings insurance would be less than $3 billion a year if it were limited to those who were employed full time on both their previous and new jobs, and if the benefits for any one individual were capped at $10,000 a year.

The Canadian government experimented with earnings insurance in the late 1990s with the Earnings Supplement Project (ESP). In this program, some individuals randomly received earnings insurance in addition to UI, while others only received UI, in order for researchers to examine the effects. Eligible displaced workers who were reemployed within twenty-six weeks at a new full-time job (minimum 30 hours per week) received supplemental payments covering 75 percent of any earnings loss for each week worked, for up to two years after initial job loss and random assignment. The supplement was capped at $250 a week, and earnings above the maximum UI amount were not counted when the ESP payment was calculated.

The Canadian ESP results showed that earnings insurance could effectively offset part of earnings losses while having little impact on other behavior (Bloom and others 1999). The primary goal of the program was to accelerate reemployment and reduce traditional UI expenditures, since every additional week unemployed was one less week that one could be receiving the earnings subsidy that ended after two years. Some observers regard the program as a failure because UI expenditures were not reduced appreciably. However, the primary motivation of the proposal presented in this chapter is not to reduce government payments but rather to target assistance to those most in need, and the Canadian results demonstrate that transfers can be targeted to those experiencing earnings losses without generating significantly adverse incentive effects.

Finally, the incentives of wage-loss insurance can be related to a past literature concerning negative wage taxes. A number of scholars have proposed and analyzed a negative hourly wage tax, where payments (which can be viewed as negative taxes) are made as a fraction of the difference between a target wage and the actual wage (see, for example, Muth 1966; Kesselman 1969; Zeckhauser and Schuck 1970). In fact, a subsidy for hourly wages was passed by the Senate in 1972 (Senate Finance Committee 1972, analyzed by Haveman 1973), although it was dropped in House-Senate conference. The approach has continued to be of interest and discussion (for example, Browning 1973; Barth 1974; Lerman 1982; Betson and Bishop 1982; Besley and Coate 1995; MaCurdy and McIntyre 2004). Wage-loss insurance operates exactly like a negative wage tax—offsetting a fraction of the difference between a target wage and the actual wage—but is restricted to those having involuntary job losses.

UI Accounts

Individual accounts have been discussed for some years as a supplement either to retirement planning or to health insurance. More recently, a number of proposals have surfaced for accounts focused on unemployment. Topel (1990) provides an early discussion of the main conceptual features of personal accounts with savings, borrowing, and repayment. Feldstein and Altman (1998) provide rough estimates of the levels of taxation and transfers that would be required under a proposed system of UI savings accounts.[5] Stiglitz and Yun (2005) show that when the duration of insured unemployment is short relative to the period of employment, the theoretical optimal system involves extensive use of a form of borrowing against individual retirement assets in order to reduce risks from unemployment while also improving job search incentives relative to a system of traditional UI. Shimer and Werning (2005) discuss the theoretical importance of ensuring that workers have sufficient liquidity to maintain living standards after job loss, and they emphasize the distinct potential role for public policy in facilitating savings and borrowing for those who become unemployed and in providing insurance.

Personal accounts for payments during unemployment have been implemented in eight Latin American countries (Ferrer and Riddell 2004). The TERA proposal in this chapter has one major difference from many existing plans: the latter are typically implemented solely by having people save in advance of the need for unemployment benefits, whereas the TERA approach involves both such advance savings and borrowing, with repayment of borrowed funds after the unemployment period is over. Despite this clear difference, some evidence on the feasibility of TERAs can be gleaned from currently functioning systems. For example, Chile uses personal accounts for protection against loss of income during unemployment, and allows withdrawals from a common fund if the individual's TERA reaches a zero balance.[6] In the mandatory Chilean system, workers contribute 2.2 percent of their wages to personal accounts. An additional 6.1 percent of total wages for up to eleven years of employment is contributed by the employee to the account if an individual had an open-ended labor contract and there was an involuntary separation. The balance in the account is paid after separation and one month of unpaid unemployment, with payments in five equal installments. If the account has a balance of less than two months' current wages, the

5. Feldstein and Altman (1998) are especially interested in whether a system of accounts could have positive balances at retirement for those who made withdrawals, rewarding individuals with shorter unemployment duration with greater retirement savings. They propose a mandatory contribution rate of 4 percent of earnings (toward both positive and negative balances in accounts). Using historical data on individual earnings, they find their system resulted in 42 to 56 percent of benefit dollars going to those with positive account balances at retirement. Graetz and Mashaw (1999) put forward a related, less detailed proposal for unemployment insurance copayments to be withdrawn from personal retirement accounts. Fernandez (2000) and Orszag and Snower (2002) also offer research focusing specifically on UI savings accounts.

6. For a description of Chile's system, see Acevedo and Eskenazi (2004); for a discussion of special challenges for developing economies, see Sehnbruch (2004).

government tops up benefits so the replacement rate is at least 50, 45, 40, 35, and 30 percent in months two through six, respectively, after the separation of worker and employer. The additional government payments are funded partially by general revenues and by a payroll tax of 0.8 percent of wages. The use of a common fund on which an individual with low balances can draw distinguishes Chile's system from others in Latin America.

The United States has recently introduced a pilot program involving accounts, although these personal reemployment accounts are not intended to provide income support during unemployment. These accounts can have $3,000, provided in addition to UI benefits, for eligible unemployed workers who are likely to exhaust their UI benefits. Factors used to determine worker eligibility for these accounts include local unemployment rates, prior employment in a declining industry, the participant's level of education, and the participant's recent job tenure. Seven states are participating in the pilot program.[7] Workers can use account funds to purchase intensive career, job training, and supportive services and products from public One-Stop Career Centers and from the private market. Workers can also use their accounts to buy services and products such as child care, clothes, tools, uniforms, transportation, and auto repairs—that is, items and services needed to help find and retain a good job. Individuals who find employment within thirteen weeks of account establishment would receive a reemployment bonus of the funds remaining in the account.

Income-Contingent Loans

Funds borrowed from TERAs would be repaid out of future income. Several countries in addition to the United States—Australia, Chile, New Zealand, South Africa, and the United Kingdom—have experimented with income-contingent loans—not for unemployment but as a way of repaying loans for higher education (Chapman 2006). Repayment of loans is typically required after income rises above some threshold. Early versions, such as that implemented at Yale University in the 1970s (Nerlove 1975) and those proposed in Congress in the 1990s (Krueger and Bowen 1993), had repayment amounts that depended on the income of other borrowers and could substantially exceed those under conventional loans if the recipient became a high earner. Later implementations in the United States and elsewhere are more similar to the TERA, where repayment depends only

7. U.S. Department of Labor, "Personal Reemployment Account Initiative" (www.doleta. gov/reemployment).

on one's own income, and social insurance repays the loan if the borrower's income turns out to be very low. For example, the Department of Education offers an income-contingent repayment plan where the monthly payments are based on those for a conventional twelve-year loan multiplied by a percentage that varies with annual income, or 20 percent of monthly discretionary income, where discretionary income is defined as adjusted gross income from one's tax return minus the federal poverty level for one's family size. The maximum repayment period is twenty-five years, after which unpaid loan amounts are forgiven (and taxes are paid on the amount discharged). This plan is seldom chosen by students, apparently because most other loans are fully repaid at the same rate of interest, yet the plan is more complex than other repayment options, and only those with extremely low incomes during the twenty-five-year period ultimately receive loan forgiveness (Johnstone 2004).

Incentive Effects and Behavioral Responses to the Proposal

Changing from UI to a combination of TERAs and wage-loss insurance would affect the incentives faced by firms and individuals in a number of ways. This section discusses the main conclusions about likely effects on firm decisions about temporary layoffs, permanent layoffs, and hiring. This is followed by an examination of the proposal's effects on the decisions of individuals immediately after job loss and during the job search, and on the work effort and wages at a new job. In making predictions about how the proposals would affect incentives, this section briefly summarizes a much more extensive discussion by Kling (2006).

Replacement of UI with TERAs should reduce temporary layoffs by 10 to 15 percent. This reduction arises from forcing firms to bear more of the direct cost of layoffs. In addition, since most employees who become unemployed would bear the costs of unemployment benefits directly, they would be much more likely to voice strong opposition to temporary layoffs than they are under UI, where they receive payments with no corresponding future obligations. Firms in industries with frequent temporary layoffs would be pressured by the labor market to raise wages in order to continue to attract workers who, under the proposal, would be self-insuring income loss during layoff through savings and borrowing.

Firms making permanent layoffs would face increased costs for doing so. For example, firms in declining industries would face the prospect of large wage-loss insurance payments because individuals who are laid off in such industries are unlikely to be reemployed doing similar work and are more likely to end up in a job where their accumulated experience is of less value. Firms with high wages and frequent permanent layoffs would feel market pressure to reduce wages to cover the cost of wage-loss insurance for workers who were likely to be laid off and who faced low prospects for finding work at similar wages. Thus firms would be effectively giving those most in need of wage-loss insurance the opportunity to pay for it themselves with lower wages on their current job, resulting in the same average future compensation (after incorporating the prospect of layoff) but lower variability due to the insurance.

As the costs of laying off longer-tenured workers increase, firms may accelerate their decisions about retaining new hires. The proposal provision that hours during the first year with an employer would not count toward potential wage-loss insurance payment duration would substantially reduce the possible disincentives to make new hires by allowing the firm to assess the fit of a new employee with the firm during his or her first year on the job. In fact, Farber (1999) shows that half of all separations occur during employees' first year on the job.

In comparison with UI, TERAs should reduce the average amount of time that people spend out of work. Use of TERAs instead of UI increases the price for additional unemployment (at least among those who do not expect to retire with an unpaid loan) because TERA withdrawals would need to be repaid from future income. As a result, the introduction of TERAs may reduce the overall duration of unemployment by 5 to 10 percent.

The duration of unemployment would also be affected by the availability of wage-loss insurance. Individuals considering a job offering a wage below their insured wage level would be more likely to accept it since the hourly rate of pay would be augmented by wage-loss insurance payments. Making employment more rewarding should reduce the tendency for some people to become discouraged and remain unemployed or even stop looking for work. This reduced duration of unemployment is unlikely to be associated with workers taking jobs too hastily, rather than waiting patiently for a more productive job match.

If wage-loss insurance is offered for a specific time period, there is an incentive for firms to offer more jobs that have lower initial earnings that would rise more rapidly over time than in the absence of wage insurance. For workers to accept offers of lower initial earnings (in the absence of a credible long-term contract), a firm would need to offer some incentive (such as on-the-job training) that would reassure workers that the firm will want to retain them at higher wages in the future. This training would most likely be firm-specific; otherwise the firm would tend to avoid such a commitment for fear of losing its investment in the training if the person left the firm. In addition, the existence of wage-loss insurance is also an incentive for firms to offer more firm-specific on-the-job training to all workers. Faced with a choice between a higher-wage job with firm-specific skills or a lower-wage job with transferable skills, most workers are likely to find the former more attractive when there is wage-loss insurance to help protect them against income loss in the event of a layoff of higher-wage jobs that are firm-specific. In addition, wage-loss insurance could also assist in the acquisition of transferable skills by financing tuition at a community college.

Increased search intensity as an effect of wage-loss insurance may increase the total labor supply and thereby reduce wage levels, as would be true with any other policy that successfully encouraged the pursuit of work. However, the impact on the labor supply is likely to be small, and thus the effect on wages is likely to be small as well. Any effect on wages from increased labor supply would be an outcome for the entire market, so no particular employer would capture a government subsidy for itself. In the presence of wage-loss insurance, if firms offer more firm-specific training (with lower initial wages but higher average wages) or new, higher-paying jobs more subject to layoff, then these factors could offset or exceed the effect of increased labor supply and could potentially lead to higher wages for nonrecipients as well. The average effect on overall wages, however, is likely to be small either way.

Implementation Issues

How Would the Transition to the Proposed System Work?

The transition to a system of TERAs and wage-loss insurance could phase in gradually. In the first year of the program, firms would be charged the full amount of withdrawals from TERAs by their former employees because those unemployed would initially have no savings, and the system would need funds to loan out from TERAs. Wage-loss insurance payments would not be paid in the first year, however, so total outlays by firms would not increase.

In the second year of the program, some workers would begin to qualify for wage-loss insurance, and firms would begin to make wage-loss insurance reimbursement payments to the government. The parameters of the system could be set so that the combined cost to firms for TERA withdrawals and wage-loss insurance payments would be no larger than the firms' costs under the current UI system.

The proposal could be adopted by one or more states, while other states could opt to remain with the existing system. Coverage for compensation after involuntary job loss would be determined by the location of the employing establishment at the time of job loss, just as under the traditional UI system. Individuals who worked in a state adopting this proposal would be covered under it even if they relocated to a state that had not adopted this proposal.

Would Administrative Problems Arise in Using Data on Hours Worked?

The proposal for wage-loss insurance relies on information about hours worked and hourly wages paid at the previous job and at the new job. Implementation would require many states to start collecting data in a systematic way on hours worked. There are two reasons for using data based on hours. First, work during part of the year or part-time work during a week is incorporated into the system in a clear, fair, and straightforward way: additional hours worked in the year before job loss would increase the number of hours covered by wage-loss insurance on reemployment. Second, using hourly wages rather than earnings as a basis for payments does not create incentives for working fewer hours on the new job. The evidence (as discussed above) indicates that people respond more to incentives to decrease hours worked than to incentives to seek lower hourly wages, perhaps because an individual's hourly wage affects self-worth and social status as well as income.

It is often argued that it is preferable to base a system on total earnings (see, for example, Carcagno and Corson 1982). This argument has become less compelling over time because information on hours is commonly available now in most firms' payroll systems, and it would be straightforward to use these data in an overhauled social insurance system for dealing with the costs of unemployment. In fact, it is often simpler to report hours worked and average hourly wages. In 1995 Oregon justified collection of data on hours for determining UI eligibility in part because employers stated that reporting hours would be much simpler than reporting weeks of work, as was previously required (Oregon House of Representatives 1995).

A number of public programs already collect data on hours worked because they base eligibility on a minimum of hours worked. For example, Oregon (500 hours a year) and Washington (680 hours a year) allow eligibility for UI to be satisfied with a minimum number of hours worked. Both states collect information on total hours worked in each calendar quarter for every employee in the state. Minnesota also collects data on hours worked, although these are currently used for research rather than for program eligibility. All three states have the information systems infrastructure in place to administer a program based on hourly wages.

Other countries also run programs that rely on data on hours worked. The United Kingdom's Working Tax Credit can be claimed by those who report working at least sixteen hours a week, with a more generous credit for those working more than thirty hours a week. In this program, the claimant reports hours worked and can be audited, but the data are not systematically reported by employers.

Numerous demonstration programs have incorporated thresholds of minimum hours. Canada's ESP (for displaced workers) and Self-Sufficiency Project (for low-income parents) both target earnings supplements to those working at least thirty hours a week. The New Hope Project in Milwaukee also requires thirty hours a week of work for an employee to become eligible for an earnings supplement. The ATAA discussed earlier requires full-time work (as defined by one's state of residence) for earnings supplements to be paid. For all these demonstrations, hours were generally verified by having individuals submit copies of their pay stubs to the program; additional information was requested or employers were contacted in cases where the stub was insufficient.

How Easy Would It Be to Game the System?

When payments to the unemployed are based on duration of unemployment, it is fairly easy to game the system: simply collect unemployment benefits while working off the books. But since TERA withdrawals either use one's own savings or are loans that must be repaid with interest, an individual gains no advantage by running up larger loans. Focusing the wage-loss insurance system on hourly wages also makes it more difficult to game the system and to extract extra payments.

Imagine, for example, that when a formerly employed worker takes a new job, the worker and the employer agree to relatively low wages and higher nonwage compensation, with the intent to take advantage of the wage-loss insurance payments. Alternatively, a firm and an employee might agree to report that the employee is working long hours for a low hourly wage when in truth the worker is putting in shorter hours for a higher hourly wage. Such a strategy could benefit the employee by qualifying that individual for higher wage-loss insurance payments. The strategy could also protect the firm, since the chance of that employee becoming unemployed and taking a job with a still lower wage—and thus making the firm responsible for future wage-loss insurance payments—would be reduced. But attempting to take advantage of wage-loss insurance in these ways certainly requires more effort than is the case when an individual extends the duration of current UI benefits by not looking very aggressively for a new job.

If firms inflate reported hours in the hope of reducing future wage-loss insurance payments, this would be against the long-term interests of the employee who might want to be protected against a genuine wage cut in the future. Such a strategy would be easily observed by the employee and fairly easily investigated by the government on request. Wages below the natural floor of the minimum wage would be especially suspicious. Firms inflating hours would also be increasing the potential duration of benefits that the firm would need to pay. If a common level of hours inflation did set in over time among all firms in an industry, then the previous job's wages and the new job's wages would be lower, duration of benefits would be longer, and more employees would be below the maximum insured wage—actually increasing insurance payments and giving incentive to the industry to police itself. Overall, firms that might be tempted to game the wage-loss insurance system would need to engage in a type of fraud that would have a fairly low payoff but would likely be observed by numerous people in the firm and would be relatively easy to investigate—all of which reduces its appeal.

What if Firms Fail to Pay Their Wage-Loss Insurance Reimbursements?

Firms would be required to purchase third-party insurance for reimbursement of wage-loss insurance claims in the event that the firm becomes insolvent. Use of private insurers would allow establishment of a market for assessing the risk of insolvency and the costs of wage-loss insurance claims. While private insurers are likely to balk at assuming the risks of individual layoffs, which are at the firm's discretion, general insolvency would take place only in special and well-defined cases where wage-loss insurance costs are likely to play a minor role in firm decisions. Insurers could hedge macroeconomic risks of recessions with economic derivatives (Baron and Lange 2003).

If firms do not have adequate insurance or do not repay the government for wage-loss insurance claims, current law contains a mechanism that could be used for collecting the money. Under current UI law, firms technically owe a federal unemployment tax of 6.2 percent of the first $7,000 paid annually to each employee. However, current law also allows the federal unemployment tax to be imposed only at a rate of 0.8 percent if the state has an approved UI program—and all fifty states have such a program. These funds are used for federal administrative costs related to UI and for funding half the cost of extending unemployment benefits from twenty-six to thirty-nine weeks in states that experience high levels of unemployment.

Any firm that does not make its required payments under the new proposal could be required to pay the full 6.2 percent on the first $7,000 of earnings paid to each employee, until the amount the firm owed was repaid. This mechanism implicitly provides an annual maximum that small firms would need to contribute in the event of a wage-loss insurance claim by a former employee. For example, a firm with four employees that laid off one worker would pay a maximum of $1,302 in taxes to the government in the following year if the firm did not fully reimburse the government for costs of a wage-loss insurance claim.

What Would Happen to TERAs at Retirement, Death, or Divorce?

On retirement a positive TERA balance would be converted to an IRA. Once an individual has elected retirement and his or her TERA has been converted to an IRA, that individual would no longer be eligible for unemployment compensation. On the death of the individual, a positive TERA balance would be transferred to the TERA of a spouse; if there were no living spouse, any positive TERA balance would be transferred to the TERA of a designated beneficiary. Upon divorce, a fraction of the TERA balance could be transferred to a spouse under a divorce agreement, as is currently the case with IRAs.

Could the Proposal Be Combined with Other Social Insurance Policies?

The proposal presented in this chapter has assumed that levels of unemployment payments, eligibility for such payments, and many other features of the current UI system will remain unchanged. Nonetheless, it could be readily adapted to changes in a number of ways. For example, if proposals for TERAs and wage-loss insurance were debated in Congress, other issues related to UI would naturally arise for reconsideration, including whether TERA loans should be the same size and of the same duration as current UI benefits.

The discussion has also assumed that other social insurance programs remain unchanged. However, beyond wage-loss insurance and income support for spells of unemployment, the scope of insurable events under the proposed system could be broadened to encompass missed work from injury or sickness. In addition to UI, income support is currently provided by workers' compensation and by temporary disability insurance. Temporary disability insurance programs provide wage replacement for non-work-connected sickness or injury in California, Hawaii, New Jersey, New York, Puerto Rico, and Rhode Island. Moreover, many states have a type of wage-loss insurance for individuals injured on the job. For example, some jurisdictions use a wage-loss approach that bases compensation for disability on the differences between the pre- and postinjury earnings, while others use a loss-of-wage or earnings-capacity approach, projecting future earnings loss based on age, education, labor market conditions, and degree of impairment (Barth and Niss 1999). An example of an integrated proposal that would include unemployment, injury, and sickness is provided by Fölster (1997, 2001), who discusses how a social insurance savings account with multiple insurable events—sickness, voluntary and involuntary unemployment, parental leave, and tertiary education—could work in Sweden. An integrated system for insuring against involuntary job loss, sickness, and disability would pool risks for diverse events of injury and unemployment that are not highly correlated, a benefit emphasized by Orszag and others (1999) and Stiglitz and Yun (2005). Broadened coverage of insurable events could be complemented by shifting to a common system of financing structured as a mandated benefit.

Conclusion

This chapter has described a proposal to replace the current unemployment insurance system with a system of wage-loss insurance and temporary earnings replacement accounts. Such a reform would be a fundamental shift toward insuring for the persistent, long-term effects of job loss. The core principle is that smaller, short-term needs can be met through savings, borrowing, and repayment, so that the funds for insurance can be targeted to assist those facing larger, longer-term losses.

Two-thirds of the financial resources currently used for UI (over $20 billion at 2005 expenditure levels) would be shifted to wage-loss insurance to augment the hourly wages of individuals who find new jobs at wages lower than their previous jobs. TERAs would provide the same amount of cash as under UI to be withdrawn during unemployment. Unemployment would be reduced by removing subsidies for temporary layoffs and by creating stronger incentives to return to work. The proposed system would provide a significantly greater share of net program benefits to workers in the lower half of the income distribution when compared to the current system of UI benefits alone. Targeting system resources to those whose hourly wages are lower on their new jobs after an involuntary job loss would reduce significant hardship.

References

Acevedo, Germán C., and Patricio A. Eskenazi. 2004. "The Chilean Unemployment Insurance: A New Model of Income Support Available for Unemployed Workers." Paper prepared for the International Workshop on Severance Pay Reform: Toward Unemployment Savings and Retirement Accounts. World Bank, Washington, November 7–8.

Advisory Commission on Unemployment Compensation. 1995. *Unemployment Insurance in the United States: Benefits, Financing, Coverage.* Washington.

Anderson, Patricia M., and Bruce D. Meyer. 2006. "Unemployment Insurance Tax Burdens and Benefits: Funding Family Leave and Reforming the Payroll Tax." *National Tax Journal* 59, no. 1: 77–95.

Baicker, Katherine, and M. Marit Rehavi. 2004. "Policy Watch: Trade Adjustment Assistance." *Journal of Economic Perspectives* 18, no. 2: 239–55.

Baily, Martin N., Gary Burtless, and Robert E. Litan. 1993. *Growth with Equity.* Brookings.

Baron, Ken, and Jeffrey Lange. 2003. "From Horses to Hedging." *Risk* 16, no. 2: 73–77.

Barth, Michael. 1974. "Market Effects of a Wage Subsidy." *Industrial and Labor Relations Review* 27, no. 4: 572–85.

Barth, Peter S., and Michael Niss. 1999. *Permanent Partial Disability Benefits: Interstate Differences.* Cambridge, Mass.: Workers' Compensation Research Institute.

Besley, Timothy, and Stephen Coate. 1995. "The Design of Income Maintenance Programmes." *Review of Economic Studies* 62, no. 2: 187–221.

Betson, David M., and John H. Bishop. 1982. "Wage Incentives and Distributional Effects." In *Jobs for Disadvantaged Workers: The Economics of Employment Subsidies,* edited by Robert Haveman and John L. Palmer, pp. 187–208. Brookings.

Blank, Rebecca M., and David E. Card. 1991. "Recent Trends in Insured and Uninsured Unemployment: Is There an Explanation?" *Quarterly Journal of Economics* 106, no. 4: 1157–89.

Bloom, Howard, and others. 1999. *Testing a Reemployment Incentive for Displaced Workers: The Earnings Supplement Project.* Ottawa: Social Research and Demonstration Corporation.

Browning, Edgar K. 1973. "Alternative Programs for Income Redistribution: The NIT and the NWT." *American Economic Review* 63, no. 1: 38–49.

Browning, Martin, and Thomas F. Crossley. 2001. "Unemployment Insurance Benefit Levels and Consumption Changes." *Journal of Public Economics* 80, no. 1: 1–23.

Carcagno, George J., and Walter S. Corson. 1982. "Administrative Issues." In *Jobs for Disadvantaged Workers: The Economics of Employment Subsidies,* edited by Robert Haveman and John L. Palmer, pp. 257–84. Brookings.

Chapman, Bruce. 2006. "Income Contingent Loans for Higher Education: International Reforms." In *Handbook of the Economics of Education,* edited by Eric Hanushek and Finis Welch, pp. 1435–1510. Amsterdam: North-Holland.

Farber, Henry S. 1999. "Mobility and Stability: The Dynamics of Change in Labor Markets." In *Handbook of Labor Economics*, vol. 3, edited by Orley Ashenfelter and David Card, pp. 2439–83. Amsterdam: North-Holland.

Feldstein, Martin, and Daniel Altman. 1998. "Unemployment Insurance Saving Accounts." Working Paper 6860. Cambridge, Mass.: National Bureau of Economic Research (December).

Fernandez, Enric. 2000. "To the Unemployed: Subsidies or Liquidity?" Unpublished dissertation. University of Chicago.

Ferrer, Ana M., and W. Craig Riddell. 2004. "Unemployment Insurance Savings Accounts in Latin America: Overview and Assessment." Paper prepared for the International Workshop on Severance Pay Reform: Toward Unemployment Savings and Retirement Accounts. World Bank, Washington (November 7–8).

Folks, Laura, Melynda Ihrig, and Karen Needels. 2001. "Study of Unemployment Insurance Exhaustees." Public Use File. Kalamazoo, Mich.: Upjohn Institute.

Fölster, Stefan. 1997. "Social Insurance Based on Personal Savings Accounts: A Possible Reform Strategy for Overburdened Welfare States." *Kyklos* 50, no. 2: 253–58.

———. 2001. "An Evaluation of Social Insurance Savings Accounts." *Public Finance Management* 1, no. 4: 420–48.

Graetz, Michael J., and Jerry L. Mashaw. 1999. *True Security: Rethinking American Social Insurance*. Yale University Press.

Haveman, Robert H. 1973. "Work-Conditioned Subsidies as an Income Maintenance Strategy: Issues of Program Structure and Integration." In *Studies in Public Welfare*, Paper 9, Part 1, Joint Economic Committee, Subcommittee on Fiscal Policy, pp. 33–67. Government Printing Office.

Jacobson, Louis, Robert LaLonde, and Daniel Sullivan. 1993. *The Costs of Worker Dislocation*. Kalamazoo, Mich.: W. E. Upjohn Institute for Employment Research.

Johnstone, D. Bruce. 2004. "Cost-Sharing and Equity in Higher Education: Implications of Income Contingent Loans." In *Markets in Higher: Education Rhetoric or Reality*, edited by Pedro Teixeira, and others, pp. 37–59. New York: Springer.

Karni, Edi. 1999. "Optimal Unemployment Insurance: A Survey." *Southern Economic Journal* 66, no. 2: 442–65.

Kesselman, Jonathan. 1969. "Labor Supply Effects of Income, Income Work, and Wage Subsidies." *Journal of Human Resources* 4, no. 3: 275–92.

Kletzer, Lori G. 2003. "Trade-Related Job Loss and Wage Insurance: A Synthetic Review." *Review of International Economics* 12, no. 5: 724–48.

Kletzer, Lori G., and Robert Litan. 2001. "A Prescription to Relieve Worker Anxiety." Policy Brief 73. Brookings (March).

Kling, Jeffrey R. 2006. "Fundamental Restructuring of Unemployment Insurance: Wage-Loss Insurance and Temporary Earnings Replacement Accounts." Hamilton Project Discussion Paper 2006-05. Brookings (September).

Krueger, Alan B., and William G. Bowen. 1993. "Policy Watch: Income-Contingent College Loans." *Journal of Economic Perspectives* 7, no. 3: 193–201.

Lerman, Robert I. 1982. "A Comparison of Employer and Worker Wage Subsidies." In *Jobs for Disadvantaged Workers: The Economics of Employment Subsidies,* edited by Robert Haveman and John L. Palmer, pp. 159–80. Brookings.

MacCurdy, Thomas, and Frank McIntyre. 2004. *Helping Working Poor Families: Advantages of Wage-Based Tax Credits over the EITC and Minimum Wages.* Washington: Employment Policies Institute.

Muth, Richard F. 1966. "Federal Poverty Programs: Assessment and Recommendations." Report R-116. Alexandria, Va.: Institute for Defense Analyses (January).

Nerlove, Marc. 1975. "Some Problems in the Use of Income-Contingent Loans for the Finance of Higher Education." *Journal of Political Economy* 83, no. 1: 157–84.

O'Leary, Christopher J., and Stephen Wandner. 1997. *Unemployment Insurance in the United States: Analysis of Policy Issues.* Kalamazoo, Mich.: W. E. Upjohn Institute for Employment Research.

Oregon House of Representatives, Committee on Labor. 1995. *Unemployment Eligibility and Reporting Requirement Change: Weeks to Hours.* Testimony of Christine Chute, Oregon Department of Labor (January 23).

Oreopoulos, Phillip, Marianne Page, and Ann Huff Stevens. 2005. "The Intergenerational Effect of Worker Displacement." Working Paper 11587. Cambridge, Mass.: National Bureau of Economic Research (August).

Orszag, J. Michael, and Dennis J. Snower. 2002. "From Unemployment Benefits to Unemployment Accounts." Discussion Paper 532. Bonn: Institute for the Study of Labor (July).

Orszag, J. Michael, and others. 1999. "The Impact of Individual Accounts: Piecemeal vs. Comprehensive Approaches." Paper prepared for the Annual Conference on Development Economics. World Bank, Washington (April 28–30).

Parsons, Donald O. 2000. "Wage Insurance: A Policy Review." *Research in Employment Policy* 2: 119–40.

Sehnbruch, Kirsten. 2004. "Privatized Unemployment Insurance: Can Chile's New Unemployment Insurance Scheme Serve as a Model for Other Developing Countries?" Working Paper 12. Berkeley, Calif.: Center for Latin American Studies (September).

Shimer, Robert, and Ivan Werning. 2005. "Liquidity and Insurance for the Unemployed." Research Department Staff Report 366. Federal Reserve Bank of Minneapolis (December).

Stiglitz, Joseph E., and Jungyoll Yun. 2005. "Integration of Unemployment Insurance with Retirement Insurance." *Journal of Public Economics* 89: 2037–67.

Topel, Robert. 1990. "Financing Unemployment Insurance: History, Incentives, and Reform." In *Unemployment Insurance: The Second Half Century,* edited by W. Lee Hansen and James F. Byers, pp. 107–35. University of Wisconsin Press.

U.S. House of Representatives. Committee on Ways and Means. 2004. *Green Book: Background Material and Data on the Programs within the Jurisdiction of the Committee on Ways and Means.* 108 Cong. 2 sess. Government Printing Office.

U.S. Senate. Committee on Finance. 1972. *Social Security Amendments of 1972.* Report 92-603. 92 Cong. 2 sess. Government Printing Office.

Zeckhauser, Richard, and Peter Schuck. 1970. "Alternative to the Nixon Income Maintenance Plan." *Public Interest,* no. 19 (Spring): 120–30.

Reforming Unemployment Insurance for the Twenty-First-Century Workforce

3

LORI G. KLETZER AND HOWARD ROSEN

The unemployment insurance (UI) system is the foundation of the U.S. government's response to the hardships associated with economic downturns and related job loss. In response to the Great Depression, the Social Security Act of 1935 established the UI and Social Security systems. Widespread economic hardship experienced in the 1930s had a huge impact on the nation's conscience and contributed to a sea change in the view of the role of the government in the United States. People in need began looking to the government, as opposed to families and other social institutions, as the primary provider of assistance. Social Security and UI constitute the most comprehensive social welfare programs in the history of the United States.

There have been no major changes in the basic structure of the UI system since then, despite significant changes in U.S. labor market conditions. Currently, just over one-third of unemployed workers actually receive assistance under the program, and that assistance is modest, at best. The fifty states, the District of Columbia, Puerto Rico, and the Virgin Islands administer and finance their own UI programs, resulting in vast differences

Lauren Malone provided excellent research assistance. The authors thank Jason Bordoff, Michael Deich, Janet Norwood, Peter Orszag, Dave Richardson, and Steven Wandner for helpful comments.

in benefit levels and tax rates, which do not appear to reflect local labor market conditions. The goals of UI are to provide income support during the period of unemployment (that is, to smooth income and thus smooth consumption) and to provide insurance against the risk of job loss. The failure to provide extended assistance in an orderly and timely fashion has seriously hindered the program's ability to achieve one of its other objectives: to provide countercyclical stimulus during periods of economic downturns.

While the basics of UI have remained unchanged, the U.S. labor market and workforce have experienced significant changes over the past half century. The agricultural-manufacturing economy of the 1940s and 1950s has been transformed into the service economy of the late twentieth and early twenty-first century. The entry of women into the labor force, the decline of traditional employer-based full-time employment, and the rise of contingent and part-time employment are just some of the sweeping changes that have taken place over the past seventy years. In addition, UI has never served the self-employed, who now total more than 10 million workers.[1]

Our starting point is that the current UI system is seriously out of date, given the needs of a twenty-first-century workforce. Although the basic structure is sound, important aspects of the system are in desperate need of reform. We are not the first to call for reform; the recommendations of the congressionally mandated Advisory Council on Unemployment Compensation (1996a, 1996b), chaired by long-time Bureau of Labor Statistics commissioner Janet Norwood, did not receive the attention they deserved when they were issued in the mid-1990s and have since been all but forgotten.

This chapter is presented in four sections. The first highlights recent changes in the U.S. labor market. This is followed by a section describing the current structure of UI and identifying its shortcomings. The third section presents several bold policy recommendations for reforming the UI system to better suit the needs of the current workforce, and the final section presents our conclusions.

---

1. Based on data from the Current Population Survey (a monthly household survey conducted by the Bureau of the Census for the Bureau of Labor Statistics), 10.3 million workers were self-employed in 2003, accounting for 7.5 percent of total employment (Hipple 2004). Self-employment as a share of employment has fallen, however, over the more than seventy years since the establishment of UI. Much of that decrease is explained by the declining importance of agriculture in employment. Incorporated self-employment has risen, as has the participation of women in self-employment (Hipple 2004).

Table 3-1. Unemployment Rate and Duration, by Decade

Units as indicated

Decade	Rate (percent)	Duration (weeks)	
		Average	Median
1960s	4.8	11.8	3.7[a]
1970s	6.2	11.9	6.3
1980s	7.3	15.0	7.1
1990s	5.8	15.7	7.6
2000s	5.2	16.2	8.3

Sources: Authors' calculations based on data from Bureau of Labor Statistics, "Overview of BLS Statistics on Employ-ment and Unemployment," various years (www.bls.gov/bls/employment.htm); U.S. Department of Labor (Series LNS14000000, LNS13008275, and LNS130008276).

a. The Bureau of Labor Statistics only reports median duration of unemployment data for 1967 to 1969. The average of these three years is 3.7 weeks.

Changes in the U.S. Labor Market

Sweeping changes have occurred in the labor force since the late 1930s. A significant rise in population, fueled in large part by the postwar baby boom, and the increasing participation of women resulted in a tripling of the labor force—from slightly more than 50 million people in 1939 to almost 150 million people in 2004. The most significant change over the past forty years has been the entry of women into the labor force. Since 1960 the female labor force participation rate has increased by 20 percent-age points, while the male labor force participation rate has declined slightly.

The composition of employment has also changed significantly. Agricultural employment, in decline for the better part of a century, stood at 6 percent of total employment in the 1960s and is currently just below 2 percent of total employment. Manufacturing employment, as a share of total employment, has fallen by half, from 34 percent in the 1960s to 17.5 percent currently. With services dominating employment since the 1960s, manufacturing employment currently accounts for only one in six jobs.

In addition to changes in the demographics and the composition of employment, there have been changes in the nature of unemployment. After rising between the 1960s and the 1980s, the average unemployment rate began falling in the 1990s, reaching a low of 4 percent in 2000 and remaining moderate over the past six years (see table 3-1). Yet despite overall declines in the unemployment rate, the average and median duration of unemployment has increased. These two conflicting trends suggest a

Figure 3-1. Variation in State Unemployment Rates, 1976–2005

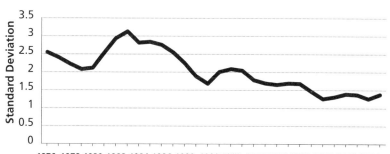

Source: Authors' calculations based on data from Bureau of Labor Statistics, "Overview of BLS Statistics on Employment and Unemployment," various years (www.bls.gov/bls/employment.htm).

change in the source of joblessness—from temporary layoff to permanent displacement. McConnell and Tracy (2005) document that from the 1960s to the mid-1980s, recessions featured surges in temporary layoffs, while for the past two recessions (early 1990s and 2001), cyclical increases in the use of temporary layoffs were not evident. (See also Groshen and Potter 2003.) Overall, new entrants account for a smaller share of the unemployed, and job losers account for a larger share of the unemployed. Compared to the 1970s, those currently unemployed have more labor force experience.

For most of the past century, employment and unemployment were highly correlated with the business cycle. This relationship appears to have changed in recent years. First, with the exception of the early 1980s, there has been a decline in the official length of recessions. Second, there has also been a decline in the magnitude of job losses occurring during economic slowdowns. Third, employment declines have continued for at least one year after the end of the last two recessions, and employment recovery has taken longer. Taken together, these three developments suggest that something has changed in the underlying structure of the U.S. labor market in recent years.

Data presented in figure 3-1 suggest that there has been a significant decline in variation across state unemployment rates over the past thirty years. During the late 1970s, states in the Northeast and Midwest—regions with high concentrations of traditional industries such as automobile manufacturing, textiles and apparel, and steel—experienced significantly higher unemployment rates than states in other regions. Beginning in the 1980s, state unemployment rates began converging toward the national average, reflecting a slow decline in overall unemployment and more similarity in state unemployment rates. This convergence suggests that during the past twenty years, unemployment has been explained more by national factors than by state or regional factors.

To summarize, we have identified the following five major developments in the U.S. labor market:

—There has been an increase in labor market participation by various demographic groups. The typical worker of 1935 was not the typical worker of 2006.

—The shift of employment from agriculture to manufacturing has been joined by a shift from manufacturing to services.

—Despite a moderate aggregate unemployment rate, the duration of unemployment has increased, with a greater incidence of permanent job loss than of temporary layoffs.

—State unemployment rates are converging, reflecting a reduction in their variation.

—Changes in employment and unemployment seem to be due more to structural rather than cyclical factors.

Firm-level employment data provide deeper insights into recent developments in the U.S. labor market. Analysis by a number of scholars reveals a high degree of labor market dynamism across all industries (Davis, Haltiwanger, and Schuh 1996; Klein, Schuh, and Triest 2003).

The high degree of employment turnover, evidenced in the firm-level data, confirms and provides deeper insights into the findings reported above, that is, a moderation in the unemployment rate, an increase in the duration of unemployment, and a reduction of the importance of business cycles in explaining unemployment. All of these labor market conditions are very different from those that existed when UI was established.

The original UI program was designed to offset income losses during cyclical periods of temporary involuntary unemployment. By contrast, current workers face short-term transitional unemployment and structural unemployment. The existing UI system is inadequate in responding to either of these labor market conditions. The system also does not assist workers who seek part-time employment, voluntarily leave one job in order to take another, or experience long-term unemployment. New entrants and reentrants into the labor market are not currently eligible for UI, since these two groups of unemployed do not fit well with one of the program's original objectives, that of insuring against the risk of involuntary job loss. Covering these workers would raise issues concerning the amount and duration of assistance, since they may not have relevant work experience.

Underlining these macroeconomic changes in the U.S. labor market is a shift from traditional employer-based full-time employment to an increased reliance on contingent and part-time employment. The shift to these non-traditional forms of employment reveals additional shortfalls in the current UI program. A system designed to provide income support during temporary layoffs for workers who were permanently attached to a single employer is not well designed for a labor market with considerable self-employment and contingent, part-time, and low-wage employment.

The Current UI Program

Federal law established the UI program in 1935 in order to provide temporary and partial wage replacement to workers involuntarily separated from their jobs. It was believed that UI would serve as a countercyclical mechanism to help stabilize the economy during economic slowdowns. In the more contemporary language of the economic analysis of insurance, the primary goal (or benefit) of UI is the ability of the government to smooth income and consumption during unemployment spells.

The UI program was modest at first. Coverage was limited to employers with more than eight employees working at least twenty weeks a year. The program did not originally cover workers employed in agriculture, non-profits, or the government. Most states set their benefit levels at 50 percent of previous earnings, up to an initial maximum benefit of $15 a week. The duration of payments ranged from twelve to twenty weeks, with most states providing assistance for a maximum of sixteen weeks. Approximately 500 million unemployed workers have received more than $600 billion in assistance since the establishment of the program (Congressional Budget Office 2004).

As established in 1935, the UI program is a federal-state system. The federal government establishes rules and standards, primarily on minimum coverage and eligibility criteria, and sets a minor tax to finance the overall administration of the program. Individual states set their own benefit amounts, duration of assistance, and means of financing that assistance.

Like Social Security and Medicare, UI, which buffers income losses associated with involuntary job loss, is a social insurance program.[2] Private UI

2. See Feldstein (2005) for a succinct exposition of social insurance.

could provide the same protection, but it is commonly thought that problems of adverse selection (of employers) would lead to private market failure. The universality of UI means that receipt of benefits is conditional only on job loss and is not based on an individual's income or wealth. That universality is commonly considered a political strength of the program, as it is with Social Security.

Some important insurance principles are built into the UI system. Premiums are paid in advance through employer taxes on wages earned. Taxes are levied on employers, but the incidence is likely passed on to employees. Individual eligibility requires earnings and employment experience above a state-specified minimum, and entry into unemployment must be through involuntary job loss resulting from a list of acceptable causes. The covered earnings requirement means that eligible workers are those with some labor force attachment. Continued receipt of benefits requires being able, available for, and actively seeking full-time work, as determined through the UI work test administered by state employment service offices.

Coverage and Eligibility

The most significant changes in UI since 1935 are related to coverage. Over the years, various changes have widened the net of covered employment to include almost all wage and salary workers, with the exception of agricultural and household workers. Self-employed workers are still not covered under the program.

Eligibility criteria for receiving assistance vary by state and are based on monetary and nonmonetary determinations:

—record of recent earnings, over a base year;

—length of job tenure (calendar quarters employed);

—cause of job loss; and

—ability and willingness to seek and accept suitable employment.

Monetary eligibility is essentially a sufficient work history before job loss. Each state determines its own sufficient work history, relying on earnings during a base period, which is generally the first four of the last five completed calendar quarters before job loss. For example, for a worker losing a job in July 2006, the base period would be April 2005 through March 2006. This lag is a remnant of a time when earnings reports had to be forwarded to a state employment office. Clearly, improved information and communications technology enables reporting on a more timely basis. Some states use an alternative base year, defined as the past four completed calendar quarters, if the standard base year calculation leaves a worker ineligible for benefits.[3] Appendix A (table 3A) reports the wide variation in monetary eligibility across states.

Nonmonetary criteria pose more significant hurdles for many workers (Levine 2006). Most state programs assist only those workers who lose their jobs through no fault of their own, as determined by state law. Reasons for UI ineligibility include:

—voluntary separation from work without good cause,

—inability or unwillingness to accept full-time work,

—discharge for misconduct connected with work,

—refusal of suitable work without good cause, and

—unemployment resulting from a labor dispute.[4]

There is enormous variation across states in the definition of *good cause* for voluntary separation, that is, leaving to accept other work, compulsory retirement, sexual or other harassment, domestic violence, and relocation to be with a spouse. Forty-three programs restrict good cause to reasons connected to work.[5] Program discretion in setting these standards results in numerous inconsistencies. For example, workers who quit to move with a spouse and meet the monetary eligibility criteria are eligible to receive UI benefits in some states—including California, Kansas, and New York—but not in others—such as Connecticut, Delaware, the District of Columbia, and Massachusetts. Workers who quit because they have been victims of sexual or other harassment are potentially eligible for UI benefits in all programs except those in Alabama, Georgia, Hawaii, Missouri, New Hampshire, and Vermont. Workers who voluntarily leave their jobs in anticipation of a plant closing in order to accept another job are potentially eligible for UI in many states, including California, Minnesota, New York, and Pennsylvania, but are ineligible in North Carolina, South Carolina, Tennessee, and West Virginia. In a highly mobile society, with integrated labor markets, it is difficult to imagine a plausible argument in support of these differences in state programs.

---

3. See U.S. Department of Labor, Employment and Training Administration, "Significant Provisions of State Unemployment Insurance Laws, July 2006" (workforcesecurity.doleta.gov/ unemploy/sigprojul2006.asp). See also Levine (2006) for a detailed discussion of the base year and its impact on benefit receipt by low-wage workers.

4. U.S. Department of Labor, Employment and Training Administration, "Comparison of State Unemployment Laws" (workforcesecurity.doleta.gov/unemploy/uilawcompar/2006/ comparison2006.asp).

5. U.S. Department of Labor, Employment and Training Administration, "Significant Provisions of State Unemployment Insurance Laws, July 2006" (workforcesecurity.doleta.gov/ unemploy/sigprojul2006.asp).

The base period monetary criteria are used as an imperfect proxy for labor market attachment. One unfortunate consequence is that some workers have insufficient work experience to meet the base period requirement, that is, reentrants into the labor market who are actively seeking employment are not eligible for UI. As a result, women who decide to postpone returning to work after childbirth and workers who return to school or who take up training after a job loss can be ruled ineligible for UI. This is true despite the fact that their current or former employers paid UI taxes, and despite the likely satisfaction of monetary eligibility requirements for the immediate base period before the job loss.

The *recipiency rate*—the percent of total unemployed workers receiving assistance—has declined over the past two decades. The recipiency rate peaked in 1975 when half of all unemployed workers received UI. The rate fell to as low as 29 percent in 1984 before rebounding to 39 percent in 1991. Receipt of benefits increased to above 40 percent in 2001, 2002, and 2003, and then fell below that in 2004 (figure 3-2). The average recipiency rate over the past twenty-seven years is approximately 37 percent. In other words, in recent years only a little more than one-third of unemployed workers actually have received assistance under the UI program.

Benefit Levels

One of the initial goals of UI was to replace half of lost wages. Because of the federal-state nature of the program, each state sets its own minimum and maximum weekly benefit amounts. Although several states have set their maximum weekly benefit at approximately two-thirds of the state weekly wage, currently only one state—Hawaii—has achieved the initial goal of actually replacing, on average, half of lost wages.

Almost all states set their maximum weekly benefits somewhere between $200 and $500, with the largest concentration of states paying between $300 and $400 (see appendix A). Puerto Rico has the lowest maximum weekly benefit ($133). States with the highest maximum weekly benefits include Massachusetts ($551 to $826), Minnesota ($350 to $515), Connecticut ($465 to $540), New Jersey ($521), and Rhode Island ($492 to $615).[6] The average weekly benefit in 2004 ranged from $106.50 in Puerto Rico to $351.35 in Massachusetts. The average weekly benefit for the entire country was $262.50 (Council of Economic Advisers 2006, table B-45). This average is almost 10 percent less than the

6. Ibid.

Figure 3-2. Comparison of Unemployed Workers, Job Losers, and UI Recipients, 1972–2004

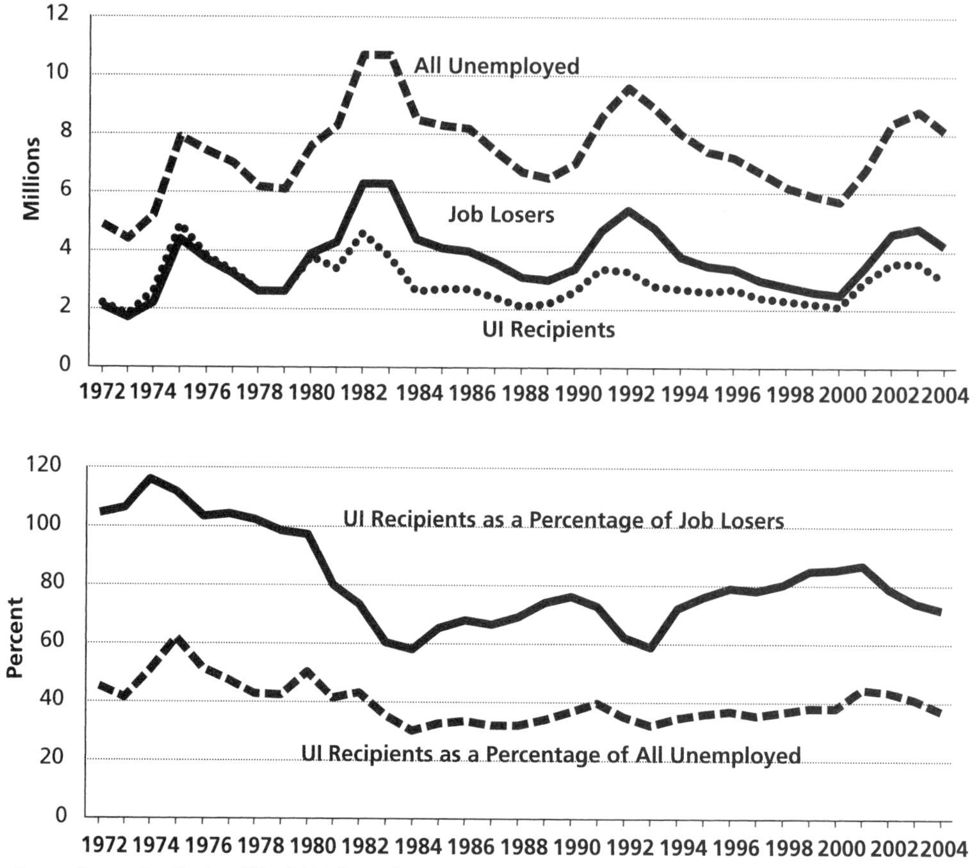

Source: Congressional Budget Office (2004, figure 3).

weekly equivalent of the poverty level for a family of three that was set by the Census Bureau.[7]

The *replacement rate,* defined as average weekly benefits as a share of average weekly earnings, is a useful measure of benefit sufficiency. The District of Columbia has the lowest replacement rate, less than one-fourth of average earnings. As mentioned above, Hawaii's UI program comes closest to replacing half of unemployed workers' average weekly earnings. Thirty-

7. Annual incomes at and below $14,974, for a family of three, with one child under the age of eighteen, were defined as poverty level for 2004 (Census Bureau 2005).

eight states have an average replacement rate of more than one-third but less than half of their workers' average weekly wages. The states with the lowest replacement rates include Alabama, Alaska, Arizona, California, Connecticut, Delaware, Louisiana, Maryland, Mississippi, Missouri, New York, Tennessee, and Virginia. The average replacement rate for the United States between 1975 and 2004 was 0.36, reaching as high as 0.38 in 1982 and as low as 0.33 in 1998 and 2000.[8]

Duration of Benefits

In the early years of the program, the duration of UI benefits was twelve to twenty weeks. Starting in the 1950s, a period of relatively low unemployment, a sizable number of states increased their UI duration to twenty-six weeks. By 1980, forty-two states had a maximum duration of twenty-six weeks, and the duration for the eleven remaining programs was between twenty-seven and thirty-nine weeks (O'Leary and Wandner 1997, table 15.3). Currently, all jurisdictions have a maximum duration of twenty-six weeks except Montana (twenty-eight weeks) and Massachusetts (thirty weeks).[9]

Over the past thirty years, the average duration for receiving UI has ranged from a low of thirteen weeks in 1989 to a high of seventeen and half weeks in 1983, hovering around fifteen weeks for most of the period (figure 3-3). A sizable fraction of UI beneficiaries exhaust their benefits, i.e., remain unemployed beyond the period for which they can receive UI. The percent of workers who exhausted the benefits before finding reemployment ranged from a low of 25.8 in 1979 to a high of 43.9 in 2003. On average, approximately one-third of UI recipients exhaust their benefits before finding new jobs.

With the trend increase in the average duration of unemployment, the maximum period that workers can receive UI has fallen from two times to a little more than one and a half times the average duration of unemployment. As with benefit levels, there does not appear to be any significant relationship between benefit duration and local labor market conditions.

Until the 1980s, the pattern of job loss in the United States was strongly cyclical. As a result, the number of unemployed and the duration

8. Authors' calculations based on U.S. Department of Labor, Employment and Training Administration, "Significant Provisions of State Unemployment Insurance Laws, July 2006" (workforcesecurity.doleta.gov/unemploy/sigprojul2006.asp).

9. U.S. Department of Labor, Employment and Training Administration, "Significant Provisions of State Unemployment Insurance Laws, July 2006" (workforcesecurity.doleta.gov/unemploy/sigprojul2006.asp).

Figure 3-3. Average Duration of Unemployment Insurance Receipt, with Periods of Recession Highlighted, 1957–2005

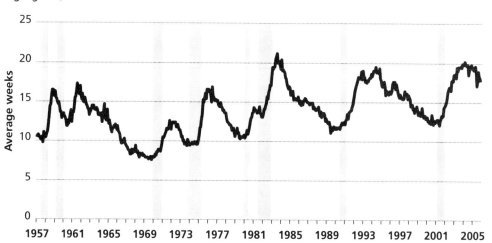

Sources: For duration, see Bureau of Labor Statistics, "Overview of BLS Statistics on Employment and Unemployment," various years (www.bls.gov/bls/employment.htm); for business cycle timing, see National Bureau of Economic Research, "U.S. Business Cycle Expansions and Contractions" (www.nber.org/cycles.html).

of unemployment tended to increase during periods of economic slow-down and decrease during periods of recovery. According to this relationship, the share of unemployed workers who exhaust their benefits before finding new jobs would be expected to rise during and immediately after recessions.

Extended Benefit Programs

The UI system proved unable to respond to surges in unemployment during most of the cyclical downturns over the past half century. Increases in the duration of unemployment during and immediately after those recessions were the primary impetus for extending statutory UI beyond its base period (figure 3-3). Congress enacted the first temporary extension of UI during the 1958 recession. In 1970 Congress enacted the extended benefits program with automatic triggers to provide assistance in a more orderly fashion. High rates of regular UI exhaustion, problems with the automatic triggers, and political pressures required subsequent congressional action to deal with heightened levels and prolonged duration of unemployment during recessions.

Under the current program, UI benefits can be extended for an additional thirteen weeks when the unemployment rate of covered workers (the insured unemployment rate, or IUR) during the previous thirteen weeks has been at least 5 percent as well as 20 percent higher than during the same thirteen-week period of the previous two years. Since states are required to finance half of the extended benefit programs, they are free to adjust this trigger.[10]

Changes in the labor market and in the UI program, combined with the static nature of the triggers, have produced an extended benefit system that is not automatic. As a result, Congress has occasionally found it necessary to extend UI through the Temporary Extended Unemployment Compensation program. Since the 1980s, the standard extended benefit program has provided a smaller share of assistance to unemployed workers than the emergency extensions of UI enacted by Congress.

Although helpful to millions of workers, these temporary stopgap measures have politicized unemployment assistance, thereby undermining one of the initial goals of the UI program. These temporary programs have proven to be clumsy, typically being enacted after hundreds of thousands of workers have already exhausted their UI. In addition, the sunset provisions are arbitrarily set and usually fall before employment has recovered. Overall, the nation's UI program has become less automatic and more dependent on congressional action in response to prolonged periods of economic slowdown.

Financing UI

UI is financed by a combination of federal and state payroll taxes. Revenue from the federal payroll tax is used to finance the costs incurred by federal and state governments in administering the UI program and to cover loans to states that exhaust their regular UI funds. States are required to raise the necessary revenue to finance regular UI benefits paid to their unemployed workers. Federal and state governments share the costs of financing benefits under the automatic extended benefit program. Currently, federal taxes finance 17 percent of the UI program. The remaining 83 percent is financed

10. Optional triggers include cases when the IUR for the previous thirteen weeks is above 6 percent, regardless of its performance over the previous two years, and cases when the seasonal adjusted unemployment rate for all civilian employment—the total unemployment rate (TUR)—is at least 6.5 percent and also 10 percent higher than that rate for the same three-month period in either of the two previous years. Benefits can be provided for an additional thirteen to twenty weeks if the TUR is at least 8 percent and also 10 percent higher than that rate for the same three-month period in either of the two previous years.

by state taxes. Temporary extended UI programs enacted by Congress have typically been financed by federal budgetary expenditures without any specific revenue offset.

The federal tax established by the Federal Unemployment Tax Act (FUTA) is currently 6.2 percent on the first $7,000 of annual salary by covered employers on behalf of covered employees.[11] Employers must pay the tax on behalf of employees who earn at least $1,500 during a calendar quarter. Employers receive a 5.4 percent credit against the tax, making the effective FUTA tax rate 0.8 percent. The bottom line is that the federal tax is trivial: a maximum of $56 is collected annually for each worker who is covered under the program.

There have been few adjustments in the FUTA taxable wage base since it was first established in 1939. The wage base, originally set at $3,000, remained fixed for thirty-two years until 1972, when it was raised to $4,200. That increase kept the taxable wage base in line with its real value in 1960. Congress raised the federal taxable wage base to $6,000 in 1978 and to $7,000 in 1983, where it has remained up to the present—more than twenty years. Had the taxable wage base been adjusted for inflation over the past sixty-five years, it would currently be about $45,000 (figure 3-4).

If the taxable wage base were adjusted to $45,000, the net federal tax rate—the tax rate minus the credit—could be reduced by half, to 0.4 percent, and generate the same amount of revenue that is currently being collected.[12] Although it is unrealistic to expect an adjustment of this magnitude anytime soon, any increase in the wage base to make up for the erosion in its real value over the past two decades could provide additional funding for assistance to workers in need or could enable the federal government to reduce the FUTA tax rate—or both. Most important, adjusting the wage base upward would reduce the regressive nature of the tax. Under the current structure, the FUTA tax accounts for a larger share of lower-income workers' wages. Adjusting for inflation alone—as many states have been doing for their own UI taxes—would increase the federal taxable wage base fivefold, make the system more progressive, and provide additional revenues to the system.

11. The 6.2 percent includes a 0.2 percent surtax initially passed by Congress in 1976, designed to replenish the UI trust fund. The surtax is scheduled to expire on December 31, 2007.
12. This estimate is based on the current number of workers covered.

Figure 3-4. Federal Taxable Wage Base, 1940–2004

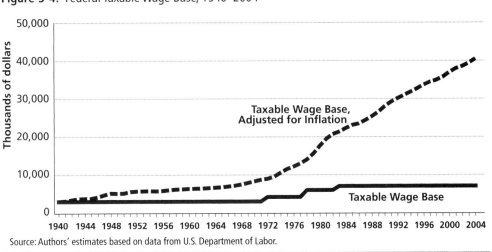

Source: Authors' estimates based on data from U.S. Department of Labor.

Twenty-seven jurisdictions set their taxable wage base below $10,000; of those programs, ten set their taxable wage base at $7,000, the same as the federal taxable wage base (see appendix A). Twelve programs set their taxable wage base above $20,000, close to three times the taxable wage base set by the federal government. The states with the highest taxable wage base are North Dakota ($20,300); Montana ($21,600); Iowa ($22,000); Minnesota, Nevada, and Utah (each with taxable wage bases of $24,000); New Jersey ($25,800); Oregon ($28,000); Arkansas ($28,700); Idaho ($29,200); Washington ($30,900); and Hawaii ($34,000). The weighted average taxable wage base for all fifty-three UI programs is $11,305.

Federal guidelines dictate that states have in place UI payroll tax systems that are experience rated. With experience rating, firms that lay off fewer workers face a lower tax rate on their payroll. States have the discretion to structure their own experience rating system, and those systems, as with the tax rates, vary considerably. The average state UI tax rates vary from 0.18 percent in the Virgin Islands to 1.89 percent in Arkansas. Forty-four jurisdictions have average state UI tax rates below 1.0 percent, while six jurisdictions—Illinois, Massachusetts, Mississippi, Pennsylvania, Puerto Rico, and Rhode Island—have average tax rates between 1.0 and 1.5 percent, and three programs—Arkansas, Oregon, and Washington—have the highest state UI tax rates, over 1.5 percent. The average tax rate for the fifty-three UI programs is 0.82 percent.[13]

Some aspects of the current UI system work well and deserve to be highlighted. Examples are the contribution of the UI program to income smoothing and consumption smoothing, and insuring workers against the risk of job loss (see Gruber 1997 and Chetty 2004, among others). UI constitutes an important source of income for unemployed workers and their families, particularly for the long-term unemployed. The Congressional Budget Office (2004) reports that UI benefits played a significant role in maintaining the family income of recipients who experienced long-term spells of unemployment in 2001 and early 2002, particularly for those families that had only one wage earner. Before becoming unemployed, recipients' average family income was about $4,800 a month. When recipients lost their jobs, that income—excluding UI benefits—dropped by almost 60 percent. Inclusion of UI benefits reduced the income loss to about 40 percent.

A Major Makeover for UI

In recent years, the U.S. labor market has come under increased pressures from intensified domestic and international competition. These pressures have changed the nature of job turnover in the United States. Unlike the cyclical job losses that characterized the labor market and economy from 1945 to the 1980s, job losses are now related more to structural factors, with workers simultaneously changing jobs, industries, and occupations. The current UI program, though, is fighting an earlier battle, one of widespread temporary layoffs, where workers were attached to a single employer.

As discussed above, current labor market conditions differ a great deal from those that existed in 1935, suggesting that it is time to revisit some of the fundamental elements of the original UI program. The reforms we outline below maintain the basic structure of UI while enhancing its efficiency, reach, and impact, to reflect the changes in the labor market since the program was designed. Before we turn to the specific changes, it is worth examining why we retain the basic structure of the program. After seven decades of experience, there is widespread agreement that the government

---

13. Tax rates equal UI tax collections as a percent of total wages in taxable employment. See U.S. Department of Labor, Employment and Training Administration, "Unemployment Insurance Chartbook" (www.doleta.gov/unemploy/chartbook.cfm).

should play an important role in providing insurance against job loss and income support to smooth consumption. Even those who call for UI reform centered on personalized accounts (for example, Feldstein 2005 and Kling 2006) agree that the government should play a central role in assisting the unemployed.

The basic structure of UI serves that function well, even though changes are necessary to update the precise details of the program. Furthermore, in our view, the current structure of UI does not create substantial economic costs. Although we acknowledge the potential distortions associated with the current UI structure, the empirical evidence on the size of the impact of these distortions is mixed. For employers, UI may subsidize the use of temporary layoffs, but experience rating is intended to address this distortion. To be sure, the degree of experience rating is imperfect; that is, the tax rate faced by a firm does not increase one for one with increased use of temporary layoffs.[14] More progress toward perfecting experience rating may reduce the subsidization of temporary layoffs, although with the trend decline in temporary layoffs, further adjustments in this area appear to be of secondary importance.

For individual workers, the most prominent distortion is the reduced incentive to save for unemployment spells and to begin a search for a new job immediately after separation (Engen and Gruber 2001). A sizable literature seeks to establish a link between receipt of UI and longer unemployment duration (Meyer 1995). The magnitude of the effect, however, is not overwhelming, and longer job searches may lead to more productive job matches, although the evidence is admittedly mixed on this latter point. Furthermore, as Feldstein (2005) states, it is important to note that these disincentives are a result of specific program designs and are not inherent in the program itself. In other words, evidence of the distortions and their effects on the overall economy should not serve as an indictment of the entire UI system; rather, they are known and understandable implications of government intervention and should be addressed when possible. The broader point is that it is important to balance any costs of the distortions against the benefits of the program.

---

14. The degree of experience rating is typically measured by the marginal tax cost (MTC) to the firm from an additional dollar of UI benefits paid to one of its (former) workers. The MTC is the present value of the additional tax payments by the firm to the state UI system, associated with the payment by the state to the worker of an additional dollar of benefits. If the MTC is less than one, the firm does not bear the full cost of the UI benefits received by its laid-off workers.

The following is an outline of proposals for reforming the current UI program. Estimates of increased costs and revenues associated with these proposals are included. Although each proposal can be evaluated and implemented separately, it would be preferable to enact them all.

Strengthen the Federal Leadership Role in UI

As documented earlier, the nature of unemployment in the United States has shifted from cyclical to structural. Although there clearly remain some differences in local labor market conditions, the current pressures on the U.S. labor market are becoming more national. Furthermore, state differences in the incidence and experience of unemployment have narrowed considerably. Local labor market conditions primarily affect the prospects for reemployment. Given the increasingly national nature of the labor market, UI would better meet its original objectives if the federal government played a more prominent role in this partnership.

When UI was created, there was considerable congressional debate over the state and federal governments' roles. At the time, there was broad consensus that Social Security, established by the same legislation that created UI, should be administered, financed, and managed by the federal government. There were no economic reasons to treat UI differently than Social Security, but Congress was concerned about infringing on states that had already established their own UI programs, such as Massachusetts, Ohio, and Wisconsin.[15] The compromise adopted by Congress was a federal-state hybrid, giving the federal government responsibility over administering and financing the costs associated with administering the UI program, and placing the responsibility for delivering the actual assistance and financing that assistance with the states. Congress agreed to rebate most of the federal tax for states that conformed to federal UI standards (Blaustein 1993).

After seventy years, the result of this compromise is a patchwork system of fifty-three UI programs, each with different eligibility criteria and benefit levels. Our analysis shows that since UI was established, unemployment and its associated costs have become more national in nature. Despite these changes, the likelihood that an unemployed worker will receive assistance, and the extent of that assistance, depends on where that worker resides.

In addition to inequities created by disparate rules across states, a significant downside of the current federal-state partnership is the states' real or perceived fears that program generosity will result in adverse changes to

---

15. For a discussion of the reasons why Social Security and UI were initially set up under different models, see Baicker, Goldin, and Katz (1997).

their business environment. Federal leadership would avoid interstate competition and a "race to the bottom" in program benefits.

An increased leadership role for the federal government would be characterized by expanding standards for eligibility, duration, and level of benefits, and for financing the program. We sketch the relevant changes below.

ELIGIBILITY. Beginning with eligibility, here is what could be recommended.

—Standardize the base period for determining eligibility to the past four complete calendar quarters before job loss. This change, already implemented by a number of states, updates the operational definition of labor market attachment and reflects the reduced time needed to report earnings.

—Use hours rather than earnings in determining eligibility (Levine 2006). The shift to hours would bring more low- and moderate-wage workers—who often need help the most during periods of unemployment—into the system.

—Harmonize nonmonetary eligibility standards. The patchwork of nonmonetary eligibility criteria, whereby some states consider voluntary separations for good cause while others do not, creates unnecessary complexity and inequities in the system.

—Enable reentrants to the labor force, if determined eligible at the time of job loss or separation, to receive the benefits they would have received at the time of job loss. In a fluid labor market, many workers may leave the labor force for some time (for example, to care for a child or parent) and then return. If the workers had been eligible for UI when they separated from their previous job but did not claim it at that time, they should be eligible for benefits when they return to the labor force.

—Amend the work test to allow job search for part-time employment. Part-time work is a common feature of the current labor market, accounting for 16 percent of employment in July 2006, and unemployed workers should not be disqualified from receiving benefits because they are searching for part-time work.

The share of unemployed workers who actually received assistance under the UI program averaged 37 percent between 1980 and 2005. The proposals outlined above are designed to increase the number and share of unemployed workers eligible to receive assistance. Given the difficulties associated with precise estimation of how much each of the individual proposals would contribute to increasing the number of potentially eligible workers, we instead estimate the costs associated with raising the recipiency rate in increments to 50 percent (table 3-2), which is a reasonable objective for the changes delineated above.

Table 3-2. Estimated Costs Associated with Increasing the Recipiency Rate[a]

Units as indicated

Recipiency rate (percent)	Increase in number of eligible workers	Increase in total benefits paid (billions of dollars)
40	220,000	1.6
45	620,000	4.5
50	1,000,000	7.4

Source: Authors' calculations.
a. Increase in workers and costs (benefits paid) relative to twenty-five-year average.

BENEFIT LEVELS AND DURATION OF BENEFIT RECEIPT. The federal government could make improvements in this area as well.

—Standardize benefit levels to at least half of lost earnings with a maximum weekly benefit equal to two-thirds of state average weekly earnings. Table 3-3 provides budgetary estimates for raising the replacement rate in this manner.

—Develop standard rules to cover benefits for partial unemployment (reduced hours). Standardizing these rules would help to update the program to reflect new labor market realities. California is among the few states with UI for partial unemployment.

—Establish uniform duration of a minimum of twenty-six weeks in all programs.

—Fix the extended benefit triggers so that they are more automatic and workers can receive assistance without disruption during economic downturns.

—Make benefits more responsive to work experience and local labor market conditions. Currently, UI benefits are set arbitrarily, based primarily on a state's ability and willingness to pay. In general, benefits do not currently reflect an employee's work experience, nor (and more important) do they reflect the costs associated with that worker's job loss, including the potential difficulty in finding a new job. We recommend setting benefit levels according to a formula based on a number of factors, including wage history, local labor market conditions, and reason for separation. Workers living in regions with poor labor market conditions might receive a higher level of assistance or receive assistance for longer periods, or both.

—Standardize allowances for dependents across all states.

FINANCING. Increase the FUTA taxable wage base, in steps, to $45,000. The last time the UI taxable wage base was adjusted was more than twenty years ago. As a result, the payroll tax is extremely regressive. Raising the

Table 3-3. Estimates of Costs Associated with Increasing the Replacement Rate[a]

Dollars, except as indicated

Replacement rate (percent)	Average weekly benefit at new replacement rate	Increase in average weekly benefit	Increase in total benefits at new replacement rate (billions)
40	295.67	34.00	0.3
45	332.63	70.96	0.7
50	369.59	107.92	1.1

Source: Authors' calculations.

a. Estimates based on the following assumptions: the average replacement rate between 1980 and 2003 was 35.4 percent; the average weekly benefit in 2003 was $261.67; the average weekly wage in 2003 was $739.18; the total number of weeks of compensation in December 2005 was slightly fewer than 10 million.

taxable wage base to $45,000 would have the benefit of making the tax more progressive while generating new revenue to finance needed reforms in the program. We estimate that increasing the taxable wage base to $45,000 while maintaining the same tax rate would generate $8.7 billion in increased revenue. This would be enough to finance the costs associated with providing more assistance (raising the replacement rate) to more workers (increasing the recipiency rate).

Local or regional wage differences, or both, would be respected under this plan because the harmonization of benefits would be in percentages of earnings, not dollar levels. Treating workers more equally in terms of program standards would remove differences that have little or no justification other than tradition. Given their long experience in providing these services, local and state providers would remain primarily responsible for reemployment assistance, job training, intake, and administration of benefits.

Enable Individuals to Contribute to Private Unemployment Accounts

Workers who do not have traditional relationships with employers are currently not covered by UI. To address this shortfall, individuals, initially the self-employed, would be able to establish and make tax-advantaged contributions up to a maximum of $200 a year to their own private unemployment accounts. Eventually this program might be extended to workers who voluntarily leave their jobs for reasons not currently allowed under the program.

Cost estimates for one version of a tax-advantaged saving program are based on the following assumptions:

—participants begin making contributions at age thirty;

—the starting wage is $30,000, and wages increase by 3 percent a year;

—the participant and the government each contribute 0.25 percent of wages each year into the fund;

—the real annual interest rate on the fund is 2 percent;

—contributions to and existing funds in these personal saving accounts would not be taxed; and

—one-fourth of the self-employed—approximately 2.5 million—would voluntarily participate in the program.[16]

Participants would be able to draw on these funds to cushion severe income losses or to finance training and job search associated with changing jobs, and withdrawals would be taxed as income. All remaining funds after age sixty-two would be transferred to existing retirement savings accounts.

Based on these assumptions, each participant's fund would grow to approximately $11,000 by the time the worker turned sixty-two. The cost to the government for each worker would be an average of approximately $125 a year, and an average of approximately $300 million a year for the entire program. This estimate does not include lost tax revenue as a result of the accounts' tax-advantaged status.

Augment UI with a Program of Wage-Loss Insurance

For some unemployed workers, particularly older workers, the costs of job loss extend beyond reemployment because earnings at a new job tend to be less than at the old job.[17] Wage-loss insurance offers assistance that is tailored to actual earnings losses. We propose that a wage-loss insurance program be offered in addition to, and not instead of, UI. As proposed in Kletzer and Litan (2001), eligible workers would receive some fraction, perhaps half, of their weekly earnings loss. The fraction could vary by age and worker tenure. Workers who find a new full-time job within twenty-six weeks of separation would be eligible for wage-loss insurance, potentially reducing the period of UI receipt.

For example, if an eligible unemployed worker earned $600 a week at her previous full-time job and found a new full-time job paying $520 (13 percent less), the supplemental payment would be $40 a week, bringing the total weekly earnings to $560. At a 30 percent earnings loss, the new

---

16. The assumed take-up rate for these private unemployment accounts is much higher than the 10 percent take-up rate for individual retirement accounts (IRAs). Unlike IRAs, private unemployment accounts would allow workers to accumulate tax-advantaged savings to be accessed in the event of unemployment. In addition, under this proposal, a worker's contribution would be matched dollar for dollar by the government.

17. This section borrows from Kletzer (2004).

job would pay $420 a week, and the weekly payment would be $90, making the total weekly earnings $510. Although wage-loss insurance might encourage a worker to take a job paying less than his previous job, the supplemental payment would reduce the earnings loss by half.

The Trade Act of 2002, in its reauthorization of Trade Adjustment Assistance (TAA), added a limited program of wage-loss insurance. Called Alternative Trade Adjustment Assistance (ATAA), workers who are more than fifty years old and earn less than $50,000 a year may be eligible to receive half the difference between their previous and new earnings, subject to a cap of $10,000, for up to two years. Workers must find a new full-time job and enroll in the ATAA program within twenty-six weeks of job loss and cannot receive other income support or training under TAA.[18]

Wage-loss insurance raises the return to job search, especially for workers with greater reemployment losses. A higher wage-loss insurance replacement rate further increases the return to job search, but it might reduce a worker's incentive to search for another, higher-paying job. If the supplement interval is fixed and limited relative to the date of job loss, the present value of the supplement declines with the duration of unemployment and acts as an incentive for a quicker return to work. As a result, workers who have difficulty finding a job, particularly if it is required to be a full-time job, will receive a smaller supplement than workers with shorter unemployment spells. This effect does not hold if the duration of wage-loss insurance is linked to time on the new job rather than time since separating from the previous job.

A wage-loss insurance program would be of greatest value to high-tenure, lower-skilled manufacturing workers, who typically earn a wage premium above what they might have otherwise earned. Wage-loss insurance is more valuable to these workers than it is to lower-wage workers, since it is less likely that lower-wage displaced workers will experience large earnings losses. This introduces a potentially important distributional issue.

Despite its benefits, wage-loss insurance is not a perfect solution to the costs associated with unemployment. Restricting wage-loss insurance eligibility to full-time employment raises some questions. Earnings losses are a product of both changes in wages and in hours. Either wages or hours, or both, could be lower on the new job. Particularly for lower-skilled workers, most readily available jobs will be part time, as well as at low wage

---

18. See Kletzer and Rosen (2005) for a detailed discussion of ATAA and possible extensions.

rates. Limiting benefits to those who find one of a scarce supply of full-time jobs is tantamount to rewarding the winners twice. On the other hand, if the supplement is applied to earnings losses arising from changes in hours worked, effective pay on new part-time jobs could be quite high. For example, as discussed by Parsons (2000), if a particular worker's earnings loss arises solely from working part time on the new job, that worker will have an opportunity to work half the hours she was working on her previous job, at three-fourths of the pay. This level of subsidy could induce a sizable shift to part-time work.

Structuring a program with a relatively short eligibility period, starting with the date of job loss, creates a reemployment incentive and addresses one of the most commonly expressed UI concerns, but it also limits the compensatory nature of the program. Displaced worker earnings losses are long term; earnings losses exist five to six years after job loss, well beyond the two years covered by ATAA (Jacobson, LaLonde, and Sullivan 1993).

The costs of a wage-loss insurance program depend critically on the number of eligible workers, the earnings losses of those reemployed at lower pay, and the duration of unemployment before reemployment. (The time it takes to find a job is a common program trigger.) Other critical program characteristics include the duration of wage-loss insurance payments, the annual cap on program payments, and the replacement rate. Based on a program with a two-year duration, a 50 percent replacement rate, and a $10,000 annual cap, Brainard, Litan, and Warren (2006) estimate that the cost of providing wage-loss insurance for all dislocated workers would have been $4.3 billion (in current dollars) based on labor market conditions in 2003. They estimate that the same basic program in 2000, when unemployment was lower and fewer workers experienced a wage loss upon reemployment, would have cost $2.6 billion.[19]

An expanded wage-loss insurance program could be financed through general government revenues or by raising the FUTA taxable wage base or tax rate. Augmenting UI, with assistance tailored to the size of reemployment earnings losses, is possible with relatively small changes in UI program parameters.

More generally, regarding reemployment, the current UI system has a limited relationship with efforts to transition workers back to employment. The worker profiling system targets resources to workers at risk of

19. These estimates do not reflect possible savings from reduced duration of UI receipt due to the reemployment incentive. For more details on the estimates, see Brainard and colleagues (2006, table 7).

exhausting benefits. Workers receiving UI are required to prove that they are actively seeking employment, primarily by documenting job inquiries and interviews. Most periods of unemployment (and benefit receipt) are too short for serious training, but job search assistance can be short term with high return given its relatively low cost. With the rise in structural unemployment, training needs are likely to expand.

Conclusion

The federal-state structure of UI is a relic of its 1935 establishment, and a Depression-era concern over the constitutionality of plans for the federal government to levy taxes for unemployment assistance. Federal programs are now well established. More important, changes necessary to move UI into the twenty-first century require significant federal leadership. The very basic structure of UI must be reformed, broadening from the single-employer, full-time worker, temporary layoff model to an approach that accommodates permanent job loss, part-time or contingent work, self-employment, and the incidence of job loss, and national, rather than local or regional, unemployment. American workers are currently facing considerable pressure due to continued technological change and intensified competition resulting from globalization. Despite significant changes in U.S. labor market conditions, there have been no major changes in the basic structure of UI since it was established seventy years ago. Reforming the nation's UI program is necessary to make it relevant to the labor market of the twenty-first century.

References

Advisory Council on Unemployment Compensation. 1996a. *Collected Findings and Recommendations: 1994–1996.* Washington.

———. 1996b. *Defining Federal and State Roles in Unemployment Insurance: Report to the President and Congress.* Washington.

Baicker, Katherine, Claudia Goldin, and Lawrence F. Katz. 1997. "A Distinctive System: Origins and Impact of U.S. Unemployment Compensation." Working Paper 5889. Cambridge, Mass.: National Bureau of Economic Research (January).

Blaustein, Saul J. 1993. *Unemployment Insurance in the United States: The First Half Century.* Kalamazoo, Mich.: W. E. Upjohn Institute for Employment Research.

Brainard, Lael, Robert E. Litan, and Nicholas Warren. 2006. "A Fairer Deal for America's Workers in a New Era of Offshoring." In *Brookings Trade Forum 2005: Offshoring White-Collar Work,* edited by Susan M. Collins and Lael Brainard, pp. 427–56. Brookings.

Chetty, Raj. 2004. "Optimal Unemployment Insurance When Income Effects Are Large." Working Paper 10500. Cambridge, Mass.: National Bureau of Economic Research (May).

Congressional Budget Office. 2004. *Family Income of Unemployment Insurance Recipients.* Government Printing Office (March).

Council of Economic Advisers. 2006. *Economic Report of the President.* Washington.

Davis, Steven J., John C. Haltiwanger, and Scott Schuh. 1996. *Job Creation and Destruction.* MIT Press.

Engen, Eric M., and Jonathan Gruber. 2001. "Unemployment Insurance and Precautionary Saving." *Journal of Monetary Economics* 47, no. 3: 545–79.

Feldstein, Martin. 2005. "Rethinking Social Insurance." *American Economic Review* 95, no. 1: 1–24.

Groshen, Erica L., and Simon Potter. 2003. "Has Structural Change Contributed to a Jobless Recovery?" *Current Issues in Economics and Finance* 9, no. 8: 1–7.

Gruber, Jonathan. 1997. "The Consumption-Smoothing Benefits of Unemployment Insurance." *American Economic Review* 87, no. 1: 192–205.

Hipple, Steven. 2004. "Self-Employment in the United States: An Update." *Monthly Labor Review* 127, no. 7: 13–23.

Jacobson, Louis, Robert LaLonde, and Daniel Sullivan. 1993. *The Costs of Worker Dislocation.* Kalamazoo, Mich.: W. E. Upjohn Institute for Employment Research.

Klein, Michael W., Scott Schuh, and Robert K. Triest. 2003. *Job Creation, Job Destruction, and International Competition.* Kalamazoo, Mich.: W. E. Upjohn Institute for Employment Research.

Kletzer, Lori G. 2004. "Trade-Related Job Loss and Wage Insurance: A Synthetic Review." *Review of International Economics* 12, no. 5: 724–48.

Kletzer, Lori G., and Robert E. Litan. 2001. "A Prescription to Relieve Worker Anxiety." Policy Brief PB01–2. Washington: Institute for International Economics.

Kletzer, Lori G., and Howard F. Rosen. 2005. "Easing the Adjustment Burden on U.S. Workers." In *The United States and the World Economy,* edited by C. Fred Bergsten, pp. 313–41. Washington: Institute for International Economics.

Kling, Jeffrey. 2006. "Wage-Loss Insurance and Temporary Earnings Replacement Accounts." Discussion Paper 2006-05. Washington: Hamilton Project (September).

Levine, Phillip B. 2006. "Unemployment Insurance over the Business Cycle: Does It Meet the Needs of Less-Skilled Workers?" In *Working and Poor: How Economic and Policy Changes Are Affecting Low-Wage Workers,* edited by Rebecca Blank, Sheldon Danziger, and Robert Shoeni, pp. 366–95. New York: Russell Sage Foundation.

McConnell, Margaret M., and Joseph M. Tracy. 2005. "Unemployment Insurance and the Diminished Importance of Temporary Layoffs over the Business Cycle." Federal Reserve Bank of New York (May).

Meyer, Bruce D. 1995. "Lessons from the U.S. Unemployment Insurance Experiments." *Journal of Economic Literature* 33 (March): 91–131.

O'Leary, Christopher J., and Stephen A. Wandner. 1997. "Summing Up." In *Unemployment Insurance in the United States: Analysis of Policy Issues*, edited by Christopher J. O'Leary and Stephen A. Wandner, pp. 669–733. Kalamazoo, Mich.: W. E. Upjohn Institute for Employment Research.

Parsons, Donald O. 2000. "Wage Insurance: A Policy Review." In *Long-Term Unemployment and Reemployment Policies. Research in Employment Policy*, vol. 2, edited by Laurie J. Bassi and Stephen A. Woodbury, pp. 119–40. Stamford, Conn.: JAI Press.

U.S. Census Bureau. 2005. *Incomes, Earnings and Poverty from the 2004 American Community Survey.* Government Printing Office (August).

Appendix 3A. State UI Program Statistics

Dollars, except where indicated

State, District, or Possession	Average annual earnings	Annual earnings required for eligibility	Maximum weekly benefit amount	Taxable base	Minimum, maximum, and new employer tax rates (percent)
Alabama	32,640	2,114	230	8,000	0.44, 6.04, 2.70
Alaska	37,179	1,000	248–320	28,700	1.21, 5.40, 4.15
Arizona	36,017	2,250	240	7,000	0.02, 5.40, 2.00
Arkansas	29,543	1,836	395	10,000	0.1, 10.00, 2.90
California	44,056	1,125	450	7,000	1.3, 5.40, 3.40
Colorado	40,139	2,500	435	10,000	0.3, 5.40, 1.70
Connecticut	52,677	780	465–540	15,000	0.5, 5.40, 2.90
Delaware	42,623	920 (in 2 HQs)[a]	330	8,500	0.3, 8.20, 2.20
District of Columbia	61,271	1,950	359	9,000	1.3, 6.60, 2.70
Florida	34,362	3,400	275	7,000	0.32, 5.40, 2.70
Georgia	38,174	1,680	320	8,500	0.03, 6.21, 2.70
Hawaii	33,223	130	459	34,000	0, 5.40, 2.40
Idaho	29,208	1,658	322	29,200	0.477, 5.40, 1.67
Illinois	42,547	1,600	350–475	11,000	0.3, 8.10, 3.40
Indiana	34,890	2,750	390	7,000	1.1, 5.60, 2.70
Iowa	31,767	1,380	334–410	22,000	0, 8.0, 1.0
Kansas	32,218	2,790	386	8,000	0.07, 7.40, 4.33
Kentucky	32,894	2,945	401	8,000	0.5, 9.50, 2.70
Louisiana	31,573	1,200	258	7,000	0.1, 6.20, industry avg.
Maine	30,818	3,612	320–480	12,000	0.53, 5.40, 1.78
Maryland	41,051	900	340	8,500	0.6, 9.0, 2.30
Massachusetts	49,892	3,000	551–826	14,000	1.12, 10.96, 2.53
Michigan	40,945	2,964	362	9,000	0.06, 10.30, 2.70
Minnesota	40,832	1,250	350–515	24,000	9.3 + 14% of taxes due, 9.3 + 14% of taxes due, 2.32 + 14% of taxes due
Mississippi	27,738	1,200	210	7,000	0.4, 5.40, 2.70
Missouri	34,822	1,950	270	11,000	0, 6.0, 2.70
Montana	26,672	5,000 (in 2 HQs)	362	21,600	0.13, 6.50, industry avg.
Nebraska	30,792	2,500	288	8,000	0.39, 6.76, 2.50
Nevada	36,073	600	362	24,000	0.25, 5.40, 2.95
New Hampshire	39,595	2,800	372	8,000	0.01, 6.50, 2.70
New Jersey	47,854	2,460	521	25,800	0.1825, 5.40, 2.68
New Mexico	29,738	1,799	312–360	17,900	0.03, 5.40, 2.0
New York	52,768	2,400	405	8,500	0.9, 8.90, 3.40

(continued)

Appendix 3A. State UI Program Statistics (*Continued*)

Dollars, except where indicated

State, District, or Possession	Average annual earnings	Annual earnings required for eligibility	Maximum weekly benefit amount	Taxable base	Minimum, maximum, and new employer tax rates (percent)
North Carolina	34,479	3,749	457	17,300	0, 5.70, 1.20
North Dakota	28,530	2,795	351	20,300	0.4, 9.44, 1.87
Ohio	36,102	3,840	343–462	9,000	0.5, 10.0, 2.70
Oklahoma	30,043	1,500	317	13,500	0.2, 7.40, 1.80
Oregon	34,982	8,080	445	28,000	1.2, 5.40, 3.10
Pennsylvania	38,166	1,320	497–505	8,000	0.3, 9.20, 3.50
Puerto Rico	20,901	280	133	7,000	1.4, 5.40, 1% of taxes due
Rhode Island	35,708	2,013	492–615	16,000	1.69, 9.79, 2.34
South Carolina	31,241	900	303	7,000	1.24, 6.10, 2.64
South Dakota	27,010	1,288	274	7,000	0, 7.0, 1.20
Tennessee	34,618	1,560	275	7,000	0.15, 10.0, 2.70
Texas	39,022	2,035	350	9,000	0.4, 7.64, 2.70
Utah	31,325	2,600	383	24,000	0.4, 9.40, 1.60
Vermont	32,626	2,582	394	8,000	0.8, 6.50, 1.0
Virginia	29,823	2,500 (in 2 HQs)	347	8,000	0.1, 6.20, 2.50
Virgin Islands	40,093	1,287	416	20,000	0, 6.0, 1.0
Washington	38,723	5,819 (in 2 HQs)	Lesser of $496 or 63% of AWW[b]	30,900	0.47, 6.12, industry avg. + 15%
West Virginia	29,105	2,200	391	8,000	1.5, 7.50, 2.70
Wisconsin	34,105	1,530	341	10,500	0, 8.90, 3.25 or 3.40
Wyoming	30,722	2,200	349	17,100	0.54, 9.04, industry avg.

Source: U.S. Department of Labor, Employment and Training Administration, "Comparison of State Unemployment Laws" (workforcesecurity. doleta.gov/unemploy/uilawcompar/2006/comparison2006.asp); "Significant Provisions of State Unemployment Insurance Laws, July 2006" (workforcesecurity.doleta.gov/unemploy/sigprojul2006.asp).

a. HQ, high quarter.

b. AWW, average weekly wage.

Improving Opportunities and Incentives for Saving by Middle- and Low-Income Households

4

*WILLIAM G. GALE, JONATHAN GRUBER,
AND PETER R. ORSZAG*

Most Americans expect a substantial period of retirement. Workers tend to leave the labor force as they approach their mid-sixties. For example, the share of men participating in the labor force falls from more than 66 percent among those ages fifty-five to sixty-four to under 20 percent for those sixty-five and older; for women, labor force participation declines from over 50 percent in the fifty-five-to-sixty-four age bracket to just slightly more than 10 percent for those sixty-five or older. Yet, in their mid-sixties, most people still have a significant life expectancy. A sixty-five-year-old man now has an average life expectancy of 17.5 more years; a sixty-five-year-old woman has a life expectancy of 19.7 additional years (Social Security Administration 2008, table V.A4). In recent decades, furthermore, life expectancies have steadily crept higher while retirement ages have moved relatively little, with the result that the expected number of years in retirement has risen.

Comments from Jared Bernstein, Doug Elliot, Doug Elmendorf, Ellen Seidman, Timothy Taylor, and the staff of the Hamilton Project are gratefully acknowledged. We would also like to thank Lily Batchelder, Esther Duflo, Mark Iwry, Jeff Liebman, Emmanuel Saez, Gene Sperling, and Steve Utkus for helpful discussions and the joint work upon which parts of this chapter are based. We also thank the Pew Charitable Trusts for its support of the Retirement Security Project, which is promoting some of the ideas presented here.

Peter Orszag, now at the Congressional Budget Office, was a senior fellow at the Brookings Institution at the time of this writing. The views expressed here should not be construed to reflect those of CBO.

What resources will elderly Americans be able to draw upon during this substantial period of retirement? Most middle- and lower-income Americans enter their retirement years having accumulated relatively little financial wealth. Social Security, the primary government program that provides income for the elderly, was never intended to provide a full retirement income by itself. Nonetheless, two-thirds of retirees depend on Social Security for half or more of their retirement income, and one-fifth depend on the program for all their income (Diamond and Orszag 2005).

Some retirees will be able to draw upon a private pension plan. But the traditional pension plans that offered lifelong benefits paid by an employer are becoming increasingly rare. An enormous shift has occurred in recent decades away from employers providing "defined benefit" pensions, in which a certain predefined level of benefits was saved by the firm in a pension fund and then paid out after retirement, and toward employers helping employees to set up personal retirement savings accounts like 401(k) plans. (We will use the broad term "401(k) plan" to refer to a retirement savings plan offered by any employer, regardless of whether the employer is a for-profit corporation, governmental entity, or nonprofit, in which employees can choose to have some of their paychecks automatically deposited in a retirement account.) Many other individuals have set up individual retirement accounts (IRAs) on their own, without the direct assistance of an employer. These 401(k) plans and IRAs have typically offered workers a tax advantage: contributions to the accounts are untaxed at the time they are made, and returns on the savings are also untaxed when they are earned, although taxes are eventually imposed when money is withdrawn from the retirement accounts, presumably after retirement.

Retirement saving accounts like 401(k)s have been increasingly dominant over the past twenty-five years. Between 1975 and 1998, the number of 401(k)-type plans more than tripled, and the number of active participants more than quadrupled. During the same period, the number of traditional defined benefit plans fell by almost half, and the number of active participants fell by one-fourth. Retirement saving plans like 401(k)s accounted for more than 80 percent of contributions to pensions in 1998, compared with just over 33 percent in 1975 (Gale and Orszag 2003). By 2004, 401(k) plans and IRAs held more than $6.7 trillion in assets (authors' calculations based on Investment Company Institute 2005, figure 2). These aggregate amounts, however, mostly reflect large balances among high-income households. Indeed, most families approaching retirement age have meager retirement saving, if any.[1] In 2001, for example, half of all households headed by adults aged fifty-five to fifty-nine had $10,000 or less in an employer-based 401(k)-type plan or tax-preferred savings plan account like an individual retirement account (Diamond and Orszag 2005).

Low retirement saving is not due to a significant lack of eligibility for tax-favored retirement accounts. Instead, about half of workers are eligible for 401(k) accounts through their employers, and almost all households lacking such an option through their employers could contribute to an IRA. The problem is instead primarily a lack of take-up—too many people fail to take adequate advantage of the tax-preferred retirement saving opportunities they have. The inadequate take-up, in turn, reflects two key factors, and our proposed policies to encourage private saving, especially among low- and middle-income households, address these two problems directly.

One reason that people do not enroll in a 401(k) plan or an IRA is that such plans typically require specific actions to join. Furthermore, the plans sometimes present a difficult and confusing array of choices regarding investment allocations and contribution levels. As a result, many people who recognize that they should be saving more end up procrastinating and avoiding any decision. In such plans, not making a decision means not enrolling. Thus inertia tends to keep workers out of 401(k) plans and IRAs, since participating in a 401(k) plan or IRA usually requires an affirmative action by the worker. Therefore, in practice, saving often becomes a

1. Significant controversy surrounds the question of how well households are preparing for retirement. However, most studies suggest that moderate- and low-income households are among the most vulnerable. Researchers have taken a wide variety of approaches to examine the adequacy of retirement saving: measuring changes in household consumption at the time of retirement, calculating accumulated wealth at retirement, comparing wealth across generations, and comparing models of optimal wealth accumulation to households' actual saving behavior. For recent overviews of this literature, see Engen, Gale, and Uccello (1999) and Congressional Budget Office (2003a). For recent work in this area, see Scholz, Seshadri, and Khitatrakun (2004). For evidence on the particular problems of middle- and lower-income households, see, for example, Banks, Blundell, and Tanner (1998); Bernheim (1993); Bernheim and Scholz (1993); Engen, Gale, and Uccello (1999); Engen, Gale, and Uccello (2004); Kotlikoff, Spivak, and Summers (1982); Mitchell, Moore, and Phillips (1998); Moore and Mitchell (1997); Robb and Burbidge (1989); and Warshawsky and Ameriks (1998). For a broader discussion of the resources available to those on the verge of retirement, see Gale and Orszag (2003); Orszag (2004); and Iwry (2003). A variety of publications related to these issues are available on the Retirement Security Project website (www.retirementsecurityproject.org).

"residual decision" for households; that is, saving is what is left over after consumption choices have been made.

In response to this problem, our first theme is that public policy should make retirement saving more of an automatic, or default, choice for households. We suggest that public policies capture the power of inertia to promote, rather than to hinder, participation in retirement plans. Congress recently took a step in this direction when it passed the Pension Protection Act of 2006 (PPA 06), which encourages employers, through a variety of means, to enroll new employees in automatic 401(k)s. Even with the passing of PPA 06, however, the majority of employers do not offer such a program. To accomplish this, we propose that every employer in the United States (with the exception of the smallest businesses) be required to ensure that all its new workers are automatically enrolled in a traditional defined benefit employer pension plan, a 401(k)-type plan through the employer, or an IRA. Defined benefit plans usually already have automatic enrollment and typically do not involve employee contributions. The automatic 401(k) and IRA plans would have a specified share of paychecks contributed to such accounts. The funds would be automatically invested in broad-based stock and bond mutual funds. The proposal, though, respects the autonomy of individuals by letting any individual choose to override these default options if he or she wishes to do so. After all, even if many people are saving too little for retirement, some households will find themselves in situations in which they do not need or want to save more. For example, someone who is working her way through law school may reasonably expect to have a much higher income in the future and thus may not wish to save in the present. These and other individuals should be permitted to opt out of the automatic saving vehicle.

A second reason that many people do not enroll in an IRA or a 401(k) plan is that the financial incentive to do so is weak or nonexistent for the vast majority of middle- and low-income households. The primary way in which the government encourages participation in IRAs and employer-based 401(k) retirement plans is that the contributions to such plans are not counted as part of the income on which federal taxes are owed. The value of excluding the contributions from taxation depends, however, on the income tax bracket into which that taxpayer would fall. For example, consider two taxpaying couples who contribute $6,000 each to a 401(k). By doing so, each couple reduces the income subject to taxation by $6,000. However, one couple has a high income and faces a marginal tax rate of 35 percent, so this couple reduces its taxes owed by $2,100 (35 percent of the $6,000 contribution). The other couple has a relatively low income and is in the 10 percent tax bracket, so this couple reduces its taxes owed by only $600. The current system thus provides the smallest immediate benefits to middle- and lower-income families, who are generally in the lowest marginal tax brackets and who are often the ones most in need of increased saving to meet basic needs in retirement.

The existing tax rules not only provide less benefit to those from low- and middle-income households but also are relatively ineffective at inducing new saving rather than simply shifting other saving into tax-preferred accounts. The contributions by high-income households to tax-subsidized retirement accounts are more likely to represent funds that are reshuffled from existing savings to take advantage of the tax benefit and thus do not represent a net new addition to saving (Engen and Gale 2000; Benjamin 2003). In other words, too much of our existing tax incentives for saving has relatively low "bang for the buck" because it merely subsidizes shifting the form of saving among higher-income households rather than raising the total amount of saving in the economy.

The tax preferences for new contributions to 401(k) plans and IRAs were estimated to reduce U.S. government tax revenues by tens of billions of dollars in 2005.[2] Instead of providing this incentive for saving so that it benefits those with high incomes proportionally more than those with lower incomes and generates little new saving to boot, we propose replacing the current deduction for contributions to these accounts with a new government program that matches households' retirement saving at a 30 percent rate up to 10 percent of their income. This matching program would significantly increase the share of the government's subsidies for saving incentives that accrue to middle- and low-income households; 80 percent of households would enjoy a stronger incentive to save under the proposal than under current law. This proposal is likely to generate both more net new saving and a more equitable distribution of retirement saving than the current system.

2. This figure should not be confused with a tax expenditure estimate, such as provided by the Office of Management and Budget (2005). The tax expenditure estimate of the present value of the revenue loss due to current 401(k) and IRA contributions is based on several factors: revenue losses due to tax-deductible contributions, nontaxation of accruing account earnings, revenue gains from taxation of withdrawals, and any early withdrawal penalties. The estimate in the text refers only to the first of these factors, namely, the revenue loss due to tax-deductible contributions. This, rather than the tax expenditure estimate, is the appropriate cost measure for comparison with our proposal since our proposal would not significantly alter the rules regarding the taxation of accruing earnings, taxation of withdrawals, or any penalties on early withdrawals.

Making retirement saving automatic and restructuring the incentive to contribute are the key elements of our reforms. Thus the next section explores in some detail what automatic retirement accounts would look like and why we expect them to increase savings even if people are allowed to opt out. The following section examines in more detail our proposal for altering the financial incentives for saving. After that, we briefly explore the challenges facing middle- and low-income households in the withdrawal stage from retirement accounts. Finally, we contrast our reforms with alternative proposals to provide greater incentives for saving by expanding the current deductions or exemptions for tax-preferred savings accounts. These alternative proposals would not target new saving among middle- and low-income households and, instead, are more likely to offer high-income households a greater opportunity to shift their assets from other forms into tax-preferred vehicles.

The Importance of Default Choices in Saving Decisions

This section explores policies designed to promote saving opportunities by making it easier for households to save. We first document the striking empirical evidence that something as simple as changing default options can be a powerful tool for increasing participation rates and contributions. We then offer a detailed description of two major elements of our proposal: the automatic 401(k) and the automatic IRA.

The Importance of the Default Option in Saving Decisions

A growing body of empirical evidence indicates that it makes a considerable difference whether people must choose to enter a retirement saving program or whether they must choose to opt out of an otherwise automatic program. Currently, 401(k)-type plans typically leave it up to the employee to choose whether to participate, how much to contribute, which of the investment vehicles offered by the employer to select, and when to pull the funds out of the plan and in what form. Workers are thus confronted with a series of financial decisions, each of which involves risk and a certain degree of financial expertise. Many workers shy away from these decisions and simply do not choose and therefore do not participate in retirement saving plans. Those who do choose often make poor choices.

A series of studies has demonstrated that automatic enrollment boosts the rate of plan participation substantially, as shown in figure 4-1 (Madrian and Shea 2001; Choi and others 2002). As the figure shows,

Figure 4-1. Effects of Automatic Enrollment on Participation Rates among New Employees

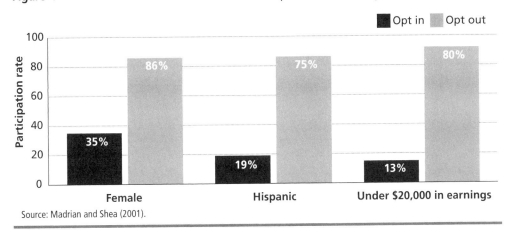

Source: Madrian and Shea (2001).

automatic enrollment is particularly effective in boosting participation among those who often face the most difficulty in saving.

One potential problem with automatic enrollment, highlighted by recent research, is that it can induce some employees to maintain the original default contribution rate passively over time when they might otherwise have elected to contribute at a higher rate (Choi and others 2004). This adverse effect can be mitigated through changing the defaults on contribution rates so that contributions rise gradually and automatically over time (for example, from 4 percent of the worker's pay in the first year to 5 percent in the second, 6 percent in the third, and so on). For example, under the Save More Tomorrow program proposed by Thaler and Benartzi (2004), workers would agree (or not) at the outset that future pay increases will generate additional contributions. In one trial, Save More Tomorrow was shown to lead to a substantial increase in contribution rates over time for those who participated, relative to other 401(k) participants at the same company. Alternatively, workers could agree to future contribution increases even in the absence of future pay raises.

The evidence on defaults underscores that even minor impediments, such as the requirement to cash a paycheck and then deposit it into another account for retirement, can have substantial effects on behavior. The payroll deduction system obviates such inconveniences and thus makes saving much easier. In particular, the payroll deduction mechanism delivers contributions to a worker's account in a "frictionless" manner; the worker does not need to receive the funds and then deposit them in the 401(k) account. The participation rate in 401(k)s, which use payroll deductions, is substantially higher than in IRAs, which typically do not use payroll deduction. For example, among those offered a 401(k), roughly three quarters typically participate (Munnell and Sundén 2004). The participation rate in IRAs is substantially lower: less than a tenth of eligible taxpayers make a contribution to an IRA in any given year (Carroll 2000; Copeland 2002). The low level of participation in IRAs, compared to 401(k)s, may reflect a variety of factors associated with the 401(k), but we strongly suspect that the higher participation rates in 401(k) plans as compared with IRAs also reflect how a payroll deduction system encourages automatic saving, and we believe that payroll deductions represent an auspicious way of promoting saving.

Our proposal combines the benefits of setting "pro-saving" defaults and exploiting the benefits of payroll deductions. Specifically, we propose that firms (except for the smallest) be required to automatically enroll all new workers in some automatic plan: either a traditional defined benefit plan, an automatic 401(k), or an automatic IRA, where the latter two terms are defined below.

Automatic 401(k)

To make saving easier, we propose an "automatic 401(k)" under which each of the key events in the 401(k) process would be programmed to make contributing and investing easier and more effective (Gale, Iwry, and Orszag 2005).

Our automatic 401(k) plan would begin with automatic enrollment. Employees would automatically become participants in their company's 401(k) plan, although they would preserve the option of declining to participate. In other words, workers would be included in the 401(k) retirement plan unless they opted out rather than being excluded unless they opted in.

The next step would be automatic escalation. Employee contributions would automatically increase in a prescribed manner over time—for example, raising the share of earnings contributed to the account whenever a worker experiences a pay increase, again with an option of declining to increase contributions in this fashion. The funds in the retirement account would be automatically invested in prudently diversified, low-cost investment vehicles, such as index funds that mimic the performance of the entire stock market or the entire bond market, again unless the employee makes other choices. Such a strategy would improve asset allocation and investment choices while giving employers reasonable protection from potential fiduciary liabilities associated with these default choices.

Finally, these accounts would have automatic rollover. When an employee switches jobs, the funds in his or her account would be either retained in the previous employer's plan or automatically rolled over into an IRA or 401(k) plan offered by the new employer. At present, many employees receive their accumulated balances as a cash payment upon leaving an employer, and most of them spend part or all of it. For example, Poterba, Venti, and Wise (1998) report that fewer than half of distributions are rolled over, although more than half of dollars are rolled over. At this stage, too, the employee would retain the right to override the default option and place the funds elsewhere or take the cash payment.

At each step—enrollment, escalation, investment, and rollover—workers could always choose to override the defaults and opt out of the automatic design. Automatic 401(k) plans thus do not dictate ultimate choices any more than does the current set of default options, which exclude workers from the plan unless they opt to participate. Instead, automatic 401(k) plans merely point workers in a pro-saving direction when workers decline to make explicit choices of their own.

Some retirement savings plans already include at least some of these automatic features. According to a recent survey, for example, about one-tenth of 401(k) plans (and one-fourth of plans with at least 5,000 participants) have switched from the traditional "opt-in" to an "opt-out" arrangement (Profit Sharing/401(k) Council of America 2004). We would mandate that all 401(k) plans move to these opt-out arrangements for new employees unless the firm is a small business, already offers a defined benefit plan, or is willing to offer an automatic IRA (defined below). The mandate is limited to new employees to avoid unnecessary disruption and to accommodate evidence that automatic enrollment in particular generates a substantially smaller gain in participation for long-tenured employees than for new employees (see, for example, Choi and others 2004). Firms would be allowed to apply the automatic features to existing employees if they so choose. Over time, as workers switch jobs or enter the labor force and become new workers at firms, a growing share of the overall workforce will be covered by the new system. We would not require that firms offering a traditional defined benefit pension plan—that is, where the firm promises to pay pension benefits based on income earned during the worker's time at the firm—also have automatic 401(k) plans for the workers covered by the traditional pension, although rules might need to be tightened to ensure that such defined benefit plans provide at least a minimum level of benefits to workers with certain levels of experience.

Several additional policy interventions would be beneficial to address various concerns firms may have about automatic 401(k) plans. Some plan administrators expressed concern that some new, automatically enrolled participants might demand a refund of their contributions, claiming that they never read or did not understand the automatic enrollment notice. This would have been costly in the past due to the required demonstration of financial hardship and 10 percent early withdrawal tax. Such claims are no longer an issue, however, as they were addressed in PPA 06. The act states that 401(k) plans are allowed to return the full amount of automatic contributions with no tax to the employee if requested within ninety days of the first contribution.

If workers are automatically enrolled, their contributions have to be invested in something, and some firms were worried about legal liability for these default investments. This is also addressed in PPA 06, which provides plan sponsors with the same protection against fiduciary liability for automatic investments (assuming they meet Department of Labor–issued regulations) as provided to employee investments.

Finally, moving to automatic enrollment could be associated with a reform of the rules governing "nondiscrimination" in 401(k) plans. These nondiscrimination standards have nothing do with discrimination by ethnicity, gender, or age. Instead, they are designed to prevent discrimination by executives and high-paid employees against others in the firm. Specifically, these rules specify that the amount of tax-favored contributions permitted for executives and other higher-paid employees depends on the contributions made by other employees. PPA 06 exempts employers who use the automatic 401(k) on new hires with a 3 percent starting rate and 1 percent escalation each year up to at least 6 percent. While this new rule encourages employers to use the automatic 401(k), it eliminates the incentive to enroll as many employees as possible because they are no longer tied to the nondiscrimination standards. This suggests that this exemption could be potentially counterproductive if PPA 06 aims to increase retirement savings. These nondiscrimination rules have become extremely complicated, and we would embrace a broad reform in this arena (for a proposed simplification, see Orszag and Stein 2001).

Automatic IRA

Since only about half of the workforce is offered an employer-based pension in each year, it is important to make it easier for workers to save even if their employers do not offer a 401(k) or other pension plan. We propose an "automatic IRA" to address this challenge.[3] As in the case of 401(k) plans, the automatic nature of the IRA would apply at each relevant step—enrollment, escalation, and investment. In the case of the IRA, automatic rollover is not an issue because these accounts would be held on an individual basis rather than through the firm. As with the automatic 401(k), workers could choose to override the IRA defaults at any stage.

Firms that do not offer qualified pension plans, of either the 401(k) or the standard defined benefit variety, would be required to set up automatic payroll deduction IRAs as a default for their workers. Firms that do offer 401(k) or other qualified plans could also set up these IRAs but would not be required to do so. Workers who did not opt out would have part of their paychecks every period flow into the automatic IRA. The share of the paycheck flowing to the account would automatically escalate over time unless the worker opted out of such increases. Legislators could provide a modest tax credit for start-up administrative costs at firms mandated to offer an automatic IRA under this plan that currently do not offer a pension plan. The funds in the IRA would be automatically invested in a limited number of diversified funds available. The specific default option could be chosen by the financial institution holding the IRA, but we envision the default investment being similar or identical to those allowed under the default investment option for the automatic 401(k).

The automatic IRA could also receive part of a household's tax refund each year. For many households, and particularly those with low or moderate income, the refund is the largest single payment that they receive all year. Accordingly, the more than $200 billion issued annually in individual income tax refunds presents a unique opportunity to increase personal saving. Beginning in calendar year 2007 for the 2006 tax season, filers have been able to split their refund among up to three different accounts via direct deposit. This makes direct contribution to IRAs more appealing for filers for whom some of the refund is needed for immediate expenses, so depositing the entire amount in an illiquid retirement savings account is not a feasible option. Though few filers took advantage of this option in the first filing season, in part due to obstacles stemming from late adoption, such deposits could increase the amounts accumulated in automatic IRAs. Families might also be able to commit to depositing an increasing share of their future tax refunds to the automatic IRA. They could always override

---

3. For details on how a related proposal for automatic IRAs would be implemented, see Iwry and John (2006).

this decision when the time came, but the default would be that a rising share of each year's tax refund was deposited into the automatic IRA over time.

Individuals could also make additional voluntary contributions to the automatic IRA to the extent that their payroll deduction contributions and refund-based contribution do not exceed the allowable limits discussed in the next major section of the paper.

Summary

The creation of the automatic 401(k) and automatic IRA, coupled with the requirement that firms enroll all workers in an automatic retirement plan of some sort, would make saving much easier for households. All workers would have the opportunity to save for retirement in a diversified manner without having to take affirmative steps. Those workers who wanted to opt out of participating, contributing at the specified levels, or the default investment choices could always do so. The two accounts, furthermore, would work together, since the automatic 401(k) could be rolled automatically into the automatic IRA if workers switch jobs. At any point in time, people would thus have a maximum of two defined contribution retirement accounts: the employer-based automatic 401(k) and the individual automatic IRA.

Restructuring Incentives for Savings

The fact that saving decisions are so heavily influenced by behavioral factors such as defaults does not mean that economic incentives are necessarily irrelevant. Indeed, recent evidence suggests that the rate at which the government matches retirement saving contributions can have a significant effect on contributions. In a recent study, households were offered at random different matching rates for making contributions to an IRA at the time they were preparing their taxes. The experiment showed that households made significantly higher contributions when offered a higher match rate (Duflo and others 2005).

Increasing retirement account contributions, though, is not necessarily the same thing as raising overall household saving. It could be that the higher rates of contributions to retirement accounts due to automatic enrollment or higher match rates result from a simultaneous decrease in other saving outside of 401(k)s and IRAs. Alternatively, people might borrow more, perhaps in the form of home equity loans, while they increase their retirement contributions by a counterbalancing amount, leaving their overall net level of personal saving unchanged. We noted earlier that evidence suggests that for many high-income households, contributions to existing retirement savings accounts largely represented a reshuffling from other assets to take advantage of the tax savings in the retirement accounts. However, this is less likely to be true for those with low and middle incomes because they have less money in other assets and thus less ability to reshuffle assets; so it is more plausible that government saving incentives will increase total household saving for these households.

This argument suggests that the current system of tax incentives for retirement savings is flawed. By providing incentives for contributions through tax provisions that are linked to the marginal tax rates that people owe, current incentives deliver their largest immediate benefits to higher-income individuals in the highest tax brackets. These high-income individuals are precisely the ones who can respond to such tax incentives by reshuffling their existing assets into these accounts to take advantage of the tax breaks rather than by increasing their overall level of saving. As a result, the tens of billions of dollars in tax expenditures associated each year with 401(k) and IRA contributions could be targeted more effectively to increasing overall saving.

Replace the Deduction for Retirement Savings Contributions with a Government Matching Contribution

We propose a new incentive structure for contributions to retirement savings accounts, which would cost roughly the same as the current tax incentives. Our plan would replace the existing tax deductions for contributions to retirement savings accounts with a government matching contribution into the account. Unlike the current system, workers' contributions to employer-based 401(k) accounts would no longer be excluded from income subject to taxation, and contributions to IRAs would no longer be tax deductible. Furthermore, any employer contributions to a 401(k) plan would be treated as taxable income to the employee (just as current wages are). However, all qualified employer and employee contributions would be eligible for the government matching contribution. Earnings in 401(k)s and IRAs would continue to accrue tax free, and withdrawals from the accounts would continue to be taxed at regular income rates, as under current law.

The qualifying government matching contribution would be 30 percent for all contributions up to the minimum of either 10 percent of adjusted gross income, which is the measure of income on which federal income taxes are imposed, or $20,000 for 401(k) accounts and $5,000 for IRAs. Thus the maximum contribution eligible for a match would be $20,000 per person under a 401(k) account and $5,000 per person under an IRA. Each spouse of a married couple could make these contributions, so each spouse would be allowed to contribute 10 percent of the household's income, and the maximum contribution for a couple could amount to $40,000 to 401(k)s and $10,000 to IRAs. These limits would be indexed for inflation.

This proposal would be roughly revenue neutral for the federal government, according to the authors' estimates using the Tax Policy Center microsimulation model. Calculations using the model show that replacing the current tax incentives with a government matching contribution, without making any change to the definition of eligible contributions, would allow a matching rate of 28 percent. Our proposal, though, restricts eligible contributions to no more than 10 percent of income up to a maximum income threshold of $200,000, which modestly restrains eligible contributions compared with current law and thus facilitates close to a 30 percent match rate on a revenue-neutral basis.[4]

Our proposal has major advantages over the existing system of savings incentives. For any given dollar deposited into an account, the match rate would depend solely on saving relative to income (up to the contribution limits), not on the level of income itself. As a result, our system provides the same proportional benefit for saving defined as a share of income (at least up to the contribution limits), unlike the existing set of tax incentives for saving. Many investment advisers counsel people to save a certain percentage of their income—advice that is in turn based on the insight that saving a certain proportion of income now will avoid sharp declines in living standards after retirement. Providing a saving incentive with a government match based on the share of income saved promotes this consistent approach to saving.

As noted above, the government matching payment would be directly deposited into the account rather than providing a reduction in tax.

---

4. Contributions currently amount to $281 billion, and eligible contributions under our proposal amount to $273 billion. The weighted average marginal tax rate on contributions is approximately 22 percent. We assume after-tax contributions would remain constant, so our match would apply to after-tax contributions of $273 billion × (1 − 0.22), or $213 billion. With a match rate of 30 percent, the cost is $63.9 billion. The cost of the 22 percent average marginal tax rate applied to $281 billion in contributions is $62 billion, suggesting that the proposal is roughly revenue neutral. The precise match rate could be adjusted to make the proposal precisely revenue neutral, based on official estimates from the Joint Committee on Taxation.

The government match is thus similar to a tax break that is required to be deposited into the account. This requirement would likely increase the probability that the matching contribution is saved when compared to the tax deduction under current law. This form of the incentive may even induce more household saving (even apart from having the incentive itself saved): although we have no direct evidence on this point in the context of retirement saving, some research suggests that direct matches are more effective than equivalent tax rebates at inducing people to contribute to charities (Eckel and Grossman 2003). Also, the match replaces the up-front tax deduction as a method of providing a government subsidy for contributions; when the matching funds are withdrawn from the account, they are therefore subject to taxation just as under an existing 401(k) or traditional IRA.

Comparison with Current Incentives

For an individual with a hypothetical marginal income tax rate of 23 percent, our proposed incentive system is very similar to the existing incentives provided under the tax code. Under the current system, for every dollar saved by that individual, the individual would receive a tax deduction worth twenty-three cents. Thus for every dollar in an account, the individual's after-tax cost is seventy-seven cents. Under our system, instead, the individual gets a matching contribution of 30 percent of the contribution, and the matching contribution is deposited into the account. If the individual makes a contribution of seventy-seven cents, the government would provide a matching contribution of twenty-three cents, so the individual would have one dollar in his or her account. Again, as with the current tax system, the individual would have one dollar in the account in exchange for an after-tax cost of seventy-seven cents. Depositing the matching contribution directly into the retirement savings account, rather than delivering it as a tax break, seems likely to significantly raise the chance that the tax break is saved rather than consumed.

Compared with the current system, our proposed incentives for saving reduce the tax subsidy to savings for high-income households—more precisely, for those with marginal tax rates higher than 23 percent—while raising it for lower-income individuals—those with marginal tax rates below 23 percent. Table 4-1 shows households at different incomes with different assumed levels of savings. Given our assumed pattern of saving, the final two columns of the table show that our proposal generally shifts the government's incentives for saving so that higher benefits flow to those with low and middle levels of income. The family with $30,000 in income,

Table 4-1. Illustrative Existing and Proposed Incentives

Dollars, except as indicated

Adjusted gross income	Pretax retirement contributions[a]	Marginal tax bracket (percent)	After-tax retirement contribution[b]	Match rate under proposal (percent)	Immediate benefit	
					Current system	Proposed system
30,000	2,000	0	2,000	30	0	600
40,000	3,000	10	2,700	30	300	810
60,000	5,000	15	4,250	30	750	1,275
150,000	10,000	25	7,500	30	2,500	2,250
250,000	15,000	28	10,800	30	4,200	3,240
500,000	20,000	35	13,000	30	7,000	3,900

Source: Authors' calculations using Tax Policy Center microsimulation model.
a. 401(k) plus IRA.
b. Assuming that after the reform, households maintain after-tax cost of contributions.

for example, receives no benefit under the existing system of tax deductions and exclusions (since the family does not have positive income tax liability) but would receive $600 under the proposal as a match for saving $2,000.

The incentive to save additional funds is determined by how much of a financial incentive is provided for an additional dollar of saving. Table 4-1 also illustrates how the proposed system creates stronger marginal incentives for most families to save that additional dollar. The family at $30,000 in income with savings of $2,000, for example, would receive a 30 percent match, rather than nothing, for saving an extra dollar. It would also receive a $600 benefit, rather than nothing, for its $2,000 contribution. By contrast, a family with $500,000 of income and $20,000 of contributions sees a reduction in its overall benefit from $7,000 to $3,900. Its marginal incentive to contribute declines, which is warranted for the reasons we discuss above. These calculations ignore the role of state taxation; for residents of most states, there will also be a loss of state tax savings from existing retirement saving vehicles—an issue discussed in more detail later in this chapter.

Table 4-1 is helpful for illustrating the mechanics of the proposal. As the table suggests, the proposal generates benefits for most middle- and low-income households while imposing costs on higher-income households. The distribution of potential winners and losers under the proposal is shown in table 4-2. As emphasized above, households facing a marginal tax rate of less than 23 percent have a stronger incentive to contribute

Table 4-2. Share of Tax Units with Marginal Tax Rate below 23 Percent Threshold for Gaining under Proposal[a]

Units as indicated

Adjusted gross income class (thousands of 2005 dollars)[b]	Tax units[c]			
	Number (thousands)	Percent of total	Number with marginal tax rate below 23 percent (thousands)	Percent within income class with tax rate below 23 percent
Less than 10	34,644	24.0	34,642	100.0
10–19	21,895	15.1	21,895	100.0
20–29	18,053	12.5	18,053	100.0
30–39	14,232	9.8	13,498	94.8
40–49	10,888	7.5	7,473	68.6
50–74	18,946	13.1	12,990	68.6
75–99	10,596	7.3	4,373	41.3
100–199	10,788	7.5	596	5.5
200–499	2,619	1.8	62	2.4
500–1,000	454	0.3	5	1.0
More than 1,000	257	0.2	5	1.9
All	144,575	100.0	114,788	79.4

Source: Authors' calculations using Tax Policy Center microsimulation model.

a. Baseline is current law.

b. Tax units with negative adjusted gross income are excluded from the lowest income class but are included in the totals.

c. Includes both filing and nonfiling units. Tax units that are dependents of other taxpayers are excluded from the analysis.

under the proposal than under current law; households with a marginal tax rate of more than 23 percent have a weaker incentive. Table 4-2 shows that approximately 80 percent of all households would enjoy a stronger saving incentive under the proposal than under current law, including all households with incomes below $30,000 and more than 40 percent of households with incomes between $75,000 and $100,000. (In this table, income is defined as adjusted gross income, the concept of income defined in the tax code. The table shows the results for tax units, which are typically similar but not identical to households.)

One concern with our proposal is the potential to erode the employer-based retirement saving structure. We agree that the available evidence suggests that individuals will respond much more to saving incentives through the workplace than they do to such incentives outside the workplace. The reason for the much tighter limit on the income to which the matching credit can be applied for IRAs than on 401(k) plans is to ensure the attractiveness of workplace-based savings plans. Indeed, our proposal may modestly encourage defined benefit plans, which would continue to enjoy the same tax treatment as under current law. For high-income workers, a defined benefit plan would provide a tax break linked to the 35 percent marginal tax rate. By contrast, as suggested by table 4-1, high-income workers would enjoy a smaller benefit under a 401(k) plan or IRA. To the extent that high-income workers influence choices made by firms about pension plans, the difference in tax treatment for such workers could encourage some defined benefit plans (which would then cover middle- and low-income workers also).

Another concern is that the matches provided through the government may displace employer matches to 401(k) plans. One motivation for these employer matches is the nondiscrimination requirements described earlier: to pass the nondiscrimination test, pension plans must ensure sufficient participation by low-income employees, and the match is an incentive to encourage such participation by low-income workers. Under this theory, to the extent that our automatic 401(k) raises participation by low-income employees, it could erode the use of matching contributions by employers (since such matches would no longer be necessary to satisfy the nondiscrimination standards). This chain of events could lead to an overall lowering of the incentive to save through employer-based retirement plans. On the other hand, many other potential motivations exist for employer matching. For example, the match may be offered as a way of furthering tax-free compensation for the highly paid employees most likely to participate in 401(k) plans; such a motivation would still exist under our proposal. Moreover, even if employer match rates decline substantially (which we do not anticipate), the overall effects of the reform may still be beneficial. If lower-income individuals participate more in 401(k) plans through defaults, but higher-income individuals receive smaller matches, the net result may still be an increase in net saving.

Withdrawal Rules

Individuals will sometimes wish to withdraw funds before retirement. The rules for preretirement withdrawal are important for any savings vehicle. In the extreme, individuals could be penalized for any withdrawal before an appointed retirement age. Yet, over time, U.S. policy has evolved to allow more generous preretirement access to funds in both IRAs and 401(k)s (National Academy of Social Insurance 2005). The argument against allowing a wide range of circumstances for early withdrawals is that preretirement withdrawals tend to harm the retirement security that is the goal of such saving. The argument for some preretirement with-drawals is that they may finance alternative forms of (physical or human) capital accumulation and that, by making access to the account balances less restrictive, such rules can raise the appeal of these accounts as savings vehicles and thus possibly increase voluntary contributions in the first place. Indeed, some argue that existing approved uses do not go far enough. Most Americans have no savings other than home equity and their retirement accounts. Thus, if they suffer adverse events such as unemployment, restricting their access to the account denies them liquid-ity that they could use to avoid severe drops in their living standards. From that perspective, it seems unfair to induce individuals to store away their savings in a mechanism that is not available should they face unfor-tunate life circumstances.

We propose a middle ground between these views. We would allow qualified withdrawals for capital accumulation like existing IRAs: that is, for first-time home purchases or college education. However, other existing exceptions to early withdrawal penalties would be disqualified. At the same time, we would allow loans from IRAs. Already, 401(k) plans allow loans of up to $50,000 or half of the employee's account balance, whichever is less.[5] Under our proposal, individuals would similarly be allowed to take loans from their IRAs for up to the lesser of $50,000 or half the accumulated balance due to their contributions (excluding the funds from the match). The loans would have to be repaid within five years, at the interest rate that the government pays when it issues five-year bonds. If individuals did not repay these loans, they would be treated as unqualified withdrawals from a retirement account, and penalties would be imposed accordingly.

Transition and Gaming Issues

This proposal represents a major change in the tax treatment of retirement saving. As such, it raises concerns about the transition from current pol-

---

5. Some 401(k) accounts accumulate balances but also require that the employee work for the employer a certain amount of time before those balances belong to, or "vest," with the employee. The rule here refers to "vested" amounts. If half the vested account balance is less than $10,000, the employee may borrow up to $10,000. The loan must be repaid within five years, unless it is used to purchase a home. To limit employees' ability to maintain outstand-ing loan balances of up to $50,000 for an indefinite time, a special rule reduces the $50,000 amount by the excess of the highest outstanding loan balance during the preceding year over the current outstanding balance. For further information, see National Academy of Social Insurance (2005).

icy to the proposed alternative. We propose that all existing 401(k) and IRA retirement savings accounts be left unchanged under this proposal but that no new savings be allowed to flow into those accounts. Ending new contributions would apply both to conventional 401(k) and IRA accounts and also to Roth 401(k)s and Roth IRAs. In Roth saving vehicles, retirement savings are taxed up front, but accumulation inside the account is not taxed, and the funds are not taxed when withdrawn.

Individuals would be encouraged to roll their existing accounts into the two proposed retirement saving vehicles. Balances in existing 401(k) and IRA accounts could be directly rolled into the new 401(k) and IRA. Balances in Roth IRA accounts could also be given the match and then rolled into the new IRA. For administrative simplicity, such rollovers should be eligible for the match under our proposal and then taxed upon withdrawal, which would eliminate the need for separate accounting.

The large matching payments also raise the possibility of gaming: individuals might invest the money, trigger the match, and then quickly withdraw the contribution. In the current context, imposing a penalty of 10 percent on early withdrawals that do not meet permissible purposes discourages gaming. The traditional IRA withdrawal rules would not be potent enough in the context of our proposed incentives since the match rate is much higher than 10 percent.[6] As a result, gaming in which people contribute money to a retirement account, receive the match of 30 percent, and then withdraw their contribution and pay the 10 percent penalty could become a problem. One possibility is to increase the penalty rate for early withdrawal. Alternatively, we would prefer that individuals would forfeit their government matching payments by an unqualified early withdrawal. As an example, consider an individual who contributes $1 to an account and receives $0.30 in matching contributions. The individual then withdraws the $1 before retirement. If the $1 withdrawal does not meet one of the specified exceptions to the early

---

6. Gaming possibilities do exist under the current Saver's Credit. This tax credit is worth between 10 and 50 percent of an individual's eligible contribution of up to $2,000 to an account like a 401(k) or an IRA. Thus a taxpayer could deposit the fund in an IRA, receive the tax credit, and then immediately withdraw the funds. As long as the tax credit reduces taxes by more than the 10 percent penalty for early withdrawal from the account, the taxpayer will come out ahead. However, the Saver's Credit is limited only to filers with incomes below $50,000, and it can only reduce taxes to zero. The gaming possibilities do not appear to be well known.

withdrawal penalties, the government would impose a penalty to reclaim the $0.30 match.[7]

State Tax Implications

This proposed reform also has important implications for state income taxation.[8] Almost all states follow the federal tax treatment of retirement saving in 401(k) accounts and IRAs: that is, income contributed to a 401(k) account is excluded from taxation, and income contributed to an IRA is deductible from income. Eliminating these tax provisions could mean that many taxpayers would face higher state income tax bills unless states took explicit actions to offer state-specific savings incentives. It seems unlikely that many states would want to take such actions since tax deferral of retirement saving makes less sense when individuals are mobile. That is, if the state of Michigan gives an up-front match to a retirement saving plan, but the taxpayer then retires to Arizona, the state tax on the withdrawals would be paid there. (If the person retires to Florida, which doesn't have an income tax, the match on the contribution would never actually be offset by a state tax bill after retirement.) Admittedly, this perspective suggests that states should not currently exclude retirement contributions from taxable income at the state level, but it may be easier for state governments not to offer a matching incentive than to include an item in taxable income that is excluded at the federal level. In other words, many state governments may view this plan as a fiscal windfall.

Reducing the Implicit Taxes on Retirement Saving Imposed by Asset Tests

Another way of increasing the incentives for middle- and low-income households to save is by removing penalties imposed on such saving. In particular, many means-tested benefit programs such as food stamps, health insurance through Medicaid, and cash welfare under Temporary Assistance to Needy Families have rules that disqualify moderate- and low-income families who have saved for retirement in 401(k)s or IRAs from receiving benefits under the program. Such asset tests can be viewed as an

---

7. We thank Emmanuel Saez and Esther Duflo for suggesting this antigaming rule. The details of the antigaming provisions for people fifty-nine and a half or older, the stacking order of withdrawals of matched principal amount and other funds (including earnings on the matched principal amount) from the account, and the tax treatment of the match itself and its withdrawal would need to be decided.

8. We are grateful to Iris Lav of the Center on Budget and Policy Priorities for laying out these issues for us.

implicit tax on retirement saving as such saving reduces government benefits that would otherwise have been available (Neuberger, Greenstein, and Sweeney 2005).

These asset tests represent one of the most glaring examples of how laws and regulations have failed to keep pace with the evolution of the U.S. pension system. At the time the asset test rules were developed, most pension plans took the form of defined benefit plans, where the employer promised to pay a future pension and in effect held the retirement assets in a pension fund on behalf of the employee. However, many firms have now shifted to providing pensions in the form of 401(k) accounts and IRAs, in which the employee holds the assets directly. Yet the asset test rules have largely not been updated, so many programs still do not treat defined benefit plans as a personal asset while counting 401(k)s and IRAs as such. Treating defined benefit and defined contribution plans similarly would be much more equitable and would remove a significant barrier to increasing retirement saving by low-income working households.

Furthermore, the rules applied under the means-tested benefit programs are confusing and often treat 401(k) accounts and IRAs in a seemingly arbitrary manner. As just one example of the complexity, workers who roll their 401(k)s over into IRAs when they switch jobs, as many financial planners would suggest, could disqualify themselves from the food stamp program.

Disregarding amounts in retirement accounts when applying the asset tests would allow low-income families to build retirement saving without having to forgo means-tested benefits at times when their incomes are low during their working years. Congress could alter the law so that retirement accounts that receive preferential tax treatment, such as 401(k) plans and IRAs, are disregarded for purposes of eligibility and benefit determinations in federal means-tested programs. Less dramatic steps to avoid the disincentives of asset tests include simply raising the amounts allowed in retirement accounts without disqualification. Any resulting increase in state government expenditures could be offset, in part or whole, by the additional revenue that states would collect from ending the deductions and exclusions associated with 401(k) and IRA plans.

Retirement Withdrawals and Annuitization

The proposals delineated in this paper would help households accumulate more funds in their retirement accounts. But the proposals would not address a major challenge for those who have accumulated such funds:

how do they make sure that whatever funds they have saved in a 401(k) or IRA are not exhausted too soon during their retirement?[9] Consider an actuarially average woman aged sixty-five. She has a life expectancy of twenty more years, according to the Social Security Administration. However, the same projections suggest that she faces more than a 30 percent probability of living past age ninety, and almost a 15 percent chance of living past age ninety-five (National Academy of Social Insurance 2005). The standard way that she could protect herself against running out of retirement funds if she lives past her average life expectancy is to convert the funds in her 401(k)-type plan or IRA into a lifetime annuity, which guarantees periodic payments for life.

We recommend that the government set as a default that the matching contributions in each person's account be annuitized. This amount would represent only a modest portion of final account balances, but it would set the precedent for individuals that annuities are a sensible use of retirement resources. Moreover, this choice would only be a default; individuals could opt out of the annuitization if they choose, allowing those with extenuating circumstances (like a family history of short life expectancies) or alternative preferences to avoid annuitization altogether.

A problem with this recommendation, however, is that for most middle- and low-income families, lifetime annuities purchased on the individual market as it currently exists may be financially unattractive, for several reasons. First, current lifetime annuity products are typically not protected against the risks of inflation. Although inflation has been low in recent years, even a low steady inflation rate can significantly erode the real value of income from an annuity over time: at 3 percent inflation, $100 today will have a buying power (expressed in current dollars) of less than $75 after ten years and less than $50 after twenty-five years. Unexpectedly higher increases in inflation could be even more devastating to the real buying power of fixed retirement income.

A second problem is that for the average purchaser, annuities are not a good deal (Brown, Mitchell, and Poterba 2000). When an individual converts a retirement account to a lifetime annuity, the value of the savings in the account is likely to be reduced by roughly 3 to 5 percent to cover the annuity company's marketing expenses, commissions to agents, other

---

9. Some of the ideas in this section are drawn from National Academy of Social Insurance (2005). Responsibility for the specific form of the ideas presented here, however, rests solely with the authors.

administrative costs, and profits. Moreover, those who buy annuities tend to have longer life expectancies than the population as a whole because those are the people who are most concerned about outliving their wealth. Because those who purchase annuities tend to have longer-than-average life expectancies, and firms that sell annuities must price the annuities to reflect that reality, the payments from an annuity are about 10 percent less than the amount that would reflect an average life expectancy. This penalty for the average person would be reduced if the market expanded, but it would likely still exist to some degree even with significant increases in market participation.

The bottom line, then, is that lifetime annuities available to individuals through private markets do not provide an attractive way for average families to protect themselves against outliving their assets. The policy question is how to facilitate better products for middle- and low-income households who want to ensure that their retirement assets are not dissipated too soon.

One option would be for the federal government to act as an intermediary between potential middle- and low-income annuitants and the private market. Under the Thrift Savings Plan, for example, the federal government acts as an intermediary between federal employees and insurance companies in providing annuities. The government selects a range of annuity products that are presented to retirees. Employees may select annuities with payments that rise by 3 percent a year or annuities that provide the same benefits to the primary annuitant as well as his or her spouse. The government then contracts with companies that will offer the annuities, making selections through a competitive bidding process. Once employees buy an annuity, they deal directly with the insurance company. It is possible that this approach could be replicated on a broader scale.

The approach we prefer, however, is for the federal government itself to provide the annuities. For example, the government could allow any household with income under a certain threshold (perhaps $100,000) to purchase an annuity of up to some amount per year (perhaps $15,000) using funds accumulated in a 401(k) or IRA. Projected life expectancy and the value of the annuity would be determined using mortality tables such as those currently employed in projecting Social Security benefit payments, and the annuity would be provided in an inflation-protected form. The Social Security Administration could process the annuities, eliminating the need for a new government agency.

One risk from this approach is that healthier individuals would be more likely to purchase the annuity from the government than those with shorter life expectancies would. After all, individuals know more about their life expectancy from their personal and family health history than overall government actuarial tables will ever reveal. The limits on how much annuity protection can be purchased may ameliorate these selection effects. Any residual losses from attracting a larger-than-expected share of healthier individuals may be a necessary price to pay to offer an actuarially fair product to middle-income households and a much more attractive product to low-income households.

Contrasts with Existing Policy Proposals

Making a retirement savings account the default option for all American workers, together with improved incentives for retirement saving by those with low and middle incomes, could significantly bolster retirement security for millions of Americans. However, some policymakers seem more inclined to pursue provisions that would expand income and contribution limits on the existing tax-preferred retirement accounts. Such proposals are fundamentally different than those advocated in this paper. Proposals to increase income and contribution limits on existing retirement saving plans would primarily benefit households who are already disproportionately well prepared for retirement. Moreover, those high-income households would probably benefit mainly from being able to place a greater share of their already existing assets into a tax-preferred account rather than by increasing their overall level of saving.

The Retirement Savings Account Proposal

As one example of a competing proposal, the retirement savings account (RSA) proposed by the Bush administration is basically a Roth IRA with no income limit. A Roth IRA, as mentioned earlier, is a specific kind of IRA plan in which the original contribution to the account is not deductible from the income on which taxes are owed. However, returns on saving that build up inside such accounts are untaxed, and no taxes are imposed on income withdrawn from a Roth after retirement. Under current law, access to Roth IRAs begins to be curtailed at $150,000 for couples and $95,000 for singles.

Removing the income limit on the existing Roth IRA would have no direct benefit for the vast majority of American households who are already under the current income limit. The only people who would directly benefit from eliminating the cap are married couples with incomes above $150,000 or singles with incomes above $95,000.[10] Analysis using the retirement saving module from the Urban–Brookings Tax Policy Center model suggests that three quarters of the tax subsidies from removing the income limit would accrue to the 3 percent of households with cash income of more than $200,000. It is very unlikely that such households would respond to this tax break by increasing their saving rather than shifting existing assets to take advantage of expanded access to the tax-preferred accounts. The Congressional Research Service has estimated that eliminating the income limit on Roth IRAs will, after two decades or so, reduce revenue by $9 billion a year (Gravelle 2004b).

Problems with Raising the Contribution Limits to IRAs and 401(k)s

Another common proposal would increase the maximum amount that can be saved on a tax-preferred basis, such as by raising the amount that can be contributed to an IRA or 401(k). Yet only about 5 percent of participants in retirement savings plans make the maximum contribution allowed by law, so increasing the maximum contribution amounts would thus be unlikely to have much effect on most families. Instead, raising the contribution limits would largely provide windfall gains to households already making the maximum contributions to tax-preferred accounts and saving more on top of those contributions in other accounts.

The 2001 tax legislation raised the allowable contribution to a Roth IRA from $2,000 to $5,000. Because of the income limits, the benefits do not accrue to those with the very highest incomes. However, the benefits all accrue to those who can save more than $2,000. In addition, this change is costly. The Congressional Research Service has estimated that perpetuating the $5,000 contribution limit on the Roth IRA, rather than allowing it to revert to the $2,000 limit, would reduce revenue in the long term by $20 billion a year (Gravelle 2004b).

---

10. Advocates of removing the Roth IRA income limits claim that eliminating the limits could allow financial services firms to advertise more aggressively and thereby encourage more saving by middle-income households. However, advertisements used in the past suggest that much advertising was designed to induce asset shifting among higher earners rather than elicit new saving among lower earners. For example, one advertisement that ran in the *New York Times* in 1984 stated explicitly: "Were you to shift $2,000 from your right pants pocket into your left pants pocket, you wouldn't make a nickel on the transaction. However, if those different 'pockets' were accounts at The Bowery, you'd profit by hundreds of dollars. Setting up an individual retirement account is a means of giving money to yourself. The magic of an IRA is that your contributions are tax-deductible."

Table 4-3. 401(k) Participants Making the Maximum Contribution in 1997

Units as indicated

Household income (adjusted gross income, dollars)	Number of total contributors (thousands)	Percent of total contributors	Percent in income class contributing maximum
Under 20,000	2,695	7.6	1
20,000–39,999	8,914	25.0	1
40,000–79,999	15,020	42.1	4
80,000–119,999	5,739	16.1	10
120,000–159,999	1,624	4.6	21
160,000 and over	1,673	4.7	40
Total	35,666	100.0	6

Source: Authors' calculations based on Congressional Budget Office (2003b, table 2).

An unpublished study by a U.S. Treasury economist found that only 4 percent of all taxpayers who were eligible for conventional IRAs in 1995 made the maximum allowable $2,000 contribution at that time (Carroll 2000; see also Copeland 2002). The paper concludes, "Taxpayers who do not contribute at the $2,000 maximum would be unlikely to increase their IRA contributions if the contribution limits were increased."

Similarly, the General Accounting Office (now known as the Government Accountability Office [2001]) found that the increase in the statutory contribution limit for 401(k)s would directly benefit fewer than 3 percent of participants.[11] Table 4-3 presents information from the Congressional Budget Office on workers constrained by the previous 401(k) limits in 1997. Only 6 percent of all 401(k) participants made the maximum contribution allowed by law, and only 1 percent of participants in households with incomes below $40,000 made the maximum contribution. Among participants in households with more than $160,000 in income, by contrast, 40 percent made the maximum contribution.

This expected and common pattern—in which those with the highest incomes are most likely to make the maximum allowable contributions to existing retirement accounts—helps to explain why subsidized retirement saving largely induces asset shifting for higher-income households. These high-income households already have levels of assets above the limits in the existing programs, so most of the funds that they hold in current retirement accounts are probably shifted from other assets, and their response to increasing the contribution limits is likely to be additional shifting of

11. See also the findings of Joulfaian and Richardson (2001).

assets from other accounts. Thus, instead of encouraging new saving, expansions of current tax preferences would mostly subsidize saving that would have occurred anyway.

Furthermore, increasing IRA contribution limits could reduce the incentives for small- and medium-sized businesses to offer employment-based payroll deduction saving plans. When the IRA limit is raised, a larger number of business owners and managers may find that they can meet all their personal demands for tax-free saving without the hassle and expense of maintaining an employer-sponsored plan. According to an analysis by the Congressional Research Service, "Some employers, particularly small employers, might drop their plans given the benefits of private savings accounts" (Gravelle 2004a). Since payroll deduction is such an important piece in encouraging savings, higher IRA limits may thus actually reduce retirement security for middle- and low-income earners by making it less likely that they would have a convenient and easy way to save through 401(k) plans.

Conclusion

A growing body of empirical evidence raises fundamental questions about the way in which the U.S. government seeks to encourage personal saving. The evidence suggests that it makes a substantial difference whether the default choice is not to participate in a retirement saving plan, with an option to participate, or whether the default choice is to participate in a retirement saving plan, with an option not to participate. However, in most cases, the default is currently set to spending rather than saving. The evidence also suggests that those with high incomes tend to respond to incentives for contributions by shifting existing assets into tax-preferred accounts rather than by increasing net saving. Current incentives for saving—which are overwhelmingly devoted to encouraging contributions to retirement accounts by high-income households rather than contributions by households with low and middle incomes—are thus upside down.

In this chapter, we have proposed a dramatic set of reforms. By creating an automatic 401(k) and automatic IRA, we would put saving first rather than treating it as the residual left over after spending decisions have been made. Inertia would allow families to be saving in sensible ways rather than missing their opportunity to save. We would also eliminate the existing system of tax deductions for 401(k)s and IRAs and replace them with a universal government matching program that would better target new saving by middle- and low-income households. This shift would be accomplished without any significant change in the government's budget position since the reduction in government revenue that currently arises because of tax incentives to encourage saving would be replaced by our system of government matching payments to encourage saving. We would also improve retirement security by having the federal government provide an actuarially fair and inflation-protected lifetime annuity. The net result of this set of policies would be a dramatic rise in the retirement income security of middle- and low-income Americans.

References

Banks, James, Richard Blundell, and Sarah Tanner. 1998. "Is There a Retirement-Savings Puzzle?" *American Economic Review* 88, no. 4: 769–88.

Benjamin, Daniel J. 2003. "Does 401(k) Eligibility Increase Saving? Evidence from Propensity Score Subclassification." *Journal of Public Economics* 87, no. 5–6: 1259–90.

Bernheim, B. Douglas. 1993. *Is the Baby Boom Generation Preparing Adequately for Retirement? Summary Report*. New York: Merrill Lynch.

Bernheim, B. Douglas, and John Karl Scholz. 1993. "Private Saving and Public Policy." In *Tax Policy and the Economy*, vol. 7, edited by James M. Poterba, pp. 73–110. MIT Press.

Brown, Jeffrey R., Olivia S. Mitchell, and James M. Poterba. 2000. "Mortality Risk, Inflation Risk, and Annuity Products." Working Paper 7812. Cambridge, Mass.: National Bureau of Economic Research.

Burman, Leonard E., and others. 2004. "Distributional Effects of Defined Contribution Plans and Individual Retirement Accounts." Discussion Paper 16. Washington: Tax Policy Center, Urban Institute and Brookings.

Carroll, Robert. 2000. *IRAs and the Tax Reform Act of 1997*. U.S. Department of the Treasury, Office of Tax Analysis.

Choi, James J., and others. 2002. "Defined Contribution Pensions: Plan Rules, Participant Decisions, and the Path of Least Resistance." In *Tax Policy and the Economy*, vol. 16, edited by James M. Poterba, pp. 67–113. MIT Press.

———. 2004. "For Better or for Worse: Default Effects and 401(k) Savings Behavior." In *Perspectives on the Economics of Aging*, edited by David A. Wise, pp. 81–121. University of Chicago Press.

Congressional Budget Office. 2003a. *Baby Boomers' Retirement Prospects: An Overview*.

———. 2003b. *Utilization of Tax Incentives for Retirement Saving*.

Copeland, Craig. 2002. "IRA Assets and Characteristics of IRA Owners." *EBRI Notes* 23, no. 12: 1–9.

Diamond, Peter A., and Peter R. Orszag. 2005. *Saving Social Security: A Balanced Approach*. Brookings Institution.

Duflo, Esther, and others. 2005. "Saving Incentives for Low- and Middle-Income Families: Evidence from a Field Experiment with H&R Block." Policy Brief 2005-5. Washington: Retirement Security Project.

Eckel, Catherine C., and Philip J. Grossman. 2003. "Rebate versus Matching: Does How We Subsidize Charitable Contributions Matter?" *Journal of Public Economics* 87, no. 3–4: 681–701.

Engen, Eric M., and William G. Gale. 2000. "The Effects of 401(k) Plans on Household Wealth: Differences across Earnings Groups." Working Paper 8032. Cambridge, Mass.: National Bureau of Economic Research.

Engen, Eric M., William G. Gale, and Cori E. Uccello. 1999. "The Adequacy of Household Saving." *BPEA*, no. 2: 65–187.

———. 2004. "Lifetime Earnings, Social Security Benefits, and the Adequacy of Retirement Wealth Accumulation." Working Paper 2004-10. Boston College, Center for Retirement Research.

Gale, William G., J. Mark Iwry, and Peter R. Orszag. 2005. "The Automatic 401(k): A Simple Way to Strengthen Retirement Savings." Policy Brief 2005-1. Washington: Retirement Security Project.

Gale, William G., and Peter. R. Orszag. 2003. "Private Pensions: Issues and Options." In *Agenda for the Nation,* edited by Henry J. Aaron, James M. Lindsay, and Pietro S. Nivola, pp. 183–216. Brookings.

Government Accountability Office. 2001. *Private Pensions: Issues of Coverage and Increasing Contribution Limits for Defined Contribution Plans.* GAO 01-846.

Gravelle, Jane G. 2004a. *Effects of LSAs/RSAs Proposal on the Economy and the Budget.* Congressional Research Service.

———. 2004b. *Revenue Effect of Restricting the Tax Preferred Savings Proposal to Retirement Accounts.* Congressional Research Service.

Investment Company Institute. 2005. *Mutual Funds and the U.S. Retirement Market in 2004.* London.

Iwry, J. Mark. 2003. "Defined Benefit Pension Plans." Testimony before Subcommittee on Employer-Employee Relations, Committee on Education and the Workforce, House of Representatives. 108 Cong. 1 sess., June 4.

Iwry, J. Mark, and David C. John. 2006. "Pursuing Universal Retirement Security through Automatic IRAs." Working Paper. Washington: Retirement Security Project.

Joulfaian, David, and David P. Richardson. 2001. "Who Takes Advantage of Tax-Deferred Saving Programs? Evidence from Federal Income Tax Data." *National Tax Journal* 54, no. 3: 669–88.

Kotlikoff, Laurence J., Avia Spivak, and Lawrence H. Summers. 1982. "The Adequacy of Savings." *American Economic Review* 72, no. 5: 1056–69.

Madrian, Brigitte C., and Dennis F. Shea. 2001. "The Power of Suggestion: Inertia in 401(k) Participation and Savings Behavior." *Quarterly Journal of Economics* 116, no. 4: 1149–87.

Mitchell, Olivia S., James Moore, and John Phillips. 1998. "Explaining Retirement Saving Shortfalls." Working Paper 98-13. University of Pennsylvania, Wharton School, Pension Research Council.

Moore, James F., and Olivia S. Mitchell. 1997. "Projected Retirement Wealth and Savings Adequacy in the Health and Retirement Survey." Working Paper 6240. Cambridge, Mass.: National Bureau of Economic Research.

Munnell, Alicia H., and Annika Sundén. 2004. *Coming Up Short: The Challenge of 401(k) Plans.* Brookings.

National Academy of Social Insurance. 2005. *Uncharted Waters: Paying Benefits for Individual Accounts in Federal Retirement Policy.* Washington.

Neuberger, Zoë, Robert Greenstein, and Eileen P. Sweeney. 2005. "Protecting Low-Income Families' Retirement Savings: How Retirement Accounts Are Treated in Means-Tested Programs and Steps to Remove Barriers to Retirement Saving." Policy Brief 2005-6. Washington: Retirement Security Project.

Office of Management and Budget. 2005. *Budget of the United States Government, Fiscal Year 2006: Analytical Perspectives.*

Orszag, Peter R. 2004. "Progressivity and Saving: Fixing the Nation's Upside-Down Incentives for Saving." Testimony before Committee on Education and the Workforce, House of Representatives. 108 Cong. 2 sess., February 25.

Orszag, Peter, and Norman P. Stein. 2001. "Cross-Tested Defined Contribution Plans: A Response to Professor Zelinsky." *Buffalo Law Review* 49, no. 2: 629.

Poterba, James M., Steven F. Venti, and David A. Wise. 1998. "Lump-Sum Distributions from Retirement Saving Plans: Receipt and Utilization." In *Inquiries in the Economics of Aging,* edited by David A. Wise, pp. 85–105. University of Chicago Press.

Profit Sharing/401(k) Council of America. 2004. *47th Annual Survey of Profit Sharing and 401(k) Plans.* Chicago.

Robb, A. Leslie, and John B. Burbidge. 1989. "Consumption, Income, and Retirement." *Canadian Journal of Economics* 22, no. 3: 522–42.

Scholz, John Karl, Ananth Seshadri, and Surachai Khitatrakun. 2004. "Are Americans Saving 'Optimally' for Retirement?" Working Paper 10260. Cambridge, Mass.: National Bureau of Economic Research.

Social Security Administration. 2008. *2008 Annual Report of the Board of Trustees of the Federal Old-Age and Survivors Insurance and Disability Insurance Trust Funds.*

Thaler, Richard H., and Shlomo Benartzi. 2004. "Save More Tomorrow: Using Behavioral Economics to Increase Employee Saving." *Journal of Political Economy* 112, no. 1: S164–87.

Warshawsky, Mark J., and John Ameriks. 1998. *What Does Financial Planning Software Say about Americans' Preparedness for Retirement?* New York: TIAA-CREF Institute.

Building a High-Skill Workforce

Success by Ten

Intervening Early, Often, and Effectively in the Education of Young Children

JENS LUDWIG AND ISABEL SAWHILL

5

Children cannot choose their parents. While people disagree about how social policy should treat adults who have been unlucky or unwise, there is something fundamentally unfair about making children's life chances hostage to the circumstances of their parents. The reality, though, is that family background has a powerful influence on how children develop, beginning early in their lives. Our society's goal should be to intervene early, often, and effectively in the lives of disadvantaged children from birth to age ten, so that by the end of this period we substantially narrow—or eliminate—disparities in cognitive and noncognitive skills across race and class lines.

The human brain grows and changes at an astonishingly rapid rate during the first few years of life (Friedman 2004; Shonkoff and Phillips 2000; Knudsen and others 2006). The brain's unusual "plasticity" seems to make young children unusually responsive to environmental influences. Children's environments during these early years differ dramatically across race and class lines. For example, compared with kindergartners from families in the bottom fifth of the socioeconomic distribution (measured by a combination of parental education, occupation, and income), children from the top fifth of all families are four times more likely to have a computer in the home, have three times as many books in the home, are read to more often, watch

Figure 5-1. Math and Reading Achievement at the Beginning of Kindergarten, by Quintiles of Socioeconomic Status[a]

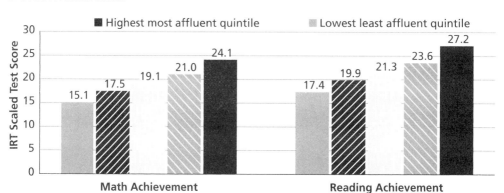

Source: Lee and Burkam (2002, figure 1.3).

a. Sample is of children who started kindergarten in 1998. Item response theory (IRT) scaling method used to equate math and reading scores.

far less television, and are more likely to visit museums or libraries (Lee and Burkam 2002).

These differences in early environments contribute to large gaps in test scores. Numerous studies have compared the outcomes of preschool children from different socioeconomic backgrounds, or racial or ethnic groups, and find large differences in cognitive skills in children as young as three or four years old (Fryer and Levitt 2004; Lee and Burkam 2002; Rouse, Brooks-Gunn, and McLanahan 2005; Rock and Stenner 2005).[1] Figure 5-1 summarizes some recent results showing marked differences in average math and reading scores by socioeconomic status for a nationally representative sample of children who started kindergarten in 1998.

The early years also appear to be a sensitive period for the development of noncognitive skills, such as those relating to emotion and affect (Nelson 2000a, 2000b). The large differences in noncognitive outcomes (such as physical aggression) between children in families above the poverty line compared with those below it have been documented at ages as young as seventeen months (Tremblay and others 2004; see also Cunha and others 2005 for a summary of other results).

1. See also Jencks, Christopher, and Meredith Phillips, 1998, "America's Next Achievement Test: Closing the Black-White Achievement Gap," *American Prospect,* no. 40, September-October, pp. 44–53.

These early gaps in cognitive and noncognitive skills tend to persist through the school years and into later life. Those who score poorly before entering kindergarten are likely to do less well in school, become teen parents, engage in crime, and be unemployed as adults (Rouse, Brooks-Gunn, and McLanahan 2005). For example, by the end of high school, the size of the gap in achievement test scores between white and African American children is not much different from the size of the gap among those groups of students in preschool (Phillips and others 1998; see Ludwig 2003 for a discussion of measurement issues).

The importance of these early years in affecting the ability of children to realize their full potential is not matched by government budget priorities. The United States currently spends around $7,300 on elementary and secondary public schooling for each school-age child, for a total of around $530 billion (see Department of Education 2005).[2] Per student spending in Head Start is similar to that in public elementary and secondary schools, but the program's annual budget of $7 billion covers only 49 percent of income-eligible three- and four-year-olds (Puma and others 2005). The newer Early Head Start program is designed to provide preschool and other services to disadvantaged children during the highly malleable years between birth and age three years, but Early Head Start's budget is only around $700 million and covers just a small fraction of all eligible children (Puma and others 2005). Most of America's social policies try to play catch-up against these early disadvantages—and most disadvantaged children never catch up.

Our Success by Ten proposal argues for a major expansion and intensification of Head Start and Early Head Start so that every disadvantaged child has the opportunity to enroll in an intensive, high-quality program of education and care during the first five years of life. Our proposal is based on a growing sense among scientists that intervening early in the lives of disadvantaged children may be particularly important and productive. The benefits of this intensive intervention may be squandered, however, if disadvantaged children go from this program to a low-quality elementary school, and there is currently little reason to believe that compensatory federal Title I spending does much to improve these children's schooling experiences. As a result, the second part of our proposal is to require that

2. The Bureau of the Census (2007, table 244) reports average per pupil spending for children in elementary and secondary schooling of around $8,200 in 2004. These data also suggest that around 89 percent of all school-age children are enrolled in public schools, so public school spending per school-age child equals about $7,300 (89 percent of $8,200).

schools devote their Title I spending to instructional programs that are proven effective, which would further improve the skills of poor children and help guard against "fade-out" of preschool gains. In short, our Success by Ten proposal argues both for more resources and for using existing resources more effectively.

The specific proposal we outline below would provide economic and social benefits that far exceed the program's costs. Moreover, over the long term, the program will even cover its costs from the narrower perspective of the government's balance sheet by increasing educational attainment and thus stimulating economic growth and consequently tax revenues, as well as reducing government costs for line items such as special education and incarceration. Finally, the proposal should help improve continuity of child care for poor families and support the bipartisan goals of the No Child Left Behind Act (House of Representatives 2001) to close educational gaps between rich and poor, and minority and nonminority children.

The remainder of our chapter fleshes out one specific proposal for achieving this ambitious set of goals. It is not intended to provide a comprehensive survey of the early childhood education literature; excellent reviews of this and related literatures can be found elsewhere (Barnett 1995; Shonkoff and Phillips 2000; Currie 2001; Carneiro and Heckman 2003; Krueger 2003; Blau and Currie 2004; Cunha and others 2005; Magnuson and Waldfogel 2005; Knudsen and others 2006). In fact, none of the ideas presented here is entirely new. Our primary goal is to selectively craft pieces of this existing literature into a coherent and specific policy proposal and to highlight the reasons why scholars working in this area believe that investing early, often, and effectively is such a promising policy.

The Principles behind Success by Ten

Our strategy rests on three central principles: intervene early, intervene often, and intervene effectively.

Intervene Early

Large disparities in children's outcomes by family background are evident, even at the age children are eligible to enroll in Head Start. We should be trying to prevent rather than remediate these educational disadvantages.

Intervene Often

Intervening early improves the ability of children to benefit from schooling in later periods (Carneiro and Heckman 2003; see also Dickens and Flynn

2001), which also implies that this benefit may be squandered if high-quality preschool programs are followed by time spent in low-quality classrooms. We need to improve the learning environments of children, not only during the preschool years but also during the elementary school years. One-shot interventions added to the existing public school options for low-income children are not enough.

Intervene Effectively

While improving the educational environments of poor children is an important goal with great potential, it is equally important to ensure that the money allocated to this goal is spent well. A central feature of Success by Ten is the requirement that all federal money that is allocated to the initiative be dedicated to proven methods—interventions that have been subjected to rigorous evaluation, have led to better outcomes for children, and have passed a benefit-cost test.

Our third principle, intervening effectively, not only guides our decisions about specific programmatic recommendations but also presents a challenge: while science is helping illuminate how human development unfolds and what types of intervention strategies might be most promising, important gaps remain (Shonkoff and Phillips 2000; Knudsen and others 2006). In our view, given the magnitude of the problem and the promise demonstrated in previous research, the combination of risks and returns justifies important new investments in this area. What follows is our attempt to spur a serious discussion about the specific form these investments should take, with the recognition (and the hope) that this dialogue and the accumulation of new research in this area will lead to the evolution of new ideas, including ones that may differ from the specific programmatic features of our proposal.

Proposal Design and Background

What would Success by Ten look like? In light of our principle to intervene effectively, and given the research evidence currently available, we think the most promising way to improve the learning outcomes of disadvantaged children would be to provide them with five years of high-quality, full-time early education and care outside the home, starting with birth. This conclusion stems in part from an unusually promising model program called Abecedarian and also from evaluations of other programs, as well as from a growing body of evidence from neuroscience, developmental psychology, and even research on animals (Shonkoff and Phillips 2000; Currie

2001; Gormley and others 2005; Barnett, Lamy, and Jung 2005; Knudsen and others 2006; Ludwig and Miller 2007; Ludwig and Phillips 2007). While there is evidence to support the cost-effectiveness of a wide variety of different programs that vary in their intensity, particularly encouraging are the results of the unusually intensive Abecedarian program, which was able to generate lasting impacts even on outcomes such as IQ scores.

To preserve and build on the gains from this type of intensive preschool program, we propose that disadvantaged children subsequently spend the first five years of their elementary school careers (from kindergarten through grade four) in a proven instructional program. One of the few elementary school programs that has been rigorously evaluated and shown to be effective is called Success for All. This program emphasizes the development of reading skills, assesses children regularly, and provides one-on-one tutoring to children who fall behind. To ensure that disadvantaged children get to participate in a high-quality program such as Success for All, we recommend that Title I funds be limited to programs certified by the National Academy of Sciences to have been rigorously evaluated and found effective.

To begin the discussion of our proposal, we first look at the two programs—Abecedarian and Success for All—whose encouraging evidence motivates the early education and elementary school follow-up components of our Success by Ten proposal, and we describe the elements and impacts of those interventions. This is followed by a discussion of the implementation of our Success by Ten proposal and the anticipated costs and benefits. Throughout this discussion, we emphasize that our proposal's structure (especially the phase-in and scale-up process) is designed to facilitate research and experimentation, with the goal of finding program alternatives that could be even more cost effective. Next we address potential questions and concerns, followed by our conclusions.

The Abecedarian Program

In 1972 a population of low-income, at-risk pregnant women (nearly all of whom were African American) was identified in Chapel Hill, North Carolina, to participate in a unique early education program called Abecedarian. The children born from this population were randomly assigned to either a control group or an Abecedarian "treatment" group. The latter received year-round, full-time care from 7:30 a.m. to 5:30 p.m., five days a week, fifty weeks a year, for five years starting in the child's first year of life. The intensity of this program is in clear contrast with Head Start, which usually provides children around age three or four years with one or two years of services during the academic year.

The Abecedarian program included transportation, individualized educational activities that changed as the children aged, and low child-staff ratios (3 to 1 for the youngest children and up to 6 to 1 for older children). Abecedarian teachers followed a clear curriculum that focused on language development, and the program explained to teachers the importance of each task and the way to teach each task. Regular assessment and monitoring was also an important part of Abecedarian: every three months, staff administered the Bayley Scales of Infant Development to children ages three to eighteen months, and every six months, they administered IQ tests to children between the ages of twenty-four and sixty months. The program also provided families with additional social services and nutritional supplements (Ramey and Campbell 1979; Campbell and others 2002; Masse and Barnett 2007).

We can draw strong conclusions about the efficacy of Abecedarian because the model program was implemented as a randomized experiment, with some mothers and their children randomly assigned to the Abecedarian program and others assigned to a control group. Parents and children in the program should be, on average, similar to those randomly assigned to the control group. Differences in outcomes for treatments and controls can therefore be attributed to the effects of the program with high confidence.

The results of Abecedarian were dramatic. Children assigned to the control group typically ended up having IQ scores that were far below the national average for that age, as one would expect for children from a lower socioeconomic group (see figure 5-1). However, children assigned to the Abecedarian treatment group had IQ scores at about the national average through age five. Similarly large effects were also observed for achievement on verbal and quantitative tests (Ramey and Campbell 1984). The implication is that if a scaled-up program (such as the one proposed in this paper) could achieve similar impacts, then most of the difference in early childhood outcomes between low- and middle-income children could be eliminated.

These impressive results motivate our decision to suggest that the early education component of our Success by Ten proposal be as intensive as that employed in Abecedarian. As discussed below, these benefits stand out even when compared with other early education programs. But in addition to being a high-benefit program, Abecedarian was also high cost, at about $16,600 a year for each of the child's first five years (Masse and Barnett 2002). The relevant column of table 5-1 summarizes many of the key features of the Abecedarian program and compares the program's features

Table 5-1. Comparison of Alternative Early Childhood Education Programs

Units as indicated (all values approximate)

Characteristics	Abecedarian	Perry Preschool	Chicago Child-Parent Center	Head Start	Early Head Start
Ages covered (years)	0–5	3–4	3–9	3–4	0–3
Quantity (coverage) per year	7:30–5:30, 5 days a week, 50 weeks a year	2.5 hours a day, 5 days a week, academic year	Half-day preschool (1.5 years), full-day kindergarten, after-school for children 3–9 years during academic year	Varied	Varied
Teacher qualifications	Mostly high school for teachers of children up to 2, mostly BA for teachers of children 3–5[a]	≥ BA plus education certificate	≥ BA plus early education teaching certificate	31 percent BA, 33 percent AA, 22 percent early education teaching certificate[b]	21 percent BA, 34 percent AA, 33 percent early education teaching certificate[c]
Teacher salaries	Comparable to public schools	Comparable to public schools (plus 10 percent)	Comparable to public schools	About half public school salaries	About half public school salaries
Pupil-staff ratios	3:1 infants and toddlers, 6:1 older children	5:1 or 6:1	17:2	9.7:1 (average)	4:1
Number of students involved in the study or program	112 (initial), 104 (end) (about 57 treatment, 54 control)	123 (58 program, 65 control)	1,539 (989 program, 550 control), 1983–86 study	855,000	62,000
Program population	Low-income African American, Chapel Hill, N.C.	Low-income, low-IQ African American, Ypsilanti, Mich.	Poor, 93 percent African American, 7 percent Hispanic, Chicago	Mostly low-income, national	Mostly low-income, national

Curricular emphasis	Communication skills plus motor, social, cognitive skills	Logic, math, literacy, creativity, social	Varied	Varied	Varied
Nonacademic services	Medical and nutrition	1.5 hours a week home visits with mother and child	Home visits, health screening, nursing service	Dental, other health, nutrition	Health and mental health services for children and mothers, nutrition
Total cost per year per student[a]	$16,600	$9,500	$5,500 (preschool)	$7,100	$10,700
Total cost per student (present value at birth, 3 percent discount rate)[a]	$78,000	$17,000	$7,500 (preschool)	$6,500[e]	$17,900[f]

Sources: Abecedarian program description and cost estimates as presented in the chapter and from Ramey and Campbell (1984), Campbell and Ramey (1994), Campbell and others (2002), and Galinsky (2006, p. 10). Perry Preschool description and estimates from Schweinhart and others (2005), Schweinhart (2003), and Heckman and Masterov (2006). Evidence on the Chicago Child-Parent Center from Reynolds and others (1998), Reynolds and others (2001,2002), and Heckman and Masterov (2006). Head Start description and data from Hamm (2006, p. 6), Currie and Neidell (2003, table 1). Office of Head Start (2006), Hart and Schumacher (2005), Zill and others (2003), and Puma and others (2005). Early Head Start description and data from Craig Turner, Administration for Children and Families, personal communication, January 29, 2007; see also Irish, Schumacher, and Lombardi (2003), Administration for Children and Families (n.d.), Love and others (2002), Hamm and Ewen (2006), and Office of Head Start (n.d.).

a. Stephen Robblee and Frances Campbell, personal communication, September 16, 2005. These data are based on Campbell's recollections rather than actual program records on teacher qualifications.

b. 2005 data.

c. 2004 data.

d. Estimated 2007 dollars.

e. Assuming one year of participation at age three years, similar to Garces, Thomas, and Currie (2002). A child who participates for two years would cost approximately $12,800. About 70 percent of Head Start participants spend one year in the program, and the remaining 30 percent usually participate for two years. Craig Turner, Administration for Children and Families, personal communication, January 29, 2007.

f. Assuming twenty-one months of participation culminating at age three years. Twenty-one months was the average duration of service reported in the study by Love and others (2002).

with the current large-scale Head Start and Early Head Start programs and with two other small-scale model programs that are often cited as evidence for the efficacy of early intervention: Perry Preschool and the Chicago Child-Parent Center.

Abecedarian cost more than other early childhood programs in large part because of differences in program duration. While most of these other programs serve children for just a few hours a day for one or two years, under the Abecedarian program, children had access to full-day, year-round services for five full years before starting school. In addition, teacher salaries under Abecedarian were comparable to those of regular public school teachers—about twice what Head Start or Early Head Start teachers are usually paid. Abecedarian also had smaller pupil-staff ratios than at least some of these alternative programs.

Table 5-2 shows how the gains from Abecedarian compare with those from other early childhood programs. The table reveals several key points. First, the increase in test scores during early childhood was much larger for Abecedarian than for either Head Start or Early Head Start—which makes sense, given that Abecedarian was a much more intensive intervention. Abecedarian and Perry Preschool generated similar gains during early childhood, but these comparisons may be misleading because the two programs served very different populations. Specifically, the average IQ of children enrolled in Perry Preschool was lower than that of children in Abecedarian because Perry explicitly selected children to participate who were "borderline educable mentally impaired" (Schweinhart and others 2005). We think Abecedarian's impacts may be more generalizable to the larger population of poor children in America.

Second, Abecedarian is the only program for which there is rigorous evidence for long-term effects on cognitive outcomes such as IQ test scores, as shown in the bottom part of table 5-2. An evaluation of Abecedarian participants at age twenty-one showed IQ scores that were about 0.38 standard deviations higher for the treatment group than for the control group, with similarly large improvements in reading and math scores.

Finally, it is important to note that all of these early childhood programs, even the large-scale Head Start and Early Head Start programs, seem to improve young children's IQ or achievement test scores. Commentators sometimes refer to these Head Start impacts as disappointing, but both the costs and benefits of Head Start during these early years are about the same size as those associated with reducing class sizes in kindergarten through grade three, as was done in the Tennessee Student-Teacher

Table 5-2. Alternative Early Childhood Education Programs: Short- and Long-Term Program Impacts[a]

Units as indicated

Impacts	Abecedarian	Perry Preschool	Chicago Child-Parent Center	Head Start	Early Head Start
Short term (standard deviation)					
Evaluation method	*Experimental*	*Experimental*	*Nonexperimental*	*Experimental*	*Experimental*
Age 3 years					
IQ scores	1.22	0.88	—	—	0.12
Reading-verbal	0.69	0.74	—	0.35	0.13
Math-quantification	0.71	—	—	0.21[b]	—
Aggressive behavior	—	—	—	−0.10[b]	−0.11
Behavior problems	—	—	—	−0.19	—
Age 4 years					
IQ scores	0.93	0.87	—	—	—
Reading-verbal	0.68	0.91	—	0.33	—
Math-quantification	0.57	—	—	0.16[b]	—
Aggressive behavior	—	—	—	−0.04[b]	—
Behavior problems	—	—	—	−0.01[b]	—
Age 5 years					
IQ scores	~0.66	—	—	—	—
Reading-verbal	—	—	—	—	—
Math-quantification	—	—	—	—	—
Age 6 years: IQ scores	—	0.32	—	—	—
Age 12 years: IQ scores	0.50	—	—	—	—
Long term (versus control)					
Evaluation method	*Experimental*	*Experimental*	*Nonexperimental*	*Nonexperimental*	—
Age outcomes measured (year)	21	40	21 (pre-K population)	23	—
High school graduation (percent)	70 vs. 67[b]	77 vs. 60	61 vs. 52	86 vs. 65 (whites)	—
College entry (percent)	36 vs. 14	—	—	—	—
School completed (years)	—	—	11.09 vs. 10.74	—	—
Ever arrested (percent)	—	71 vs. 83	17 vs. 22 (by age 18)	—	—
Arrested 5 or more times (percent)	—	36 vs. 55	—	—	—
Employment rate (percent)	26 vs. 45	76 vs. 62	—	—	—
Teen parent (percent)	18 vs. 39	—	—	—	—

(continued)

Table 5-2. Alternative Early Childhood Education Programs: Short- and Long-Term Program Impacts[a] (*Continued*)

Units as indicated

Impacts	Abecedarian	Perry Preschool	Chicago Child-Parent Center	Head Start	Early Head Start
Long term (versus control)					
Evaluation method	Experimental	Experimental	Nonexperimental	Nonexperimental	—
Marijuana use (percent)	—	48 vs. 71 (males)	—	—	—
IQ scores (standard deviation)	0.38	—	—	—	—

Sources: Abecedarian program description and impacts from Ramey and Campbell (1984), Campbell and Ramey (1994), and Campbell and others (2002). Evidence on the Chicago Child-Parent Center from Reynolds and others (2002) and Reynolds (1998). Results from Head Start from Hart and Schumacher (2005), Zill and others (2003), Garces, Thomas, and Currie (2002), and Puma and others (2005). Results for Early Head Start from Puma and others (2005), Irish, Schumacher, and Lombardi (2003), Administration for Children and Families (n.d.), and Love and others (2002). Results for Head Start short-term impacts are estimates from Ludwig and Phillips (2007) for the effects of Head Start participation per se, calculated based on data from the recent randomized Head Start experimental evaluation (Puma and others 2005).

a. Unless otherwise indicated, standard deviation values are significant at the conventional 5 percent cutoff. Abecedarian test score impacts for reading and math achievement reported for age four and five years in our table were actually measured for Abecedarian participants at forty-two and fifty-four months. For Perry Preschool, the results are actually for "end of first preschool year" and "end of second preschool year," which should roughly correspond to ages three and four years, respectively (Schweinhart and others 2005). The effects of Head Start participation presented in the table equal the effects of assignment to the Head Start experimental treatment group on children's outcomes divided by the effects of treatment-group assignment on the probability of participating in Head Start.

Results for Head Start's long-term impacts come from Garces, Thomas, and Currie (2002) and show the mean high school completion rate among all Head Start children in their sample versus this mean added to the estimated Head Start effect for whites (the white mean is not reported separately in the paper). Note that Ludwig and Miller (2007) find complementary evidence suggesting that Head Start's impact on schooling attainment is large for African Americans as well as whites.

b. Not statistically significant; while a difference was found, it was small enough to be statistically indistinguishable from chance variation.

Achievement Ratio (STAR) experiment (Krueger 1999, 2003).[3] The perceived success of STAR has been one motivation for the statewide class size reduction efforts that took place recently in California and Florida.

Other early education programs have also demonstrated encouraging evidence for long-term effects, such as the randomized experimental evaluation of Perry Preschool. Unfortunately, the experimental studies of Head Start and Early Head Start followed children for only one or two years after program participation, so ironclad evidence for the long-term effects on participants from these two large-scale programs is currently not available. Nevertheless, a growing body of research provides at least suggestive evidence that even Head Start may generate lasting impacts on children that yield benefits to society that are large enough to justify program costs

3. Class sizes were reduced from an average of twenty-two to an average of fifteen students per class.

(Currie and Thomas 1995; Currie 2001; Garces, Thomas, and Currie 2002; Ludwig and Miller 2007; Ludwig and Phillips 2007). Hence, while Abecedarian's benefits were impressive compared with these other early education programs, it is also true that early education programs have generally demonstrated benefits exceeding their costs.

Success for All

The original Abecedarian experiment included a follow-on elementary school component that did not seem to do much good for children who participated (Campbell and others 2002). This means that, in practice, the children who received Abecedarian's intensive, high-quality early childhood services went on to experience a learning environment that was essentially equivalent in quality to whatever the usual elementary school offerings were for low-income African American children in that part of North Carolina. One of the important differences between our own proposal and Abecedarian is that we believe more can be done to improve the learning environments of children in elementary school than the limited intervention that followed the original Abecedarian project.

We strongly believe that early childhood intervention should be followed up with additional support, at least in the early grades of school, but the current evidence available on most schooling interventions is limited. Based on our reading of available research, one of the few programs supported by evidence from a rigorous randomized experiment is Success for All, a comprehensive, whole-school reform model focusing on reading achievement that is already in operation in more than 1,200 schools.

The philosophy of the Success for All elementary school reading program is to focus on the prevention of reading problems. Other subjects are important, but Success for All emphasizes the development and use of language through the reading of children's literature. Consistent with this emphasis, children receive ninety minutes each day of reading instruction in groups that are organized across grade levels, based on each child's current reading level, which helps teachers to target instruction. Students engage in cooperative learning exercises in which they discuss stories or learn from each other, which helps to reinforce what teachers do and builds social skills. Children are assessed at eight-week intervals, using both formal measures of reading competency and teacher observations. Children who are falling behind are given extra tutoring or other help with whatever might be impeding success (such as health or behavior problems).

A recent evaluation of Success for All funded by the Department of Education's Institute for Educational Sciences provides rigorous evidence of the program's effectiveness (Borman and others 2005). Because the schools were randomly assigned to Success for All or to the control group, comparing the results of the two groups becomes much more credible and meaningful. Two years later, the differences between children in the treatment and control schools were positive and statistically significant, usually on the order of about 0.2 standard deviations (about one-fifth the gap between low- and high-socioeconomic-status children).[4]

Our current recommendation for use of Title I money on Success for All in kindergarten through grade four is motivated by the fact that this is one of the only programs we have found that, in a rigorous experimental evaluation, has been demonstrated to be successful. If and when new evidence develops, schools would be eligible to use their Title I money on other proven programs. In fact, our requirement that programs be proven successful to be funded under Success by Ten provides a powerful financial incentive for increased experimental evaluation of new curricula and reform models.

Clues about what program ingredients might prove to be most important over time come from some of the striking similarities between Abecedarian and Success for All. These similarities include an emphasis on the development of language and reading skills; frequent assessments of children's developmental progress through regular testing; and clear, prescriptive curricular materials for teachers to follow (in contrast with more open-ended teacher- and student-initiated learning environments).

Program Implementation and Governance

The preschool piece of our proposal could in some sense be thought of as "Head Start on steroids." It involves combining, expanding, and transforming the current early education infrastructure, including Early Head Start and Head Start, into a program that is much more intensive, on the scale of the Abecedarian program. The second part of our proposal calls for adding an elementary school component that emphasizes the effective use of existing Title I funding streams. While the evidence in favor of such an approach is quite strong, it comes from a set of experiments that are relatively small in number and scale. Therefore, we recommend that this transformation be phased in over ten years in a way that fosters rigorous evaluation of the program's impacts and allows experimentation with alternative interventions that might prove to be even more cost effective than the specific proposal outlined here.

4. For a discussion of concerns about the Success for All study, see Ludwig and Sawhill (2007).

Our proposal would work as follows: a high-poverty school (defined as a school in which at least 40 percent of the children are eligible for the school lunch program) would form a partnership with a local Head Start program or another early childhood program. This partnership would apply to the federal government for the extra funds that would be needed to serve all of the poor children in the local area. Eligibility for the preschool component would be based on family income.

Funding would be jointly administered by the Department of Education and the Department of Health and Human Services. As with the current Head Start system, the federal government would provide funding directly to the local providers instead of using state governments as intermediaries. Competitive grants would be made based on the quality of the local plan, based on, among other things, a willingness to implement the key elements of Success by Ten, assurances that the Head Start and the local school could work together, a commitment by the school system to maintain electronic student-level data on children in their enrollment areas that would be made available to program evaluators, and a willingness to allow the program's impacts and implementation to be independently evaluated.

The key to our implementation strategy is to use lotteries to decide which of the communities submitting acceptable proposals would receive Success by Ten funding during the early years of the phase-in. We expect that more communities would submit acceptable proposals than could be initially funded. Using lotteries to determine which of these communities would receive funding not only would be fair but also would support real-time program evaluation that would be as rigorous as a controlled, randomized experiment. Our proposal thus departs dramatically from the conventional practice of paying lip service to the importance of evaluation but then implementing programs in ways that all but rule out the chance for truly rigorous study.

The lottery would assign acceptable proposals to one of three possibilities: Success by Ten, an experimental version of Success by Ten, or no services. The experimental versions of Success by Ten would vary specific programmatic elements to try to identify program models that might be more cost effective than the very intensive default version of our early childhood program. Particularly important is to learn more about the role played by the duration of the intervention. Previous studies suggest that even early childhood interventions that begin at age three or four years can achieve long-term benefits for participants' schooling attainment, earnings, and other outcomes, even if the program models that have been tried to date have not been able to achieve lasting impacts on IQ scores. So there remains an important question about how the cost-effectiveness of the intervention we propose would change if we started at age three years rather than at birth, which would at the very least substantially reduce the overall cost of the program.

In addition, the experimental versions of Success by Ten could include controlled alterations in pupil-staff ratios, teacher qualifications and salaries, the nature of the curriculum, the nature of nonacademic services, and eligibility rules. For example, eligibility rules could be modified to allow all children living in the area of a high-poverty school to participate in Success by Ten. Such an approach would be simpler to administer, less stigmatizing for families, and not require that families whose incomes change from one year to the next be dropped or added to the program. It would assume that if a family lives in a low-income neighborhood, the family's children are at risk. A possible downside of this approach, however, is that it would be more expensive and less effective than a more highly targeted program. An alternative, therefore, would be to limit eligibility of schools to those that have particularly high proportions of children from low-income families and limit eligibility for the preschool component not only to those children who live in the neighborhood of a high-poverty school but also to those in families with below-poverty-line incomes.

Such controlled variations also might identify ways in which the program could be tailored to the particular needs of local communities—for example, low-income children in rural parts of West Virginia might benefit from slightly different types of early childhood learning activities than would immigrant children in New York City.

Children living in communities that receive funding for some version of Success by Ten would be compared with children in surrounding communities that had applied for Success by Ten resources but were not selected in the lottery. Ideally, we would like to follow up with children over time to understand fade-out and the general persistence of program impacts. Given that some children will move across communities over time, this evaluation strategy would classify children into "treatment" and "control" groups based on their community of residence at the time of the initial lottery, regardless of whether or where children moved subsequently; this is known in the program evaluation literature as the "intent to treat" effect.

We propose phasing in Success by Ten over ten years. An initial six-year phase would be designed to allow one cohort of children to complete the entire five-year early education program and give researchers an additional year to rigorously study and evaluate the results from that cohort. The program would be scaled up to full implementation over the following four years.

Estimates of Costs and Benefits

What would our proposal cost, and what would be the benefits? Federal spending would be approximately $6 billion higher than it is now during each of the first six years, enough to serve about 500,000 children, which is almost the same as Head Start began with in 1965 (and more than half of what Head Start serves today). If all eligible children participated when the program was fully implemented, federal spending would be approximately $56 billion higher than it is under current law. Ultimately, the take-up rates would almost certainly fall somewhere below full participation. There is unavoidable uncertainty as to what that lower rate would be, but based on the experiences of other prekindergarten (pre-K) programs, it seems reasonable to make the rough guess that no more than 75 percent of eligible children would participate in the program. In that case, federal outlays would be no more than $40 billion higher than under current law, after taking into account the reallocation of current federal funds (as discussed below). The estimated benefits to American society from these outlays would be on the order of about two times that amount.

For our cost calculations, our starting point is to assume that the costs per child would be about the same as the costs and benefits per child for Abecedarian and the Success for All programs. We then calculate the costs of implementing this program nationwide for children in families below the poverty line in the United States.

To maximize the chances that a large-scale intensive preschool program achieves large, long-term effects on participants, the preschool part of our proposal should be as intensive as the Abecedarian model program, including five full years of eligibility from birth through the start of kindergarten, full-day full-year services, teacher salaries that are competitive with regular public schools, and low pupil-staff ratios. Ideally, we would like to know exactly which of these program features are crucial for achieving important gains for children and preserve those features while cutting program costs wherever possible. Right now, though, the independent contribution of each feature in existing early childhood programs is not well understood. Under our proposal, local providers assigned by lottery to the main Success by Ten phase-in group would implement a program that includes all of the big-ticket items associated with the Abecedarian model program, while those communities assigned to the experimental group could scale back

Table 5-3. Summary of Existing Federal Early Childhood Education and Child-Care Expenditures

Billions of dollars

Program	Green Book, fiscal year 2003	White House, fiscal year 2002
Child Care and Development Block Grant	3.9	4.8
Temporary Assistance for Needy Families[a]	2.1	4.0
Title XX[b]	0.2	0.165
Head Start	6.7	6.5
Title I	0.2	. . .
Early Reading First	0.075	. . .
Even Start	0.25	. . .
Special education grants for preschool and infants	0.551	. . .
Total	14.0	15.5

Sources: U.S. House of Representatives Ways and Means Committee (2004, table 9–15), and White House, "Executive Summary" (www.whitehouse.gov/infocus/earlychildhood/earlychildhood.pdf), on President Bush's "Good Start, Grow Smart" plan to strengthen early learning.

a. Child-care estimate for fiscal 2002 is an estimate that captures all federal and state spending, while the figure for 2003 reflects federal funds transferred in 2002.

b. Figures for Title XX of the Social Services Block Grant reflect spending on child care services.

along important dimensions to help identify ways of reducing program costs without compromising the program's effectiveness.

We assume a cost per pupil of $16,600 a year, about what has been estimated for the preschool component of Abecedarian (see footnote 3). The actual cost per pupil for the preschool part of our proposal could be somewhat lower than with the small-scale Abecedarian program if there are economies of scale in service provision. The costs could be somewhat higher if salaries need be increased to secure enough talented teachers for the program.

There are approximately 4.1 million children under age five living in households that are below the poverty line (Bureau of the Census 2006). Multiplying the per child cost by the number of children, the gross cost of the program's preschool part each year would be $68 billion if all eligible children were to participate in the program. Actual participation rates would likely be lower and would probably be no more than around 75 percent, which would yield gross early education program costs of about $51 billion a year.

However, not all of this spending would need to be new money. Table 5-3 shows that the federal government currently spends $16 billion a year for Head Start and other childcare or preschool programs that are targeted mainly at poor children. Our proposal would obviate or build on some of these programs. Assuming that we could redirect three-quarters of the $16 billion to our proposal, then the estimated net new cost of the preschool share of our program would be about $39 billion a year. We would add another $1 billion for research, technical assistance, and teacher training, for a total of about $40 billion.

The elementary school follow-up component to Success by Ten would require schools to dedicate Title I money to "proven effective" programs, which, based on evidence available to date, would default to the Success for All program described above. Title I is a funding program rather than a defined intervention, so school districts have wide latitude in determining how Title I funds are spread across schools or classrooms and in choosing the programs or services paid for with federal funds. Current law requires that Title I funds be used for activities that are backed up by scientifically based research, although what this means in practice remains ambiguous (Jacob and Ludwig 2005). Moreover, school districts can currently pick and choose components of several tested programs without evidence that their specific recipe will lead to better outcomes. A key aspect of our proposal is that it would require elementary schools to faithfully implement interventions that have been rigorously tested in random-assignment studies.

Assuming that Success for All is the only rigorously evaluated program identified at the time our proposal goes into effect, how much of this program could schools implement with existing Title I funding? Success for All costs about $930 per student per year, after averaging higher start-up costs with lower ongoing costs of the program (Borman and Hewes 2002). About two-thirds of this cost is associated with the tutoring component of Success for All. Currently, spending under Title I is around $880 per eligible student. If we make the simplifying assumption that nonpoor students would not need tutoring, then schools in which at least 75 percent of students are eligible for Title I could implement Success for All "as is" schoolwide without many additional resources. The No Child Left Behind Act allows schools that have at least 40 percent of Title I–eligible students to implement schoolwide programs that use Title I funds to benefit all children at the school. Other schools would have the option of either implementing less intensive versions of Success for All (for example, by reducing the number of hours of tutoring for children) or redirecting Title I funding from grades five and up, to kindergarten through grade four. Currently, 64 percent of Title I funds go to students in grades one through six, while another 12 percent is dedicated to kindergartners or pre-K children, so our proposal would not require a major reallocation of existing funds.

The cost to society from redirecting Title I resources in the way that is proposed here depends in part on what is being accomplished now with Title I funds. The most recent large-scale study of Title I finds that children who received Title I services did no better academically than those who did not (Puma and others 1997). Other studies, such as Kosters and Mast (2003) come to a similar conclusion. One partial explanation for these discouraging results could be that school districts may offset extra Title I money, to some degree, by reducing local spending on schools (Gordon 2004).

In sum, after taking into account program take-up, offsetting reductions in expenditures for related programs, and a reallocation of Title I funding, we estimate that the additional costs for our proposal would be no more than about $40 billion annually.

What would be the benefits of our proposed preschool and elementary school intervention? A starting point for thinking about the answer to this question is the benefit-cost analysis of the Abecedarian model program by Leonard Masse and Steven Barnett (2007). The costs of early childhood intervention are incurred relatively soon whereas many of the benefits are received much later. In comparing costs and benefits, this difference in timing matters. Policy analysts use the tool of "present discounted value" to adjust for the timing of costs and benefits. The present discounted value of costs is the total amount that would need to be set aside right now, in the present, so that it would be enough with accumulated interest earned over time to cover all current and future costs. Similarly, the present discounted value of benefits is the total amount that would need to be received right now, in the present, so that it would be equal with accumulated interest earned over time to the sum of all future benefits.

Using an annual interest rate of 3 percent to discount future costs and benefits, the present value of the gross costs of these preschool services is about $78,000 per pupil. With the offsetting cost savings in other programs, our best guess is that the net cost to the federal government for each child of participating in the expanded preschool intervention would be about $60,000 in present value terms.

Masse and Barnett (2007, table 2) estimate that the present value of the benefits from Abecedarian is about $147,000 per child. Listing all these benefits in terms of their present discounted value, they include approximately $9,940 in savings to the kindergarten through grade twelve schooling system from reductions in special education placements, $20,000 from improvements in health, $42,200 in increased earnings for participants, $6,400 from the increased earnings of their children, $77,300 from increased maternal earnings, and $220 in social program (welfare) savings. These benefits are partially offset by costs of $9,100 resulting from the program's positive effect on college enrollment rates (all estimated 2007 dollars).[5]

The Masse and Barnett calculations may understate the benefits in one important way: the Abecedarian benefit calculations do not include any estimate of savings from a reduction in criminal activity. As noted earlier, those who received the Abecedarian intervention had a crime rate about one-third lower than the rate for those in the control group, a proportionately large difference. However, the number of criminal participants in both groups was small enough that it is impossible to state with a high degree of confidence whether this decline was a result of the Abecedarian program or simply a statistical fluke (Campbell and others 2002).

Our own hunch is that Abecedarian would be found to reduce criminal involvement of participants if there were a larger group to study. After all, Abecedarian had statistically significant effects on IQ scores, college enrollment, teen parenthood, and drug use. Given that all of these characteristics are highly correlated with the likelihood that people become involved with crime, it would be surprising if Abecedarian had *not* affected criminal behavior. If the Abecedarian program did, in fact, reduce criminal activity by about one-third, then the benefits to society might be on the order of an additional $20,000 to $40,000 per person.[6] Thus, adding the potential benefit of reduced crime to the other benefits would make the expected benefits of Abecedarian more than two times the costs.

What about the benefits of implementing the Success for All program? Studies suggest that this program might increase achievement test scores by around one-fifth of a standard deviation (Borman and others 2005). If these gains persisted over time, the benefits would be quite substantial—for example, the increase in lifetime earnings alone might be worth between $5,000 and $45,000 per child (Krueger 2003). However, we have no way of knowing how the benefits from an intensive early childhood program

5. All values from Masse and Barnett (2007) are discounted and deflated values in 2002 dollars, converted to estimated 2007 dollars. All of these benefits are calculated with a 3 percent discount rate. Masse and Barnett's cost-benefit analysis, however, shows that benefits exceed costs even above a 7 percent discount rate when avoided childcare costs are taken into account.

6. A rough estimate of the average social costs of crime might be $60,000 per person in poor neighborhoods, an estimate that is based on the lifetime arrests of poor urban youth aged fifteen to twenty-five from highly disadvantaged neighborhoods in Baltimore, Boston, Chicago, Los Angeles, and New York (Kling, Ludwig, and Katz 2005). The costs might be twice as high when we account for the fact that not all crimes result in arrest. If the per person costs of criminal activity among disadvantaged populations is $60,000 to $120,000, then the value of a one-third reduction in these costs is $20,000 to $40,000.

and Success for All would interact. Rather than giving a best-case scenario, we conservatively assume that the main effect of Success for All would be to reduce the chances of fade-out after the proposed intensive preschool component and to increase the odds that our large-scale early childhood intervention would achieve large gains similar—if not exactly equal—to those of the Abecedarian model program.

Another way to measure the possible benefits of our Success by Ten proposal is in terms of its impact on productivity and economic growth in the United States. Technology has increased the demand for skilled labor in recent decades, as evidenced by a sharp increase in the earnings of more-educated workers relative to their less-educated counterparts. In a knowledge-based economy, the productivity of the workforce depends not just on the amount invested in plants and equipment but also on the skills and education that workers bring to their jobs. If Success by Ten is as successful as we hope, then eventually educational attainment will rise in the United States, which will translate into more growth and a higher standard of living.

Although many people have made these arguments at a general level, we have taken a well-specified model of economic growth and asked what the effects would be if our proposal could achieve impacts such as those of the Abecedarian model program. Suppose the intervention were successful in increasing educational attainment by 0.6 years by age twenty-one among participating children relative to those who did not participate. Assuming that about 15 percent of all children participated (equal to about 75 percent of all children below the poverty line), educational attainment would increase by 0.09 years for the population as a whole (0.15 times 0.6). Based on analysis with a preferred set of assumptions, we project that a 0.09-year increase in average educational attainment would boost the rate of growth and produce about a 0.8 percent higher real GDP by 2080, which translates to an extra $493 billion (Dickens, Sawhill, and Tebbs 2006).

All these estimates clearly have an element of uncertainty. However, we think the chances are extremely good that the benefits to society from our proposal would outweigh the costs. If our proposal achieved the same benefits as the small-scale Abecedarian program, we would expect the present value of benefits to outweigh the costs by more than two times. But even if we assume that the benefits would be somewhat attenuated by the scaling-up process, they would still likely outweigh costs by about two times. The large-scale version of the intensive program that we are proposing here would need to be *substantially* less effective than earlier model programs before it would fail a benefit-cost test.

As more early childhood and elementary school interventions are identified as successful through ongoing research, the specifics of this intervention package could, in principle, change over time or vary from district to district. But based on current evidence, this intervention portfolio, which uses an intensive early childhood program design that incorporates features from the Abecedarian program from birth to age five and the Success for All model for kindergarten through grade four, seems to us to be the one that has the strongest supporting evidence.

Questions and Concerns

Will the Benefits Persist in a Large-Scale Program?

Possibly the most important concern with our proposal is that we are arguing for an investment of up to an estimated $40 billion a year in additional federal spending on preschool without direct evidence that a similarly intensive large-scale program would achieve the impacts that we hope for. How can we be sure that we could achieve improvements in children's lives that are as impressive as those found with smaller-scale early childhood model programs? (There is less concern with the Success for All component to our proposal, since it has already been widely adopted.)

The answer is that we cannot be sure. In fact, we are pretty sure that we cannot achieve gains of the sort found with the Abecedarian model program on a massive national scale. The model Abecedarian program that was implemented in Chapel Hill almost surely drew from a pool of teachers who were more committed and perhaps more talented than the average teacher, and the fidelity with which the program was implemented would surely be much better replicated in a small-scale model than in a national program.[7]

How can we justify our proposal in the face of this uncertainty? We have five responses:

First, our proposal for increased investment in early childhood education for disadvantaged children does not rest solely on the encouraging results from the Abecedarian model program. As summarized in table 5-2, we now have ample evidence that, in principle, early childhood intervention can improve the life chances of disadvantaged children.

Second, we have examples of other preschool programs that have been successfully taken to scale. The early days of Head Start in 1964 and 1965

---

7. One complication with this simple calculation is that the experimental estimates for the effects of Head Start apply to recent cohorts of children; thus the effects Head Start had during the early years might differ because earlier cohorts of participating children came from even more disadvantaged family backgrounds, on average, than recent participants.

were filled with debates about whether to focus on implementing small experimental programs that could be evaluated and refined or instead follow what was ultimately President Johnson's wish to immediately implement a large nationwide program (Gillette 1996; Greenberg 2004). How much of a problem was scaling up Head Start? It is difficult to answer definitively, but here is our rough-and-ready guess. Table 5-1 shows that per child spending for Head Start is about 40 percent of that for Perry Preschool, a model program that started just a few years before Head Start. If we are willing to assume that effects on children are proportional to spending, then we would expect the impacts of Head Start to be about 40 percent of the impacts of Perry Preschool, if nothing were lost during the scale-up process. The recent randomized experimental study of Head Start (summarized in table 5-2) suggests that the program has impacts at age four that are about one-third as large as those of Perry.[8] This simple exercise suggests that scale-up might reduce the effectiveness of the program by around 15 percent.[9]

Third, the phase-in design of our proposal would generate rigorous evaluation evidence for at least short-term impacts and highlight whether and how the scaled-up preschool piece was working. Planned deviations from the proposed model in some localities might uncover ways to make the program more effective, less expensive, or both.

Fourth, our strongest hedge against the risk that a scaled-up version of an intensive early childhood program will produce smaller benefits than previous model programs is our proposal to strengthen the elementary school follow-up component compared to previous model early childhood interventions. The elementary school follow-up piece adopted as part of the original Abecedarian model program in Chapel Hill did not seem to

---

8. The benefits of Head Start recorded in table 5-2 reflect results achieved after children had been in the program for only one year; the benefits of Perry Preschool reflect results achieved after children had been in that program for two years. Accordingly, table 5-1 compares the cost of providing one year of Head Start and two years of Perry Preschool.

9. One reason the intervention could have more modest effects than the original program when implemented on a large scale has to do with the program population itself. The added value of an Abecedarian-style intervention comes from the difference in the developmental environment for the child between the program and the child's alternative care arrangements. Abecedarian's program population was quite disadvantaged—on average, mothers were about twenty years old with around a tenth-grade education (Ramey and Campbell 1984). While eligibility under our proposal is limited to families below the poverty line, the population of children served under our proposal may, on average, have developmentally "better" family environments than those in Abecedarian, if only because of the widespread increase over time in parental schooling levels.

have much of an independent effect on children (Campbell and others 2002). Our proposal instead follows an Abecedarian-like preschool component with a proven elementary school intervention (Success for All) that yields impressive program impacts in its own right.

Finally, we do not *need* Success by Ten to be as effective as model programs such as Abecedarian in order for our proposal to substantially change future economic growth and improve the life chances of disadvantaged children. In fact, Success by Ten would pass a benefit-cost test even if the combined preschool and elementary school components that we propose were even half as effective as the small-scale Abecedarian preschool program alone. Thus we think the chances are good that our proposal would pass a benefit-cost test despite the inevitable problems associated with bringing programs to scale.

Is it Desirable and Feasible to Reallocate Title I Dollars?

Title I is essentially a block grant that provides enormous flexibility to local school districts. As one education researcher put it:

> Although the Title I program was a massive funding program, it did not represent a unified or coherent treatment program. . . . There did not seem to be any one, or even small, set of programs that could be classified Title I [and] any attempt to evaluate the effectiveness of the Title I program is faced with the problem that Title I was better defined as a funding program than as an educational treatment (Carter 1984, p. 11).

Local districts like this kind of flexibility and predictably will resist any effort to dictate to them how to spend these funds. But the overwhelming evidence is that these funds have not been used in ways that improve student performance. That said, schools face major challenges in implementing the provisions of the No Child Left Behind Act, and it may be necessary to provide them with some additional funding to make the elementary school component of our proposal feasible. It may also be necessary to give them some flexibility in the design of the program, subject to continued evaluation and assessment of the results.

Why Not Universal Pre-K?

Why not finance a universal rather than targeted early childhood program? After all, more than forty states are adopting pre-K programs, and the momentum for extending the public education system down the age scale is currently quite strong.

Our proposal targets disadvantaged children in part to maximize the benefits per federal dollar. Most studies of early childhood interventions, including those of Head Start (Love and others 2002), the Tennessee STAR class-size experiment (Krueger 1999), and Abecedarian itself (Campbell and others 2002) find larger impacts for disadvantaged or minority children than for nonpoor or white children. One exception seems to arise in the evaluation of Oklahoma's pre-K program in Tulsa (Gormley and others 2005).

In any case, states would be free to use their own funds to expand the scope of our proposal to include children in families above the poverty line. This possibility would lead to even greater benefits for poor children if peer effects in learning are important. Expanding the program to include nonpoor students might also provide some—if more limited—benefits for these children and help build a larger political constituency for the program.

Why Not Expand Head Start?

A number of people argue that Head Start is a strong program with a network of centers around the country providing a base on which to build. They assert that all that is needed is to provide the system with additional resources so that all eligible children aged three or four years can be served for at least one year. While there is a growing body of evidence to suggest that Head Start may have important long-term benefits, whether these long-term impacts generalize to current cohorts of poor children is subject to some uncertainty, as is our ability to scale up more intensive programs to a national level. Given the scale of the problem we are trying to address, our default position is to suggest a more rather than less intensive intervention and then use controlled variation during the implementation stage to determine whether modified versions of the program are capable of generating similarly large benefits at lower cost.

In our view, there is also a general argument to be made in favor of prevention over remediation; family background generates large differences in outcomes across children even before they are old enough to enroll in Head Start. While Early Head Start was launched for this reason, Abecedarian seems to be a more cost effective intervention for the first few years of life; the evidence from tables 5-1 and 5-2 suggests that Early Head Start costs around one-quarter of what Abecedarian costs per child but yields a short-term impact on children's test scores (measured at age three years) that is only about one-tenth as large.

Finally, we note that Early Head Start and Head Start providers would be eligible for funding under Success by Ten and, in fact, would be eligible for much more federal funding than they currently receive. In that sense,

Success by Ten can be thought of as a major expansion and intensification of Head Start.

Should States Be Given More Responsibility and Control?

Education is primarily a state responsibility in the United States, with the federal government providing no more than 7 percent of the total funding for elementary and secondary schooling. Moreover, states are especially active right now in their attempts to add a pre-K component to the existing system. However, states have different fiscal capacities, and these, together with the exigencies of local politics, can produce unequal chances for poor children. Moreover, with an increasingly mobile population, a poor child who grows up in Mississippi may end up living as an adult in Illinois, whose residents then bear the costs if that child has not been given a good education earlier in life. For these reasons, we believe that there is a federal role in funding a program such as Success by Ten.

How Should Success by Ten Be Funded?

The challenge of the growing fiscal deficit is great, but many feasible options have already been put forward for tackling the nation's long-term fiscal situation. The principal problem now is one of political choice and will; what is most needed is a bipartisan political process for deciding among the options. We recommend that funding for Success by Ten be part of a broader deficit-reduction package that allows increased public investment in select growth-enhancing programs while reducing the overall deficit through both revenue increases and spending reductions, as proposed in several recent publications (see, for example, Rivlin and Sawhill 2004; Frenzel and others 2007).

Conclusion

Ideally, we would prefer no uncertainty about what our proposal will accomplish. But, of course, this is not how real life works, either for private individuals or for government policymakers. People make decisions in the face of uncertainty all the time: which job to take, how to invest, whom to marry. Government policymakers similarly are forced to make policy decisions before the available science is perfect.

It is also important to note that there is unlikely to be much new information in the foreseeable future that could substantially reduce the uncertainty associated with launching a large-scale intensive early childhood program. Even if a government agency or private foundation launched a randomized evaluation of a large-scale version of an intensive early child-hood model program, we would not know about the scaled-up intervention's effects on people at, say, age forty, for another . . . forty years. At that point there would still be uncertainty about whether a yet larger version of the program would produce the same average treatment effects, which would require another forty years to evaluate.

The real question is whether the uncertainty associated with this policy change is tolerable in light of the alternative of doing nothing. The growing body of research from neuroscience, developmental psychology, and even animal studies about the developmental importance of the early years of life; the existing evidence supporting model programs such as Abecedarian and Perry Preschool; and the fact that a number of these interventions—Head Start, a number of state universal pre-K programs, and Success for All, among others—operate with apparent beneficial impacts on a large scale suggest to us the value of proceeding. We propose moving forward with some built-in features that facilitate evaluation, such as phased-in implementation over a random selection of localities to generate reliable estimates of at least short-term effects. Preserving the status quo has its own consequences. Specifically, a course of inaction runs the risk that our society forgoes the chance to help all our children realize their full potential and to improve the skills (and consequent competitiveness) of America's future workforce. Based on the available evidence, we think that present knowledge strongly favors our proposal of stepped-up investments in early education from birth to age ten.

References

Barnett, W. Steven. 1995. "Long-Term Effects of Early Childhood Programs on Cognitive and School Outcomes." *Future of Children 5*, no. 3: 25–50.

Barnett, W. Steven, Cynthia Lamy, and Kwanghee Jung. 2005. "The Effects of State Prekindergarten Programs on Young Children's School Readiness in Five States." Working Paper. National Institute for Early Education Research, Rutgers University.

Blau, David, and Janet Currie. 2004. "Preschool, Day Care, and After-School Care: Who's Minding the Kids?" Working Paper 10670. Cambridge, Mass.: National Bureau of Economic Research.

Borman, Geoffrey D., and Gina M. Hewes. 2002. "The Long-Term Effects and Cost-Effectiveness of Success for All." *Educational Evaluation and Policy Analysis* 24, no. 4: 243–66.

Borman, Geoffrey D., and others. 2005. "The National Randomized Field Trial of Success for All: Second-Year Outcomes." *American Educational Research Journal* 42, no. 4: 673–96.

Campbell, Frances A., and Craig T. Ramey. 1994. "Effects of Early Intervention on Intellectual and Academic Achievement: A Follow-Up Study of Children from Low-Income Families." *Child Development* 65, no. 2: 684–98.

Campbell, Frances A., and others. 2002. "Early Childhood Education: Young Adult Outcomes from the Abecedarian Project." *Applied Developmental Science* 6, no. 1: 42–57.

Carneiro, Pedro, and James Heckman. 2003. "Human Capital Policy." Discussion Paper 821. Bonn: Institute for the Study of Labor (July).

Congressional Budget Office. 2007. *The Budget and Economic Outlook: Fiscal Years 2008 to 2017.*

Cunha, Flavio, and others. 2005. "Interpreting the Evidence on Life Cycle Skill Formation." Working Paper 11311. Cambridge, Mass.: National Bureau of Economic Research.

Currie, Janet. 2001. "Early Childhood Education Programs." *Journal of Economic Perspectives* 15, no. 2: 213–38.

Currie, Janet, and Matthew Neidell. 2003. "Getting inside the 'Black Box' of Head Start Quality: What Matters and What Doesn't?" Working Paper 10091. Cambridge, Mass.: National Bureau of Economic Research.

Currie, Janet, and Duncan Thomas. 1995. "Does Head Start Make a Difference?" *American Economic Review* 85, no. 3: 341–64.

Dickens, William T., and James R. Flynn. 2001. "Heritability Estimates versus Large Environmental Influences: The IQ Paradox Resolved." *Psychological Review* 108, no. 2: 346–69.

Dickens, William T., Isabel Sawhill, and Jeffrey Tebbs. 2006. "The Effects of Investing in Early Education on Economic Growth." Policy Brief 153. Brookings (April).

Frenzel, William, and others. 2007. "Taming the Deficit." Budget Option Series. Brookings.

Friedman, Dorian. 2004. "What Science Is Telling Us: How Neurobiology and Developmental Psychology Are Changing the Way Policy Makers and Communities Should Think about the Developing Child." National Scientific Council on the Developing Child, Brandeis University.

Fryer, Roland G., and Steven D. Levitt. 2004. "Understanding the Black-White Test Score Gap in the First Two Years of School." *Review of Economics and Statistics* 86, no. 2: 447–64.

Galinsky, Ellen. 2006. "The Economic Benefits of High Quality Early Childhood Programs: What Makes the Difference?" Washington: Committee for Economic Development.

Garces, Eliana, Duncan Thomas, and Janet Currie. 2002. "Longer-Term Effects of Head Start." *American Economic Review* 92, no. 4: 999–1012.

Gillette, Michael L. 1996. *Launching the War on Poverty: An Oral History.* New York: Twayne Publishers.

Gordon, Nora. 2004. "Do Federal Grants Boost School Spending? Evidence from Title I." *Journal of Public Economics* 88, no. 9–10: 1771–92.

Gormley, William T., Jr., and others. 2005. "The Effects of Universal Pre-K on Cognitive Development." *Development Psychology* 41, no. 6: 872–84.

Hamm, Katie. 2006. "More than Meets the Eye: Head Start Programs, Participants, Families, and Staff in 2005." Head Start Series Brief 8. Washington: Center for Law and Social Policy.

Hamm, Katie, and Danielle Ewen. 2006. "From the Beginning: Early Head Start Children, Families, Staff, and Programs in 2004." Policy Brief 7. Washington: Center for Law and Social Policy.

Hart, Katherine, and Rachel Schumacher. 2005. "Making the Case: Improving Head Start Teacher Qualifications Requires Increased Investment." Head Start Series Policy Paper 1. Washington: Center for Law and Social Policy.

Heckman, James, and Dimitriy Masterov. 2006. "The Productivity Argument for Investing in Young Children." Early Childhood Research Collaborative Paper Series. Center for Early Education and Development at the University of Minnesota and Federal Reserve Bank of Minneapolis.

Irish, Kate, Rachel Schumacher, and Joan Lombardi. 2003. "Serving America's Youngest: A Snapshot of Early Head Start Children, Families, Teachers, and Programs in 2002." Head Start Series Policy Brief 3. Washington: Center for Law and Social Policy.

Jacob, Brian, and Jens Ludwig. 2005. "Can the Federal Government Improve Education Research?" In *Brookings Papers on Education: 2005*, edited by Diane Ravitch, pp. 47–88. Brookings.

Kling, Jeffrey R., Jens Ludwig, and Lawrence F. Katz. 2005. "Neighborhood Effects on Crime for Female and Male Youth: Evidence from a Randomized Housing Voucher Experiment." *Quarterly Journal of Economics* 120, no. 1: 87–130.

Knudsen, Eric I., and others. 2006. "Economic, Neurobiological, and Behavioral Perspectives on Building America's Future Workforce." *Proceedings of the National Academy of Sciences* 103, no. 27: 10155–62.

Kosters, Marvin H., and Brent D. Mast. 2003. *Closing the Education Achievement Gap: Is Title I Working?* Washington: American Enterprise Institute.

Krueger, Alan B. 1999. "Experimental Estimates of Education Production Functions." *Quarterly Journal of Economics* 114, no. 2: 497–532.

———. 2003. "Economic Considerations and Class Size." *Economic Journal* 113, no. 485: F34–F63.

Lee, Valerie E., and David T. Burkam. 2002. "Inequality at the Starting Gate: Social Background Differences in Achievement as Children Begin School." Washington: Economic Policy Institute.

Love, John M., and others. 2002. *Making a Difference in the Lives of Infants and Toddlers and Their Families: The Impacts of Early Head Start.* Report prepared for the Administration for Children and Families, U.S. Department of Health and Human Services.

Ludwig, Jens. 2003. "Educational Achievement and Black-White Inequality: The Great Unknown." *Education Next* 3, no. 3: 79–82.

Ludwig, Jens, and Douglas L. Miller. 2007. "Does Head Start Improve Children's Life Chances? Evidence from a Regression-Discontinuity Design." *Quarterly Journal of Economics* 122, no. 1: 159–208.

Ludwig, Jens, and Deborah A. Phillips. 2007. "The Benefits and Costs of Head Start." *Social Policy Report* 21, no. 3: 3–19.

Ludwig, Jens, and Isabel Sawhill. 2007. "Success by Ten: Intervening Early, Often, and Effectively in the Education of Young Children." Hamilton Project Discussion Paper 2007-02. Brookings (February).

Magnuson, Katherine A., and Jane Waldfogel. 2005. "Early Childhood Care and Education: Effects on Ethnic and Racial Gaps in School Readiness." *Future of Children* 15, no. 1: 169–96.

Masse, Leonard N., and W. Steven Barnett. 2002. "A Benefit Cost Analysis of the Abecedarian Early Childhood Intervention." Washington; National Institute for Early Education Research.

———. 2007. "Comparative Benefit-Cost Analysis of the Abecedarian Program and Its Policy Implications." *Economics of Education Review* 26, no. 1: 1–144.

Nelson, Charles A. 2000a. "How Important Are the First Three Years of Life?" *Applied Developmental Science* 3, no. 4: 235–38.

———. 2000b. "Neural Plasticity and Human Development: The Role of Early Experience in Sculpting Memory Systems." *Developmental Science* 3, no. 2: 115–36.

Phillips, Meredith, and others. 1998. "Family Background, Parenting Practices, and the Black-White Test Score Gap." In *The Black-White Test Score Gap,* edited by Christopher Jencks and Meredith Phillips, pp. 103–46. Brookings.

Puma, Michael J., and others. 1997. *Prospects: Final Report on Student Outcomes.* Cambridge, Mass.: Abt Associates.

———. 2005. *Head Start Impact Study: First-Year Findings.* Report prepared for the Administration for Children and Families, U.S. Department of Health and Human Services.

Ramey, Craig T., and Frances Campbell. 1979. "Compensatory Education for Disadvantaged Children." *School Review* 87, no. 2: 171–89.

———. 1984. "Preventive Education for High-Risk Children: Cognitive Consequences of the Carolina Abecedarian Project." *American Journal of Mental Deficiency* 88, no. 5: 515–23.

Reynolds, Arthur J. 1998. "The Chicago Child-Parent Center and Expansion Program: A Study of Extended Early Childhood Intervention." In *Social Programs That Work,* edited by Jonathan Crane, pp. 110–47. New York: Russell Sage.

Reynolds, Arthur J., and others. 2002. "Age 21 Cost-Benefit Analysis of the Title I Chicago Child-Parent Centers." Discussion Paper 1245-02. Madison, Wisc.: Institute for Research on Poverty (February).

Rivlin, Alice, and Isabel Sawhill. 2004. *Restoring Fiscal Sanity: How to Balance the Budget.* Brookings.

Rock, Donald A., and A. Jackson Stenner. 2005. "Assessment Issues in the Testing of Children at School Entry." *Future of Children* 15, no. 1: 15–34.

Rouse, Cecilia, Jeanne Brooks-Gunn, and Sara McLanahan. 2005. "Introducing the Issue." *Future of Children* 15, no. 1: 5–14.

Schweinhart, Lawrence. 2003. "Benefits, Costs, and Explanation of the High/Scope Perry Preschool Program." Paper presented at the meeting of the Society for Research in Child Development. Tampa, Florida, April 26.

Schweinhart, Lawrence J., and others. 2005. *Lifetime Effects: The High/Scope Perry Preschool Study through Age 40.* Ypsilanti, Mich.: High/Scope Press.

Shonkoff, Jack P., and Deborah A. Phillips. 2000. *From Neurons to Neighbor-hoods: The Science of Early Childhood Development.* Washington: National Academies Press.

Tremblay, Richard E., and others. 2004. "Physical Aggression during Early Child-hood: Trajectories and Predictors." *Pediatrics* 114, no. 1: e43–e50.

U.S. Census Bureau. 2006. *Current Population Survey, 2006 Annual Social and Economic (ASEC) Supplement.*

———. 2007. *Statistical Abstract of the United States: 2007.* 126th ed.

U.S. Department of Education. 2005. *10 Facts about K–12 Education Funding.*

U.S. Department of Health and Human Services. Administration for Children and Families. n.d. *Early Head Start Fact Sheet.*

———. Office of Head Start. 2006. "Head Start Program Factsheet: Fiscal Year 2006."

———. Office of Head Start. n.d. *Early Head Start Almanac.*

U.S. House of Representatives. 2001. *Elementary and School Education Act* (No Child Left Behind Act). 107 Cong. 1 sess.

———. Ways and Means Committee. 2004. "Section 9: Child Care." In *2004 Green Book.* Government Printing Office.

Zill, Nicholas, and others. 2003. *Head Start FACES 2000: A Whole-Child Per-spective on Program Performance.* Fourth Progress Report prepared for the Administration for Children and Families, U.S. Department of Health and Human Services.

Summer Opportunity Scholarships

A Proposal to Narrow the Skills Gap

6

ALAN B. KRUEGER AND MOLLY F. MCINTOSH

Even in relatively early grades, a large gap in skills is apparent between students from economically advantaged and disadvantaged households. One way to measure the skills gap is to look at the differences between students who were eligible for free or reduced-price lunch and those who were ineligible for the lunch program in their performance on the National Assessment of Educational Progress (NAEP), a test given to a nationally representative sample of fourth-, eighth-, and twelfth-graders. In the 2003 NAEP, which was given to approximately 343,000 fourth-grade students, those who were eligible for free or reduced-price lunch scored an average of 28 points lower in reading and 22 points lower in math than students not eligible for free or reduced-price lunches (on a test in which a perfect score would be 500 points).[1] To put this in perspective, the score of the average fourth-grade low-income student falls just below the 25th percentile of the distribution of reading and math scores for the remaining students.

The authors would like to thank Peter Orszag, Timothy Taylor, the members of the Hamilton Project, the Hamilton Project Authors' Conference participants, and Michele McLaughlin for their many helpful suggestions and comments.

1. Authors' analysis of the NAEP using the NAEP Data Explorer (www.nces.ed.gov/nationsreportcard/nde/).

Figure 6-1. Gap in Average Reading and Math Fourth-Grade NAEP Scores, Higher Income versus Free or Reduced-Price-Lunch–Eligible Students, 1996–2003

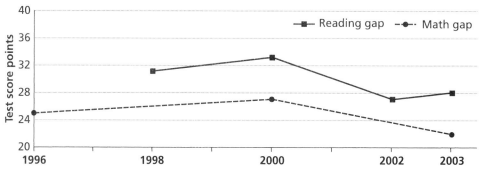

Source: NAEP Data Tool using the 1998, 2000, 2002, and 2003 fourth-grade reading and the 1996, 2000, and 2003 fourth-grade mathematics assessments. See NAEP Data Explorer (www.nces.ed.gov/nationsreportcard/nde/).

Since African Americans are relatively more likely to be found in these low-income households than whites, there is little surprise in discovering that the African American–white gap in test scores is similar to that based on income levels. In 2003 white students in fourth grade scored, on average, 31 points higher than African American students on reading and 27 points higher on math. Similar gaps in skills across African American and white students have been found in a variety of studies using a variety of different tests (Rock and Stenner 2005). Trends in these gaps by free or reduced-price lunch eligibility or race over time, using data available from NAEP, are displayed in figures 6-1 and 6-2. As is evident from the figures, some progress has been made in closing these gaps, but they remain sizable.

Much of the discussion of the skills gap has implicitly assumed that this gap reflects circumstances and events—whether at school, at home, or in the community—that occur during the standard school year from September to June. However, a body of evidence suggests that a substantial share of the skills gap emerges during summer vacation. For many American children, the traditional three-month summer vacation is a time when their skills atrophy by as much as a third of a school year of learning (Cooper and others 1996). Moreover, during the summer vacation, students are more likely to be victims of violent crimes and to engage in risky behaviors than they are during the school year (Snyder and Sickmund 1999). Summer learning loss is well known by teachers, who routinely anticipate dedicat-

Figure 6-2. Gap in Average Reading and Math Fourth-Grade NAEP Scores, White versus African American Students, 1990–2003

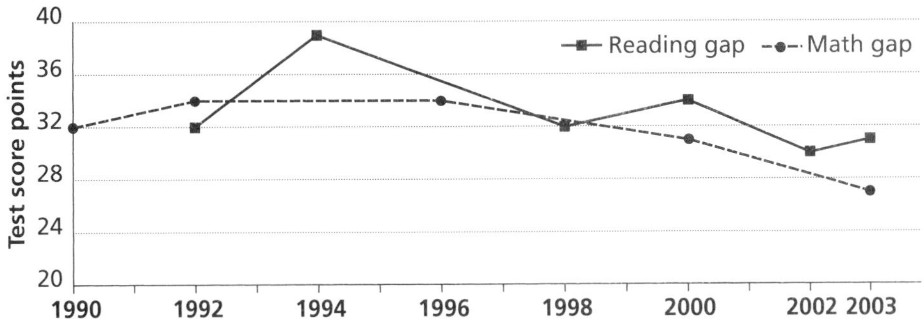

Source: NAEP Data Tool using the 1992, 1994, 1998, 2000, 2002, and 2003 fourth-grade reading and 1990, 1992, 1996, 2000, and 2003 fourth-grade mathematics assessments. See NAEP Data Explorer (www.nces.ed.gov/nationsreportcard/nde/).

ing one or two months at the start of each school year to reviewing forgotten material (Fairchild and Boulay 2002).

Several studies confirm the existence of summer learning loss and find that it is not evenly distributed among advantaged and disadvantaged students. In a groundbreaking study, Barbara Heyns (1978) compared reading and math school year and summer achievement gains among 1,128 sixth- and seventh-graders in Atlanta, Georgia. While achievement gains over the school year were moderately associated with family income, gains over the summer were very strongly associated with family income. High-income white students gained 0.29 grade equivalents in their test scores over the summer, while middle-income white students gained 0.18 grade equivalents and low-income white students gained just 0.07 grade equivalents. The situation was even more lopsided for African American students: while high-income African American students made achievement gains of 0.22 grade equivalents over the summer, on average, middle-income African American students suffered losses of 0.12 grade equivalents, and low-income African American students suffered losses of 0.28 grade equivalents. Heyns (1978, p. 187) summarized the evidence as follows: "The gap between black and white children, and between low- and high-income children, widens disproportionately during the months when schools are not in session. Schooling apparently attenuates the influence of socioeconomic status on achievement and thereby reduces the direct dependence of outcomes on family background."

Numerous other studies have documented the disparate effects of summer vacation on disadvantaged students. Cooper and others (1996) conducted a meta-analysis that pulled together data from thirteen previous studies that examined the effects of summer vacation on achievement, including Heyns (1978). A proper meta-analysis can draw on a greater body of data than any single study and can also adjust for different methodologies that may have been used in the literature. Taking all the studies as a group, Cooper and colleagues found that, among students as a whole, fall test scores were slightly lower than they were in the previous spring, consistent with a modest overall summer loss. All students suffered summer learning losses in math, regardless of family income. However, the reading skills of middle-income students actually improved over the summer while those of low-income students deteriorated, so that a three-month reading achievement gap emerged during the summer.

A similar result emerged from a recent analysis by Alexander, Entwisle, and Olson (2004) of Baltimore's Beginning School Study. The researchers used three factors—family income relative to family size, parents' education levels, and parents' occupations—to classify students according to socioeconomic status. They found compelling evidence that the negative effects of summer vacation are attenuated or reversed for students with higher socioeconomic status. This pattern is depicted in figures 6-3a and 6-3b, which display school year and summer reading comprehension and mathematics gains over time for a random sample of 665 first graders from twenty Baltimore public schools who entered school in the fall of 1982. These figures suggest three conclusions. First, if one accepts the scaling of the exams, achievement gains are generally greater in the earlier elementary grades for both reading and math, suggesting the existence of a peak learning period in a child's education. Second, student performance during the school year is not significantly influenced by socioeconomic status. Figure 6-3a shows that the school year gains in reading and math among students of low and high socioeconomic status are virtually indistinguishable. Third, student performance during the summer is strongly correlated with socioeconomic status, especially for math. Figure 6-3b shows that while students from high-socioeconomic-status families make gains during the summer months, students from low-socioeconomic-status families, on average, experience relatively large losses, especially in the early grades. Indeed, Alexander, Entwisle, and Olson conclude that the widening skills gap is due almost exclusively to differential rates of summer learning, since all students experience parallel gains during the school year, but students of higher socioeconomic status

Figure 6-3a. School Year Gains by Socioeconomic Status, California Achievement Test, Beginning School Study, Fall 1982–Spring 1987[a]

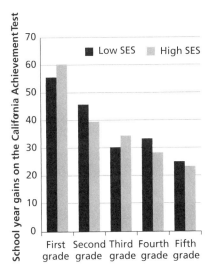
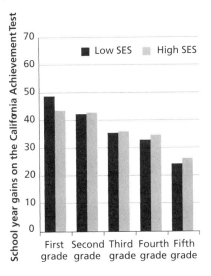

Figure 6-3b. Summer Gains by Socioeconomic Status, California Achievement Test, Beginning School Study, Spring 1983–Fall 1986[a]

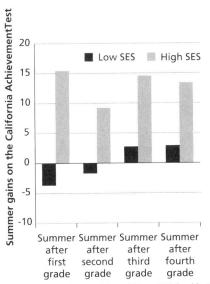
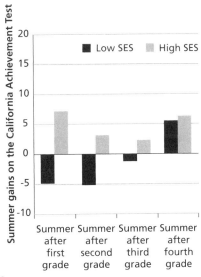

Source: Alexander, Entwisle, and Olson (2004), table 2.3, p. 33.
a. The sample consists of 665 Baltimore public school students who entered first grade in 1982. SES = socio-economic status.

pull ahead during the summer while students of lower socioeconomic status fall behind.[2]

In an earlier study, Entwisle, Alexander, and Olson (1997) attributed this pattern of summer learning loss to "faucet theory," since when school is in session, the faucet of learning is turned on and achievement rises for all children. During the summer, however, the faucet is turned off for children of lower socioeconomic status, while the faucet is left on for children with higher socioeconomic status since they often continue to participate in some form of educational activity, either at home or in an organized program away from home. Common elements of socioeconomic status, such as poverty status, parental education, and family structure, all influence a child's home learning environment (Schacter 2001). Children from poor families are read to less often, own fewer books, and watch more television. The more education a mother has, the more likely she is to read to and introduce literacy techniques to her child. Never-married mothers are least likely to monitor a child's schoolwork or to supervise a child at home. By many measures of "disadvantaged," the home environments of disadvantaged students are considerably less conducive to continuous academic achievement from the school year through the summer. Krueger called this phenomenon the "Harry Potter divide," as low-income children are much less likely to read the Harry Potter books, or any other book for that matter, over the summer than are high-income children.[3] (Indeed, the lower rate of reading Harry Potter is borne out by Gallup poll data.)[4]

But despite the phenomenon of summer learning loss, surprisingly few children are attending summer school. Using data from the October Current Population Survey, the National Center for Education Statistics estimated that among children enrolled in grades one through seven,

---

2. One recent study by Fryer and Levitt (2004) contradicts the evidence presented here on the disparities in summer learning loss by race. Using data from the Early Childhood Longitudinal Study (ECLS), Fryer and Levitt found that the summer setback among African American kindergarten students was not significantly different from that of white kindergarten students and that African Americans' scores decreased, not increased, in both math and reading during the school year. However, it is our opinion that this contradiction does not undermine the motivation for our proposal for two reasons. First, the results using the ECLS data are substantially different from those from all other studies (Rock and Stenner 2005). Second, unlike Fryer and Levitt, our research is focused primarily on disparities in summer learning loss across income levels, not race.

3. Alan B. Krueger, "Vouchers for Summer School Could Help Halt the Learning Slide," *New York Times*, August 17, 2000, p. C2.

4. Jeffrey M. Jones, "Even Adults Familiar with Harry Potter Books," Gallup News Service, July 13, 2000 (www.gallup.com/poll/2740/Even-Adults-Familiar-Harry-Potter-Books.aspx).

7.5 percent, or just under 2 million children, attended summer school in 1996 (Department of Education 1998).[5] Rates of summer school attendance are slightly higher, but still notably low, for children in families with incomes in the bottom quintile of the income distribution, with only 9.4 percent attending summer school. Parents from many of these families recognize the potential problem. A recent study by the Council of Chief State School Officers (2005) reports that 60 percent of low-income parents are concerned that their children will fall behind during the summer, compared with only 32 percent of higher-income parents, where low income is defined as below $25,000 and higher income as above $50,000. In addition, more than two-thirds of low-income students and four-fifths of minority students showed an interest in participating in a summer program that would help them manage their work during the school year or prepare them for the upcoming school year. As argued below, several studies on the effects of summer school, most notably a summary by Cooper and others (2000) of the summer school literature, provide firm evidence that summer school is an effective tool for stanching summer learning loss.

The policy prescription in this situation seems clear: to reduce the negative impact of summer learning loss, expand access to summer school and other academic enrichment programs among those who experience the greatest learning losses. We propose a policy of summer opportunity scholarships (SOS), which will allow students from low-income families to participate in summer school or other summer enrichment programs chosen by the child's parent(s). The program would target economically disadvantaged children: students who are eligible for free school lunches under the National School Lunch Program (NSLP), which requires that a child's family income is below 130 percent of the federal poverty line, will be eligible for SOS. The program we outline will apply to kindergarten through fifth-grade students because programs initiated for younger cohorts may put the children on a higher learning trajectory (Entwisle, Alexander, and Olson 1997).

In the following section, we describe in some detail the design and costs of our proposal for summer opportunity scholarships. The next section compares and contrasts our proposal with some other interventions commonly proposed as remedies for summer learning loss: spreading the exist-

5. Since the survey questions regarding a child's summer activities were included as a one-time supplement to the 1996 October Current Population Survey, we are unable to produce more recent estimates using this data set. In addition, there seems to be no other centralized data source gathering information on summer school participation. Thus, to our knowledge, this 1996 estimate of summer school participation is the best available.

ing number of school days more evenly across the calendar year, a longer school year, and summer school. The final section discusses the possible gains from our proposal.

Designing Summer Opportunity Scholarships

Our proposed summer opportunity scholarships will pay for economically disadvantaged children to attend a six-week summer school program or summer enrichment camp, of their parents' choosing, that offers five days of at least half-day instruction per week. Limiting the program to six weeks of the summer will allow students to enjoy the vacation aspect of summer as well. Eligible providers for the summer programs will include school districts, for-profit companies, nonprofit organizations, summer enrichment camps, and possibly faith-based institutions. Summer enrichment camps are often held at college campuses or community centers; some examples include computer, science, theatrical, and public speaking camps for students in the fourth grade and higher, hosted at college campuses such as Stanford, the University of California–Berkeley, UCLA, or Tufts. There are also camps that offer programs for children as young as four years old, for instance, Education, Sports, and Fun (ESF) Summer Camps.[6]

Eligible Students

A child's grade level and family income will determine eligibility. In studies of summer school, the most successful summer school interventions take place in the early elementary school grades (Cooper and others 2000). For this reason, SOS phase-in will occur in two waves, concentrating on children in the early grades. In the first wave, spanning the first three years of the phase-in, students who have just finished kindergarten through third grade will be eligible. In the second wave, beginning in the fourth year of the phase-in, eligibility will be extended to students finishing the fourth and fifth grades. Students may participate in successive summers, as long as they remain eligible for the program. The decision to cap SOS eligibility at fifth grade was largely influenced by a desire to keep costs down when the program is first being implemented. However, it would be reasonable to extend eligibility to students through the eighth grade or higher once a successful implementation for the younger students has taken place.

6. For more information, see www.educationunlimited.com and www.esfcamps.com/index.htm.

In addition to grade level, eligibility will be determined by a child's family income. We use eligibility for free school lunches from the National School Lunch Program, where students with family incomes below 130 percent of the federal poverty line are eligible, as the cutoff based on economic status. This is our preferred measure of economic status for two reasons: this information is easily obtained and verified with the use of school- or district-level records, and it will allow for comparisons with results from other studies that also use this measure. As an alternative, the program could be made accessible to more students if we based participation on eligibility for free *or* reduced-price lunches from the NSLP. In this instance, students with family incomes below 185 percent of the federal poverty line would be eligible. In our discussion of program participation and the budget below, we describe the expected effect on costs of such an extension of eligibility.

Finally, we propose that a child be eligible for multiple summers, or for every summer between the end of kindergarten and the end of third or fifth grade, depending on the extent to which the program has been phased in. Some studies express a concern that achievement gains associated with summer school might fade over time (Cooper and others 2000; Grossman and Sipe 1992). However, there is also some encouraging evidence that when children from low socioeconomic backgrounds participate in summer school for multiple years, it can have positive long-term effects on the development of their skills (Borman and others 2005). These results will be discussed at greater length later in the chapter.

Participation Estimates

To get a sense of how many students are likely to participate in SOS, we first estimated how many children would be eligible, based on the eligibility criteria for free school lunches through the National School Lunch Program. The results from this exercise are displayed in the first section of table 6-1. We estimated that for the entire United States, approximately 3.7 million kindergartners through third graders in 2006 and an additional 1.9 million fourth and fifth graders in 2009 would meet the income qualification for NSLP. If eligibility were to be extended to students who are eligible for reduced-price, not just free, school lunches from NSLP, these numbers would have risen to approximately 5.4 million kindergartners through third-graders in 2006 and 2.8 million fourth and fifth graders in 2009.

However, as with any government program, we expect that less than 100 percent of those who are eligible will actually take advantage of the

Table 6-1. Five-Year Budget for Summer Opportunity Scholarships[a]

Units as indicated

Components	Calendar year					Five-year total
	2006	2007	2008	2009	2010	
Annual participation						
Number of eligible children per year						
Grades kindergarten (K)–3	3,703,988	3,706,870	3,709,755	3,712,643	3,715,532	. . .
Grades 4–5	. . .	. . .	. . .	1,850,500	1,851,940	. . .
Total	3,703,988	3,706,870	3,709,755	5,563,142	5,567,472	. . .
Take-up rate (percent)						
Grades K–3	25	30	35	40	45	. . .
Grades 4–5	. . .	. . .	35	35	40	. . .
Number of participating children per year						
Grades K–3	925,997	1,112,061	1,298,414	1,485,057	1,671,989	. . .
Grades 4–5	. . .	. . .	. . .	647,675	740,776	. . .
Total	925,997	1,112,061	1,298,414	2,132,732	2,412,765	. . .
Annual per pupil cost						
Mean school year expenditure per pupil in average daily attendance, per year (dollars)	9,421	9,704	9,995	10,295	10,604	. . .

Number of days in the school year	180	180	180	180	180	. . .
Total number of days in a six-week SOS summer program	30	30	30	30	30	. . .
Scaling factor: (number of days in SOS)/ (number of days in school year)	0.17	0.17	0.17	0.17	0.17	. . .
Per pupil cost of SOS, per year (dollars)	1,570	1,617	1,666	1,716	1,767	. . .
Annual total cost (millions of dollars)						
Total annual cost of SOS						
Grades K–3	1,454	1,799	2,163	2,548	2,955	10,919
Grades 4–5	. . .	. . .	. . .	1,111	1,309	2,420
Total	1,454	1,799	2,163	3,659	4,264	13,339
State annual 50 percent match	727	899	1,081	1,830	2,132	6,670
Federal annual 50 percent match	727	899	1,081	1,830	2,132	6,670

Sources: Estimates for annual participation were calculated using the Census Bureau's online "Current Population Survey Table Creator" (www.census.gov/hhes/www/cpstc/cps_table_creator.html) and projected population growth rates from Bureau of the Census, "Table 1: Annual Estimates of the Population by Sex and Five-Year Age Groups for the United States: April 1, 2000, to July 1, 2004" (www.census.gov/popest/national/asrh/NC-EST2004-sa.html). Calculations for annual per pupil cost are based on data from the National Center for Education Statistics (Department of Education 2003).

a. All dollar figures are reported in real 2005 dollars. Projections for annual per pupil cost estimates are calculated assuming a 3 percent annual growth rate. Since the Current Population Survey Table Creator does not include data on grade in school, we placed children ages six through nine in the kindergarten through third-grade (K–3) group and children ages ten and eleven in the fourth- and fifth-grade (4–5) group. While these age groups may not perfectly correspond with the grade levels, there is sufficiently little variation in the number of children per age such that using ages five through eight and nine through ten for the K–3 and 4–5 grade groups, respectively, would not substantially change the results. Also, the Current Population Survey Table Creator allows an income threshold of 125 percent of the federal poverty line, not 130 percent. So these estimates might marginally underestimate the actual number of eligible children.

program. A good benchmark is Head Start, the forty-year-old federal program that provides support for mothers with children younger than school age. For Head Start, approximately 60 percent of eligible children currently participate in the program. However, the Head Start program is relatively well established and well known. Given that it would take time for parents to learn about SOS, we estimate a lower initial take-up rate of 25 percent for the first year of the program and then assume the rate will increase over time. In the first part of the phase-in, when only kindergarten through third-grade students are eligible, we postulate that the take-up rate among eligible families will rise by 5 percentage points annually. During the second part of the phase-in, we predict that the rate of growth in the take-up rate among eligible families with students in kindergarten through third grade will remain unchanged, but the initial take-up rate among fourth- and fifth-grade students will be 35 percent. This is slightly higher than the initial 25 percent take-up rate for the younger group since the program will have already been in operation for three years, and therefore we expect there to be greater program awareness among the older students and their parents.

Based on these assumptions, we projected that in 2006, the first year of the program phase-in, approximately 926,000 children would have participated in SOS. That number rose to 2.4 million by 2010, the fifth year of the phase-in. Again, if the broader eligibility criterion is used, whereby students eligible for free *or* reduced-price lunches can participate, approximately 1.4 million children in 2006 and 3.6 million children in 2010 were projected to participate in SOS.

Eligible Providers

Providers' eligibility will be based largely on their mode of instruction and curricular content. SOS will require that providers use small-group, scientifically based instruction, akin to that required by the No Child Left Behind Act, with a strong emphasis on improving basic reading and math skills, which have been shown to be responsive to such settings (Cooper and others 2003) and which are a particular concern for many disadvantaged children. An effort should be made to align the summer and school year curricula to capitalize on the greatest potential achievement benefits. However, remedial reading and math will not be the exclusive focus of the program, since many researchers argue that one of the beneficial features of summer that affluent students enjoy is the chance to have new educational and cultural experiences that are not feasible during the regular school year (Schacter 2001; Fairchild and Boulay 2002).

There are many potential SOS providers, and much can be learned about which providers are most appropriate from the implementation of an already existing special provision of No Child Left Behind (NCLB): Supplemental Educational Services. This provision funds tutoring services for children attending schools that fail, three years in a row, to meet the academic standards set under NCLB. In particular, when a school is labeled as "failing," the school district is required to set aside funds from its allotment of federal Title I funds to pay for additional tutoring services for that school's students. Parents choose a tutor for their children from a pool of eligible providers, and while school districts can be providers, so can private institutions. Such private institutions may include large for-profit providers, such as Catapult Learning and Kumon; smaller and less well known for-profit providers; and nonprofit community-based providers, including faith-based institutions (Gorman 2004). For SOS all these providers would be eligible to provide services. This list of potential providers also includes summer enrichment camps, on the condition that scientifically based instruction is a component of the camp curricula.

Schacter's review (2001) of a summer literacy day camp is a useful illustration of what the key features of summer enrichment camps are for the purposes of SOS. This camp featured an eight-week literacy program for disadvantaged first-grade students from poorly performing schools where at least 75 percent of the student population received free or reduced-price lunches. The program allotted thirty-two days for instruction and eight days for testing or field trips. On each instructional day, students received two hours of reading instruction from a credentialed elementary school teacher, who was assisted by camp counselors. In addition, each student received at least one hour of tutoring a week with a volunteer tutor. Students were tested at the beginning and the end of the intervention. The remaining hours of the instructional days were spent doing typical summer camp activities, such as arts and crafts, drama, music, and sports. Since the goal of a program like SOS is to strike a balance between the dual objectives of accelerating students' learning in an academic setting and maintaining the freedom to explore less traditional avenues of learning through arts and outdoor activities, this literacy day camp exemplifies what an SOS summer enrichment camp should provide.

It is sometimes claimed that a lesson to be learned from the implementation of NCLB's Supplemental Educational Services is that the school district should not play the dual role of program administrator and service provider. In the case of Supplemental Educational Services, critics argued that school districts were too involved in the administration of the program to be able to act as an independent service provider. In particular, districts often had the most direct contact with parents and therefore developed a monopoly power over the market for the provision of Supplemental Educational Services (Gorman 2004). This reduced the incentive for private providers to enter the market, resulting in fewer providers from which parents could choose. Under SOS, districts would still be eligible to provide services, but the SOS program itself would be administered by an independent, state-level official to avoid such a conflict of interest. Among other responsibilities, this official would be charged with producing and maintaining a list of approved providers, while local superintendents and district-level officials would be responsible for determining if the summer and school year curricula are aligned and if the state education standards are being met.

A final issue to consider when determining provider eligibility is whether providers will be allowed to reject students with disabilities or limited English proficiency. This issue is also currently being faced by NCLB's Supplemental Educational Services. Supplemental Educational Services providers claim that they lack the resources and the expertise to educate these special needs children properly. Given that children from a lower socioeconomic background are more likely than other children, all else being equal, to be identified as special needs students, this issue cannot be overlooked (Entwisle, Alexander, and Olson 1997). We propose that in every local area, there be at least one designated provider, perhaps an institution that specializes in the education of special needs children, that will serve students with disabilities and limited English proficiency. An important consideration is whether such providers should receive a higher payment per student than other SOS providers.

Evaluating Student Progress

Under SOS, student testing will be conducted twice a year, during the last week of the year in the spring and during the first week of the year in the fall. Of course, if any school year instruction takes place between the dates of the spring and fall tests, then the effects of the summer program may be estimated inaccurately (Cooper and others 1996). For this reason, it is crucial that testing take place as close as possible to the end of the school year in the spring and the beginning of the school year in the fall. When school calendars differ substantially across school districts, data on the number of days of summer vacation each student receives should be used to adjust the achievement gains. In addition, a formal evaluation of the program's impact should be conducted. One especially useful approach would be to assign children randomly into SOS scholarships in a certain school district or region, which allows a straightforward comparison of how the program works compared with students who were randomly assigned to a control group.

Regulating SOS Providers

Informal regulation of SOS providers may occur through market forces: parents who are dissatisfied with their children's achievement gains may choose to move their children to a different approved provider for subsequent summers. However, additional funding will not be awarded for children who want to switch providers in midsummer.

Still, a parent may not have access to all the information necessary to choose the best summer school program for a child. To inform parents and to align the providers' incentives with SOS's goals, a list of top-performing providers in each geographic area will be maintained and distributed by a state-level official. In addition, providers reporting achievement effects below a certain threshold, or who deviate from the specified instructional and curricular guidelines, may be disqualified from receiving future SOS funding. However, this disqualification may be temporary, with reentry into the SOS program dependent upon evidence of a fundamental change in instructional practices or curricula. A state-level official will be in charge of ensuring that all participating providers are financially sound institutions, while local superintendents and district-level officials—either or both—will be responsible for determining if the summer and school year curricula are well aligned and if the state education standards are being met.

Budget

To make budgetary calculations for SOS, it is necessary to have an estimate of the average cost of providing approved summer school or summer enrichment services. Because SOS would provide much of the same resources as are provided during the regular school year, we estimated the cost of the scholarship by scaling down average school year per-pupil expenditure by the length of the SOS summer program. As displayed in the middle section of table 6-1, we estimated the mean per pupil annual expenditure for the years 2006 through 2010 using estimates from the National Center for Education Statistics and assuming a 3 percent rise in costs each year. For example, the projected mean per-pupil school-year expenditure in 2006 is $9,421. (The estimates of school-year expenditure used here do not include capital expenditures or interest on school debt.) The regular school year spans 180 days of instruction. The SOS program would meet five days a week for six weeks, for a total of thirty instructional days—or one-sixth of a school year. The amount could be less (for example, if the program met only for half days), but for the sake of erring on the side of overstating costs, we use one-sixth of a school year. Taking one-sixth of the mean per-pupil annual expenditure projections, we obtained an estimated annual per-pupil cost for SOS of approximately $1,600 for 2006, rising to nearly $1,800 by 2010. We believe this is a reasonable prediction of per pupil expenditures for SOS, especially since several major private learning centers we interviewed remarked that they would be willing to act as SOS providers at this estimated cost.

Multiplying the estimated annual per-pupil cost by the number of students who are projected to participate in each year, the total annual cost for SOS, as displayed in the bottom section of table 6-1, will grow from approximately $1.5 billion in 2006 to $2.2 billion in 2008. In addition, the total cost jumps to $3.7 billion in 2009 and $4.3 billion in 2010 with the introduction of fourth and fifth graders into the program. If SOS eligibility is extended to students who qualify for free or reduced-price lunches, these estimated cost figures would increase by approximately one-third.

SOS will be funded by a combination of federal and state funds. States wishing to make SOS available to their students will be required to make a contribution that will be matched by the federal government. Many education-related programs are funded in this way. For example, Head Start is funded by a federal-nonfederal match in which the federal government pays for 80 percent of program costs, and the rest is made up by the state or locality.[7] Also, the National School Lunch Program and Even Start, a program that is designed to improve the academic achievement of low-income children and their parents, are funded by federal-state matches. For NSLP, states are required to make a minimum expenditure of 30 percent of the amount of federal school lunch funds received for the school year starting in 1980 (*Richard B. Russell National School Lunch Act* 1966). For Even Start, the federal government pays 90 percent, and the state pays the remaining 10 percent of operating costs during the first year of operation; over time the federal government's share of the fiscal responsibility decreases, down to 35 percent by the ninth year of operation.[8]

7. See Head Start Information and Publication Center, "A Head Start Dictionary" (www.headstartinfo.org/infocenter/hsdictionary.htm).

8. Even Start program staff, telephone discussion with authors, August 8, 2005.

We recommend that the fiscal responsibility for SOS be split evenly: the federal government and the state will each contribute 50 percent of the total cost of the scholarship. With such a match, the states and the federal government will each face an annual cost of approximately $727 million in 2006, rising to just over $2.1 billion in 2010, as displayed in the bottom section of table 6-1. The estimated five-year cost to the federal government is approximately $6.7 billion. Again, if SOS eligibility is extended to those who qualify for free and reduced-price lunches, these cost figures would increase by approximately one-third.

Why Scholarships?

Some may wonder why scholarships in the form of vouchers are the preferred mode of funding for SOS, instead of direct provision of summer school through a child's existing school. We would argue that vouchers are preferable for four reasons. First, vouchers provide parents with more choice than mandatory summer school when it comes to deciding what their children do during the summer or whether to send their children to summer school at all. Particularly during the summer months, parents will value this flexibility. Second, while the best available evidence suggests that low-income students who have been provided private school vouchers for the 180-day school year have not performed better than a control group of students who were not provided such vouchers, there is no compelling evidence that students who were given vouchers performed worse, either (Rouse 1998; Krueger and Zhu 2004). In our view, there is thus little reason to suspect that mandatory summer school provided by public school districts will outperform the scholarship approach.

Third, experimentation with vouchers to provide education is valuable in its own right, since there is a lack of consensus on their likely effects. Fourth, since vouchers have produced mediocre results, at best, during the regular school year, a proposal to use vouchers in the summer may provide a new and more productive outlet for the voucher movement, but in a manner that shifts the focus away from disrupting the regular school year.

Distributing the Scholarships

The funds can be distributed to one of two parties: the parents or the providing institution. If distributed to the parents, the funds could come in the form of a check or a refundable tax credit. A refundable tax credit may be an unattractive avenue for distribution since low-income parents are often cash constrained and would be unable to pay for their children's participation in a summer program up front. In addition, both these methods of distributing the scholarship directly to the parents share a major drawback: the risk of fraud, in which no educational services are provided but the check is cashed or the tax credit is claimed nonetheless. The payment system in school voucher experiments during the 180-day school year—like the PACE program in Dayton, Ohio; the DC Opportunity Scholarship Program in Washington, D.C.; and the Milwaukee Parental Choice Program in Milwaukee, Wisconsin—offers a model that would reduce the risk of fraud: a check, made out to the parents, would be sent to the providing institution in which the child has been enrolled; the parent must sign the check over to the school, thereby ensuring not only that the funds are not misused but also that the funds pass through the parents' hands and not directly to the provider.

Policy Interventions to Remedy Summer Learning Loss

Three main types of interventions have been suggested to prevent or to minimize summer learning loss: a modified school calendar to shorten the summer break, a longer school year, and summer school. In particular, we view the evidence on the effect of summer school programs as especially relevant to our SOS proposal.

The proposals for a modified school calendar typically call for the redistribution of vacation days such that the total number of days of instruction remains unchanged, but any extended breaks are eliminated. Proponents of this sort of intervention argue that by eliminating "summer," you can eliminate summer learning loss. However, the evidence on the effectiveness of such an intervention is weak, at best. In a comprehensive synthesis of existing literature on modified school calendars, Cooper and others (2003) conclude that the potential effect of shifting from a traditional to a modified school calendar is small. In fact, the estimated effect of a modified school calendar on student achievement is only one-fifth to one-third of the effect of summer school, as measured by Cooper and his colleagues in an earlier paper (2000). The authors do qualify this conclusion with two caveats: a modified school calendar may have a cumulative effect that has not been adequately observed in the data, and it may have a greater effect for lower socioeconomic students.

In another review of school reform proposals, Glass (2002) cites some early findings from the 1982 implementation of a modified school calendar by Chatfield Elementary, a school in Colorado's Mesa County Valley School District. Glass finds that compared with districtwide gains, students in the Chatfield implementation experienced statistically insignificant improvements in reading, math, and language achievement. Glass adds that these early findings have been replicated across the United States in more recent years (Naylor 1995; Zykowski and others 1991; Carriedo and Goren 1989). Thus the available evidence on modified school calendars does not suggest that it should be the centerpiece of a reform package aiming to close the achievement gap.

Proponents of extending the school year argue that the United States lags behind many other countries in terms of the number of days children attend school in a year and that this deficit in instructional time is at least partially responsible for the mediocre ranking of U.S. students in international comparisons of student test scores. We think the jury is out regarding the effectiveness of extending the school year as a tool for improving student achievement. In part, the lack of variation in the length of the school year across school districts in the United States makes this issue very difficult to study.

Regardless of the evidence, however, the institutional and financial obstacles to extending the school year are quite substantial. First, some parents are voicing strong disapproval of such an intervention. Recently, some school districts have begun starting classes in late July or early August to have more instructional time before spring standardized testing takes place, as required by the No Child Left Behind Act. In response, parent-initiated grassroots organizations are springing up across the nation in opposition.[9] Parents argue that an earlier start to the school year disrupts family vacationing, summer camps, and sports activities. It is important to note that the mandatory nature of an extended school year is what creates the parental dissent. SOS, on the other hand, is entirely voluntary, thereby eliciting participation only among those students who have the desire to attend school for more than the typical 180 days a year. While some parents are in direct opposition to lengthening the school year, data we cited earlier from the National Center for Education Statistics (Department of Education 1998) showed that other parents, namely those with low incomes, support increasing the amount of time their children spend in school via summer school. SOS would give parents an opportunity to opt into a lengthened school year via their children's voluntary participation in a summer school program.

9. Michael Janofsky, "As More Schools Open Earlier, Parents Seek to Reclaim Summer," *New York Times*, August 6, 2005. For examples, see Save Our Summers (www.saveour summers.com/index.asp) and Texans for a Traditional School Year (www.traditional schoolyear.org).

Second, teachers often oppose extending the school year, anticipating an increase in their workload and a greater chance of teacher or student burnout. In addition, a longer school year would result in reopening labor negotiations with teachers' unions across the country.

Finally, lengthening the school year is an expensive intervention (Aronson, Zimmerman, and Carlos 1999) since the costs must be paid for all students, not just those eligible for our SOS proposal. If all students were eligible for a full nine-week summer term, then the program would involve eight times as many students and one and half times as much instruction, so the total cost would be twelve times as high as the estimates for the SOS program. In contrast, summer school programs are voluntary for both students and teachers. They can be targeted to a smaller number of students, which holds down costs.

Most important for our purposes, summer school programs have shown some success in combating summer learning loss and improving academic achievement. In a meta-analysis of ninety-three studies on the effects of summer school programs, Cooper and others (2000) conclude that programs focusing on remedial instruction substantially increased participating students' scores. In fact, students from families with lower socioeconomic status attending a remedial summer program increased scores by a magnitude that is about as large as the summer learning loss that others have found typically occurs for low-income students. The authors also found that programs focusing on accelerated learning (as opposed to remedial instruction) had positive effects but remarked that this conclusion is tenuous since it is based on only a handful of studies. In addition, Cooper and his colleagues report that effects from accelerated learning programs were greater for students with middle socioeconomic status compared with students with lower socioeconomic status (although, as described above, the effects were still positive for the latter group). Effects were also greater when small group or individualized instruction was used, when parents were actively involved, and when the intervention took place in early elementary school grades or in secondary school.

Dozens of studies have been done regarding the effects of different summer school programs, and of course, the results are not unanimous. When social scientists and policy analysts are confronted with enough studies to fill a file cabinet, one important way they gain confidence in their conclusions is to examine whether similar answers emerge from studies that use both different data and different analytical approaches. In the case of summer school, studies of the intervention's effectiveness are conducted using three broad analytical approaches: an observational study, an experimental study, and a natural experiment.

The first approach, called an "observational study," looks at the performance of students who have entered a summer school program under the natural circumstances that lead students to go into such programs. An advantage of observational studies is that a large quantity of data is often available from programs about the students who enrolled and how they performed. An inherent difficulty with observational studies of summer school, however, is the possibility that in some way, perhaps obvious or perhaps not, those who entered the summer school program were a group that would be expected to perform better or worse (or improve more quickly or more slowly), on average, than the comparison students who did not go into the program. For example, if participation in a summer school program requires that students and their families sign up, then those who sign up will tend to come from families with the desire and ability to take the initiative to improve their children's learning, a factor that may have more influence on a child's academic achievement than the summer school program itself. Alternatively, if students who score below a certain cutoff are the ones who attend summer school, we might expect their average scores to be lower than those of other, nonparticipating students.

A second methodology for summer school studies is called an "experimental study." Controlled experiments in public policy, of course, are not quite the same as experiments in a science laboratory. The simplest and probably most persuasive design of an experiment in social science is to randomly assign students into two groups: those who are eligible to participate in the program—the "treatment" group—and those who are not—the "control" group. That is, eligible students are assigned based on the equivalent of a coin flip. Setting up a policy experiment in this way can be politically and administratively difficult. But an experimental study has a major advantage over an observational study: namely, the interpretation of the results is much more straightforward. The average characteristics of those in the treatment and control groups should be much the same, since selection into the program is at random. As a result, if randomization is successfully done, studying the effects of the program simply involves comparing outcomes between members of the treatment and control groups. Other than the treatment, there is no reason to suspect outcomes would be different for the two groups, on average.

A third method is sometimes called a "natural experiment." This approach refers to a situation in which events conspire to more or less randomly allocate some students to receive the treatment (summer school in this case) and some not to receive the treatment. Quirky changes in laws or the interaction between program requirements and individuals' characteristics are common circumstances that create natural experiments researchers can exploit. For example, imagine a summer school program that is available only for students born after February 1, 2000. A policy analyst could compare the change in test performance over the summer of those who were born just before the February 1 cutoff with the change for those who were born just after it, on the assumptions that the two groups are otherwise probably highly similar (given that birthdays are almost randomly distributed) and that individuals cannot intentionally manipulate their birthdays to be on one side of the threshold or the other to change their eligibility status.

A recent example of an observational study of summer school comes from John Portz (2004) on the Boston Public Schools Transition Services Program, a reform package that sought to end "social promotion"—the automatic grade-level advancement of students without regard to achievement. This program includes a package of reforms. During the school year, there is additional instructional time, a modified curriculum, and before- or after-school support for targeted students. In addition, students in the second, fifth, and eighth grades who fail to meet a promotion standard are required to attend summer school. If these students still cannot meet the promotion standard at the end of the summer, they face grade retention. In his review, Portz found that among those students who could not pass the promotion standard for math and reading at the beginning of summer, roughly half met the benchmark by the end of the summer. In addition, students who completed the summer program were more likely to be promoted to the next grade, compared with students who were also required to attend summer school but did not complete it. However, since this is an observational study, the validity of these results is threatened by "mean regression"—the phenomenon by which the performance among individuals with initially below-average scores is generally expected to improve over time, while the performance among individuals with initially above-average scores tends to deteriorate.

An experimental program is Teach Baltimore, a remedial summer school program for ten high-poverty urban Baltimore schools. From a pool of applicants, Teach Baltimore randomly assigns kindergarten and first-grade students to treatment and control groups, where the treatment group is eligible to participate in a six-week summer program with a focus on reading and writing instruction, and the control group is ineligible for the program. A series of studies by Geoffrey Borman and colleagues have examined the effects of Teach Baltimore on student achievement and found that a simple comparison of summer reading gains for kindergarten students reveals that treatment students outperformed control students in all three summers during which the program took place (Borman and others 2004).

After taking a variety of other factors into account, Borman, Benson, and Overman (2005) conclude that just being assigned to the Teach Baltimore treatment group had no effect on summer learning loss. However, the number of weeks a student actually attended the program was found to have a positive impact on achievement. Still, the authors acknowledge that this effect could be due to self-selection: students whose parents ensured that their child kept good attendance may differ from other parents in systematic ways that could be related to a child's expected achievement gains, independent of his or her program attendance. Borman and others (2004, 2005) found that treatment assignment was a significant predictor of test score gains when students participated for multiple summers. However, the effect of treatment assignment was close to zero after the first year of participation. Thus Borman and his colleagues conclude that while the single-year effect of summer school may be trivial, there could be substantial cumulative effects that should not be overlooked.[10]

In an example of a natural experiment study, Jacob and Lefgren (2002) consider the implementation of the Chicago Public Schools Summer Bridge school reform. This program requires students in the third, sixth, and eighth grades who fail to meet a promotion standard to attend summer school. Thus the researchers may compare those students just below the promotion standard to those just above the standard—creating a situation that the researchers describe as almost as good as random assignment to summer school. Jacob and Lefgren found that, for third graders, the effect in the first year after the completion of summer school was approximately 20 percent of a year's worth of learning. By the second year, the effect for third graders was an attenuated but still significant 14 percent of a year's worth of learning. For sixth graders, however, the effects of the summer program were essentially zero in the first and second years after the program.

Roderick, Jacob, and Bryk (2004) take a different approach when analyzing the natural experiment created by the implementation of Chicago's

---

10. Results are murkier when student background characteristics are taken into account (Borman, Benson, and Overman 2005).

Summer Bridge program. In particular, they use data from students' testing histories to predict what students' summer learning gains would have been in the absence of the intervention. Then the authors compared the actual scores that students received after the summer program against their projected gains. They found increases in achievement among third graders in the first year after summer school: reading skills increased modestly while math skills increased by as much as six months. This study found that sixth graders' reading and math skills, unlike in the previous study, improved by four months. The authors conclude that Summer Bridge's relatively large test score effects, especially the notably positive results for sixth graders, may be credited to the high-stakes nature of the intervention (whereby students face grade retention should they not pass the promotion standard at the completion of the summer program), the extent to which the summer and school year curricula were aligned, and the small class sizes in the summer program.

We also acknowledge that some evidence on the long-term impacts of summer school programs is less encouraging. Grossman and Sipe (1992) studied the long-run effects of the Summer Training and Education Program (STEP) that was implemented in five U.S. cities (Boston, Massachusetts; Fresno, California; Portland, Oregon; San Diego, California; and Seattle, Washington) in the mid-1980s. STEP participants were teenage students, aged fourteen to fifteen, who faced a high risk of dropping out of high school and becoming teenage parents. In this experimental program, some participants were randomly assigned into a fifteen-month program that coupled remedial summer education and life skills instruction with work opportunities, while others were offered a single-summer job. Studies on the short-term effects found that those in the fifteen-month program outperformed the control group in reading and math achievement (Sipe, Grossman, and Milliner 1988). Achievement scores fell for the control group over the summer but not for the treatment group. Despite this short-term benefit, three to four years after the program was completed, students in both groups were equally as likely to drop out of school, to graduate from high school, to get a GED, to go to college, and to be employed (Grossman and Sipe 1992). These results cast some doubt on the overall effectiveness of summer school programs. However, there are three important caveats to consider with regard to this study. First, the results are likely to have been more promising if the intervention had started earlier in a child's education. Second, if the program had lasted for more than two summers, it might have had lasting effects. Third, the educational treatment in the STEP program involved just ninety hours of reading and math remedial education and eighteen hours of life skills whereas we are proposing a more intensive summer academic program.

Other studies have examined less conventional approaches to curbing summer learning loss. As mentioned above, Schacter (2001) studied the effects of summer literacy day camps, which combine reading instruction and recreation into a single summer program. Schacter found that participating students considerably outperformed their nonparticipating counterparts. However, the validity of this finding is subject to two criticisms: it does not take into account the extent to which more motivated or more talented students might have been disproportionately likely to join the program, and the number of students involved is relatively small. Therefore, the extent to which the results of this study can be extrapolated is unclear.

In another approach, Kim (2005) designed and implemented a randomized controlled experiment to reduce summer reading loss by increasing students' access to books that were matched to their skill level and preferences. From a multiethnic public school including kindergarten through sixth grade, Kim randomly selected 355 students to receive ten books from the Scholastic Guided Reading series, which categorizes books into twenty-six reading levels. In addition, each of the ten books was accompanied by a letter from the teacher and a postcard that helped educate students about skill-level-appropriate strategies to increase reading comprehension and word recognition. Kim found that the greatest reading gains were among third and fifth graders: for third graders, scores increased by 5 points, on average, from a mean initial score of 620; for fifth graders, scores increased by 11 points, on average, from a mean initial score of 658. Statistical tests suggest that the third-grade reading gains were small enough that they might have been produced by chance variation, but the gains for fifth graders are quite unlikely to have been the result of chance variation. Still, the effects of this intervention are likely attenuated due to the fact that, in spite of the randomization, treatment students had significantly lower preintervention reading attitudes than control students, and this difference may have biased the results. In addition, the mode of instruction for the younger grades was arguably less conducive to improving a student's independent reading skills since it did not include one-on-one reading instruction from a teacher or parent. Finally, the sample sizes in each grade level were small, perhaps contributing to difficulty in determining whether the effects are reliably different from chance outcomes. A replication of this study with a larger sample size and improvements in the randomization and the mode of reading instruction for younger students might produce more favorable results.

From this review of the evidence on summer school programs—and particularly the systematic review of the literature by Cooper and coworkers (2000)—we conclude that summer school programs have generally been found to have ameliorative effects when it comes to summer learning loss. Furthermore, the gains associated with summer school seem to be larger and better targeted than those caused by a modified or extended school year. Of course, it would be preferable if the estimates of summer school effects using different data sets and methods were perfectly aligned. Still, taking the evidence as a whole, we believe that improving summer school is a promising approach to eliminating summer learning loss. Indeed, the attentive reader may have noticed that several aspects of our proposal for summer opportunity scholarships are based on the evidence from existing studies. For example, studies suggest that a six-week program is long enough to produce desirable results. In addition, the evidence on the benefits of summer school for younger children is stronger than that for older children. Last, nontraditional programs such as the summer literacy camps, run outside of a conventional school setting, seem capable of producing the desired results.

Conclusion

A considerable academic literature has developed on the topic of summer learning loss, affirming that students' basic reading and math skills suffer during summer vacation. Furthermore, summer vacation deepens the skills divide: children from affluent families maintain their pace while children from disadvantaged families fall further and further behind. Our proposal for summer opportunity scholarships aims to reverse the summer slide among students from lower-socioeconomic-status families and therefore to make strides toward closing the skills gap. We believe that the key stakeholders would support such a program.

Summer opportunity scholarships will provide a chance for lower-socioeconomic-status children to attend the same sort of summer school programs and enrichment camps that are already available to many of their affluent counterparts. As noted earlier, survey results suggest that more than two-thirds of low-income students and four-fifths of minority students are interested in a summer program (Council of Chief State School Officers 2005). The same survey shows that low-income parents are concerned about their children falling behind. For such parents, summer opportunity scholarships offer both better opportunities for their children and a chance to reduce worries over day care and safety, because the SOS program will provide child supervision for a substantial portion of the summer.

Some teachers' unions may hesitate to support this program, fearing that if their school districts opt to provide services to children receiving SOS, additional burdens will be placed on the existing school staff, as was frequently the case with the implementation of NCLB's Supplemental Educational Services (Sunderman, Kim, and Orfield 2005). Furthermore, teachers' unions will object if the federal or state monies used to fund SOS are transferred from other education spending. Teachers' unions might also lobby that the SOS program be required to employ only certified teachers.

But these concerns are not insurmountable. The SOS program need not place additional burdens on existing school staff or require a transfer of funds currently being spent on other education needs. Participation by teachers will be entirely voluntary; so while many teachers may welcome an opportunity to increase their incomes over the summer months, others can choose not to participate. Perhaps more to the point, school districts now bear substantial costs as a result of summer learning loss. Fairchild and Boulay (2002) estimate that two months of lost instruction, at a median annual expenditure of $7,000 per pupil, can cost a school district approximately $1,500 per student annually in remediation. If summer learning loss of this magnitude occurs each year, one child's cumulative summer learning loss could cost the district more than $18,000 in teaching time (not to mention teacher frustration from reviewing material at the beginning of each year). For large urban school districts, the potential for reallocating resources to more gainful uses than dealing with summer learning loss would be quite substantial.

Finally, we conducted informal interviews with several of the major for-profit learning centers that provide private tutoring or who are approved providers, or both, for NCLB's Supplemental Educational Services program. The feedback gathered from these interviews suggests that the learning centers are generally amenable to SOS's curricular and instructional requirements. In addition, many providers expressed a strong interest in being a potential provider for the SOS program and remarked that our estimated cost figures seem reasonable.

For society as a whole, summer opportunity scholarships offer an investment with a potentially high rate of return. An intervention, such as summer opportunity scholarships, that takes place during the summers following the elementary school grades could produce a lasting positive impact on a child's lifetime learning trajectory.

References

Alexander, Karl L., Doris R. Entwisle, and Linda S. Olson. 2004. "Schools, Achievement, and Inequality: A Seasonal Perspective." In *Summer Learning: Research, Policies, and Programs*, edited by Geoffrey D. Borman and Matthew Boulay, pp. 25–51. Mahwah, N.J.: Lawrence Erlbaum Associates.

Aronson, Julie, Joy Zimmerman, and Lisa Carlos. 1999. *Improving Student Achievement by Extending School: Is It Just a Matter of Time?* San Francisco: WestEd.

Borman, Geoffrey D., James Benson, and Laura T. Overman. 2005. "Families, Schools, and Summer Learning." *Elementary School Journal* 106, no. 2: 131–50.

Borman, Geoffrey D., and others. 2004. "Can a Multiyear Summer Program Prevent the Accumulation of Summer Learning Losses? In *Summer Learning: Research, Policies, and Programs*, edited by Geoffrey D. Borman and Matthew Boulay, pp. 233–53. Mahwah, N.J.: Lawrence Erlbaum Associates.

———. 2005. "The Longitudinal Achievement Effects of Multi-Year Summer School: Evidence from the Teach Baltimore Randomized Field Trial." University of Wisconsin–Madison.

Carriedo, Ruben A., and Paul D. Goren. 1989. "Year-Round Education through Multitrack Schools." Policy Brief 10. San Francisco: Far West Laboratory for Education Research and Development.

Cooper, Harris, and others. 1996. "The Effects of Summer Vacation on Achievement Test Scores: A Narrative and Meta-Analytic Review." *Review of Educational Research* 66, no. 3: 227–68.

———. 2000. "Making the Most of Summer School: A Meta-Analysis and Narrative Review." *Monographs of the Society for Research in Child Development* 65, no. 1: 1–127.

———. and others. 2003. "The Effects of Modified School Calendars on Student Achievement and on School and Community Attitudes." *Review of Educational Research* 73, no. 1: 1–52.

Council of Chief State School Officers. 2005. *Summer Learning Opportunities in High-Poverty Schools*. Washington.

Entwisle, Doris R., Karl L. Alexander, and Linda Steffel Olson. 1997. *Children, Schools, and Inequality*. Boulder, Colo.: Westview Press.

Fairchild, Ronald A., and Matthew Boulay. 2002. "What If Summer Learning Loss Were an Education Policy Priority?" Presentation for the 24th Annual Association for Public Policy Analysis and Management Research Conference. Dallas, November 7–9.

Fryer, Roland G., Jr., and Steven D. Levitt. 2004. "Understanding the Black-White Test Score Gap in the First Two Years of School." *Review of Economics and Statistics* 86, no. 2: 447–64.

Glass, Gene V. 2002. "Time for School: Its Duration and Allocation." In *School Reform Proposals: The Research Evidence*, edited by Alex Molnar, pp. 79–93. Greenwich, Conn.: Information Age Publishing.

Gorman, Siobhan. 2004." The Invisible Hand of NCLB." In *Leaving No Child Behind? Options for Kids in Failing Schools*, edited by Frederick M. Hess and Chester E. Finn Jr., pp. 37–62. New York: Palgrave Macmillan.

Grossman, Jean Baldwin, and Cynthia L. Sipe. 1992. *Summer Training and Education Program (STEP): Report on Long-Term Impacts*. Philadelphia: Public/Private Ventures.

Heyns, Barbara. 1978. *Summer Learning and the Effects of Schooling*. New York: Academic Press.

Jacob, Brian A., and Lars Lefgren. 2002. "Remedial Education and Student Achievement: A Regression-Discontinuity Analysis." Working Paper 8918. Cambridge, Mass.: National Bureau of Economic Research.

Kim, James S. 2005. "Does Increased Access to Books and Opportunities to Practice Comprehension Strategies Improve Children's Reading Skills during Summer Vacation? Results from a Randomized Experiment." Paper presented at the Annual Meeting of the American Educational Research Association. Montréal, Quebec, April 11–15.

Krueger, Alan B., and Pei Zhu. 2004. "Another Look at the New York City School Voucher Experiment." *American Behavioral Scientist* 47 (5): 658–98.

Naylor, Charlie. 1995. *Do Year-Round Schools Improve Student Learning? An Annotated Bibliography and Synthesis of the Research*. Vancouver: British Columbia's Teachers' Foundation.

Portz, John. 2004. "Summer School 2000 and 2001: The Boston Public Schools Transition Services Program." In *Summer Learning: Research, Policies, and Programs*, edited by Geoffrey D. Borman and Matthew Boulay, pp. 103–19. Mahwah, N.J.: Lawrence Erlbaum Associates.

Richard B. Russell National School Lunch Act. 1966. *U.S. Code*. Vol. 42, secs. 1751 and following, as amended.

Rock, Donald A., and A. Jackson Stenner. 2005. "Assessment Issues in the Testing of Children at School Entry." *Future of Children* 15, no. 1: 15–34.

Roderick, Melissa, Brian A. Jacob, and Anthony S. Bryk. 2004. "Summer in the City: Achievement Gains in Chicago's Summer Bridge Program." In *Summer Learning: Research, Policies, and Programs*, edited by Geoffrey D. Borman and Matthew Boulay, pp. 73–102. Mahwah, N.J.: Lawrence Erlbaum Associates.

Rouse, Cecilia Elena. 1998. "Schools and Student Achievement: More Evidence from the Milwaukee Parental Choice Program." *Economic Policy Review* 4, no. 1: 61–76.

Schacter, John. 2001. *Reducing Social Inequality in Elementary School Reading Achievement: Establishing Summer Literacy Day Camps for Disadvantaged Children*. Santa Monica, Calif.: Milken Family Foundation.

Sipe, Cynthia L., Jean B. Grossman, and Julita A. Milliner. 1988. *Summer Training and Education Program (STEP), Report on the 1987 Experience*. Philadelphia: Public/Private Ventures.

Snyder, Howard N., and Melissa Sickmund. 1999. *Juvenile Offenders and Victims: 1999 National Report.* U.S. Department of Justice, Office of Juvenile Justice and Delinquency Prevention.

Sunderman, Gail L., James S. Kim, and Gary Orfield. 2005. "Increasing Bureaucracy or Increasing Opportunities? School District Experience with Supplemental Educational Services." In *NCLB Meets School Realities: Lessons from the Field.* Thousand Oaks, Calif.: Corwin Press.

U.S. Department of Education. National Center for Education Statistics. 1998. *The Condition of Education 1998.*

———. 2003. *Projections of Education Statistics to 2013.*

Zykowski, Jane L., Douglas E. Mitchell, David Hough, and Sandra E. Gavin. 1991. *A Review of Year-Round Education Research.* Riverside, Calif.: California Educational Research Cooperative.

Identifying Effective Teachers Using Performance on the Job

7

*ROBERT GORDON, THOMAS J. KANE,
AND DOUGLAS O. STAIGER*

O ver the last two decades, policymakers have fretted over the quality
of elementary and secondary education in the United States. Worried
that the public education system has become a constraint on future productivity growth and a root cause of income inequality, leaders have champi-
oned a succession of reforms—from test-based accountability to smaller
class sizes. But, ultimately, the success of U.S. public education depends
upon the skills of the 3.1 million teachers managing classrooms in elementary and secondary schools around the country. Everything else—educational standards, testing, class size, greater accountability—is background,
intended to support the crucial interactions between teachers and their students. Without the right people standing in front of the classroom, school
reform is a futile exercise.

Traditionally, policymakers have attempted to raise the quality of the
teaching force by raising the hurdles for those seeking to enter the profession. For instance, the federal No Child Left Behind Act requires all
teachers of the core academic subjects to be "highly qualified"—with a

The authors thank Jason Bordoff, Cindy Brown, Michael Cohen, Michael Deich, Kati
Haycock, Richard Kahlenberg, Goodwin Liu, Richard Murnane, Ann O'Leary, Peter Orszag,
Mike Petrilli, Michelle Rhee, Andrew Rotherham, Richard Rothstein, Ross Wiener, and Amy
Wilkins for comments. Timothy Taylor suggested a number of helpful revisions to an earlier
draft. Amanda Major and Jerilyn Libby provided excellent research assistance.

minimum of a bachelor's degree, full state licensure and certification (generally requiring that teachers graduate from a teacher education program), and demonstrated subject area competence (through completing academic coursework or passing a standardized test).

Once teachers are hired, however, school districts typically do very little additional screening. Tenure is awarded as a matter of course after two or three years of teaching. Very few teachers are involuntarily discharged from a school or school district. And the very best teachers receive no financial incentives to go where they are needed most.

The current credential-centered regime is built upon two questionable premises. The first premise is that the paper qualifications required for certification are strongly related to a teacher's effectiveness. The second premise is that school districts learn nothing more about teachers' effectiveness after the initial hire.

A growing body of research, however, suggests that neither of these premises is valid. According to recent evidence, certification of teachers bears little relationship to teacher effectiveness (measured by impacts on student achievement). The differences between the stronger teachers and the weaker teachers only become clear once teachers have been in the classroom for a couple of years.

In response to this evidence, our proposal aims to improve average teacher effectiveness by increasing the inflow of new teachers and requiring minimum demonstrated competency on the job. It also aims to alter the *distribution* of high-performing teachers by encouraging more of the most effective teachers to work in high-poverty schools. Moreover, by removing barriers to entering the teaching profession, our proposal would enable many people interested in pursuing teaching as a second career to become teachers. This is particularly important at a time when our nation faces a looming teacher shortage because a large share of our nation's teachers is nearing retirement.

These policies require consistent and reliable measurement of teacher performance. States and districts will need funding and technical support to build the requisite data infrastructure if these policies are to succeed. This infrastructure will not only make decisions about tenure and pay easier but will also help identify which teachers need help, which teachers are succeeding and should serve as mentors to others, and which teaching approaches are proving most effective.

We make five specific recommendations:

—Reduce the barriers to entry into teaching for those without traditional teacher certification.

—Make it harder to promote the least effective teachers to tenured positions.

—Provide bonuses to highly effective teachers willing to teach in schools with a high proportion of low-income students.

—Evaluate individual teachers by using various measures of teacher performance on the job.

—Provide federal grants to help states that link student performance with the effectiveness of individual teachers over time.

Recent Evidence on Teacher Quality

Recent evidence demonstrates that teacher certification is a poor predictor of teacher effectiveness. Figure 7-1 shows the differences in performance that emerge when similar students—with similar baseline scores and similar demographics—are assigned to different teachers. The figure plots the distribution of teacher impacts on average student math performance in grades three through five in Los Angeles Unified School District (LAUSD), based on the performance of roughly 150,000 students in 9,400 classrooms each year from 2000 through 2003. Three different groups of teachers were evaluated: those who were certified when hired, those who were uncertified when hired but participating in an alternative certification program, and those who were uncertified and not participating in an alternative certification program. Controlling for baseline characteristics of students and comparing classrooms within schools, there is no statistically significant difference in achievement for students assigned to certified and uncertified teachers (Kane and Staiger 2005).[1]

While the differences *between* the three groups are small, the differences *within* the three groups are quite dramatic. Effectiveness varies substantially among both certified teachers and uncertified teachers. The difference between the 75th percentile teacher and the 50th percentile teacher for all three groups of teachers was roughly five times as large as the difference between the average certified teacher and the average uncertified teacher. The difference between the 25th percentile teacher and the 50th percentile teacher is also about five times as large. And those larger differences are

1. In the analysis reported here, we controlled for demographic factors. We later reran our analysis without including such factors and found only modest differences from the results presented here. We conclude that when the policies advocated here are implemented by the state, rather than simply proposed by researchers, controls for demographic factors should not be used (see discussion under "Use of Control Factors").

Figure 7-1. Teacher Impacts on Math Performance by Initial Certification[a]

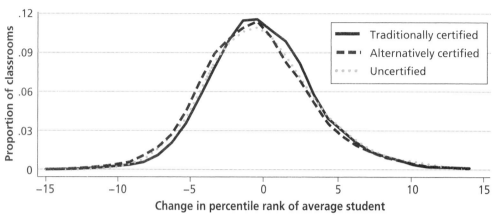

Source: Authors' calculations.

a. Estimated impact of LAUSD elementary teachers, grades three through five, on the mean percentile score of students in a classroom, controlling for baseline scores, student demographics, and program participation. Each student's score is measured on a percentile basis, with each score representing the percentage of students with scores at the student's level or lower in the national norm sample. On the horizontal axis, a value of 5 implies that the *average* student in the class moved ahead 5 percentile points relative to students with similar baseline scores and demographics. A value of –5 implies that the average student fell behind an additional 5 percent of students with similar baseline scores and demographics. The height of the curves represents the proportion of teachers with a given impact. About 90 percent of the teachers' estimated impacts were between –5 and 5 percentile points.

For details of how an ordinary least squares regression was used to adjust for student background, baseline performance, and other factors, see the online technical appendix at www.brookings.edu/~/media/Files/rc/papers/2006/04education_gordon/200604 hamilton_1.pdf.

evident even after one adjusts for the obvious socioeconomic and educational factors that affect student performance. A similar analysis for distributions of reading scores yielded comparable results: certification does not seem to affect classroom performance much, but there is wide variation across teacher effectiveness.

To put it simply, teachers vary considerably in the extent to which they promote student learning, but whether a teacher is certified or not is largely irrelevant to predicting his or her effectiveness. But could school district leaders learn anything useful about a teacher's likely future impacts by measuring that teacher's impact on student test scores in the past? How long would it take to make reliable distinctions between more and less effective teachers? To test how well a district could predict future effectiveness using performance during the first couple of years on the job, we focused on a sample of teachers whom we observed in their first, second, and third year of teaching. We measured their students' performance dur-

Figure 7-2. Teacher Impacts on Math Performance in Third Year by Ranking after First Two Years[a]

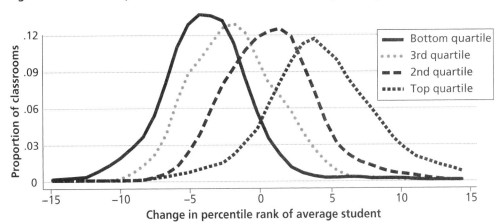

Source: Authors' calculations.

a. LAUSD elementary teachers with less than four years' experience. Classroom-level impacts on average student performance, controlling for baseline scores, student demographics, and program participation.

ing each of those three years, controlling for students' previous test scores and demographics. We then ranked teachers based on their estimated impact on their students during their first two years of teaching, sorting them into quartiles. Figure 7-2 reports the distribution of estimated impacts of teachers during their third year, using four separate curves, with each one representing the quarter of the distribution of effectiveness in which the teacher was categorized during the first two years of teaching.

While certification status was not very helpful in predicting teacher impacts on student performance, teachers' rankings during their first two years of teaching do provide a lot of information about their likely impact during their third year. The average student assigned to a teacher who was in the bottom quartile during his or her first two years lost on average 5 percentile points relative to students with similar baseline scores and demographics. In contrast, the average student assigned to a top-quartile teacher gained 5 percentile points relative to students with similar baseline scores and demographics. Therefore, the average difference between being assigned a top-quartile or a bottom-quartile teacher is 10 percentile points.

Moving up (or down) 10 percentile points in one year is a massive impact. For some perspective, the black-white achievement gap nationally is roughly 34 percentile points. Therefore, if the effects were to accumulate, having a top-quartile teacher rather than a bottom-quartile teacher four years in a row would be enough to close the black-white test score gap. A random assignment evaluation of a classroom size reduction in Tennessee found that schools could improve achievement by half as much—5 percentile points—by shrinking class size in early grades (Krueger 1999). But class size reduction of the magnitude considered in that experiment is expensive: shrinking average class size from twenty-two to sixteen students per class would require a 38 percent increase in the number of teachers and the amount of classroom space in those early grades.

Although the data for our figures come from only one school district, they illustrate three conclusions widely accepted among education researchers and consistent with results from many other places. First, there is wide variation in the effectiveness of teachers, even after one adjusts for student characteristics such as baseline test performance, race-ethnicity, family income, gender, and so on.[2] Second, with only one or two years of student outcome data, a district learns a lot about which teachers are likely to generate large student learning gains and which are not (as shown in figure 7-2).

And, third, these differences in teacher effectiveness are largely unrelated to whether a teacher is certified. The above results—that those with traditional certification do not outperform those without such certification in promoting student achievement—are mirrored in several recent papers (Jepsen and Rivkin 2002; Hanushek and others 2005; Ballou and Podgursky 2000; Raymond, Fletcher, and Luque 2001). But even when researchers have found differences in mean performance between certified and uncertified teachers, those differences are usually quite small. For example, a recent study by Darling-Hammond and others (2005, table 5) found that students assigned to uncertified teachers performed 0.5 percentile points worse on an achievement test than those assigned to traditionally certified teachers, and those assigned to alternatively certified teachers underperformed by 2.5 points.[3] Indeed, even in our own work in New York City, we have found that the average traditionally certified teacher raised reading scores about 1 percentile point more than the average alternatively certified teacher (Kane, Rockoff, and Staiger 2005). But a statistically significant difference is not necessarily an important difference: a 1 percentile point difference between groups is dwarfed by the differences within groups. Moreover, a recent random assignment evaluation found

2. For further evidence, see Rockoff (2004); Rivkin, Hanushek, and Kain (2005); Aaronson, Barrow, and Sander (2003); Kane, Rockoff, and Staiger (2005); and Nye, Konstantopoulos, and Hedges (2004).

3. These are Stanford 9 math and reading normal curve equivalent points.

that Teach for America corps members considerably outperformed tradi-tionally certified teachers (Decker, Mayer, and Glazerman 2004).

The evidence described above sets the stage for the five recommendations in our policy proposal for improving the quality of the teacher workforce. The next five sections of this paper lay out each of these five recommenda-tions in more detail. We then pose and answer a number of questions, including how much this proposal would cost, how practical it is, and other issues.

Recommendation 1: Reduce the Barriers to Entry into Teaching for Those without Traditional Teacher Certification

The central provision of the No Child Left Behind Act related to teacher quality is the requirement that teachers of core academic subjects be highly qualified by the close of the 2005–06 school year. "Highly qualified" means having a bachelor's degree and obtaining (or being on the way to obtaining) full state certification. It then means different things for differ-ent teachers depending on when they were hired and whom they teach. For new elementary school teachers, highly qualified status also requires that they pass a "rigorous" subject matter test; new middle and high school teachers must pass such a test or have an academic major in the relevant subject; and veteran teachers must be in compliance with these standards or with an alternative "high objective uniform state standard of evalua-tion" (HOUSSE) established by the state. Although the Department of Education's data show a sharp increase in the number of teachers deemed highly qualified, it is unclear how much this increase corresponds to any increase in actual teaching effectiveness, as opposed to teachers and admin-istrators becoming more skilled at checking statutory boxes.

We would broaden the definition of a highly qualified teacher. Under our proposal, a new teacher would still be required to have a four-year undergraduate bachelor's degree and to demonstrate content knowledge. There is fairly consistent evidence that teachers' test scores and subject matter expertise are modestly related to their classroom performance (Goldhaber and Anthony 2004; Cavalluzzo 2004; Vandevoort, Amrein-Beardsley, and Berliner 2004). Such evidence is somewhat more robust for teachers of students in later grades. Therefore, we would allow teachers who met these basic requirements to be deemed highly qualified if they also demonstrate effectiveness in the classroom, regardless of whether they had met a state's other certification requirements. Specifically, any new teacher scoring above the 50th percentile on the scale of teacher effectiveness at the end of two years would be deemed highly qualified, regardless of his or her ability to meet existing certification requirements. Moreover, all current experienced teachers who are rated above the median would be deemed highly qualified, regardless of their certification status or compliance with other state systems.

Why a Performance-Based Option Is Preferable for Teachers

Under the regime we propose, novice teachers will have two routes into teaching. One point of entry would be via the current model, in which they follow the existing rules leading to certification. However, another route would be provided to novice teachers who have the undergraduate degree and subject knowledge and are looking for a teaching job.

Schools will, of course, remain free to screen for the qualities they deem most important in the classroom; certification simply will not be an iron-clad requirement. And school systems likely will provide training short of that required for full certification. For example, most principals judge novice teachers who complete Teach for America's intensive six-week summer training program as at least as well trained as other novice teachers.

Once hired, teachers will have a trial period of a couple of years, and then they can receive tenure based on performance. We expect that this additional option will encourage many of those who suspect that they might have the makings of a good teacher, but are unwilling to commit several years to education school, to enter the teaching profession. Given the large variation in teacher effectiveness, we expect that the full range of good, average, and ineffective teachers will enter the teaching profession in this way. But as a group, those who enter the teaching profession in this way will not be noticeably less effective than those who have pursued traditional certification.

For experienced teachers, who nonetheless need to be certified as "high quality" under the No Child Left Behind Act, most states have established HOUSSE standards that are easily met based on assorted past activities; these provide little evidence of genuine subject matter expertise (Walsh and Snyder 2004; Education Trust 2003). At the same time, the HOUSSE standards have become genuinely burdensome to many good teachers who are forced to rummage through transcripts of classes they took years or decades earlier to demonstrate knowledge that they deploy every day.[4]

---

4. National Education Association, "Time Is Almost Up! Do You Meet the No Child Left Behind 'Highly Qualified' Teacher Rules?" (www.nea.org/esea/qualification/teacher/images/hqteacherchart.pdf).

Allowing experienced teachers with above-average results to be deemed highly qualified—whether or not they satisfy the other HOUSSE provisions—would simplify the lives of many high-quality experienced teachers by requiring less paperwork and hassle. In addition, meeting a performance-based tenure standard is a better guarantee of a quality teacher than HOUSSE because it reflects actual success in raising student performance. This could be a win-win arrangement for many teachers and schools.

The Coming Teacher Shortage

Encouraging more recent college graduates and midcareer professionals to enter a teaching career, without requiring them to take (or commit to taking) years of education school classes, should substantially expand the pool of eligible candidates. Recent experience has shown that there is a reserve army of Americans who are interested in teaching. When the Los Angeles Unified School District needed to triple its hiring of elementary teachers following the state's class size reduction initiative in 1997, the district was able to do so without experiencing a reduction in mean teacher effectiveness, even though a disproportionate share of the new recruits were not certified (Kane and Staiger 2005). New York City's Teaching Fellows program, geared to young and midcareer professionals and still requiring alternative certification, had 16,700 applicants for 1,850 spots. Similarly, Teach for America had 17,000 applicants last year for only 2,000 openings.

Expanding the pool of teacher recruits is especially important now because America's schools will soon face a growing teacher shortage. The age of primary and secondary school teachers has increased substantially over the last twenty-five years. The median age of a public school teacher (that is, the threshold at which half the teachers are older and half are younger) rose from thirty-three in 1976 to forty-six in 2001 (Snyder, Tan, and Hoffman 2004). There are two underlying reasons for this demographic bubble. First, there was a persistent decline in the proportion of younger women choosing teaching as a career, which occurred in the late 1960s and early 1970s. As career opportunities for women expanded (Blau and Ferber 1992), the proportion of female college freshmen interested in teaching fell precipitously in the early 1970s. Despite a small rebound in interest since that time, the proportion remains below the high levels of the early 1960s (Higher Education Research Institute 2002). Second, elementary and secondary school enrollment started declining in 1970, and districts were hiring fewer teachers (Murnane and others 1991). Indeed, the decline in job opportunities in teaching may have accelerated the declining interest of college students in teaching.

Figure 7-3. Age Distribution of Elementary and Secondary School Teachers, by Five-Year Age Groups, Selected Years 1979–2004[a]

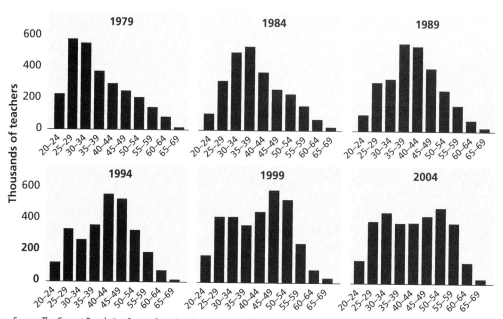

Source: The Current Population Survey Outgoing Rotation Group files, a household-based survey administered monthly by the Bureau of the Census that covers a nationally representative sample of more than 100,000 individuals, including more than 5,000 teachers each year.

a. Teachers are measured in "full-time equivalents," which means that a full-time teacher is counted as 1, a part-time teacher is counted as 0.5.

Thus the college freshmen of the late sixties were the last cohorts to enter teaching in large numbers. That group is now nearing sixty. Therefore, it is not surprising that 40 percent of public school teachers plan to exit the profession within five years (National Center for Education Information 2005). Similar trends have occurred in other professions traditionally dominated by women, such as nursing (Buerhaus, Staiger, and Auerbach 2000; Staiger, Auerbach, and Buerhaus 2000).

Figure 7-3 shows the evolution of the age of teachers in recent decades. We plot the number of teachers by five-year age groups for selected years from 1979 through 2004. Two large cohorts can be seen working through the age distribution, for example, ages 25–29 and 30–34 in 1979, ages 30–34 and 35–39 five years later in 1984, and eventually ages 50–54 and

55–59 in 2004. These are the same cohorts who expressed the highest interest in teaching as college freshmen in the late 1960s. These large cohorts are also now approaching retirement.

Over the next twenty years, the U.S. Census Bureau projects that the school-age population aged five through seventeen will increase by 10 percent.[5] To maintain pupil-teacher ratios at their current levels, the number of teachers must also grow by 10 percent, from their current level of 3.1 million to 3.4 million. Based on the data in figure 7-3, we extrapolated the future supply of teachers by aging the current cohorts and assuming that new cohorts will enter teaching at about the same rate as people have for the last two decades. Under this scenario, the supply of teachers will decline over the next decade and then remain at about 3 million through 2025—nearly half a million teachers below what would be required to maintain current student-teacher ratios.

The bottom line is rather stark. *Simply to maintain pupil-teacher ratios, we must increase the number of people entering teaching by roughly 35 percent—back to levels not seen since the cohorts that came out of high school in the 1960s.* Rather than raise class sizes or dig further down in the pool of those willing to consider teacher certification programs, we need to expand the pool of those eligible to teach. It is time to encourage young people to begin a teaching career without needing to invest in two years of education school first, and to encourage older people to try teaching as a second career.

Recommendation 2: Make It Harder to Promote the Least Effective Teachers to Tenured Positions

Because paper qualifications are not very useful in identifying effective teachers, school districts will inevitably make some mistakes in choosing whom to hire in the first place. But our results above suggest that if states or school districts were to assemble the evidence available to them, by linking student performance and teacher effectiveness data over time, they could learn a lot about which teachers are likely to be effective in the future. States should establish a presumption, but not a requirement, that teachers in the bottom quartile of effectiveness after two years do not qualify for tenure and are not allowed to continue teaching.

5. U.S. Census Bureau, "U.S. Interim Projections by Age, Sex, Race, and Hispanic Origin," March 18, 2004 (www.census.gov/ipc/www/usinterimproj/).

Current Teacher Tenure Laws and Procedures

State statutes typically provide considerable protections to teachers who are already granted tenure (often formally known as permanent, continuing contract, or postprobationary teachers). Tenured teachers may be removed only after an adversarial hearing before a neutral arbiter and often only on specific grounds, which may be exacting (such as requiring proof of incompetence). In most states, nontenured teachers may be removed for any reason except grounds prohibited by generally applicable federal or state laws or by the Constitution—for example, racial discrimination, sex discrimination, or politically motivated discharge. Furthermore, nontenured teachers generally are entitled to no hearing on their discharge. Most states award tenure after three years of teaching; smaller numbers of states require two or four years; a few states do not have tenure at all.

Even though school districts have the opportunity to discharge nontenured teachers, they seldom do so. It is rare for public or private school teachers to report being laid off or transferred involuntarily. Table 7-1 reports tabulations of a survey of public and private school teachers who left teaching or moved between schools after the 1999–2000 school year. Very few public or private school teachers report that being laid off or involuntarily transferred was a "very important" or "extremely important" reason for their decision. Less than 1 percent of all public or private school teachers moved and cited being laid off or transferred as the reason. For those in their first three years of teaching, less than 2 percent report that they moved schools because of a layoff or involuntary transfer.

It may be that teachers are hesitant to admit that they were laid off or involuntarily transferred, or principals may find ways to persuade ineffective teachers to move "voluntarily." However, even if the proportion being laid off or transferred involuntarily is understated by a factor of five, less than 10 percent of new teachers are terminated involuntarily. Given the evidence on the wide variability in teacher performance, it seems clear that schools regularly award tenure to teachers who are quite ineffective in the classroom compared with other teachers who have similarly situated students.

Impact on Student Achievement of a More Selective Teacher Tenure Policy

Schools could substantially increase student achievement by denying tenure to the least effective teachers. Suppose that teachers were ranked at the end of their first two years of classroom performance according to test score gains among their students. What might a school system expect to gain if the

Table 7-1. Teachers Leaving the Profession or Moving between Schools in the Following Year, 1999–2000[a]

Percent

Teaching venue and experience	Moved schools or left teaching	Moved to a new school	Cited layoff or involuntary transfer	Left teaching	Cited layoff or involuntary transfer
Public schools					
Total	15.1	7.7	0.8	7.4	0.2
By years of experience					
1–3	22.7	13.8	1.9	8.9	0.8
4–9	17.7	10.8	0.9	6.9	0.1
10–19	12.8	6.7	0.6	6.1	0.1
20+	11.5	3.5	0.4	8.0	0.1
Private schools					
Total	20.9	8.4	1.0	12.5	1.4
By years of experience					
1–3	34.1	10.8	0.7	23.3	1.5
4–9	24.6	11.6	1.9	13.0	0.3
10–19	12.5	5.9	0.4	6.6	0.7
20+	13.6	5.4	0.8	8.2	0.9

Sources: Estimates in columns 1 through 4 are drawn from Luekens, Lyter, and Fox (2004, tables 6 and 7). Values listed in column 5 are from unpublished estimates from the Schools and Staffing Survey provided by Deanna Lyter.

a. Movers are teachers who were still teaching in 2000–01 but had moved to a different school. Leavers are teachers who left the teaching profession between 1999–2000 and 2000–01. Respondents were asked to rate the importance of various reasons in their decision to move or to leave teaching. Columns 3 and 5 include those who stated that a layoff or involuntary transfer was "very important" or "extremely important" in their decision.

bottom quarter of teachers were not renewed for the following year? The outcome would depend on two effects. First, establishing a minimum threshold of effectiveness will raise the average quality of the remaining retained teachers. But second, each teacher not given tenure would be replaced with a novice teacher, who would have less experience. Depending upon the magnitude of learning teachers do on the job, this latter effect could be quite costly. How is the net balance of these two effects likely to work out?

Considering the risks of false positives and negatives, the potential effects on recruitment of teachers, and the overriding goal of increasing student achievement, we focused on quartiles of teachers. Based on the Los Angeles data, a policy that dropped the bottom quartile of teachers after their first year of teaching would increase the average impact of retained teachers by about 1.5 percentile points.[6] This policy would also require an

---

6. The gain would be $(3.16 + 5.46 + 10.08)/3 - (0 + 3.16 + 5.46 + 10.08)/4 = 1.49$ percentile points.

increase in the hiring of novice teachers in order to maintain class size. The evidence suggests that the average "value-added" of novices is about 4 percentile points lower than for teachers with two years of experience. For example, Los Angeles would have to increase its number of novice teachers from the current level of 9 percent of teachers to 12 percent of teachers, since one quarter (3 percent) of these would not be retained under the new policy. We could expect a 1.5-percentile-point increase in higher student performance among 88 percent of teachers who were not novices. This would be offset by a 4-percentile-point decline among the 3 percent of additional novice teachers, for a net increase in student test score gains of around 1.2 percentile points a year.[7]

The cumulative impact of such a policy could be substantial. If the effects of a good teacher in early grades were to persist through high school (a hypothesis that has not been tested in education research), an annual increase in test scores of 1.2 percentile points at each grade over the course of twelve years in a school system would raise student test scores by roughly 14 percentile points by the time students graduated.

The economic value of such an increase could be enormous. To estimate the dollar value of an increase in academic achievement, we needed some means of converting test scores into dollars. To do so, we used alternative estimates of the relationship between test scores and earnings among young adults (see Murnane, Willett, and Levy 1995; Neal and Johnson 1996). Using these estimates, we calculated the value of a test score increase over a student's career.[8] The increase in career earnings from a 14-percentile-point increase in achievement test scores would be worth about $72,000 to $169,000 per high school graduate.[9] When multiplied by 3 million public high school graduates a year, such an increase would be worth $216 billion to $507 billion a year, if the policy were applied nationwide.

These rough estimates may overstate the gains somewhat. For instance, the estimates assume that the impact of having a particularly effective teacher in an early grade persists over a student's career. It is not uncommon for learning gains produced in one year to fade somewhat over time. We may be too optimistic about the quality of the novice teachers that would be attracted, particularly at a time when larger numbers of novices

7. The gain would be 0.88 * 1.49 − 0.03 * 4 = 1.2 percentile points.
8. For details on the net present value calculation, see Kane and Staiger (2002).
9. In Kane and Staiger (2002), we estimate that a 1 standard deviation increase in test scores is associated with a $110,000 to $256,000 increase in the present value of lifetime earnings for an eighteen-year-old. A 14-percentile-point increase would represent 0.66 standard deviations in normal curve equivalents.

would need to be hired. The greater uncertainty about tenure prospects for new teachers might also make it harder to recruit teachers. Finally, there are difficulties with implementing the system among younger and older students (because of the lack of availability of baseline test scores or standardized tests that all students take).

Nevertheless, even if only a quarter of the gains suggested above were realized, such an improvement in student performance would represent substantial economic value.

Changing the Default for Ineffective Teachers

After a phase-in period, states receiving federal teacher quality funding would no longer be able to grant tenure so easily to teachers performing in the bottom quartile during their first two years. Generally, these teachers should not be able to continue teaching in the jurisdiction, but we would not want to require districts to fire these teachers; there may be circumstances in which teachers should be retained or granted tenure notwithstanding being ranked in the bottom quarter. For example, a principal may be able to identify certain cases where teachers were inaccurately identified as ineffective or where there were factors beyond the teacher's control affecting classroom performance.

When a principal wishes to allow a low-performing teacher to continue teaching, we would require the principal to meet two requirements: receive a waiver from local district authorities and provide public notice of the waiver, through both letters to parents and some other form of public notification (perhaps on a school website, for example). Such a rule would create costs to keeping lower-achieving teachers in the classroom or granting them tenure but would permit overrides when principals can make a case for them.

Within such a regime, teachers should receive the support needed to maximize their chances for success. New teachers should have access to mentoring and support during their first year of teaching. Such support is particularly important for those without traditional certification, who often will not have had prior experience in the classroom (Johnson, Birkeland, and Peske 2005). Schools should give teachers notice of how they are performing as frequently as possible—at the latest, after their first year in the classroom. Indeed, just as the presence of high-stakes testing for students may encourage schools to target necessary resources to students in danger of failing, we hope that raising the stakes for new teachers will increase the pressure on districts to ensure that new teachers receive the support they need. Teachers should have a reasonable opportunity to improve before the tenure decision at the end of the second year.

Although denying tenure to many low-achieving teachers would mark a sharp break from what actually happens in schools today, it is consistent with the views of many of the key players in education. In a Public Agenda survey, 78 percent of teachers recognized that at least some of their colleagues in the same school "fail to do a good job" (2003). Principals report that they believe many teachers remaining in the classroom do not belong there (Bradley 1999).[10] According to one new study, principals regularly deal with low achievers by "passing them around from school to school" rather than terminating them (Levin, Mulhern, and Schunck 2005). The problem may be, in the words of Michael Ward, North Carolina's superintendent of public instruction, the limited "willingness of school leaders to confront unpleasant tasks associated with dealing with performance problems" (Bradley 1999). Our proposal would shift the default for bottom-quartile teachers: rather than make it costly to terminate ineffective teachers, we would make it costly to keep them.

Maintaining Commitments to Teachers Who Already Have Tenure

We do not intend that the policy suggested here be applied to already tenured teachers. These teachers have legal rights and legitimate expectations under both state statutes and local collective bargaining agreements. Moreover, given the coming wave of teacher retirements, the new teachers hired will quickly become the majority of the teaching force anyway.

Recommendation 3: Provide Bonuses to Highly Effective Teachers Willing to Teach in Schools with a High Proportion of Low-Income Students

If current tenure practices screen out too few of the weakest teachers, current pay practices encourage too few of the strongest teachers to work in the schools where they are needed most. Teacher pay scales typically increase salaries based on only two criteria—years of experience and educational qualifications—neither of which is strongly related to teacher effectiveness beyond the first few years of teaching.

Today, only a few school districts offer rewards for high-performing teachers, and these are often modest. Denver is one of the few to do so, yet even there the performance bonus amounts to only 5 percent of base pay (Jupp 2005). According to recent surveys, only eight states provide bonuses

---

10. Robert Gordon, "Class Struggle," *New Republic*, June 6, 2005.

of at least $5,000 for teachers with certification from the National Board for Professional Teaching Standards, which has been shown to be correlated with improved performance (Goldhaber and Anthony 2004; Cavalluzzo 2004; Vandevoort, Amrein-Beardsley, and Berliner 2004). At present, a distinct minority of districts offer differential pay to teachers in schools with a high proportion of low-income students, and among those that do so, many fail to screen for teacher quality (Rotherham 2005).

Salary increases for high-performing teachers are particularly critical in schools where a large share of the children comes from low-income families. These schools tend to have the weakest teachers. They have the fewest teachers with relevant subject matter expertise (Education Trust 2003). They also have the fewest teachers certified by the National Board for Professional Teaching Standards (Humphrey, Koppich, and Hough 2005). Using our own data, we find that in Los Angeles, students in the poorest schools (where more than 90 percent of the students qualify for free or reduced-price school lunch) were more than 2.5 times as likely to have teachers in the bottom quarter of all teachers than were students in the wealthiest schools (where fewer than 10 percent of students qualified for free or reduced-price lunch).

The inequitable distribution of effective teachers within school districts has many causes. Uniform salary schedules, under which teachers with the same experience and educational attainment are paid the same regardless of their skills or where they work, are an important contributing factor. Uniform pay may sound fair, but it leads to an inequitable distribution of teachers. For many teachers, high-achieving students with parents who are supportive of education are simply easier to teach. Schools with those students often also have better facilities and safer environments. If teacher salaries are based solely on educational attainment and experience of the teacher, and any teacher would earn the same salary whether he or she taught in a high- or low-achieving school, there is no way for low-achieving, low-income schools to compensate teachers for the additional challenges of working there. Understandably, once teachers accumulate sufficient seniority, they frequently exercise contractual rights and transfer into wealthier schools (Lankford, Loeb, and Wyckoff 2002; Levin and Quinn 2003; Prince 2002).

School finance rules facilitate the inequitable distribution of teachers. Because dollars typically follow teachers within districts, more experienced and better-paid teachers who transfer into schools with less taxing teaching environments effectively bring their higher salaries with them. Schools with students from low-income families not only are left with less costly, less experienced teachers but also receive no additional funding to raise salaries, hire additional staff, or provide additional services (Roza and Hill 2004).

Salary increases targeted to high-performing teachers in poor schools could help counter all these effects. They could also attract more high-performing individuals to become teachers rather than go into other professions. There is some evidence that the inverse of that effect has already occurred. Hoxby and Leigh (2005) find that as the teacher pay scale became compressed and the premium available to women teachers educated at elite schools declined, the number of elite-educated women going into teaching also dropped. This finding is consistent with a broader literature concluding that the aptitude of individuals entering public sector fields like teaching has declined as compensation in those fields relative to other professions has dropped (Bok 1993; Miller 2003).

To encourage better teaching and to attract more high-quality teachers, we recommend bonus pay for teachers who are ranked in the top quarter by effectiveness and who teach in schools where at least 75 percent of the students come from families with incomes low enough to be eligible for free or reduced-price school lunches. Some states now offer bonuses to teachers willing to work in high-poverty schools, but we do not see the point in offering bonuses to *any* teacher willing to do so—there will be a lot of low-performing as well as high-performing teachers willing to take that offer. Our proposal would provide large bonuses only to teachers with a proven track record who are willing to teach in high-poverty schools.

How Large Should Bonuses Be and How Should They Be Distributed?

There is no settled answer to the question of how large incentives must be to attract and retain high-quality teachers in low-performing schools. Kate Walsh (2005) of the National Center for Teacher Quality suggests that bonuses would need to be 10 to 20 percent of base pay. Others have suggested that even 15 percent is inadequate (Miller 2003), that bonuses would need to be at least $20,000 to have an impact (Rothstein 2004), or that bonuses would need to range between 20 and 50 percent of base salary to attract teachers to the highest-poverty schools (Hanushek, Kain, and Rivkin 2001).

We propose that top-quartile teachers willing to teach in high-poverty schools be provided at least $15,000 in bonus money above and beyond their current salaries. In a profession where salaries currently start at about $30,000 and average about $45,000, this is a substantial increase. As noted above, we would define a high-poverty school as one where more than 75 percent of the students qualify for the federal free or reduced-price lunch program. Such schools represent about 21 percent of public school enrollment.

Alternative approaches to raising pay are possible. One could offer bonuses of differing amounts, graduated according to the poverty rate in the school, with some bonuses for teachers at all schools. Still another approach, with more flexibility, would be to send money for salary bonuses to the district and school, based on the percentage of students in poverty, and then require those districts and schools to allocate the bonuses to the highest-achieving teachers. Some bonuses might also be provided to all teachers at high-need schools that show large improvements. Our proposal would provide bonuses only after the second year, when teachers have already typically achieved their largest improvement. To address regional variation, the $15,000 might be reformulated as a percentage of base pay for starting teachers.

Teachers who wish to be eligible for additional compensation would need to be reassessed periodically. As a matter of fairness, we would give new teachers two years to get their feet under them, provide notice of their performance after the first year, and make decisions after their second year. We also would require reassessments every five years. Such reassessments would recognize when teachers burn out or when they sharply improve over time. But the reassessments would not be so frequent that they would become a constant presence in a teacher's life.

We do not suggest that increasing pay alone is a complete strategy for attracting more high-quality teachers into poor districts. The quality of school facilities, school supports, and school safety all play important roles in teachers' choices of where to go. Our proposal is not a cure-all for the maldistribution of teachers, but it will help significantly.

Recommendation 4: Evaluate Individual Teachers by Using Various Measures of Teacher Performance on the Job

Each of the first three steps relies on a working definition of classroom effectiveness. States and districts will need to implement a practical definition of classroom effectiveness. In establishing such systems, several challenges arise:

—balancing objective and subjective factors;

—using appropriate control factors;

—applying the system to teachers in grade levels and subjects where there is currently no testing;

—measuring performance relative to other teachers or relative to an absolute standard;

—addressing concerns about fairness;

—addressing the role of principals; and

—choosing the appropriate level at which the measures should operate—state, district, or school.

We consider each of these issues in turn.

Objective and Subjective Factors

Impacts on measured student achievement should be a substantial factor in teacher evaluations. Such changes are the most tangible evidence of a teacher's accomplishment. Simply providing such estimates to principals may prove particularly valuable in teacher promotion decisions. A measure of students' growth in performance, benchmarked against the performance of similar classrooms of students elsewhere, may be the first piece of "objective" evidence principals have been given to make difficult decisions regarding tenure.

However, no single measure of performance is a perfect measure of what students should be learning, and statistical evidence from student scores should not be the only measure by which teachers are evaluated (Walsh 2005; Feldman 2004). There is growing evidence that the tests and assessments now in use are not adequately aligned with state standards and not sufficiently sophisticated to measure high-level student skills.[11] And as states have implemented systems to increase accountability for student test scores, researchers have documented troubling evidence of teachers and principals cheating (Jacob and Levitt 2003), the narrowing of curriculum to tested subjects such as reading and math (Koretz 2002), and instruction increasingly geared to particular tests. If the stakes are too high on student test performance, the looming presence of such tests can distort the classroom learning experience.

A wide range of other methods for evaluating teachers are possible. Principals, teachers, and other educators can evaluate teacher performance based on both classroom observation and reviews of student work. The use of multiple evaluators from inside and outside of a particular school can reduce the risk that any individual evaluator lets personal biases color his or her judgment. Parent evaluations can also be taken into account. The National Board for Professional Teaching Standards has its own multifaceted method for certifying effective teachers, including videotapes of

11. Thomas Toch, "Measure for Measure," *Washington Monthly*, October–November.

classroom instruction, examples of student assignments, and teacher feedback to students.

Sound objective and subjective measures of teacher quality are likely to converge, at least for those teachers at the top and bottom of the distribution of teacher quality. For example, Jacob and Lefgren (2005) recently asked principals to subjectively rate teachers' ability to raise the math and reading achievement of their students. Nearly 70 percent of those who received top ratings from their principals in their ability to raise math achievement were in the top of the distribution of value-added on test scores. In reading, more than 50 percent of those who were in the top of the subjective ratings were in the top of the value-added metric using test scores. In general, although there was more disagreement in the middle of the distribution, principals' subjective impressions lined up with the quantitative evidence for the most and least effective teachers. Murnane (1975) and Armor and others (1976) also found that subjective ratings by principals were correlated with value-added measures.

We propose that states be offered funding to establish systems for evaluating teacher performance. As there is no consensus on the single best way to evaluate teachers, states should be allowed to develop different methods of evaluation that weight different items in different ways. We would impose only three substantive constraints. First, states would not be permitted to use measures such as licensure status, degrees awarded, or courses or tests taken. Second, a substantial portion of the evaluation—perhaps one-third to two-thirds of a total score, but not the entirety—should be tied to student test scores in one form or another. Third, states would be required to ensure that data collected over a period of time, not just a single school year or a few months within a year, represent a substantial aspect of the evaluation.

Many school districts already provide evaluations of individual teachers. Unfortunately, in many districts, virtually every teacher gets a satisfactory evaluation because principals have little incentive to make distinctions among teachers. Under our proposal, if all teachers were evaluated as "satisfactory," such evaluations would play little role in determining who was in each quartile. The measures along which teachers varied—such as student achievement impact—would account for much more of the variation in teacher rankings. However, it is hard to imagine that a system driven solely by the test-based measures of value-added would ever be viewed as fully legitimate. To earn legitimacy, school systems will have to develop alternative ways to discern among their teachers beyond simply test scores.

Use of Control Factors

A performance-ranking system must control for baseline test scores so that teachers are held accountable for their ability to raise achievement, not for students' preexisting knowledge and skills. Thornier questions arise about whether to control for other characteristics such as income, gender, and race.

Controlling for these characteristics, as we have done here, ensures that each teacher is in effect compared only against other teachers with demographically similar classrooms. In theory, if background characteristics are not controlled, expectations for teachers with disadvantaged students could be higher than the historical performance of those students could justify. Teachers might then be effectively punished for having poorer students. This could bring about the perverse effect of discouraging teachers from going into these students' classrooms.

On the other hand, by using control factors, the government would effectively be instituting different standards for students based on race, gender, or income. For example, where poorer students have shown lower gains in the past—perhaps in part due to lower expectations—their teachers would face a lower threshold of expected gains. Particularly given the abundant evidence that academic expectations can be self-fulfilling, such controls could send a destructive signal to teachers and students.

We considered a practical question: to what extent does this trade-off actually arise? How much does controlling for racial composition and other student background characteristics actually matter for the teacher evaluations?

To gain some insight into this question, we first estimated teacher impacts on math performance, controlling only for student baseline test scores in reading, math, and language arts and an indicator for whether the student is currently repeating a grade (as well as the interactions of all these with academic year and grade level). We did not include any direct socioeconomic background measures. Second, we added indicators for student race-ethnicity, gender, participation in federal lunch subsidy programs, and English language learner status. The correlation between the two measures was 0.98. Ninety percent of those who were in the top (and bottom) quartile on one measure were in the top (and bottom) quartile on the other measure. So, as long as the estimates are controlling for student baseline test scores, it made only a modest difference whether or not there were additional controls for demographic characteristics and family background.

Given the evidence that expectations can be self-fulfilling, and given the absence of evidence that correcting for socioeconomic characteristics significantly affects which teachers are rewarded, we recommend that the state not control for income, gender, and race.

Evaluating Teachers in Early Grades and High Schools

Nearly every state now tests students annually in reading and math in grades three through eight. Therefore, it should be possible to construct a system to evaluate the performance of those teaching math and reading in grades four through eight. Such an analysis can adjust for baseline academic performance by relying on student performance data from the previous spring. But in most states, a number of K–12 teachers will not be covered well by the current tests, including teachers in kindergarten through second grade, middle school teachers teaching subjects other than math and reading, and many teachers working at the high school level.

For those teaching in elementary schools, a state could require probationary teachers to start teaching in grades four or five, where their performance could be monitored using the student test score data. However, to the extent that there are specific talents and skills appropriate for teaching in kindergarten through third grade, this option may not be attractive. In middle schools, the typical student receives instruction from several different teachers over the course of a day. To the extent that the quality of instruction in one subject (like science), spills over and affects a student's performance in another subject (like math), it may be difficult to separate out the contributions of individual teachers. In high schools, there is the additional problem that students generally self-select into courses and take courses at different difficulty levels. The problem of controlling for all the relevant baseline differences between students, which is a distinct challenge in elementary grades, would be even more of a challenge in high school.

For those teachers working in grades and subject areas that do not lend themselves to value-added assessments, states and districts will have to rely on other measures to evaluate their performance. For these teachers, evaluations by principals, peers, or parents will necessarily play a larger role.

One option is simply to focus the new evaluation systems on teachers in tested grades and subjects. This would create unhelpful incentives for low-achieving teachers to leave the tested fields and high-achieving teachers to enter them. It is important to avoid such distortions and, more important, to develop sound methods for evaluating teaching performance in all fields. After all, even though we do not currently have national mandates for testing of first-graders or eleventh-grade social studies students, there is no reason to believe that the distribution of quality among teachers in these fields is less broad than the distribution for teachers in the tested subjects and grades.

For these reasons, we would encourage states to develop alternative evaluation systems for teachers in nontested grades and subjects where value-added measures may not be practical. One potential model is Connecticut's Beginning Educator Support and Training program in which new teachers submit portfolios of their work, including lesson logs, videotaped segments of teaching, examples of student work, and reflective commentaries on the goals during the lesson. Portfolios are scored by multiple external assessors with experience in the same content area as the beginning teacher. The assessors go through approximately fifty hours of training to able to score portfolios. Measures along these lines provide a promising model for evaluations on grounds other than test scores.

Absolute and Relative Standards

Should teachers be evaluated on an absolute scale, where in theory all could succeed or all could fail? Or should they be graded on a curve and evaluated on a relative scale, where inevitably some will be at the top, the middle, and the bottom? Each approach has advantages and disadvantages. With an absolute standard, evaluators may be pushed by political and personal considerations to dilute the standards so that few teachers face negative consequences. (States have already responded to No Child Left Behind's demand for rising student "proficiency" by defining the definition of proficiency downward.)

Relative standards have other pitfalls. If performance is measured relative to other teachers in the same school or district, teachers will be competing for a finite number of tenure positions or performance awards. In such a system, teachers may be discouraged from collaborating. The ultimate goal of performance reviews is not to pit teachers against one another but to encourage excellence among all teachers.

An alternative approach would be to use a combination of relative and absolute standards. A threshold could be established using a relative comparison in the first year of a program but then could be held constant over time. For example, a state might set an absolute cutoff at the level of achievement growth attained by the 25th percentile teacher in the first year. If average teacher effectiveness improves, more than 75 percent of teachers might exceed that threshold in future years. But such systems also have problems: to the extent that subjective measures such as peer evaluations are included, future evaluations could be artificially inflated. In addition, as performance measures are added or improved, it will be difficult to continue using the original benchmark.

Although we recognize that no solution is without problems, we believe it is essential to use a measure that resists manipulation. Given the options currently available, we would require evaluation of teachers relative to each other and would impose consequences based on relative rankings at the state or district (but not the school) level. Potentially unfair consequences would be mitigated by permitting principals to make exceptions when they are willing to justify their actions to district officials and to parents in their schools.

Ensuring Quality, Fairness, and Teacher Participation

A rigorous performance-based system will succeed over the long run only if it is perceived as fair by teachers who must live with it. As a result, it will be critical that performance measures be developed through an open process in which teachers fully participate. Indeed, the full array of stakeholders—including parents, teachers, and principals—should be involved in the design of such measures. In addition, not only should the process be open, but the measures themselves should also be transparent. "Merit pay" has often become a synonym for principals handing out rewards to favorite teachers based on grounds only the principals themselves know. The grounds for performance measurements should be subject to public review.

The Role of Principals

Beyond their important general role in schools, principals also play a critical part in the success of evaluation systems as we propose. They are likely to be invested with significant authority for evaluating teachers and deciding whether exceptions to quartile rankings should be offered. Principals must have incentives to make judgments based on teacher performance rather than personal preference. Although beyond the scope of this chapter, a parallel incentive system should ultimately apply to principals with regard to any tenure they may enjoy, as well as pay. Principals could be evaluated based on the performance of the teachers they allowed to earn tenure on their watch. So even if a principal were to move between schools, his or her evaluation could depend upon the learning gains generated by all the teachers that principal ever recommended for tenure.

State, District, or School Evaluations

Another key design question is whether teachers are measured against teachers in the same school, the same district, or the same state. To ensure that the students compared are as similar as possible, one may be tempted to compare teachers within the same school, on the assumption that students attending the same school may be similar in ways that justify such a comparison. This might also help ensure that the teachers are operating in similar facilities and with similar administrative supports. As noted above, however, making comparisons within the same school weakens incentives for teachers to collaborate. Moreover, making comparisons within schools disadvantages those teaching in schools where the average teacher is high-performing—and gives undeserved credit to those teaching in schools where the average teacher is low-performing.

Our preference would be to measure teacher quality at the district or state level. To address concerns about comparing teachers with very different student populations, a state or district could rank teachers within peer groups of comparable schools (for example, based on size or location). A big advantage of a state system is that it would be able to track students moving across school district lines. However, this requires the states to institute a statewide student identification system. At least initially, districts may be in a better position to launch such a system. As a result, districts would be eligible to apply for federal funds to develop their data systems if the states are not in a position to do so. This necessity leads to our final proposal.

Recommendation 5: Develop Data Systems to Link Student Performance with the Effectiveness of Individual Teachers over Time

If a system for evaluating teacher effectiveness is to work well, data systems are needed that can track the performance of individual students from year to year and link these results with their teachers. Technical assistance must also be provided on how to use these data systems.

Although the No Child Left Behind Act requires states to test in grades three through eight in reading and math, only a subset of districts and states have linked student outcomes to teacher identifiers and followed students over time. Tennessee began doing so in 1992, developing measures of teacher value-added similar in spirit to those described above. Ohio, Florida, and Colorado have created or are creating such tracking systems. Some cities, such as Dallas, have created these systems as well (Carey

2004).[12] However, most states currently do not have the needed longitudinal data systems (National Center for Educational Accountability 2005). The Institute for Education Sciences at the U.S. Department of Education has a modest grant program designed to support states' development of data systems that provide raw material for measuring the value that teachers add in the classroom.

The federal government should expand its support of state efforts to assemble data and provide sufficient funding for all states to develop and implement longitudinal data systems linking teachers and students. The costs of supporting the development of improved data systems would not be great. Dallas estimates that its value-added system, serving 160,000 students, cost about $210,000 to start up and now costs about $100,000 a year to operate. Hoxby (2002) has suggested that the costs of starting up and administering a wide range of accountability systems have been similarly small.

Implementation and Costs of Our Five Recommendations

We propose a two-phase implementation of our proposals. The first phase would last three years. During this phase, the federal government would support all states in adopting our fifth recommendation: developing the data infrastructure required to track students on a longitudinal basis. Initially, participation would be voluntary. However, by 2009 we would require states receiving funding under Title II of the Elementary and Secondary Education Act to have in place operational longitudinal data systems for linking student performance and teacher effectiveness. Assuming a cost of approximately $4 per youth for start-up and $2 per youth for operating the system, the cost of the implementation of these data systems should be $200 million in one-time start-up costs and $100 million in annual operating costs.

During phase one, the federal government would also fully fund implementation of our four other recommendations in up to ten states. These states would be selected by the Department of Education based on a competitive application process. To encourage states to compete based on quality rather than financial resources, the federal government would pay for the main programming costs in this phase. This means the federal government would pay for the implementation of teacher ranking systems (recommendation 4), the pay bonuses for teachers (recommendation 3), and the new tenure policies (recommendation 2). Without cost, we would also modify No Child Left

---

12. See also Toch, "Measure for Measure."

Behind so that these states could (and would be required to) provide a performance-based path to "highly qualified" status (recommendation 1).

At the end of the first implementation phase, we would evaluate the success of the initiative, including comparisons between states inside and outside the new initiatives. We could see, for example, if states that denied tenure to bottom-quartile teachers saw higher gains in student achievement than states that did not. As part of the first phase, some states outside the pilot might also be funded to establish evaluation systems for their teachers but not yet act on the results of those evaluations. These states could keep track of the teachers ranked in the bottom quartile and observe how their students perform in subsequent years.

The cost of our proposals depends on many variables. We assume the following:

—participation by ten states having typical proportions of the U.S. and low-income populations;

—$15,000 bonuses for top-quartile teachers in the 21 percent of schools meeting our high-poverty definition, with proportional representation of top-quartile teachers in these schools; and

—additional funding, equal to 25 percent of the amounts spent on bonuses, to implement the evaluation system and enhance professional development.

Based on these assumptions, costs in phase one would be about $600 million a year. Together with the costs of the data systems nationally, the costs in the first five years would total perhaps $800 million a year.

Based on the results of phase one, we would expect modifications to be made. If the initiative broadly succeeded, we would propose to implement it nationwide. In the national phase, we would require states receiving any Title II funding to have in place new systems for evaluation, tenure, and pay in poor districts. We would also allow teachers in all these states to be deemed highly qualified based on performance.

Our proposal assumes that the federal government would bear the full cost of this program, just as it now pays the entire cost of existing teacher quality programs under the Elementary and Secondary Education Act. When fully implemented, the salary bonuses and operation of the data systems would cost slightly more than $3 billion a year. Even if costs ultimately proved higher for various reasons, they would still be relatively small in context. The nation currently spends more than $500 billion a year on K–12 education, of which the federal government pays nearly $38 billion a year. For a small fraction of those sums, our proposal could begin to change the way American schools induct, tenure, and pay American teachers.

Questions and Concerns

Won't These Proposals Undermine the Status of Teaching as a Profession?

To attract and retain highly skilled individuals, teaching must be an honored profession. Many high-status professions, like law and medicine, have high barriers to entry. One concern is that our proposal, by lowering barriers to entry into teaching, will diminish the social status of teaching as a profession.

Barriers to entry may be one element of high-status professions, but they are neither necessary nor sufficient. There are plenty of modestly regarded professions with distinctive certification requirements, from forensic scientists to real estate agents. Today, obtaining an education degree and certification is not perceived as a large challenge for talented individuals. Adoption of our proposal would signal that long-term standing in the teaching profession depends on a more demanding achievement: some success in the classroom. The higher pay offered to teachers who demonstrate excellence could be coupled with other steps to elevate such high-performing teachers, such as use of career ladders and master teacher status. These measures together could improve the standing of teaching as a profession built not on paper qualification but on excellence.

Aren't Involuntary Layoffs Rare in the Private Sector?
Why Are Teachers Different?

According to the U.S. Bureau of Labor Statistics (2005), 1 to 1.4 percent of employed persons are laid off or discharged every month.[13] As table 7-1 shows, a similar percentage of teachers report moving schools or leaving teaching involuntarily during an entire year.

However, the production process in education is very different from other sectors. An employee hired in the mail room in a modern corporation can remain in the mail room or be promoted. The same is true for employees hired to be stock analysts, accountants, or salespeople. When employees meet expectations, they are promoted; when they fall below expectations, they remain at the entry level. Firing may be rare, but it is not at all rare for employees to be passed over for promotion.

For teachers, there is no equivalent to the mail room. A low-performing teacher has as much responsibility for a class of students as a high-performing teacher. When a low-performing teacher is retained, his or

---

13. This is based on the layoff and discharge rate from the Job Openings and Labor Turnover Survey (JOLTS), 2000–2005.

her students pay the price. All else equal, particularly given the difficulty in identifying effective teachers based on paper qualifications, one might even expect to see higher discharge rates in schools than in other industries. At present, they seem to be considerably lower.

How Reliable Are Quantitative Measures of Teacher Effectiveness?

One concern is that quantitative measures of teacher effectiveness will be unreliable because of statistical noise. Even if a teacher's skills and effort remain largely the same from one year to the next, the average performance of students in the classroom will differ from year to year. In a typical fifth-grade classroom, with only about twenty-five students taking the test each year, a few particularly bright or particularly rowdy pupils can substantially affect the average performance of the class. A teacher may look good either because the students in that year did unusually poorly on the baseline test or unusually well on the follow-up test. Some years a construction crew may be working loudly across the street on the day students take their evaluation exam, driving down the test scores for the class, or perhaps two of the low-scoring students in a class will come down with flu on the day of the test, bringing up the class average.

These extraneous sources of variation mean that evidence on teacher effectiveness mixes together true differences between teachers and other, potentially random factors. As described in the technical appendix, we have attempted to adjust downward the variation in teacher effectiveness reported in figures 7-1 and 7-2, using our best estimates of the proportion of the variation that is due to nonpersistent or random factors.[14]

While there is a degree of randomness in evaluating teachers, the evaluation does capture actual aspects of performance. Our proposal does not attempt to use measures of teacher performance to make fine gradations but instead focuses on who will look either quite effective or quite ineffective largely regardless of the evaluation system that is used.

Why Not Focus on Improving Teacher Quality by Investing in Training for Existing Teachers?

Many school districts currently invest heavily in professional development for existing teachers. However, we believe that efforts to selectively retain the most effective teachers are more likely to generate large increases in average teacher effectiveness than additional training of the existing teaching force.

14. The technical appendix is available online at www.brookings.edu/~/media/Files/rc/papers/2006/04education_gordon/200604hamilton_1.pdf.

Figure 7-4. Teacher Impacts on Math Performance by Year of Experience[a]

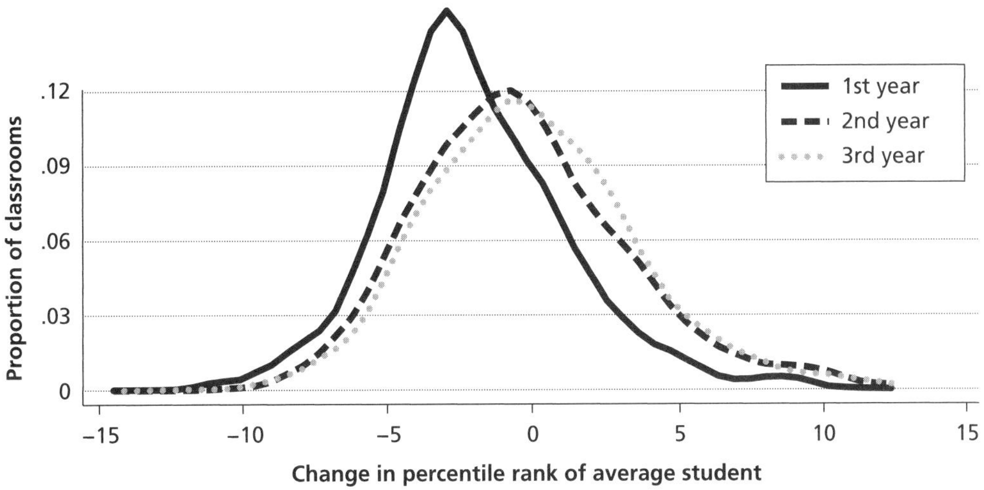

Source: Authors' calculations.

a. LAUSD elementary teachers with less than four years' experience. Classroom-level impacts on average student performance, controlling for baseline scores, student demographics, and program participation.

As evidence for this admittedly provocative proposition, we present data from the Los Angeles Unified School District (LAUSD) about how teacher effectiveness changes with experience. Figure 7-4 shows the distribution of the estimated impacts on performance by year of experience for the sample of teachers whom we observed throughout their first three years of teaching. As is the case with the preceding figures, these average scores for a classroom can be taken to represent the statistically average student—that is, they have been adjusted for race-ethnicity, gender, family income, and scores on an earlier baseline test.

Figure 7-4 illustrates three interesting facts. First, there are large gains in teacher effectiveness between the first and second year of teaching but much smaller gains between the second and third year. The difference in mean math impacts is approximately 3 percentile points between the first and second year of teaching and roughly 1 percentile point between the second and third year of teaching.

Second, the distribution of teacher effectiveness does not seem to become narrower by the third year: the curve for teachers in their third year is slightly wider than the curve for teachers in their first year. In other words, as teachers gain experience on the job, their effectiveness does not seem to converge. This has potentially important implications. For example, suppose that some teachers started out effective and remained so, and other teachers started out ineffective but improved. We would expect the distribution of teacher impacts to become narrower with each year of experience. This does not happen. In other work, we have shown that the reverse is true: those who start out effective in their first years of teaching tend to get better faster than those who start out ineffective (Kane and Staiger 2005; Kane, Rockoff, and Staiger, 2005).

Third, the magnitude of the payoff to experience—about 4 percentile points over the first three years of teaching—is small relative to the difference in effectiveness between those identified in the top and bottom quartile. Recall from a previous section that, as measured by the impact of top-quartile versus bottom-quartile teachers on math scores during their first two years, the difference in teacher effectiveness is 10 percentile points. That is, the return to moving from one to three years of experience is less than half as large as the difference between teachers identified to have been in the top and bottom quartile in their first two years.

Districts invest considerable resources in the professional development of their teachers (much of it through salary points for teachers completing graduate coursework). Without attempting here to assess the vast evidence on how well these programs work, or how they might work if they were better designed, it is hard to imagine that such retraining efforts could generate the same learning that each teacher experiences in the first year on the job. Anyone who has ever taught knows how steep the learning curve is during the first year or two in the classroom. Thus the return to experience during the first few years of teaching appears to be an upper bound on the potential effectiveness of later investments in professional development.

All this said, changes to tenure policies should be complements to, not substitutes for, teacher training efforts. One possible use of the evaluation systems described in this paper would be to help identify the forms of professional development that are most effective. Our point is that rather than simply invest in professional development in the hope of solving the problem of ineffective teaching, districts should place greater emphasis on selectively retaining effective teachers.

What Other Potential Uses Do We See for New Teacher Evaluation Systems?

The system for evaluating teacher effectiveness outlined in this chapter could be put to many uses. Given that there is a degree of randomness in any method of evaluation, we would not support using the results of this evaluation system to, say, fine-tune teacher salaries on an annual basis.

However, we would tend to welcome uses of this system that rely mainly on very large distinctions, such as those between teachers who are consistently in the lowest quarter or the highest quarter of effectiveness over time. For example, as just noted, we could identify which teachers improve the most over time and ask about their characteristics and the training they receive.

We expect that the availability of better data on teacher effectiveness will set off a cascade of other activities at the district and school level: to study the characteristics of effective teachers, to measure teacher effectiveness more carefully, to target effective teachers as mentors, to identify teachers who need additional assistance during the school year, and so on. These systems will also permit more sophisticated evaluation of school performance than the "adequate yearly progress" measure now used under the No Child Left Behind Act.

Are There Potential Legal Barriers to Implementing This Proposal?

One important advantage of our proposal is that it is consistent with many existing tenure laws and collective bargaining agreements. We are not contemplating a wholesale shift to performance-based pay. Likewise, we are not proposing to revoke tenure for existing teachers or dismantle the system for future teachers. Indeed, our proposal may well help provide legitimacy to teacher tenure in the future by ensuring that teachers clear a real hurdle before being granted tenure.

Most collective bargaining agreements already allow for careful scrutiny during the initial probationary period; our proposals would simply apply the scrutiny that these agreements allow. The proposals also do not alter the fact that teachers will be paid according to years of experience and paper qualifications—except for the bonuses proposed here. Moreover, the proposal would help schools meet the federal requirement that all teachers be "highly qualified" by offering an alternative avenue for other professionals to get into teaching.

Conclusion

Although it can be difficult to know with much certainty who is likely to be an effective teacher during a job interview, we have shown that school districts can learn a lot about teachers' future effectiveness simply by scrutinizing their record during their first few years on the job. Currently, such information is not being used. Indeed, it is usually not even assembled since most districts now cannot link individual student test scores to teachers.

Over many years, American schools have experimented with various reform strategies, from increasing accountability to reducing class sizes. Given that history, we are unlikely to get dramatic new results from pushing a little harder on these familiar levers for reform. For instance, in school systems that already have good accountability systems, further ratcheting up the pressure is not likely to produce sudden improvements. But partly because most districts have never assembled the data required to calculate the value-added of individual teachers, the payoff to doing so could be enormous.

Traditionally, policymakers have tried to raise teacher quality by raising the hurdles for those entering teaching. But our results suggest that those hurdles are often not related to teacher effectiveness. Rather than continuing to focus on teacher *credentials,* our proposal would build the infrastructure to measure teacher *effectiveness* on the job and to encourage states and districts to use that information.

References

Aaronson, Daniel, Lisa Barrow, and William Sander. 2003. "Teachers and Student Achievement in the Chicago Public High Schools." Working Paper 2002–28. Federal Reserve Bank of Chicago.

Armor, David, and others. 1976. *Analysis of the School Preferred Reading Program in Selected Los Angeles Minority Schools.* Santa Monica, Calif.: Rand Corporation.

Ballou, Dale, and Michael Podgursky. 2000. "Reforming Teacher Preparation and Licensing: What Is the Evidence?" *Teachers College Record* 102, no. 1: 5–27.

Blau, Francine D., and Marianne A. Ferber. 1992. *The Economics of Women, Men and Work.* 2nd ed. Englewood Cliffs, N.J.: Prentice-Hall.

Bok, Derek. 1993. *The Cost of Talent.* New York: Free Press.

Bradley, Ann. 1999. "Confronting a Tough Issue: Teacher Tenure." *Education Week* 18, no. 17: 48.

Buerhaus, Peter I., Douglas O. Staiger, and David I. Auerbach. 2000. "Implications of an Aging Registered Nurse Workforce." *Journal of the American Medical Association* 283, no. 22: 2948–54.

Bureau of Labor Statistics. 2005. *Job Openings and Labor Turnover Survey.* U.S. Department of Labor.

Carey, Kevin. 2004. "The Real Value of Teachers." *Thinking K–16* 8, no. 1: 3–42.

Cavalluzzo, Linda C. 2004. "Is National Board Certification an Effective Signal of Teacher Quality?" Working Paper. Alexandria, Va.: CNA Corporation.

Darling-Hammond, Linda, and others. 2005. "Does Teacher Preparation Matter? Evidence about Teacher Certification, Teach for America, and Teacher Effectiveness." Working Paper. Stanford, Calif.: Stanford University.

Decker, Paul T., Daniel P. Mayer, and Steven Glazerman. 2004. *The Effects of Teach for America on Students: Findings from a National Evaluation.* Princeton, N.J.: Mathematica Policy Research.

Education Trust. 2003. *Telling the Whole Truth (or Not) about Highly Qualified Teachers*. Washington.

Feldman, Sandra. 2004. "Rethinking Teacher Compensation." *American Teacher,* March.

Goldhaber, Dan, and Emily Anthony. 2004. "Can Teacher Quality Be Effectively Assessed?" Working Paper. Washington: Urban Institute.

Hanushek, Eric A., John F. Kain, and Steven G. Rivkin. 2001. "Why Public Schools Lose Teachers." Working Paper 8599. Cambridge, Mass.: National Bureau of Economic Research.

Hanushek, Eric A., and others. 2005. "The Market for Teacher Quality." Working Paper 11154. Cambridge, Mass.: National Bureau of Economic Research.

Higher Education Research Institute. 2002. *The American Freshman: Thirty-Five Year Trends*. University of California–Los Angeles.

Hoxby, Caroline M. 2002. "The Cost of Accountability." In *School Accountability,* edited by Williamson M. Evers and Herbert J. Walberg. Stanford, Calif.: Hoover Institution Press.

Hoxby, Carolyn M., and Andrew Leigh. 2005. "Wage Distortion." *Education Next* 5, no. 2: 50–56.

Humphrey, Daniel C., Julia E. Koppich, and Heather J. Hough. 2005. "Sharing the Wealth: National Board Certified Teachers and the Students Who Need Them Most." *Education Policy Analysis Archives* 13, no. 18.

Jacob, Brian A., and Lars Lefgren. 2005. "Principals as Agents: Subjective Performance Measurement in Education." Working Paper 11463. Cambridge, Mass.: National Bureau of Economic Research.

Jacob, Brian A., and Steven D. Levitt. 2003. "Rotten Apples: An Investigation of the Prevalence and Predictors of Teacher Cheating." *Quarterly Journal of Economics* 118, no. 3: 843–78.

Jepsen, Christopher, and Steven G. Rivkin. 2002. "What Is the Tradeoff between Smaller Classes and Teacher Quality?" Working Paper 9205. Cambridge, Mass.: National Bureau of Economic Research.

Johnson, Susan Moore, Sarah E. Birkeland, and Heather G. Peske. 2005. *A Difficult Balance: Incentives and Quality Control in Alternative Certification Programs*. Harvard University, Project on the Next Generation of Teachers.

Jupp, Brad. 2005. "The Uniform Salary Schedule." *Education Next* 5, no. 1: 10–12.

Kane, Thomas J., Jonah E. Rockoff, and Douglas O. Staiger. 2005. "Identifying Effective Teachers in New York City." Paper presented at NBER Summer Institute. Cambridge, Mass. July.

Kane, Thomas J., and Douglas O. Staiger. 2002. "The Promise and Pitfalls of Using Imprecise School Accountability Measures." *Journal of Economic Perspectives* 16, no. 4: 91–114.

———. 2005. "Using Imperfect Information to Identify Effective Teachers." University of California–Los Angeles, School of Public Affairs.

Koretz, Daniel M. 2002. "Limitations in the Use of Achievement Tests as Measures of Educators' Productivity." *Journal of Human Resources* 37, no. 4: 752–77.

Krueger, Alan B. 1999. "Experimental Estimates of Education Production Functions." *Quarterly Journal of Economics* 114, no. 2: 497–532.

Lankford, Hamilton, Susanna Loeb, and James Wyckoff. 2002. "Teacher Sorting and the Plight of Urban Schools: A Descriptive Analysis." *Education Evaluation and Policy Analysis* 24, no. 1: 37–62.

Levin, Jessica, Jennifer Mulhern, and Joan Schunck. 2005. *Unintended Consequences: The Case for Reforming the Staffing Rules in Urban Teachers Union Contracts.* New York: The New Teacher Project.

Levin, Jessica, and Meredith Quinn. 2003. *Missed Opportunities: How We Keep High-Quality Teachers out of Urban Classrooms.* New York: The New Teacher Project.

Luekens, Michael T., Deanna M. Lyter, and Erin E. Fox. 2004. *Teacher Attrition and Mobility: Results from the Teacher Follow-Up Survey, 2000–01.* U.S. Department of Education, National Center for Education Statistics.

Miller, Matt. 2003. *The Two Percent Solution.* New York: Public Affairs.

Murnane, Richard J. 1975. *The Impact of School Resources on the Learning of Inner City Children.* Cambridge, Mass.: Ballinger.

Murnane, Richard J., John B. Willett, and Frank Levy. 1995. "The Growing Importance of Cognitive Skills in Wage Determination." *Review of Economics and Statistics* 77, no. 2: 251–66.

Murnane, Richard J., and others. 1991. *Who Will Teach? Policies That Matter.* Harvard University Press.

National Center for Education Information. 2005. *Profile of Teachers in the U.S. 2005.* U.S. Department of Education.

National Center for Educational Accountability. 2005. "Results of 2005 NCEA Survey of State Data Collection Issues Related to Longitudinal Analysis." Austin, Tex.

Neal, Derek A., and William R. Johnson. 1996. "The Role of Premarket Factors in Black-White Wage Differences." *Journal of Political Economy* 104, no. 5: 869–95.

Nye, Barbara, Spyros Konstantopoulos, and Larry V. Hedges. 2004. "How Large Are Teacher Effects?" *Educational Evaluation and Policy Analysis* 26, no. 3: 237–57.

Prince, Cynthia D. 2002. "Higher Pay in Hard-to-Staff Schools: The Case for Financial Incentives." Arlington, Va.: American Association of School Administrators.

Public Agenda. 2003. *Stand by Me.* New York.

Raymond, Margaret, Stephen H. Fletcher, and Javier Luque. 2001. *Teach for America: An Evaluation of Teacher Differences and Student Outcomes in Houston, Texas.* Stanford, Calif.: Hoover Institution, Center for Research and Education Outcomes.

Rivkin, Steven G., Eric A. Hanushek, and John F. Kain. 2005. "Teachers, Schools and Academic Achievement." *Econometrica* 73, no. 2: 417–58.

Rockoff, Jonah E. 2004. "The Impact of Individual Teachers on Student Achievement: Evidence from Panel Data." *American Economic Review* 94, no. 2: 247–52.

Rotherham, Andrew J. 2005. "Credit Where It's Due: Putting Nationally Certified Teachers into the Classrooms That Need Them Most." *Education Week* 24, no. 29: 34, 48.

Rothstein, Richard. 2004. *Class and Schools: Using Social, Economic, and Educational Reform to Close the Black-White Achievement Gap.* Washington: Economic Policy Institute.

Roza, Marguerite, and Paul T. Hill. 2004. "How Within-District Spending Inequities Help Some Schools to Fail." In *Brookings Papers on Education Policy: 2004*, edited by Diane Ravitch. Brookings.

Snyder, Thomas D., Alexandra G. Tan, and Charlene M. Hoffman. 2004. *Digest of Education Statistics 2003*. U.S. Department of Education, National Center for Education Statistics.

Staiger, Douglas O., David I. Auerbach, and Peter I. Buerhaus. 2000. "Expanding Career Opportunities for Women and the Declining Interest in Nursing as a Career." *Nursing Economics* 18, no. 5: 230–36.

Vandevoort, Leslie G., Audrey Amrein-Beardsley, and David C. Berliner. 2004. "National Board-Certified Teachers and Their Students' Achievement." *Education Policy Analysis Archives* 12, no. 46: 1–117.

Walsh, Kate. 2005. "Merit Pay: Not So Fast, Governors!" *Education Gadfly* 5, no. 27.

Walsh, Kate, and Emma Snyder. 2004. *Searching the Attic: How States Are Responding to the Nation's Goal of Placing a Highly Qualified Teacher in Every Classroom*. Washington: National Council on Teacher Quality.

College Grants on a Postcard
A Proposal for Simple and Predictable Federal Student Aid

SUSAN M. DYNARSKI AND JUDITH E. SCOTT-CLAYTON

8

State and federal governments spend billions on financial aid for college students each year. Pell Grants, Stafford Loans, the Hope and Lifetime Learning Tax Credits, and a host of other programs make college less expensive (see table 8-1). The intent of this aid is to increase college attendance. The idea is straightforward: people buy more of a product (college) when its price (tuition) is lower. Price drops, demand increases: that is a lesson learned in any introductory economics course.

Economics 101 says that federal student aid should increase college attendance. The United States needs aid programs to work: college entry and completion rates are low among poor people in our country, with college attendance lowest among the fastest-growing segments of our population.[1] Just 7 percent of high school sophomores from the lowest quartile of socioeconomic status eventually earn a bachelor's degree, compared with

We are indebted to the many colleagues who have shared their ideas and criticism. While they are too numerous to list, we would like to extend special thanks to Sandy Baum, Sandy Jencks, and, especially, Tom Kane, whose insights into financial aid policy have consistently inspired our research.

1. See College Board (2005b) for statistics of college enrollment by family income and race. The Census Bureau shows growth estimates for 2000–10 of 7.2 percent for whites (any ethnicity), 12.9 percent for African Americans (any ethnicity), and 34.1 percent for Hispanics (any race). See U.S. Bureau of the Census, "U.S. Interim Projections by Age, Sex, Race, and Hispanic Origin," 2004 (www.census.gov/ipc/www/usinterimproj/).

Table 8-1. Summary of Pell Grant Program and Federal Tax Benefits for Higher Education, 2003–04[a]

Units as indicated

Aid	Income eligibility	Number of applicants	Number of recipients	Average benefit	Maximum benefit	Total cost
Pell Grant	No cutoff but almost all recipients have income below $40,000	9,567,023	5,387,000	$2,354	Up to $4,050	$12.7 billion
Hope Credit and Lifetime Learning Credit (LLC)	Must have tax liability (credits are not refundable); income limit is $107,000 for a joint return	7,180,884	5,114,143	$838	Up to $1,500 (Hope) or $2,000 (LLC)	$4.4 billion[b]

Sources: Pell Grant statistics are for 2003–04 from the College Board (2006). Tax credit statistics are from the Internal Revenue Service, *Statistics of Income: Individual Complete Report 2004,* table 3.3 (www.irs.gov/pub/irs-soi/04in33ar.xls).

a. Number of applicants represents the number of returns claiming the tax credits and includes nontaxable returns, but number of recipients and average benefits are based on taxable returns only. The Joint Committee on Taxation (2005) estimated that the cost of the tax credits for 2005 would be $5.2 billion.

b. Of this total, we estimate approximately $3 billion flows to undergraduate students, based on 2003–04 National Postsecondary Student Aid Survey data on income and student type (National Center for Education Statistics 2005). Hope credits are restricted to undergraduates whereas Lifetime Learning credits are not.

60 percent of those from the highest quartile. Moreover, only 12 percent of Hispanics and 16 percent of African Americans eventually earn a B.A., compared with 33 percent of non-Hispanic whites (National Center for Education Statistics 2006, table 306). Racial and socioeconomic gaps in attainment are rooted in multiple causes, including weak academic preparation in high school. Even among well-prepared students, however, these gaps persist, suggesting that the cost of college is at least partly to blame.

We expect that student aid could help close these troubling and persistent gaps in educational attainment. Puzzlingly, there is little firm evidence that federal Pell Grants or the federal education tax credits actually get more young people into college.[2] Why is this? One clue lies in the fact that the aid programs that researchers have found to be most effective are simple and certain.[3] These key attributes—simplicity and certainty—are sorely

2. Two well-designed studies have found no effect of the Pell Grant on schooling decisions (Hansen 1983; Kane 1995), while one has found no effect for the tax credits (Long 2004).

3. We have strong evidence on the effectiveness of state merit aid (Abraham and Clark 2006; Cornwell, Mustard, and Sridhar 2006; Dynarski 2004b; Dynarski 2005; Kane 2003), the GI Bills (Bound and Turner 2002; Stanley 2003; Turner and Bound 2003); and the Social Security student benefit program (Dynarski 2003). Much of this evidence is reviewed in Dynarski (2002).

lacking in the current aid system, which is a tangled web of tax, grant, loan, and savings programs, with rules and regulations so complicated and fraught with uncertainty that many prospective students do not know how affordable college can be.

Applying for Aid Is Too Complicated

Families have to fight through a maze of paperwork to get aid. Prospective aid recipients must file the Free Application for Federal Student Aid (FAFSA) to determine their eligibility for federal grants and loans.[4] Nearly 10 million students fill out FAFSAs each year. Table 8-2 compares the FAFSA to the Internal Revenue Service (IRS) 1040, 1040A, and 1040EZ income tax forms. The FAFSA is lengthier than Form 1040EZ (one page, with 37 questions) and Form 1040A (two pages, with 83 questions), and is comparable to Form 1040 (two pages, with 118 questions).

The U.S. tax system is no paradigm of simplicity: the President's Advisory Panel on Federal Tax Reform (2005) extensively documents its mind-numbing complexity. However, for the low-income families targeted by the Pell Grant, the complexity of the aid application dwarfs the complexity of the tax form. Most families eligible for the Pell Grant file the shorter 1040A or 1040EZ; 86 percent of filing households with income below $50,000 (and two-thirds of all households) use these simplified IRS forms. Ninety percent of Pell funds flow to families with incomes below $40,000. The contrast between Form 1040EZ and the FAFSA is especially informative: with one-third of the FAFSA's questions and one-fifth of its pages, the 1040EZ captures the information needed to determine tax liability for the very population that is targeted by Pell Grants.

The time cost alone of filling out these forms is enormous, although the Department of Education seems blind to this fact. The Department of Education improbably estimates that it takes one hour to complete the five-page, 127-question FAFSA. The IRS more realistically estimates that it takes sixteen hours to complete a 1040, thirteen hours to complete a 1040A, and eight hours to complete a 1040EZ.[5] The one-hour figure

---

4. Some websites offer expected family contribution (EFC) calculators, which require the same data as does the FAFSA. An enterprising student or parent could therefore calculate the EFC without completing a FAFSA. However, a student able to do this sort of sleuthing is likely to go to college with or without a federal Pell Grant.

5. Even these are probably conservative estimates: Blumenthal and Slemrod (1992) conclude that the time required for tax compliance averages twenty-seven hours per filing household and is longer for low- and high-income households.

Table 8-2. Complexity of the FAFSA versus IRS 1040[a]

Units as indicated

Measure	1040 2005	1040A 2005	1040EZ 2005	FAFSA 2006–07
Number of pages (excluding instructions)	2	2	1	5
Total number of questions	118	83	37	127
Nonfinancial items				
Identifying information	6	6	6	22
Demographic and family information	8	8	2	18
Enrollment status and school information	0	0	0	7
Signature and preparer information	12	12	12	8
Other	1	1	1	10
Financial items				
Earned income	1	1	1	5
Other income	19	12	2	33
Assets	0	0	0	6
Deductions, credits, allowances	39	22	2	12
Tax amounts from tables, calculation lines	21	12	6	6
Withholdings, refund preferences	11	9	5	0
Number of items required for computation of tax, refund, or aid amount[b]	71	43	8	72
Length of signing statement (number of words)	49	64	59	232
Official estimate of time to prepare (hours)[c]	16	13	8	1

Source: Authors' counts unless otherwise noted.

a. Counts for the FAFSA are for dependent students with two parents and include questions on required student and parent worksheets. Total number of questions includes subquestions and nonnumbered questions, and ensures that items such as name and address are counted in the same way on both IRS and FAFSA forms.

b. For the FAFSA, this excludes items required only to determine dependency status or general eligibility for federal aid.

c. Estimates from official Paperwork Reduction Act notices in the instructions accompanying each form. IRS-reported estimates of time and cost of preparation are based on nonbusiness filers who self-prepare without tax preparation software (these estimates can be found in each form's instructions, on page 78, 58, and 23, respectively). The FAFSA time estimate can be found on page 7 of the FAFSA (Office of Federal Student Aid 2005b).

would be plausible if filling out the FAFSA were simply a matter of copying data from a completed tax form. This is not the case, for two reasons: first, the FAFSA asks about items that are not on the 1040 (such as assets and food stamps); second, many schools require that the FAFSA be submitted in January or February, before the arrival of documents required to complete the 1040 (such as W-2 and 1099 forms). When the 1040 is submitted after the FAFSA, the Department of Education requires that the FAFSA be updated, initiating another round of paperwork.

We conservatively estimate that an average applicant needs ten hours to complete the FAFSA. With 10 million FAFSAs filed a year, that means 100 million hours a year spent filling out financial aid forms, or the equivalent of fifty-five thousand full-time jobs. Reams of paperwork impose significant administrative and verification costs on colleges, who handle much of the aid process. Families also pay for this complexity in their capacity as taxpayers, since a complicated system requires more administrative resources than a simpler system would.

Information about Aid Arrives Too Late

Paperwork is not the only or even gravest problem with the aid system. Our student aid system delivers information about aid for college too late for it to affect schooling decisions. The federal tax system is a maze of paperwork, but we give the IRS this much: once taxpayers fill out their 1040, they know how much tax they owe. Upon completing the FAFSA, aid applicants are no more informed about their financial aid eligibility than they were when they began. Consider the parents of a high school student, concerned that college is beyond their financial reach. They will not get definitive information about aid eligibility until after their child has applied to and been admitted to colleges in the spring of senior year in high school (see figure 8-1). The education tax credits are even worse on this dimension because they are calculated as much as sixteen months after a student has enrolled and paid tuition.

This brings us to another commonsense concept from Economics 101: a consumer has to know about a price discount in order to respond to it. Delivering a subsidy after a person has made a purchase is no way to increase demand. Imagine a car dealer who told customers about a rebate incentive only after they had agreed to purchase a car. What would happen? Customers who were willing to buy at the prerebate price would be pleasantly surprised and drive out of the dealership with their wallets a little fuller than they had anticipated. Customers scared off by the sticker price would never even learn about the rebate and would walk out not knowing that the car they wanted was affordable.

Our complex system of delivering aid and tax credits for college back-loads information about college discounts. This surely reduces the efficacy of the subsidies since many high school students will not start on the path to college if they are not certain that it is affordable. Confusion about college aid is of the greatest consequence for low-income students, who (unlike their upper-income counterparts) are pessimistic about their ability to pay for college (Avery and Kane 2004). For those teetering on the margin of college entry, there is too little concrete information about aid, and what little information there is arrives far too late. These marginal students

Figure 8-1. Student Aid Application Process

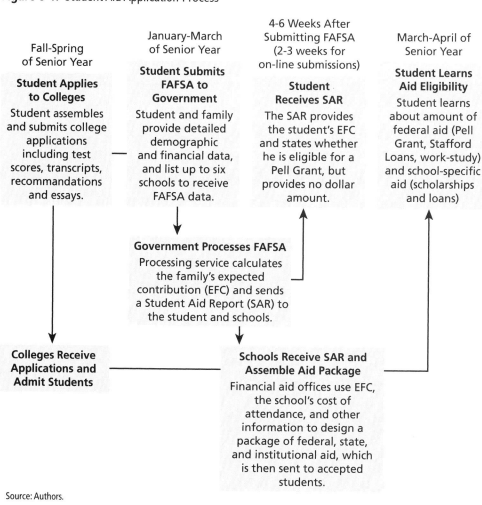

Source: Authors.

are discouraged from going to college by its price, even though aid is available to help them. This is a waste of human potential.

Federal aid inarguably eases the sting of college costs for those who go to college. But many who fear college is unaffordable will never even apply to college, much less apply for aid and matriculate. Many who fear college is unaffordable will give up on their studies while they are in high school, making the inaccessibility of college a self-fulfilling prophecy. Low-income and nonwhite youths are less likely than their better-off peers to take college preparation classes and achieve in high school. This achievement gap in high school may be driven by a gap in expectations and aspirations. Knowing that college is affordable could push kids to work harder in high school instead of giving up on themselves.

Does Complexity Improve the Targeting of Aid?

The costs of complexity and uncertainty in college aid are potentially quite high. What benefits, if any, arise from all this complexity and uncertainty? Financial aid officers and education specialists have patiently explained that the complexity of aid is a necessary evil, without which aid could not be targeted to students with the greatest need. The FAFSA is long, they argue, to enable precise measurement of who needs aid the most. The calculation of aid eligibility is delayed until the spring before the student enters college so that complete and up-to-date information about schooling costs and family finances can be compiled.

We decided to take this argument at face value and measure empirically how much complexity in aid applications contributes to the targeting of funds. We examined detailed data from nearly 52,000 aid applications and aid packages, using the nationally representative 2003–04 National Postsecondary Student Aid Survey (NPSAS; National Center for Education Statistics 2005). With these data, we examined how the distribution of federal aid would shift if the FAFSA were drastically scaled back.

How much does complexity help with targeting? The answer shocked even us. Out of more than 100 questions on the FAFSA, only a few have any substantial impact on grant eligibility. Dozens of questions contribute virtually nothing to the determination of grant aid.

Take a look at figure 8-2: the light grey bars show the current distribution of the Pell Grant. When the number of items that go into the aid formula is cut from seventy-two to fourteen, Pell eligibility changes by the amount shown by the dark bars. As the figure demonstrates, there is virtually no change in the distribution of the Pell: it changes by less than $100 for 76 percent of students and less than $500 for 88 percent of students (table 8-3). The small shifts in aid eligibility that occur are highly progressive, with more money flowing to low-income families. Even if we go further and throw out 90 percent of the questions used in the aid calculation, there is still virtually no change in the distribution of Pell Grants (figure 8-3).

The questions needed to determine aid in this last approach could fit on a postcard. In fact, all of these questions are already asked of us when we

Figure 8-2. Effects of Estimating Pell Grants Using Only Income and Assets of Parents and Students, and Family Structure, 2003–04[a]

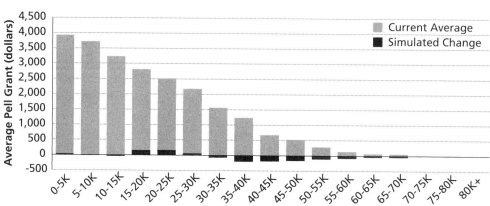

Income, head of household (thousands of dollars)

Source: Authors' estimates based on a sample of 51,822 full-time, full-year undergraduates from the 2003–04 NPSAS (National Center for Education Statistics 2005).

a. Simulated change with the number of items used in the calculation cut from seventy-two to fourteen.

file our annual tax forms. Effectively, the federal government has all the information it needs to determine Pell Grants, even if no application is filed at all. Complexity is not a prerequisite for progressivity (Dynarski and Scott-Clayton 2006b).

The current aid system creates formidable barriers to college. A key lesson of our research is that these barriers can be dismantled if we are willing to tolerate minor imperfections in measuring ability to pay. This is a worthwhile trade-off since both economic theory and empirical evidence suggest that reducing complexity and uncertainty in the aid system will increase its efficacy. This will allow aid to serve its intended goal: opening the doors of college to those with the ability but not the means to pursue higher education.

Our Proposed Solution: College Grants on a Postcard

The federal system of student financial aid is broken. Small tweaks and Band-Aid solutions are likely only to add to the complex, confusing, and uncertain situation faced by students and their families. Building

Table 8-3. Consequences of Aid Simplification for Full-Time, Full-Year Undergraduates, 2003–04[a]

Units as indicated

		Simulations keeping FAFSA formula, dropping items sequentially	
	Baseline	Drops taxes paid, type of tax form, and worksheets	Additionally drops assets
Percent of all full-time, full-year applicants whose Pell:			
Remains the same (within $100)	100	76	75
Increases by $500 or more	0	5	7
Decreases by $500 or more	0	7	6
Correlation between new and old Pell Grant	1.00	0.96	0.95
R^2	1.00	0.92	0.90
Change in average Pell (per full-time, full-year applicant)	0	−13.61	53.79
Percentage change in total program costs[b]	0	−0.84	3.34
Variables included in simulation			
Assets	Y	Y	N
Dependent students' adjusted gross income (AGI)	Y	Y	Y
Parental AGI, or independent student–spouse's AGI	Y	Y	Y
Parental or independent students' marital status	Y	Y	Y
Family size	Y	Y	Y
Number of family members in college	Y	Y	Y
Number of FAFSA items required for simulation[c]	72	14	8

Source: Authors' calculations using FAFSA data from the 2003–04 NPSAS.

a. Sample is limited to 24,253 students (dependent or independent) who attended a single institution full-time for the full school year and who were not missing key data elements such as income or actual EFC. Baseline calculations based on the federal aid formula as described in the *2003–2004 Federal Student Aid Handbook* (Office of Federal Student Aid 2003a).

b. Estimated total Pell expenditures for this sample of full-time, full-year aid applicants were $7.6 billion. Total Pell expenditures across all applicants were $12.7 billion in 2003–04.

c. Count refers to the number of questions on the 2003–04 FAFSA (Office of Federal Student Aid 2003b) required to elicit the items used in the simulated needs analysis for a dependent student. For example, eliciting AGI requires three questions on the FAFSA because non–tax filers must report their earnings and their spouses' earnings. The count does not include questions used only to determine dependency status or questions unrelated to the calculation of need. The differences between the 2003–04 FAFSA and the 2006–07 version described in table 8-2 are minor.

a workforce for the twenty-first century requires a system for funding college that is up to the task. Our proposal drastically simplifies the system for students and parents, allowing them to know the aid they can get for college years before they need it. This set of reforms will improve the effectiveness of the dollars we have already committed to higher education.

Figure 8-3. Effects of Estimating Pell Grants Using Only Income of Parents and Students, and Family Structure, 2003–04[a]

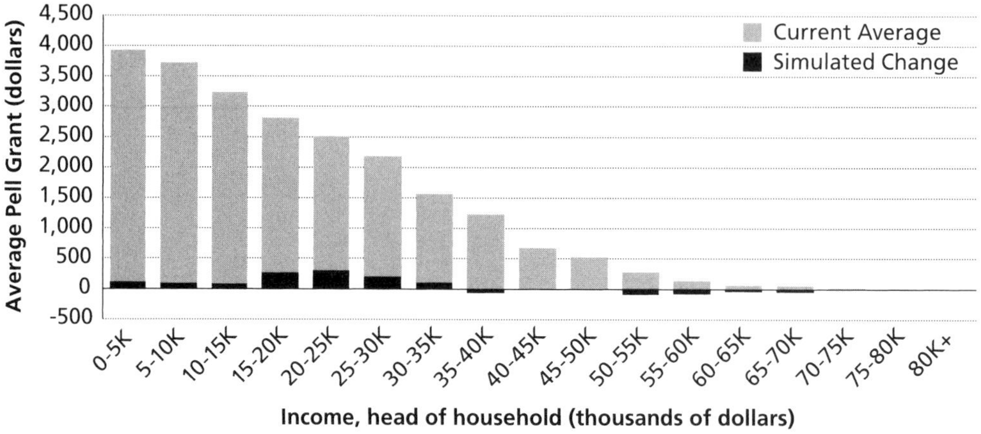

Source: See figure 8-2.
a. Simulated change with the number items used in the calculation cut by 90 percent.

Eligibility

A proposed grant table is shown in box 8-1. This grant would replace the Pell, Hope, and Lifetime Learning benefits for undergraduates. Such a table can fit on a postcard and be prominently displayed on posters in high school hallways. The amounts listed in the grant table roughly correspond to the average combined benefits from Pell Grants and the Hope and Lifetime Learning Tax Credits for each income category (see figure 8-4), with increases for lower-income groups in order to minimize adverse impacts on the most vulnerable students. Families with more than one child (and independent students with any children) are eligible for slightly larger grants. Grants would be prorated for part-time or part-year attendees. (Average grant amounts, accounting for this proration, are illustrated in figure 8-5.) Subsidized student loan eligibility can be assigned using the same table; as is true with grants, a handful of questions can explain the overwhelming majority of variation in loan eligibility (see Dynarski and Scott-Clayton, 2008).

Application Process

Families will apply for the grant by checking off a box on their income tax form, and they will receive a voucher, by mail or through the Internet, that

Box 8-1. Federal Student Aid on a Postcard

How much federal aid can I get to help pay for college?

If your parents' adjusted gross income is . . .	then your annual grant is . . .
$0–$14,999	$4,050
$15,000–$19,999	$3,700
$20,000–$24,999	$3,300
$25,000–$29,999	$3,000
$30,000–$34,999	$2,400
$35,000–$39,999	$1,600
$40,000–$44,999	$800
$45,000–$49,999	$600
$50,000–$74,999	$450
$75,000–$99,999	$300

. . . *plus* $250 for each dependent child other than the student, up to an additional $1,000. If you are legally independent from your parents, your aid will be based on your (and your spouse's) income.

　　Grants will be adjusted for attendance status. For example, if you attend half-time, your grant would be half the amount listed.

Figure 8-4. Distribution of Spending on Undergraduates under Current System and Proposed System, 2003–04[a]

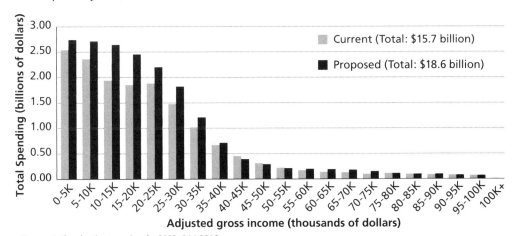

Source: Authors' estimates using the 2003–04 NPSAS.

a. Estimates for the cost of current benefits (Pell Grants plus Hope and Lifetime Learning Credits) and our proposal are based on the 2003–04 population of undergraduate federal aid applicants and 2004 tax benefits.

Figure 8-5. Average Benefits for Undergraduates under Current System and Proposed System, 2003–04[a]

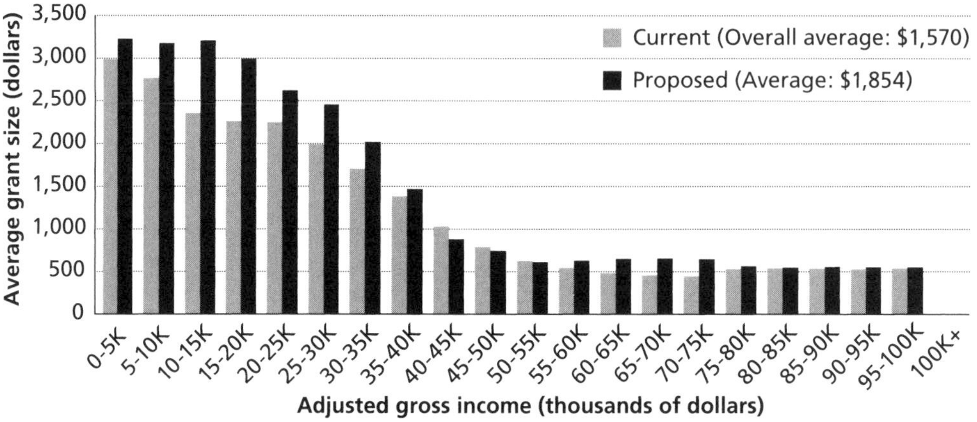

Source: Authors' estimates using the 2003–04 NPSAS.

a. Estimates are based on the 2003–04 population of undergraduate federal aid applicants. Average grants are lower than maximums because of proration for less than full-time attendees.

can be applied toward the cost of the student's attendance at any eligible higher education institution. Students will notify schools of their grant eligibility as part of the normal application process. Schools will verify this information with the Department of Education, just as they now verify data from the FAFSA and Student Aid Report. Financial aid administrators will provide verifications of students' enrollment status to the Department of Education.

Program Administration

While the IRS has all the data needed to determine grant eligibility, the Department of Education has the infrastructure in place to deliver funds to schools. We therefore suggest that the role of the IRS be limited to forwarding applicants' adjusted gross income, dependency status, and number of dependents to the Department of Education, which will calculate aid eligibility and send vouchers to students. As in the current system, the students' aid eligibility for the 2006–07 school year would be based on 2005 income, as reported to the IRS in early 2006. Unlike the current system, students would not have to wait for their voucher to arrive to know exactly how much they will receive because they can look it up in the simple table at any time (box 8-1).

Delivery of Funds

The Department of Education will deliver funds directly to the school. As in the current federal student aid system, schools would then refund to the student any portion of the grant that remains after covering tuition and fees; the student could use this excess for books and for food, housing, transportation, and other living expenses. As in the current system, funds could be recouped from the student in cases of fraud or error. Our proposed system is less vulnerable to fraud and error than is the current system since our system relies on IRS reports of income rather than on self-reports. With an eye to fraud, the Department of Education currently audits 30 percent of aid applications; these audits require that applicants provide supporting tax documents from the IRS. In our proposal, these time-consuming audits are unnecessary since the eligibility data will come from the IRS. In other words, the audit rate in our proposed program is effectively 100 percent but places no burden on families or schools.

Advantages over the Current System

Simplicity

Our approach combines the Pell Grant and tax credits into a single, unified program with eligibility based simply on income and number of children in the household. Unifying the tax credit and grant programs removes the confusion over which credit is best to take for a given student and eliminates the complicated rules that determine how tax credits and Pell Grants interact.

Predictability

The grant schedule we propose is so straightforward that parents can easily determine their eligibility well before their child applies to college. The grant schedule can easily be communicated to students through postcards, posters, and targeted mailings. This eliminates a critical weakness in the current aid system: delayed and unpredictable information about aid eligibility. There are multiple proposals to simplify the aid system. Many of these simplification proposals will not make aid predictable, which is central to making it effective. In particular, any proposal that merely shortens the FAFSA while still postponing the determination of aid eligibility until after college admission will be ineffective. Families need certain information about aid eligibility, and they need it early, when their children are preparing academically for the rigors of college coursework.

Less Paperwork

Families applying for aid will report their income to the IRS as usual when they file their taxes. They will not make a separate application to the Department of Education. Time savings will be upward of 100 million hours, or the equivalent of 55,000 full-time jobs.[6] In addition, since income information will come directly from the IRS rather than from students' self-reports on a FAFSA, individual institutions will no longer need to verify students' financial information. Currently, schools are legally required to audit 30 percent of FAFSAs submitted, at an estimated cost of $432 million a year (Advisory Committee on Student Financial Assistance 2005).

Families Get Funds When They Need Them

Currently, the tax credits arrive as much as sixteen months after families have paid for college tuition. The credits do nothing for the strapped family who cannot come up with the funds for college. By delivering funds at the time of enrollment, our approach gets money into families' hands when they need it most.

Single Program

The current system of college finance shunts low-income families into one program (the Pell Grant) and middle- and upper-income families into another (the education tax credits).[7] Perhaps unsurprisingly, funding for the Pell Grant has stagnated while tax benefits for middle-class families have skyrocketed. Our approach would combine the Pell Grant and tax credits into a single, unified program that benefits families across the income distribution. By applying a consistent standard of need to all families, this approach would yield a broad-based yet progressive system of student aid.

Stops Penalizing Work

The aid system's treatment of student earnings is deeply flawed; it is both inequitable and inefficient. The aid formula taxes student earnings (above a

6. Approximately 6 percent of FAFSA applicants do not currently file income taxes but would need to under our proposal (authors' estimate using NPSAS data). The families of these students would trade the time spent filling out the FAFSA for the time spent filling out an IRS 1040, most likely the shorter 1040A or EZ form. If we conservatively treat this as a time-neutral trade-off, then our overall estimates of time saved would decrease by 6 percent, to 94 million hours.

7. Skocpol's review of major American antipoverty programs over the past two centuries concludes that strictly targeted policies "have not been politically sustainable" (1991, p. 414).

very low threshold) at a rate of 50 percent.[8] This onerous tax on labor applies to both dependent and independent students. Such a high tax on students' earnings penalizes those who work their way through college and especially hurts dependents from low-income families, who work more than their better-off dependent peers. It also punishes students who have a full-time job while attending school because their aid is reduced or eliminated due to their hard work.[9]

Assists Nontraditional Students

The typical college student is no longer in her teens or early twenties, attending college full-time. Instead, she is in her late twenties or thirties, working while she studies part-time for her degree. Roughly 40 percent of part-time, independent students are African American or Hispanic (see table 8-4). These students typically work twenty-eight hours a week while they are going to school. Our current aid system, designed for full-time students supported by their parents, shortchanges this large and rapidly growing population. Their earnings are taxed very heavily by the aid formula, penalizing students who work hardest. In our proposal, part-time and older students get higher grants than they do now, largely because we stop penalizing their work effort. Independent, part-time students, on average, currently get a Pell Grant of $1,235 and tax credit of $118. Our proposal would give these students a grant averaging $1,740, an increase of about 30 percent.

Increases College Enrollment

Because of its simplicity and predictability, our proposal could increase college enrollments where the Pell Grants and tax credits have not. Economic research suggests that simple programs can increase enrollments by 3 to 4 percentage points per $1,000 in aid (Dynarski 2002). If our proposed program had the same effects as other simple programs, there could be an increase of 5.6 to 7.4 percentage points in college enrollments among the grant eligible population (given an average expected grant size of $1,854). We would expect to see the effects concentrated

8. In 2003–04 the earnings threshold was $2,400 for dependent students, $5,400 for unmarried independent students, and $8,640 for married independent students.

9. Among dependent students from lower-income families, 73 percent have positive earnings; among such students from upper-income families, that figure is 62 percent. Median student earnings are $2,730 for the lower-income group versus $2,231 for the upper-income group.

Table 8-4. Characteristics of Traditional and Nontraditional Students, 2003–04

Units as indicated

Characteristic	Dependent		Independent	
	Full-time	Part-time	Full-time	Part-time
Age (years)	19.9	20.2	30.0	31.1
Family income (dollars)	63,673	51,801	21,553	25,240
Hours worked per week	15.9	20.9	24.2	27.5
White, non-Hispanic (percent)	67	57	58	53
Black, non-Hispanic (percent)	12	15	20	24
Hispanic (percent)	12	17	13	15
Asian (percent)	6	5	3	3
Neither of student's parents earned a high school diploma (percent)	4	9	14	17
Neither of student's parents earned a B.A. (percent)	53	64	72	75
Male (percent)	44	44	37	32
Parents are married (percent)	71	63	. . .	. . .
Student is married (percent)	. . .	. . .	32	34
Student has dependent children (percent)	. . .	. . .	50	55
Estimated average Pell Grant (dollars)	1,139	821	2,636	1,235
Estimated average tax credit (dollars)	332	201	173	118
Proposed benefit (dollars)	1,594	1,159	3,398	1,740
Percent increase in benefit	8	13	21	29

Source: Authors' estimates using a sample of 51,822 undergraduates from the 2003–04 NPSAS.

among students from families earning less than $50,000, since their grants are largest and their attendance rates have substantial room to grow.

How Much Would This Cost?

We could design a simplification plan that is perfectly revenue neutral, but such an arrangement would create losers as well as winners—and it will be difficult to sell a program that causes some groups to get less funding and others to get more. Since our goal is to minimize losses while maximizing simplicity, we have chosen to design the plan to spend slightly more so that no group is penalized by simplification.

Currently $15.7 billion is spent on Pell Grants and education tax incentives for undergraduates. Our unified grant program for undergraduates would cost $18.6 billion, an increase of $2.84 billion, or 18 percent.[10] This is in line with recent growth in aid for college: between academic years 2001–02 and 2002–03, spending on the education tax incentives increased by $1 billion, and spending on the Pell Grant increased by $1.6 billion, for a total increase of $2.6 billion, or 17 percent.

As is always the case with budget projections, a few cautions are in order. First, our calculations assume that college attendance patterns do not change after our program is introduced, but we hope that the new aid program could increase college attendance rates among the eligible population by about 9 percent. In this case, program costs would be about 9 percent higher than projected above, rising to $20.3 billion. While costs would be higher under this scenario, so too would be the education, productivity, and taxable earnings of our workforce. A college graduate working full-time pays $5,300 more *each year* in federal income taxes than does a full-time worker with only a high school diploma (College Board 2005, p. 2). Even those who attend college without completing a degree pay significantly more in federal taxes than do those who never attend.

Our second caution is along the same lines: our cost projections assume that the take-up rate for student aid stays as it is today. The take-up rate in the Pell Grant program is currently quite low. Research shows that roughly 25 percent of Pell dollars are left on the table by students who either do not apply or fail to follow through on their applications. Take-up of the education tax credits appears to be even lower (Long 2004; Bershadker and Cronin 2002).

Low take-up of the Pell Grant and tax credits is likely due to complexity and uncertainty in the application process. Our proposed program is much simpler and substantially reduces uncertainty, in the hope that many more students will step forth and take advantage of the resources for which they are eligible. Some have cautioned that a high take-up rate would make our approach "too expensive." Currently, complexity and uncertainty keep program costs down by discouraging the neediest students from applying. This is a cowardly way to ration scarce aid funds. If aid must be rationed,

10. All cost estimates are based on NPSAS 2003–04 data (National Center for Education Statistics 2005). Using income data provided in this survey, we calculate aid eligibility under our proposal and use survey weights to calculate national estimates. To estimate costs under the current system for the same students, we use detailed information from FAFSA applications included in the survey data to replicate Pell eligibility, and then add to this amount the average education tax credit claimed by individuals in the students' income category.

it should be done honestly by designing a program that in practice as well as in principle reflects national distributional priorities.

Costs and Benefits of Simplification

As discussed above, losses are inevitable when simplification is constrained by revenue neutrality.[11] The only way to simplify while ensuring that no one is worse off is to increase spending. Even producing winners can cause political problems. Winners are those whose aid eligibility increases with the shift to a simpler measurement of income. By implication, many families who do not currently "deserve" aid will get it under a simplified system. Some will perceive the receipt of aid by such students as fraud, evasion, or a policy failure. Creating winners and losers is an inevitable cost of simplification, but one we believe is ultimately outweighed by the benefits conferred on the vast majority of students and especially on those teetering on the margin of entering college.

The average student gains nearly $300 from our proposal (see first row of table 8-5). The gains are concentrated among those whose family income is less than $30,000 a year; they do not vary substantially across type of school attended (that is, public, private, two-year, or four-year). Working students see large gains, as do independent students, primarily because of the reduced tax on their work effort.

A cost of simplification is that some funds will flow to those we do not currently consider needy. A small number of families have low income but substantial assets; under the proposed system, they will get grants. Among dependent aid applicants, 1 percent of parents have financial assets of more than $390,000, and their grants will rise by $330, to $510.[12] Since they are such a small slice of the population, the cost of this increase is just $17 million.

This small increase in costs should be weighed carefully against the substantial decrease in complexity conferred by dropping assets from the federal aid formula. When assets are part of the aid formula, the tax system cannot be used to determine aid eligibility since it does not collect asset

11. In its final report, the President's Advisory Panel on Federal Tax Reform (2005) makes this point very nicely in the context of tax simplification.

12. The asset figures quoted in this paragraph are for those assets that are counted by the federal aid formula. The federal formula does not count housing equity or retirement assets when considering a family's ability to pay. Few families have substantial financial assets outside of their retirement accounts (especially families with income in the Pell range), which is why excluding all assets from the aid formula has very little impact on the distribution of Pell Grants.

Table 8-5. Changes in Average Grants and Total Funding by Selected Characteristics, 2003–04[a]

Units as indicated

Distribution of changes in funding	Percent of student population	Median change	Mean change per student	Total change (billions)
			Dollar amount	
Total change for undergraduates	100.0	121	284	2.840
Income less than $15,000	25.3	250	497	1.260
Income $15,000–30,000	24.0	53	525	1.260
Income $30,000–45,000	15.2	137	105	0.160
Income $45,000–60,000	10.6	144	3	0.003
Income $60,000–75,000	8.0	189	184	0.148
Income over $75,000	16.9	0	5	0.009
Four-year public students	34.9	48	283	0.989
Four-year private student	23.4	17	264	0.619
Two-year public students	33.1	184	299	0.989
Two-year private students	4.3	236	409	0.013
Dependent students	52.5	0	128	0.673
Independent students	47.5	203	456	2.170
Total change for dependent undergraduates	100.0	0	128	0.673
Students with no earnings	25.5	0	−78	−0.104
Students with earnings	74.5	18	198	0.776
Earnings above $6,200 (75th percentile)	24.9	200	491	0.642
Parental assets below $1,500	50.3	84	122	0.322
Parental assets above $1,500	49.7	0	134	0.351
Assets above $15,600	25.0	0	184	0.242
Assets above $76,000	10.0	0	257	0.135
Assets above $390,000	1.0	0	330	0.017
Income less than $15,000	10.7	250	444	0.250
Income $15,000–30,000	17.8	−52	252	0.236
Income $30,000–45,000	16.4	123	75	0.065
Income $45,000–60,000	13.7	164	−4	−0.003
Income $60,000–75,000	12.1	189	188	0.119
Income over $75,000	29.3	0	4	0.006
Total change for independent undergraduates	100.0	203	456	2.170
Student assets below $1,500	85.7	209	455	1.830
Student assets above $1,500	14.3	178	458	0.334
Income less than $15,000	41.5	250	512	1.010
Income $15,000–30,000	30.8	153	699	1.020
Income $30,000–45,000	13.8	146	145	0.095
Income $45,000–60,000	7.0	116	17	0.006
Income $60,000–75,000	3.5	122	172	0.028
Income over $75,000	3.3	0	17	0.003

Source: Authors' estimates using a sample of 51,822 undergraduates from the 2000–04 NPSAS.

a. All increases and decreases are relative to the current Pell Grant plus estimated tax credit.

information. If we keep assets in the formula, we have to require a separate application for student aid.

We have tried to minimize losses under our proposal. The correlation of current aid with our radically simplified grant table is 84 percent. Overall, 49 percent of current aid applicants would see their grants change by less than $250 (we consider such applicants neither winners nor losers). About 34 percent would gain more than $250, and about 14 percent would lose more than $250. Only 8 percent would lose more than $500.

Grandfathering in current Pell recipients would be a relatively inexpensive way to ensure that no current students see reductions in their grants. This approach would guarantee that new grants going to current Pell recipients would be no smaller than current grants to those recipients. While this would impose small transition costs in the first few years, it would allow certainty in aid for current students and increase the political viability of the proposal.

Questions and Concerns

Doesn't Complexity Help Target Limited Funds to Those Most in Need?

The design of the current student aid system shows that the nation wants to give more money to needy students; otherwise, we would have no application and just give everyone the same grant amount. In this sense, complexity in aid is well intentioned: it aims to measure precisely each family's ability to pay for college. It is equitable and efficient to tolerate some complexity in order to target funds to those who are neediest. But diminishing marginal returns can set in, and at some point, the additional questions do more to increase costs than they do to improve targeting (Kaplow 1990, 1996). First, there are compliance costs for applicants, such as time spent learning about the rules and formulas, collecting the required documents, and completing forms. Second, there are administrative costs borne by schools and the government, which ultimately fall on students and taxpayers in the form of higher tuition, higher taxes, or reduced services. While such costs are high, our research (Dynarski and Scott-Clayton 2006a, 2006b) shows that the benefits are remarkably small. Out of more than 100 questions on the FAFSA, only a few have any substantial impact on grant eligibility.

How Does Complexity in the Aid System Harm Needy Families?

Complexity in student aid disproportionately burdens the very groups we are trying to target. We have heard repeatedly from college-educated professionals (including college professors!) that they have suffered through many nights on the home computer and Internet, filling out the FAFSA for their college-bound child. Imagine, then, the time, stress, and effort the aid process imposes on parents who have never gone to college, those who do not speak English, and those who have no computer at home, much less an Internet connection. On all of these key dimensions, low-income families—the target of need-based aid—are the worst off:

—Half of low-income high school seniors have no parent who attended college (National Center for Education Statistics 2002).[13]

—Thirteen percent of low-income youth live in families in which English is not the primary language; this is double the rate of high-income youth.[14]

—Low-income families typically do not have Internet access at home. In 2003 more than two-thirds of children from families with incomes below $25,000 had no Internet access at home, compared with 12 percent of families with incomes above $50,000.[15] Families may be reluctant to take their financial documents to a school or a library in order to enter data into a public computer. Even locating financial records is an obstacle for poor students due to higher mobility rates and separation of children from parents. The bottom line is that the costs of complexity are highly regressive, falling heavily on low-income, nonwhite, and non-English-speaking youth whose lagging educational levels are repeatedly cited as a justification for need-based financial aid. Complexity arises from well-intentioned efforts to target funds, but in practice this complexity significantly reduces both the efficiency and equity of federal student aid.

Won't Lots of Wealthy Families Start Applying for Aid If We Stop Taxing Assets in the Aid Formula?

In practical terms, assets have little impact on the calculation of federal grants. We checked this by dropping assets from the aid formula, leaving all other aspects of the aid calculation intact. The Pell Grant did not change at all for 75 percent of the sample. Total Pell expenditures in this simulation increased by just 3.3 percent.

Assets have little effect on aid eligibility because few households have assets that are included in the formula. Families hold the vast majority of their wealth in homes and retirement funds, both of which are protected by

13. Authors' calculations, comparing families with income below $25,000 to those with income above $50,000.

14. Ibid.

15. Authors' calculations using published tables from the computer and Internet supplement to the Current Population Survey (Day, Janus, and Davis 2005).

the aid formula. Other financial assets count only if they are above a threshold (up to $54,500) that increases with the age of the parents. Among dependent students who file a FAFSA, 85 percent have no assets above the disregard. Among those from families with income below $50,000, 93 percent have no assets above the disregard. As a result, for the overwhelming majority of families, the effective tax rate on assets is already zero—yet data on assets are still gathered.[16]

It could be true, however, that families with substantial assets simply do not file a FAFSA since they know they will not be eligible for aid. We checked this by comparing assets of current FAFSA applicants to assets of all households with similar incomes, using data from the Survey of Consumer Finances.[17] We find that the assets of households currently applying for aid are quite similar to the population that could apply for aid. The statistics offer no support for the concern that a substantial, hidden population of low-income, high-asset families will gain Pell eligibility if assets are completely removed from taxation. This is not to say that no such families will gain eligibility: 0.25 percent of families with income in the Pell range have more than $250,000 in nonretirement financial assets. This is a minute portion of the population, and so the program costs of "wrongly" giving Pell Grants to such asset-rich, income-poor families are low. By contrast, the resulting reduction in compliance costs is large once it is aggregated across the other 99.75 percent of households.

If People Are Dissuaded from College Just Because They Do Not Want to Fill Out a FAFSA, Doesn't That Suggest That They Are Not Really "College Material"?

The problem with federal student aid goes far beyond the aggravation of filling out a confusing form. The FAFSA and the aid process highlight costs, obscure benefits, generate uncertainty, and ignore well-understood behavioral phenomena that can limit participation. For all of these reasons, complexity is not just an annoyance but rather a serious barrier to the efficiency and equity of student aid. Theory and empirical evidence both suggest that the federal aid system is poorly designed if the goal is to get more people into college.[18]

16. For 99 percent of aid applicants, the marginal tax rate on assets is zero. We obtain this figure by adding $100 to every applicant's financial assets and recalculating aid. For 99 percent of the sample, Pell eligibility is unchanged.

17. Federal Reserve Board, "2004 Survey of Consumer Finances" (www.federalreserve.gov/pubs/oss/oss2/2004/scf2004home.html).

18. A fuller exposition of the theoretical and empirical insights into aid provided by behavioral economics can be found in Dynarski and Scott-Clayton (2006a).

Economists and psychologists have found that individuals' decisions are strongly influenced by their default course of action (Samuelson and Zeckhauser 1988). An influential study by Madrian and Shea (2001) is illustrative. They examined retirement saving at a large financial firm where 401(k) participation required that new employees check a box on a form; the consequence of not checking that box was not participating in the 401(k). That is, the default option was nonparticipation. Despite the low transaction costs of enrollment and strong financial incentives (tax advantages plus an employer match of savings), participation rates were low. The company made a minor change: nonparticipation now required that the new employee check a box on a form, making participation the default option. This small change in program design had a profound effect on behavior, increasing participation by 50 percentage points.

Seemingly minor obstacles put low-income youth off the path to college, much as adults are put off the path to saving by bureaucratic details. A study of high school seniors in Boston found that few low-income youth make a deliberate choice not to go to college. Rather, they miss a key deadline or incorrectly fill out a form or fail to take a required class, and thereby fall off the path to college (Avery and Kane 2004).

For upper-income teenagers, the affirmative actions of their parents and schools establish college entry as the default path. Their high schools guide them through the multiple steps and deadlines of the college and financial aid process. Schools provide on-site SAT preparation, schedule exams for students, organize the writing of recommendations, and repeatedly remind students about relevant deadlines. Informal guidance and support is also provided by their college-educated relatives and neighbors, who act as de facto guidance counselors.

By contrast, due to their comparatively weak institutional and social supports, the default option for low-income students is not to go to college. Navigating the maze of college and aid applications requires both formal and informal support. Lower-income schools receive fewer visits from college representatives and have fewer guidance counselors per student. Parents and siblings are not as likely to have gone to college and so cannot compensate for this lack of institutional support.

What Is the Evidence That This Proposal Would Increase College Enrollments?

There is plenty of evidence that simple student aid programs can increase college enrollments by about 3 to 4 percentage points per $1,000 in grants (Dynarski 2002). Successful college aid programs include the Social Security student benefit program (Dynarski 2003), Georgia's HOPE (Helping

Outstanding Pupils Educationally) Scholarship program (Dynarski 2000, 2005), and similar state merit aid programs (Kane 2003; Dynarski 2004b, 2005). The common denominator of successful programs is that they have simple eligibility requirements, making it easy for families to discern their likely benefits well in advance.

By contrast, there is little to no persuasive evidence that the current Pell Grant program affects the college enrollment decisions of young people.[19] A plausible explanation is that the aid process effectively screens out students who are teetering on the margin of college entry. As described earlier, if our proposed program had the same effects as other simple programs, we might anticipate a 5.6 to 7.4 percentage point increase in college enrollments.

If Taxes Are Not Filed until Mid-April and Students Enroll in September, Will There Be Enough Time to Get Aid Vouchers to Students?

Note that students and families can closely estimate their eligibility simply by looking at the eligibility table, well before they even start thinking about filing their taxes. The question is whether and how this information can be forwarded from the IRS to the Department of Education in time for college enrollment, when funds are needed.

There are at least two ways around this problem. First, eligibility could be based on income from a previous tax year. Currently, aid eligibility for 2006–07 is based on income from the 2005 tax year. If it were instead based on the 2004 tax year, eligibility could be confirmed a full year prior to enrollment—in the fall of a student's senior year of high school, for example. Because the IRS can provide transcripts of up to three years of prior taxes (and does so for thousands of "no paperwork" mortgage applications each year), eligibility could even be based on an average of several prior years of income.

---

19. An early study by Hansen (1983) examined enrollment rates before and after implementation of the Pell Grant program. Hansen found that while enrollment rates of all income groups increased during the 1970s, enrollment among low-income students (the targets of the Pell Grant) did not increase. Kane (1995) used more years of data and limited the sample to women, whose enrollment patterns were less disrupted by the Vietnam War; he was also unable to find an effect. Seftor and Turner (2002) found a small effect of Pell Grants on college enrollment for older, independent students. Bettinger (2004) found suggestive evidence that Pell Grant size affects college completion but noted that his results were very sensitive to specification.

A second possible solution is for the IRS to forward preliminary income information to the Department of Education as soon as it is submitted, before the IRS completes its verification processes. Vouchers could then be mailed out on the basis of this preliminary information, with the understanding that awards will be adjusted if the information is found to be incorrect.

How Would This System Work for Students Who Are Not Required to File Taxes?

Approximately 640,000 (6 percent of) federal student aid applicants do not currently file a tax return (National Center for Education Statistics 2005). As with the Earned Income Tax Credit, families would have to file taxes if they wish to receive program benefits.[20] Many of these families would be able to file the 1040EZ tax form, which—at one page and only 37 questions—is significantly less burdensome than the FAFSA (five pages and 127 questions).

If a nonfiling student decides after the April 15 tax deadline to enroll in college, that individual could complete and submit an income tax form late, providing a copy to the school. While the student and school wait for eligibility to be verified, a compromise might be to require the school to apply the expected grant amount to tuition and fee charges but not allow the school to refund any excess funds to the student until eligibility can be verified.

Doesn't the FAFSA Already Provide Simplified Options for the Poorest Applicants?

Over the years, Congress has passed several provisions aimed at simplifying the aid formula. In 1992 Congress mandated an automatic-zero expected family contribution (EFC) for families with taxable income below $15,000 who are also eligible to file an IRS Form 1040A or 1040EZ. These applicants can potentially skip more than fifty of the financial questions on the FAFSA. In 1986 Congress mandated a "simplified needs test" for families earning less than $50,000 who are eligible to file the 1040A or 1040EZ; for these families, asset information can be disregarded.

---

20. For those rightly concerned about undocumented, immigrant students, such students are currently ineligible for federal student aid and the education tax incentives. They fare no better and no worse in our proposed system than they do in the current system.

While laudable in intent, these efforts have been ineffectual. As implemented, these simplifications have had virtually no impact on the aid system as it is experienced by students and their families. In our sample, just half of applicants from families with income between $5,000 and $15,000 had their applications processed using the automatic-zero EFC or the simplified needs test. Even among the applicants whose FAFSAs were flagged as having received this simplified treatment, the evidence indicates that the student's own application experience was not simplified. Among those who had their FAFSA processed using the simplified needs test and who were eligible to skip the asset questions, at least 48 percent provided asset information. Among those who had their application processed under the automatic-zero EFC formula, 90 percent had responded to questions that they were not required to answer.

In effect, these simplifications have only made things easier for the computer that processes aid applications. Simplifications are not communicated to students and their families; they are never mentioned on the paper FAFSA, which is used by about half of dependent, undergraduate applicants whose families' incomes are below $50,000 (National Center for Education Statistics 2005).[21] Even the online FAFSA only offers the option to skip the relevant questions midway through the application, and then it warns that some schools may require that the questions be answered.[22] This phrasing will frighten many students into filling in the complete application.

A critical shortcoming of these past efforts at simplification is that they have focused too heavily on simplifying the aid form itself, without adequate attention given to reducing complexity and uncertainty in the overall process. We must do more than simplify the application form; we must make it easier for students and their families to predict, years in advance of the college decision, how much aid they are likely to get.

21. Authors' calculations. Note that the Department of Education frequently claims that less than 10 percent of applicants use the paper form (see, for example, LeBlanc and Brown 2006, slide 43). However, this statistic is heavily weighted by renewal applicants, who are much more likely to use the online process. Nearly 30 percent of first-time applicants still use the paper form according to Office of Federal Student Aid (2005a) filing statistics, including the 6 percent of applicants who fill out a paper form and then have their school file their application electronically. Applicants from low-income families are even more likely to rely on the paper form.

22. Office of Federal Student Aid, "FAFSA on the Web—2006–2007 FAFSA on the Web Screen Shots," U.S. Department of Education October 25, 2005 (ifap.ed.gov/eannouncements/1025fotwscreenshot0607.html).

How Will States React to Federal Simplification?

One concern is that the states will not go along with the proposed program and will demand that students fill out complicated aid forms for state aid. This could make things worse for students if every state creates its own aid form to replace the FAFSA. Before the FAFSA was introduced in the early 1990s, different states had different aid application forms, generating confusion and duplicative paperwork for families. The goal of the FAFSA was to replace these multiple forms with a single form. The unfortunate product of this well-intended effort was a form that includes every data item needed by any state.

The Department of Education's timidity and the states' foot-dragging have crippled the effectiveness of two attempts to reduce complexity: the simplified needs test and the automatic-zero EFC. Both of these provisions should allow very low income aid applicants to skip many questions on the FAFSA. But the Department of Education does not provide a shortened FAFSA in paper form. All applicants who use the paper FAFSA are required to fill out the entire form. And in the online application process, the option to skip questions only appears if the student is from a state that has agreed to accept the shortened FAFSA, which thirty-two states have refused to do. Even for students from the remaining states, skipping questions is presented as an option, with the warning that it could compromise aid eligibility. Unsurprisingly, many students end up answering questions they do not have to.

So how do we keep the states from derailing this simplification effort? There are two questions to ask in this context. First, how much need-based state aid is there, and is that amount commensurate with the complexity its distribution imposes on millions of college students and their families? Second, is there a way to convince states to distribute their aid using less information?

How much state aid is there? The states give out a total of $4.2 billion in need-based grants (National Association of State Student Grant and Aid Programs [NASSGAP] 2005), about one-third as much grant aid as the federal system. And one-third of that amount is given out by states that have already agreed to the simplified data for low-income students described above. Moreover, a few generous states skew these figures; the typical state gives out less than $200 per undergraduate (NASSGAP 2005). That is a lot of complexity for not much money.

Can the states be convinced to make do with less data from aid applicants? No one likes change, but positive incentives can help elicit cooperation. We suggest that the federal government match state grants that determine need using only the data required for our proposal (adjusted gross income and household composition).[23] The Leveraging Educational Assistance Partnership Program could be the vehicle for such a matching program.[24]

How Will Colleges React to Federal Simplification?

One concern is that colleges will not agree to the change and will demand that students fill out complicated aid forms in order to get aid that is paid for out of the colleges' coffers ("institutional aid"). This could make things worse for students if every school creates its own aid form to replace the FAFSA. Schools that disburse substantial amounts of their own aid and enroll wealthy students already supplement the FAFSA with additional aid forms, such as the College Board's College Scholarship Service (CSS) PROFILE. About 270 schools (including only 6 public institutions) currently use the CSS PROFILE, out of more than 4,200 two- and four-year colleges nationwide. We anticipate that these schools will continue to use these forms in distributing their own aid, and we see no problem with that.

Why don't we care if elite schools use complicated forms to give out their own aid funds? First, it is their money. Second, any student who is confident enough to apply to an elite college is clearly not dissuaded from college by complexity and uncertainty in aid. Students discouraged by complexity and uncertainty in the aid system are more likely to attend community colleges and state universities.

For the typical student who attends a community college or state university, government aid is the only aid. These schools do not have their own funds of any consequence to distribute. Yes, a few have small pots of money, but then the costs and benefits of complexity must be considered. Should a community college impose a lengthy aid application on all its students in order to give out a tiny grant to a few students? They should not, we would argue, but they may do so, nonetheless. Therefore they should be provided with incentives to do the right thing. For example, a bonus could be added to the federal grants of students at schools who agree to use the simplified formula. The rule could be that any student who is eligible for the grant

23. This incentive could be put in place even if our full proposal is not implemented. As described above, many states refuse to accept simplified FAFSAs for low-income students. A carrot of matching grant funds might give those states the impetus to allow existing simplifications to work.

24. Thanks to Brian Fitzgerald for suggesting this approach.

shown in box 1 cannot be required to fill out a complicated form to access institutional funds, or else the school forfeits the bonus for its students.

Aid simplification could substantially benefit public colleges that are stressed by shrinking state support. Think about all of the money that goes into processing aid forms, verifying applications, and sending out award letters. Imagine if all the money and labor spent on these tasks could instead go into counseling and teaching students!

What about Loans?

The grants proposed are sufficient to cover tuition at community colleges and many public universities. They will not cover living expenses, or tuition at the more expensive public universities. As is the case now, loans would be necessary to cover the shortfall. We chose to focus our proposal on grants, to emphasize the point that existing grants and tax credits could be distributed simply while still maintaining the same distribution of aid. We can apply the same concepts and analysis to subsidized Stafford Loans and assign them based on income alone. In Dynarski and Scott-Clayton (2008), we show that this simplified approach has little effect on the targeting of loans.

In an ideal world, we would pair the simplified grant discussed in this chapter with an income-contingent loan program similar to those operating in Australia, New Zealand, and the United Kingdom (Chapman 2005; Barr 2004). In these programs, former college students repay their loans as a percentage of their payroll earnings. This forward-looking needs-analysis approach has good distributional characteristics: the beneficiaries of college pay for its costs, but they are insured against bad labor market draws that would saddle them with unsustainable loan payments.

Conclusions

There is no doubt that the federal aid system provides grants and loans to many families who would be worse off without it. There is little evidence that this aid gets more young people into college, however. In this chapter, we have proposed a radical simplification to the aid system that will preserve its distributive properties while enhancing its positive impact on schooling decisions.

The basics of need determination have changed little since they were laid out more than fifty years ago. At a College Board conference in 1953, John Monro, then dean of admissions at Harvard College, described to his colleagues at other elite colleges the formula he had been using to distribute aid to Harvard admits. The assembled college administrators were eager to establish a common formula for assigning aid so that they could quash the competitive bidding for the best students that had recently developed. Within a year, a common aid application was in use (the Parents' Confidential Statement) and the new CSS had been established by ninety-four charter members (Duffy and Goldberg 1998; Wilkinson 2005).

Then, as now, Harvard and other elite schools sought exhaustive measures of wealth and income to tailor their scholarships. Until 1973 the aid application asked about make and model of the family car (Wilkinson 2005). Today's FAFSA and aid formula reflect this peculiar history, providing extremely fine measures of ability to pay at levels of income that far exceed the effective cutoffs for federal aid. While these distinctions are critical at institutions that provide need-based grants to families with incomes well above $100,000 (Dynarski 2004a), we have shown that such fine measures are irrelevant for the distribution of Pell Grants.

The U.S. system for subsidizing college students hides information about the affordability of college behind a thicket of paperwork, and it delays sharing this information until it is too late. It is time for the federal aid system to uncouple itself from the needs of elite schools such as Harvard and Princeton, and concentrate on the needs of young people unnecessarily dissuaded from college by the impression that it is not affordable.

References

Abraham, Katharine G., and Melissa A. Clark. 2006. "Financial Aid and Students' College Decisions: Evidence from the District of Columbia Tuition Assistance Grant Program." *Journal of Human Resources* 41, no. 3: 578–610.

Advisory Committee on Student Financial Assistance. 2005. *The Student Aid Gauntlet: Making Access to College Simple and Certain.* Washington (January 23).

Avery, Christopher, and Thomas J. Kane. 2004. "Student Perceptions of College Opportunities: The Boston COACH Program." In *College Choices: The Economics of Where to Go, When to Go, and How to Pay for It,* edited by Caroline Hoxby, pp. 355–91. University of Chicago Press.

Barr, Nicholas. 2004. "Higher Education Funding." *Oxford Review of Economic Policy* 20, no. 1: 264–83.

Bershadker, Andrew, and Julie-Anne Cronin. 2002. "Winners (and Losers?) in the Search for Higher Education Tax Subsidies." Unpublished draft. U.S. Department of the Treasury, Office of Tax Analysis.

Bettinger, Eric. 2004. "How Financial Aid Affects Persistence." In *College Choices: The Economics of Where to Go, When to Go, and How to Pay for It,* edited by Caroline Hoxby, pp. 207–33. University of Chicago Press.

Blumenthal, Marsha, and Joel Slemrod. 1992. "The Compliance Cost of the U.S. Individual Income Tax System: A Second Look after Tax Reform." *National Tax Journal* 45, no. 2: 185–202.

Bound, John, and Sarah Turner. 2002. "Going to War and Going to College: Did World War II and the GI Bill Increase Educational Attainment for Returning Veterans?" *Journal of Labor Economics* 20, no. 4: 784–815.

Chapman, Bruce. 2005. "Income-Contingent Loans for Higher Education Reform: International Reform." Discussion Paper 491. Canberra: Australian National University, Centre for Economic Policy Research (June).

College Board. 2005. *Education Pays 2005*. New York.

———. 2006. *Trends in Student Aid 2006*. New York.

Cornwell, Christopher, David Mustard, and Deepa Sridhar. 2006. "The Enrollment Effects of Merit-Based Financial Aid: Evidence from Georgia's HOPE Program." *Journal of Labor Economics* 24, no. 4: 761–86.

Day, Jennifer Cheeseman, Alex Janus, and Jessica Davis. 2005. *Computer and Internet Use in the United States: 2003*. Publication P23–208. U.S. Bureau of the Census (October 2005).

Duffy, Elizabeth, and Idana Goldberg. 1998. *Crafting a Class: College Admissions and Financial Aid, 1955–1994*. Princeton University Press.

Dynarski, Susan M. 2000. "Hope for Whom? Financial Aid for the Middle Class and Its Impact on College Attendance." *National Tax Journal* 53, no. 3 (part 2): 629–61.

———. 2002. "The Behavioral and Distributional Implications of Aid for College." *American Economic Review* 92, no. 2: 279–85.

———. 2003. "Does Aid Matter? Measuring the Effect of Student Aid on College Attendance and Completion." *American Economic Review* 93, no. 1: 279–88.

———. 2004a. "Tax Policy and Education Policy: Collision or Coordination?" In *Tax Policy and the Economy*, vol. 18, edited by James M. Poterba, pp. 81–116. MIT Press.

———. 2004b. "The New Merit Aid." In *College Choices: The Economics of Where to Go, When to Go, and How to Pay for It*, edited by Caroline Hoxby, pp. 63–97. University of Chicago Press.

———. 2005. "Building the Stock of College-Educated Labor." Working Paper 11604. Cambridge, Mass.: National Bureau of Economic Research (September).

Dynarski, Susan M., and Judith E. Scott-Clayton. 2006a. "The Cost of Complexity in Federal Student Aid: Lessons from Optimal Tax Theory and Behavioral Economics." *National Tax Journal* 59, no. 2: 319–56.

———. 2006b. "The Feasibility of Delivering Aid for College through the Tax System." Paper presented at the National Tax Association Ninety-Ninth Annual Conference on Taxation. Boston, November 17.

———. 2008. "Complexity and Targeting in Federal Student Aid: A Quantitative Analysis." In *Tax Policy and the Economy*, vol. 22, edited by James M. Poterba, pp. 109–50. University of Chicago Press.

Hansen, W. Lee. 1983. "The Impact of Student Financial Aid on Access." In *The Crisis in Higher Education*, edited by Joseph Froomkin, pp. 84–96. New York: Academy of Political Science.

Joint Committee on Taxation. 2005. *Estimates of Federal Tax Expenditures for Fiscal Years 2005–2009*. JCS-1-05. Government Printing Office.

Kane, Thomas J. 1995. "Rising Public College Tuition and College Entry: How Well Do Public Subsidies Promote Access to College?" Working Paper 5164. Cambridge, Mass.: National Bureau of Economic Research.

———. 2003. "A Quasi-Experimental Estimate of the Impact of Financial Aid on College Going." Working Paper 9703. Cambridge, Mass.: National Bureau of Economic Research.

Kaplow, Louis. 1990. "Optimal Taxation with Costly Enforcement and Evasion." *Journal of Public Economics* 43, no. 2: 221–36.

———. 1996. "How Tax Complexity and Enforcement Affect the Equity and Efficiency of the Income Tax." *National Tax Journal* 49, no. 1: 135–50.

LeBlanc, Marilyn, and Michelle Brown. 2006. "Application Processing System Update." PowerPoint presentation by the Office of Federal Student Aid to the 2006 National Association of Student Financial Aid Administrators (NASFAA) Conference. Seattle, July.

Long, Bridget Terry. 2004. "The Impact of Federal Tax Credits for Higher Education Expenses." In *College Choices: The Economics of Where to Go, When to Go, and How to Pay for It,* edited by Caroline Hoxby, pp. 101–65. University of Chicago Press.

Madrian, Brigitte C., and Dennis F. Shea. 2001. "The Power of Suggestion: Inertia in 401(k) Participation and Savings Behavior." *Quarterly Journal of Economics* 116, no. 4: 1149–87.

National Association of State Student Grant and Aid Programs. 2005. *Thirty-Fifth Annual Survey Report on State-Sponsored Student Financial Aid: Academic Year 2003–04*. Washington.

National Center for Education Statistics. 2002. *National Education Longitudinal Survey of 1988: Public-Use Data and Electronic Codebook, Base Year through Fourth Follow-Up*. U.S. Department of Education. CD-ROM.

———. 2005. *2003–04 National Postsecondary Student Aid Survey: Restricted-Use Data and Electronic Codebook*. U.S. Department of Education. CD-ROM.

———. 2006. *Digest of Education Statistics: 2005*. U.S. Department of Education.

Office of Federal Student Aid. 2003a. *2003–2004 Federal Student Aid Handbook*. U.S. Department of Education.

———. 2003b. *2003–2004 Free Application for Federal Student Aid*. U.S. Department of Education.

———. 2005a. *2005–2006 Federal Student Aid Handbook*. U.S. Department of Education.

———. 2005b. *2006–2007 Free Application for Federal Student Aid*. U.S. Department of Education.

President's Advisory Panel on Federal Tax Reform. 2005. *Final Report of the President's Advisory Panel on Federal Tax Reform*. Government Printing Office.

Samuelson, William, and Richard Zeckhauser. 1988. "Status Quo Bias in Decision Making." *Journal of Risk and Uncertainty* 1, no. 1: 7–59.

Seftor, Neil, and Sarah Turner. 2002. "Back to School: Federal Student Aid Policy and Adult College Enrollment." *Journal of Human Resources* 37, no. 2: 336–52.

Skocpol, Theda. 1991. "Targeting within Universalism: Politically Viable Policies to Combat Poverty in the United States." In *The Urban Underclass,* edited by Christopher Jencks and Paul Peterson, pp. 411–36. Brookings.

Stanley, Marcus. 2003. "College Education and the Mid-Century GI Bills." *Quarterly Journal of Economics* 118 (May): 671–708.

Turner, Sarah, and John Bound. 2003. "Closing the Gap or Widening the Divide: The Effects of the GI Bill and World War II on the Educational Outcomes of Black Americans." *Journal of Economic History* 63, no. 1: 145–77.

Wilkinson, Rupert. 2005. *Aiding Students, Buying Students.* Vanderbilt University Press.

Investing in the Best and Brightest

Increased Fellowship Support for American Scientists and Engineers

9

RICHARD B. FREEMAN

There is widespread concern that the United States faces a problem in maintaining its position as the scientific and technological leader in the world and that loss of leadership threatens future economic well-being and national security. Business, science, and education groups have issued reports that highlight the value to the country of leadership in science and technology. Many call for new policies to increase the supply of scientific and engineering talent in the United States (see box 9-1). While the reports differ in emphasis, the basic message is uniform: the United States should spend more on research and development (R&D) and increase the number of young Americans choosing scientific and technological careers. In his 2006 State of the Union address, President Bush announced the American Competitiveness Initiative that concurred with these assessments: "For the U.S. to maintain its global economic leadership, we must ensure a continuous supply of highly trained mathematicians, scientists, engineers, technicians, and scientific support staff" (Office of Science and Technology Policy 2006, p.15).

In 1957, faced with the analogous challenge of Sputnik, the United States responded with increased R&D spending and by awarding large

I have benefited from the assistance of Holly Ming and from comments summarized by Timothy Taylor.

Box 9-1. Drumbeat of Concern about the Science and Engineering Workforce

We must "enhance the science-technology enterprise so the U.S. can compete, prosper, and be secure." (Committee on Prospering in the Global Economy 2005)

The Department of Defense and the defense industry are "having difficulty attracting and retaining the best and brightest students to the science and engineering disciplines relevant to maintaining current and future strategic strike capabilities." (U.S. Department of Defense 2006)

"To maintain our leadership amidst intensifying global economic competition, we must make the best use of talented and innovative individuals, including scientists, engineers, linguists, and cultural experts. . . . The nation must cultivate young talent and orient national economic, political, and educational systems to offer the greatest opportunities to the most gifted American and international students." (American Association of Universities 2006)

"If trends in U.S. research and education continue, our nation will squander its economic leadership, and the result will be a lower standard of living for the American people." (Council on Competitiveness 2005)

"Together, we must ensure that U.S. students and workers have the grounding in math and science that they need to succeed and that mathematicians, scientists and engineers do not become an endangered species in the United States." (Business Roundtable 2005)

"It is essential that we act now; otherwise our global leadership will dwindle, and the talent pool required to support our high-tech economy will evaporate. . . . This is not just a question of economic progress. Not only do our economy and quality of life depend critically on a vibrant R&D enterprise, but so too do our national and homeland security. . . . A robust educational system to support and train the best U.S. scientists and engineers and to attract outstanding students from other nations is essential for producing a world-class workforce and enabling the R&D enterprise it underpins." (Task Force on the Future of American Innovation 2005)

There is "a shortage of U.S. citizen scientists to work in sensitive national security programs." (Lewis 2005)

"The message is clear. Today's relentless search for global talent will reduce our national capacity to innovate unless we develop a science and engineering workforce that is second to none." (Building Engineering and Science Talent 2004)

"The United States is facing a crisis in science and engineering talent and expertise. For the United States to remain competitive in a vibrant global innovative and research environment, it must . . . attract, educate, recruit, and retain the best S&E workers. Assuring that the nation has the number and quality of scientists and engineers is a national imperative upon which the nation's security and prosperity rests entirely." (Jackson 2003)

"The Federal Government and its agencies must step forward to ensure the adequacy of the U.S. science and engineering workforce. All stakeholders must mobilize and initiate efforts that increase the number of U.S. citizens pursuing science and engineering studies and careers." (National Science Foundation 2003) numbers of National Science Foundation (NSF) Graduate Research and National Defense Education Act fellowships, which together induced a large number of young Americans to invest in science and engineering careers. In the early 1960s, the country gave about 1,000 NSF graduate research fellowships per year (Freeman, Chang, and Chiang 2005, p. 4). Forty-five years later, despite a more than threefold increase in the number of college students graduating in science and engineering and a global challenge from the spread of technology and higher education to the rest of the world, the United States still gives the same number of NSF fellowships (see figure 9-1).[1] With so many more college students, current U.S. NSF fellowship policy provides less of an incentive for students to enter science and engineering than did policies in the earlier period.

And yet, for all the concern about the number of scientists and engineers, there is no evidence of a classic labor market shortage for these specialists: no abnormally large numbers of vacancies, slow growth of employment, or rising wages for scientists or engineers. From the 1990s to 2004, employment in science and engineering increased at an annual rate of 3.2 percent to reach approximately 5.8 million in 2004—around 3.9 percent of the workforce (see figure 9-2).[2]

The number of employed PhD scientists and engineers increased from about 396,000 in 1990 to 581,800 in 2003.[3] This occurred while the earnings of scientists and engineers fell relative to those in some other occupations that use highly educated workers. Employment of computer specialists, which boomed in the 1990s, fell short of Bureau of Labor Statistics projections as many firms offshored work to lower-wage countries.[4] Enrollments

1. The NSF includes social science and psychology in its definition of sciences and awards graduate fellowships in those fields, which makes this expansive definition the appropriate one for analysis. The story is much the same if one considers degrees solely in engineering and the natural and biological sciences, however. In 1960 the United States graduated 89,443 persons with natural science and engineering bachelor's degrees (NSF 1965, table V-13); by 2002 that number had risen to 219,175 (NSF 2006c, table 2–26), a 2.45-fold increase.

2. Estimates of the number of scientists and engineers vary with the definition used and source of data (NSF 2006c, table 3–1; Pollak 1999).

3. The 2003 figures are for employed doctorate scientists and engineers (NSF 2005, table 1). The 1990 data are estimated from NSF (1995, table 2) and Lehming (1998); I have averaged the numbers for data from 1991 and 1989. I use the word "about" for the 1990 statistics because they come from two separate surveys.

4. Between 2000 and 2002, the Bureau of Labor Statistics reduced its projected increases in demand for computer and mathematical scientists over the next decade by half, or 1 million jobs (Sargent 2004).

Figure 9-1. Graduate Research Fellowships (GRFs) as Proportion of Science and Engineering (S&E) Bachelor's Graduates, 1952–2004

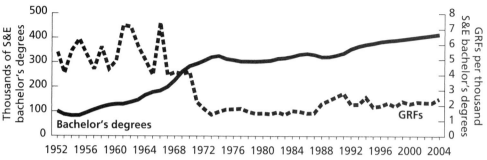

Sources: Cumulative index and related data sets are from NSF-DGE (various years). Bachelor's degree data tabulated by NSF Division of Science Resources Studies; data from U.S. Department of Education.

Figure 9-2. Science and Engineering Workforce in the United States, 1983–2004

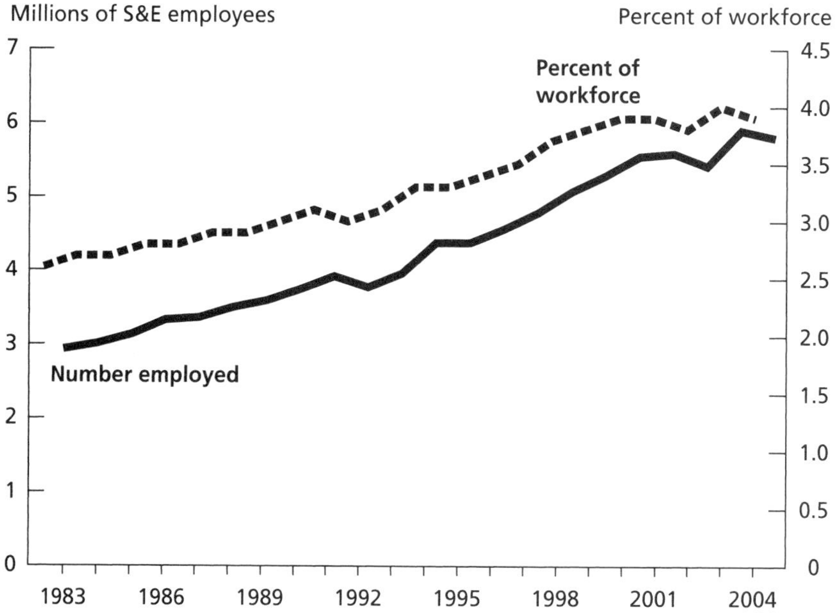

Millions of S&E employees   Percent of workforce

Source: NSF (2006c, figure 3-04).

in computer sciences fell.[5] From the perspective of persons choosing a career, the prospects in science and engineering seemed highly uncertain.

Past experience with alleged shortages of science and engineering workers shows, moreover, that just because the scientific and technological establishment declares that the country needs more scientists and engineers does not make it so. The United States has sometimes erroneously rung alarm bells about a shortage of scientists and engineers.

The country first became concerned with shortfalls in the science and engineering workforce in the late 1950s and early 1960s, prompted by the Soviet Union's surprise launch of Sputnik in 1957 and the failure of the first two U.S. attempts to launch a satellite into space. Congress enacted the *National Defense Education Act of 1958* and increased federal R&D. In this period, the earnings of scientists and engineers rose rapidly, so the labor market confirmed that demand had grown relative to supply. In the early 1980s, however, NSF proclaimed a shortage of scientists and engineers that turned out to be unjustified. The shortage was based on policymakers' erroneous use of data, possibly motivated by a desire to reduce the cost of scientists and engineers to large firms.[6]

In 1990 Richard C. Atkinson (1990), then president of the American Association for the Advancement of Science, predicted that by the year 2000, demand for scientists in the United States would outstrip supply by almost 400,000. He recommended programs to encourage more young people to pursue doctorates in science and engineering. But four years later, there was no evidence of a shortage.[7]

Is there a real problem in the job market for scientists and engineers today? If so, what sort of policies might resolve the problem? This chapter argues that the country's problem in the science and engineering job market differs greatly from a classical labor market shortage. The problem is twofold: first, inadequate investment in R&D for the economic and security well-being of the country, which keeps earnings and opportunities in science and engineering occupations below what would attract large numbers of young Americans from competing occupations; and second, unlimited access

5. Ed Frauenheim, "Students Saying No to Computer Science," August 11, 2004 (www.news.com/Students-saying-no-to-computer-science/2100-1022_3-5306096.html).

6. See Eric Weinstein, "How and Why Government, Universities, and Industry Create Domestic Labor Shortages of Scientists and High-Tech Workers" (www.nber.org/~peat/PapersFolder/Papers/SG/NSF.html).

7. See Sharon Begley, Lucy Shackelford, and Adam Rogers, "No PhDs Need Apply: The Government Said We Wouldn't Have Enough Scientists. Wrong," *Newsweek*, December 5, 1994, pp. 62–63.

to immigrant scientists and engineers, who can fill demands at going wages. As long as the United States enjoys an ample supply of immigrant scientists and engineers, it cannot have a classic labor market shortage. The worst it can have is an imbalance between the supply of citizens and immigrants.

I present a policy—increasing the number and value of graduate fellowships in science and engineering—that can augment the supply of U.S. students in science and engineering without impairing access to immigrant scientists and engineers, and I give evidence that this policy would work. If the United States increases research spending, as laid out in the American Competitiveness Initiative and other proposals, and if the nation takes steps to improve the career opportunities for young scientists and engineers, the expanded fellowship policy would help solve the science and engineering workforce issues that have produced the outpouring of concerns documented in box 9-1.

Understanding the Problem

Since the end of World War II, the United States has had a disproportionate share of the world's science and technology resources. The reasons are largely historic: the destruction of European higher education and science by the Nazis and World War II; development of mass college education in the United States before Europe; R&D expansion after Sputnik; and the low investment in higher education in China, India, and other developing countries. In 2005 the United States employed about 31 percent of the world's science and engineering researchers and financed 35 percent of R&D while accounting for 5 percent of the world's population and 21 percent of the world's GDP (Freeman 2006, p. 123). Excellence in science and engineering has spurred U.S. economic growth and created a comparative advantage in high-tech industries.

The U.S. share of global science and engineering activity is declining, however, and will continue to decline in the next decade or so. Some loss is inevitable, as the rest of the world catches up in higher education and R&D from low baselines. Between 1970 and 2000, the U.S. share of college students in the world fell from 30 to 14 percent (United Nations Educational, Scientific and Cultural Organization [UNESCO] 2004).[8] The U.S. share of science and engineering graduates was lower than its share of

---

8. I have filled in missing observations by taking the enrollments from the nearest year for which data are available. Tertiary-level students are not always college students, so these data are imperfect. However, using data for college enrollments reported by individual countries, I obtain estimates of the U.S. share comparable to the tertiary enrollment figures of UNESCO.

college students overall because science and engineering attract large proportions of students from overseas (NSF 2006c, appendix table 2–38). At the doctorate level, the U.S. share of science and engineering degrees fell from about 40 percent in 1970 to 20 percent in 2000, and is expected to reach 15 percent in 2010 (Freeman 2006, exhibit 5.1). The U.S. share of world R&D spending has been declining for decades, and that trend continues today: between 1990 and 2003, it declined from 40 to 35 percent (Organization for Economic Cooperation and Development [OECD] 2006).[9]

Commensurately, the U.S. share of scientific publications and citations has also fallen. Data from the Chemical Abstracts Services show that in 1980 the United States had published 73 percent of papers in the field, whereas in 2003 U.S. researchers had published 40 percent of the papers (Heylin 2004, p. 40). The NSF has documented a downward trend in the U.S. share of citations and of the most cited articles in science and engineering. Between 1992 and 2003, the U.S. share of the top 1 percent of cited articles fell from 64.6 to 56.6 percent, while its share of the top 10 percent of cited articles fell from 56 to 46.5 percent (NSF 2006c, figure O-18).

Responding to the spread of scientific and engineering talent around the world, the multinational firms who undertake most industrial R&D are investing in R&D in China and India. In 2004 China reported that multinationals had established more than 600 R&D facilities, whereas in 1990 they had none.[10] In 1990 the United States spent 7.1 times as much on R&D as China spent; in 2003 it spent only 3.3 times as much.[11]

While the United States will not have the dominance in science and technology in the future that it had from the 1950s through 2000, it can still be the leading center in scientific and technological progress if it invests more in R&D and undertakes policies to make science and engineering careers more attractive to young people.

Why Care?

Expansion of modern scientific and technological activity throughout the world will make the lives of Americans better in many ways. More research

9. Since these data cover only nine non-OECD countries, U.S. shares given are upper bound estimates (NSF2006c, figure O–1).

10. "Multinational Corporations Establish 600 R&D Centers in China," *Financial Times*, August 23, 2004.

11. The NSF (1993) estimates that China spent $21.4 billion on R&D in 1990, while the Census Bureau (1995, p. 611, table 979) reports that the United States spent $151.5 billion in that year. The 2004 figures are from OECD (2006). All estimates for China in the earlier period are problematic.

will produce more knowledge, innovation, and technological change and advance productivity, which should improve living standards. If a medical scientist in China, India, or anywhere else finds a cure for cancer, we will be ecstatic about the spread of scientific excellence around the world. If a German innovation lowers the price of goods and services, we all benefit. Scientific advances and innovations overseas that lead firms to set up production facilities in the United States will create jobs as well as better products. So why do the reports on science and engineering quoted in box 9-1 view expansion of the science and engineering workforce overseas with concern?

There are three arguments for greater investment in science and engineering and for increasing the supplies of scientists and engineers. First, since the United States is at the frontier of modern technology, American economic growth depends on technological and scientific advances. Other economies can grow by moving their production to the frontier of modern knowledge, but the United States must advance that frontier. The United States is more likely to maintain a healthy share of leading-edge industries—which have the fastest productivity growth, pay higher wages to production workers, and offer spillovers of knowledge to other sectors—if it pioneers scientific advances than if other countries do.[12] The growth of high-tech employment in Silicon Valley and in university-based locations of scientific excellence suggests that innovation, production, and employment in high-tech fields occur largely in areas strong in basic science.[13] The supply of scientists and engineers is a major factor in the location of these centers of excellence.

Second, the comparative U.S. advantage in trade lies in high-tech research-intensive industries. Were the United States to lose its advantage in those sectors, it would have to sell goods or services with lower technological content on the global market. The gains from trade would lessen, and wages would fall for American workers. The United States needs topflight researchers advancing the technological frontier to maintain its advantage

12. For evidence on the impact of R&D on productivity, see Jones and Williams (1998). Earnings of production and nonsupervisory workers in the three high R&D intensive sectors—aerospace, chemicals, and computers and electronic products—are $26.48, $19.17, and $19.15 per hour, respectively, compared to $16.70 per hour for production and nonsupervisory workers in other sectors in the country (Census Bureau 2006, table B-16).

13. Darby and Zucker (2006) show that industry develops in areas where star researchers work in nearby universities. Similarly, U.S. states with greater supplies of university graduates have been in the forefront of the new economy (Atkinson, Court, and Ward 1999).

in the face of the growth of scientific and technological capacity in China, India, and other developing countries, which will have a cost edge in high-tech as well as in other sectors until their wages approach ours.[14]

Third, U.S. defense depends on a technically sophisticated military, which requires an ample supply of scientists and engineers to the U.S. Department of Defense and to defense-related industries. Science and technology offer the best defense against chemical, biological, or radiological attacks by terrorists. In addition, the National Security Agency and some Defense Department laboratories hire only U.S. citizens, so the country must ensure a healthy supply of citizens in the relevant fields. The science and engineering workforce in security areas has become top-heavy with older workers, which will create large replacement demands for citizen researchers. In sum, there are good reasons for the United States to want to maintain a large science and engineering workforce for the economic strength of the country and national security. But "where's the beef" in the labor market?

Indicators of the labor market for scientists and engineers—salaries, unemployment rates, the length of time it takes graduates to obtain work, the proportion who obtain jobs in their area of specialization—show no sign of shortages. Rather, the data suggest that the job market has weakened for young workers in science and engineering relative to many other high-level occupations, which discourages U.S. students from pursuing these fields. For example, between the 1990 and 2000 censuses, earnings increased more for lawyers and doctors than for Ph.D. scientists and engineers (Freeman 2006, exhibit 5.3).

A major reason for the absence of any shortage of scientists and engineers is that the United States attracts large numbers of international science and engineering students and immigrant employees to its universities and workplaces. Table 9-1 shows that the share of immigrant scientists and engineers in 1990 and 2000 increased greatly at every educational level, helping to fuel the 1990s boom. As long as the United States remains a highly desirable worksite for scientists and engineers, the country cannot face a classic labor shortage. It can import scientists and engineers just as it

---

14. During the cold war, the Soviet Union challenged U.S. technological dominance in the military area only. The challenge from Japan in the 1980s in high-tech was limited because Japan had a much smaller population than the United States and had labor costs only modestly lower than those in the United States. It is the combination of large numbers of scientific and engineering workers with low wages that differentiates the current situation from the earlier one.

Table 9-1. Trend in Immigrant Share of Science and Engineering Employment, 1990 versus 2000

Percent

	Year	
Degree level	1990	2000
Bachelor's	11	17
Master's	19	29
All Ph.D.'s	24	38
Ph.D.'s less than 45 years old	27	52
Postdoctorate[a]	49	55

Source: Freeman, Chang, and Chiang (2005, exhibit 5.2). The census sources were from the 1990 and 2000 censuses and IPUMS data (Ruggles and others 2004).The source for postdocs was the NSF (2006c, figure 2-29).
a. For postdocs, the numbers refer to temporary residents rather than all immigrants.

imports goods and services, and can obtain whatever number of scientists and engineers it desires.

So why do the groups quoted in box 9-1 want to encourage domestic production of scientists and engineers? One reason is that the United States has the leading university system in the world, so that U.S.-trained scientists and engineers tend to be of higher quality than those trained elsewhere. This favors domestic production of graduates, some of whom will be U.S. natives, and some of whom will be international students. Another reason is that reliance on immigrant supplies involves the risk of a sudden cutoff of international students or immigrant workers due to political problems or to decisions to return home in large numbers. The post–September 11 fears about visa restrictions on international scholars exemplify this problem. U.S. students are also more likely to respond to the U.S. job market and changes in national priorities than are international students. U.S. students' knowledge of American society and its can-do culture might also enable them to make unique contributions to the scientific endeavor and to economic innovations, though I know of no evidence to support this possibility. Finally, the National Security Agency and government labs that limit hires to U.S. citizens rely on U.S. Ph.D.'s in science and engineering.

I conclude that the United States should seek some reasonable balance of native and immigrant scientists and engineers in the workforce. The "best and brightest" fellowship policy that I describe next is designed to accomplish this by increasing the supply of citizens in science and engineering without restricting the flows from overseas.

The Proposal: More and Higher-Paying Stipends

If the United States wants to increase the flow of citizens choosing scientific and engineering careers, an appropriate policy to achieve this would be to increase the number and value of fellowships for graduate work. I propose that the National Science Foundation triple the number of graduate research fellowships (GRFs) for science and engineering work and increase the value of those awards relative to earnings elsewhere in the economy. The increased number of fellowships would induce students who have an interest and ability in science and engineering to proceed to graduate training and research careers. The increase in the value of the awards would keep the quality of awardees high even with the larger number of fellowships being granted.

As noted at the outset, current NSF fellowship policy offers less incentive for young students to enter science and engineering than it did in the 1950s because NSF gives approximately the same 1,000 GRFs that it did in the 1950s and 1960s when the United States had far fewer undergraduate degrees in science and engineering. Tripling the number of NSF awards would roughly restore the ratio of GRFs to undergraduate science and engineering degrees that the country had after the Sputnik challenge. It would send a dramatic signal to American students that the country wants them to specialize in these areas.

To be sure, NSF is one of many government agencies that award fellowships for graduate study, and fellowships are only one way the government supports graduate students. Seventy percent of government-supported science and engineering graduate students receive research assistantships. In 2004, 7,301 full-time graduate students in science and engineering fields in doctorate-granting institutions received federal government fellowships. Approximately 3,300 were NSF GRF recipients, which makes NSF the largest grantor of fellowships (NSF 2006a). The second-largest awarder of fellowships is the National Institutes of Health (NIH), which in fiscal 2005 supported 1,267 fellowships and funded 8,367 students on training grants to institutions in the biomedical fields relevant to its mission.[15]

---

15. See National Institutes of Health, "Number of Pre-Doctoral and Post-Doctoral Research Training Positions on NIH Training Grants and Fellowships," PowerPoint chart, National Research Service Awards (NRSA), Fiscal Years 1996–2005. Among the other agencies granting awards are the U.S. Department of Defense, which gives National Defense Science and Engineering Graduate three-year fellowships annually; the U.S. Department of Homeland Security, which gives graduate fellowships; different parts of the Department of Energy, which provide awards to fields relevant to their mission; and NASA, which grants 300 awards annually as part of its Graduate Student Researchers Program. The NSF (2006a, table 41) provides the numbers for some of these agencies, as well.

NSF GRFs operate differently from fellowships that come from other agencies. NSF awards students depending on the number of qualified applicants in different fields rather than according to disciplines to meet some agency goal. Thus NSF GRFs are the only awards that can ensure a comprehensive research base and that allow the market, through student choice, to determine the attractiveness of different fields.

Can Fellowship Policy Affect Supply?

Increasing the incentives for students to invest in science and engineering can affect the number of young people pursuing these fields if the supply of scientific talent is constrained due to economic factors rather than to lack of interest or ability in science and engineering on the part of young Americans. The evidence in figure 9-1 of large rising numbers of graduates with bachelor of science or engineering degrees suggests that the country has many able candidates for further education. More and higher-valued fellowships are likely to increase the number of these graduates going on to advanced training for two reasons. First, coming early in someone's career, fellowships represent a large proportion of discounted lifetime earnings for science and engineering specialists. Second, fellowships signal that the person has the talent to have a successful career. Receipt of a prestigious fellowship carries nonmonetary as well as monetary weight in career considerations.

Between 1999 and 2005, NSF altered its GRF policies in a way that allows researchers to estimate the response of students to changes in policies. In 1999 the NSF's Committee of Visitors noted "the GRF awards are no longer as attractive as they once were" and recommended that the stipend value be raised from $15,000 to $18,000. NSF went much farther, raising the value of the stipend to $27,500 in 2002 and to $30,000 in 2005 without increasing the number of rewards. As can be seen in figure 9-3a, the result was that the number of applicants per bachelor's degree in science and engineering nearly doubled. Figure 9-3a shows a tight link between the number of applicants relative to the number of science and engineering bachelor degrees and the total amount spent on NSF awards relative to GDP. The statistical analysis in Freeman, Chang, and Chiang (2005, table 6, column 4) suggests that a 10 percent increase in the number of NSF awards granted increases the number of applicants by 0.349 log points, or 41 percent, while slight variants of the model give modestly different estimates (author's calculations). While it is difficult to determine if the increase in awards attracts students on the margin of going into science, or if the increase goes largely to students who would study

Figure 9-3a. Science and Engineering Bachelor's Graduates Applying to the GRF Program and Total GRF Budget as a Fraction of GDP, 1952–2004

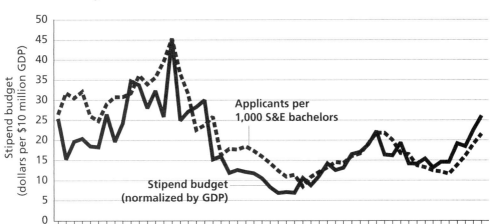

Sources: NSF-DGE (various years) for cumulative index of the GRF program and related data sets. Data on the GDP from the Bureau of Economic Analysis.

science and engineering in any event, the available evidence supports the notion that an increase of NSF awards raises the supply of students. Figure 9-3b shows that the fraction of bachelor's graduates enrolled in science and engineering programs is positively related to the NSF stipend budget relative to GDP. Statistical analysis suggests that a 10 percent increase in NSF spending on GRFs increases the number of graduate enrollments by 7 to 15 percent (depending on the statistical model; author's calculations, available on request). Since NSF supports a relatively small number of graduate students, this smaller impact on total enrollments than on applicants for awards makes sense. That the estimates are positive suggests that the spending affects students on the margin, though the channels by which it does so may be complicated.

Another way to assess potential student response to fellowship incentives is to ask students how fellowship support would affect their career decisions. In winter 2006, one of my students asked nearly 1,800 Harvard undergraduates, "If you won a national fellowship for graduate study of a year, would you go on to graduate work in science and engineering?" (Shukla 2006). Seventy-three percent of the science concentrators said that they would go on. Forty percent of all students said they would go on to

Figure 9-3b. Fraction of Science and Engineering Bachelor's Graduates Enrolling in Science and Engineering Graduate Programs versus Total GRF Budget as a Fraction of GDP, 1966–2003

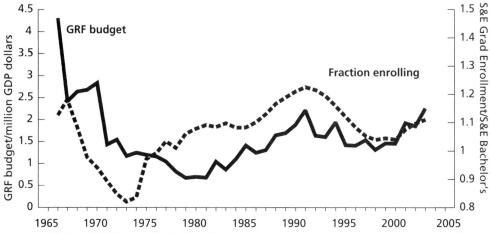

Source: GRF budget divided by GDP and bachelor's graduates in science and engineering as shown in figure 9-3a. For enrollments in science and engineering graduate programs, see NSF (2006a).

graduate study in science—which was more than twice the 18 percent who said that they intended to go on to careers in science and engineering. She also asked the students, "If you were offered a scholarship of $20,000 annually in college to pursue a career in science and engineering research, would this affect your career choices?" Fourteen percent of all students said they would change their career plans and pursue a science and engineering career, which would bring the proportion to 32 percent. While the questions are hypothetical, the responses show potentially sizable responsiveness to fellowship support.

Can the Number of Fellowship Awards Be Increased without Greatly Reducing the Quality of Those Obtaining the Awards?

Figure 9-4 shows that a significant number of applicants who did not receive awards have characteristics only modestly weaker than those of awardees, so that the number of awards can be increased substantively without greatly reducing the quality of students. In addition, the fact that higher-value stipends attract some applicants that are more able could offset any potential reductions in quality.

Figure 9-4. Quality of GRF Program Applicants on the Margin of Receiving an Award Compared to the Quality of Awardees, 2004[a]

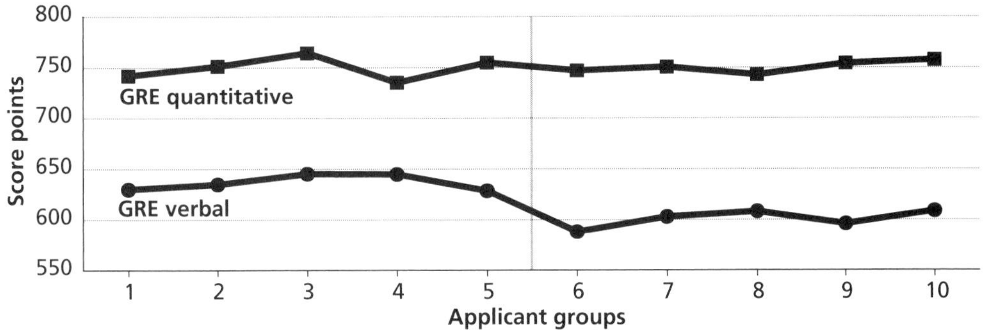

Source: Author's calculations.

a. All persons to the *left* of the line were given awards; all persons to the *right* of the line were not given awards. Applicant groups consisted of fifty persons, ordered by the estimated probability they would win an NSF award. The group 5 consists of fifty awardees with the lowest probability of getting an award, group 4 consists of fifty awardees with the next lowest probability, and so on. Group 6 consists of the fifty nonawardees with the highest probability of getting an award. The probabilities are predicted values from an ordinary least squares regression of an award receipt dummy variable on panel rating, female dummy, underrepresented minority dummy, and eight field dummies.

How Would Other Stipend Providers React if NSF Raised the Number and Value of Awards?

Universities, foundations, and other agencies responded to the large 1999–2005 increased value of NSF awards by raising the value of their own awards. Some complained to NSF about this. Because universities depend greatly on direct government moneys for research and indirect government moneys for teaching, the government ultimately paid some of these added costs. However, the propagation of the increase beyond the 1,000 recipients presumably helped boost overall graduate enrollments. Increasing the number of fellowship awards is unlikely to have such an effect, since the other awards will remain competitively valued with the NSF's awards.

Would an Expanded NSF Fellowship Program Largely Benefit the Elite Universities?

The elite universities would undoubtedly attract a large share of an increased number of graduate fellowship awards, as they do currently, but the growth of Ph.D. production in the United States from the 1960s to the present has not been at these universities. Most of the growth in science

Figure 9-5. Percentage of NSF Fellowships Awarded to Women, 1952–2004[a]

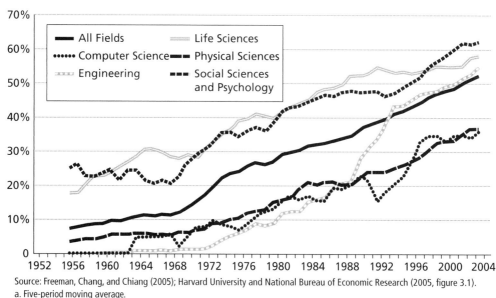

Source: Freeman, Chang, and Chiang (2005); Harvard University and National Bureau of Economic Research (2005, figure 3.1).
a. Five-period moving average.

and engineering doctorate production has occurred at less prestigious universities (Freeman, Jin, and Shen 2004), some of which have become world-class universities—for example, the University of California, San Diego. The reason why the growth of science and engineering Ph.D.'s has been concentrated among newer programs is that many elite universities have reached what they view as optimal size and are not eager to expand their enrollments. Thus the benefits of the proposed new NSF GRFs are likely to be spread widely among research universities.

To What Extent Will an Enhanced Fellowship Program Attract More Women and Minority Students?

Figure 9-5 shows the sizable increase in the proportion of NSF GRFs awarded to women from the onset of the program in the 1950s though 2004. The proportion of women winning these fellowships has increased from fewer than 10 percent to more than 50 percent. The proportion of underrepresented minority students winning fellowships has also increased (Freeman, Chang, and Chiang 2005, figure 5). Analysis of the responses of female and minority undergraduate science and engineering majors to changes in the NSF graduate fellowship program shows similar behavior to the responses of men: more apply to the program when the rewards are greater or the number of NSF awards increases.

This evidence, together with analyses of student career choices that find substantial responses to economic incentives, implies that fellowship policies are likely to have an impact on enrollments in science and engineering.

Costs and Benefits

Suppose that more students will continue in science and engineering if they can gain graduate fellowship support for their studies. With NSF having established high values for awards, the appropriate margin on which to adjust awards is in the number granted. If the country takes seriously the various reports quoted in box 9-1, a reasonable target would be to restore to post-Sputnik levels the number of NSF awards relative to the number of bachelor of science and engineering graduates. This means increasing the number of NSF GRFs granted per year from about 1,000 to about 3,000. Since NSF selects persons with the highest measurable qualifications, such a large increase would risk some decline in the quality of awardees. To counterbalance this, I propose increasing the value of the fellowships. Higher-valued fellowships will attract more highly able candidates, from which NSF can select the best.

Box 9-2 summarizes the costs of the proposed fellowship policy. Currently, the NSF gives about 1,000 awards, each of which provides $30,000 to the student and $10,500 to the university they attend to help pay for the cost of their education. Since the awards are for three years of graduate training, the total cost to the taxpayer is $121.5 million a year. Tripling the number of awards without changing their value would increase NSF spending to $364.5 million. If, in addition, the value of fellowships were to be increased to $40,000 and the support to universities increased commensurately to $14,000, the total annual cost of the program would rise to nearly $500 million a year.

What would the country get for this expenditure? It would get more top students studying and earning doctorate and master's degrees in science and engineering. Even if the new fellowships went entirely to students who would go into science and engineering in any case, funding those students would free money for universities and other funders to support additional students in science and engineering. In this case, graduate enrollments and master's or doctorate degrees would increase by approximately the additional 2,000 awards. In 2004, 15,721 U.S. citizens earned science and engineering Ph.D.'s, down from 18,997 in 1995 (NSF 2006b, table 3). An increase of 2,000 Ph.D.'s would be a 13 percent increment on the

Box 9-2. Costs and Outcomes from Expanded GRF Program

Current costs of NSF GRF program: 1,000 GRFs of $30,000 for each fellow and $10,500 as cost of education allowance to the university, for a total cost of $40.5 million per cohort. Since awards are for three years, the commitment is approximately $122 million in a given year.

Proposed Change 1: Increasing the Number of Awards

Increase awards from 1,000 to 3,000 a year, at $30,000 per award and $10,500 to the university. Costs:
  —year 1: $81 million additional cost over current program;
  —year 2: $162 million additional cost over current program;
  —year 3: $243 million additional cost over current program (steady-state cost).

Proposed Change 2: Increasing the Number of Awards and Increasing the Value of Awards, to Keep the Quality High

Increase the number of awards from 1,000 to 3,000 a year, at $40,000 per award and $15,000 to the university. Costs:
  —year 1: $125 million additional cost over current program;
  —year 2: $250 million additional cost over current program;
  —year 3: $375 million additional cost over current program (steady-state cost).

Outcomes

  —An increase in the number of top students getting science and engineering degrees, producing an increase of about 13 percent or more in U.S.-born science and engineering Ph.D.'s per year.
  —Greater ability to meet the labor demands from prospective increased R&D spending and the retirement of baby-boom scientists and engineers, without raising salaries.
  —Additional supplies that strengthen the scientific and technology-intensive parts of the economy and help maintain comparative U.S. advantage in high tech.
  —Increase in the supply of citizen scientists and engineers available for defense and national security projects.

current rate (see figure 9-6). If, as some of the estimates suggest, a 10 percent increase in the NSF budget would boost graduate enrollments by 7 to 15 percent, then the proposed quadrupling of the budget would imply even larger increases. Even with an expanded number of NSF awards, most students who applied for the awards would not win one. Nevertheless, many young people would be thinking seriously about scientific careers as a result of their application and might seek other support.

The benefit to the country is not, however, an increased supply of U.S. citizen scientists or engineers, but rather the economic and security gains that they might bring. While no one can be sure of the particular areas

Figure 9-6. Expected Impact of Increasing NSF GRFs on the Number of U.S. Citizens Graduating with Ph.D.'s in Science and Engineering, 2009–2015

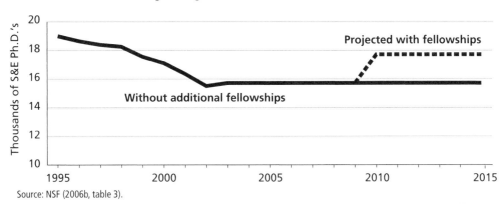

Source: NSF (2006b, table 3).

where an increased number of scientists and engineers might make their greatest contribution, our recent history is filled with examples where young innovative researchers have made major contributions to economic progress: the Internet, the biotech industry, the personal computer, and the mathematics of cryptography that underpins Internet commerce. The buzz today is about nanotechnology, though no one is sure in what areas (if any) it will pay off. Given the potential dangers from global warming and climate change, rising costs of energy, terrorist threats of diverse forms, and environmental pollution, there are many places where a larger supply of scientists and engineers could pay off in higher productivity and better lives. But simply producing more graduates will not by itself produce scientific and technological advances nor will it substantially affect the future supply of such workers. There must also be a commensurate increase in R&D spending that raises the demand for scientists and engineers.

The Demand Side of the Equation

Assuming that more and better-paying fellowships induce more people to become scientists and engineers, what will happen to them after they graduate? If R&D spending does not increase more rapidly than in recent years, and if federal spending for basic research languishes, the new doctorate graduates will find that the job market does not live up to their expectations. The increase in U.S.-born scientists and engineers would reduce wages and opportunities, which in turn would reduce the impact of the fellowships on the future supply of such professionals. The citizen share of the nation's science and engineering workforce would be higher than otherwise, which could help meet some of the national security concerns, but the overall supply would not increase much. Many young scientists would likely leave science in their thirties and forties for other jobs, or decide to pursue their science careers in other countries where they might find adequate funding, as MIT has recently reported about two young physicists to whom it had offered employment.[16] In this case, I would see little value to expanding the number of GRFs.

But both the executive and legislative branches of government have proposed sizable increases in research spending that should create greater demand for scientists and engineers. The Bush administration's American Competitiveness Initiative commits $50 billion to increase funding for research over ten years. NSF spending would double between 2007 and 2016 from $5.6 billion to $11.2 billion (Office of Science and Technology Policy 2006). In addition, the initiative promises $86 billion for R&D tax incentives, which would further increase demand. In the *National Innovation Act of 2005* (U.S. Senate 2005), a bipartisan group of senators committed to science and innovation called for doubling the NSF budget by 2011. Such increases are necessary to improve the career prospects of young scientists and to justify a large increase in the number of NSF graduate research fellowships.

Still, the experience in doubling NIH research spending from 1996 through 2002 suggests that increasing research spending by itself does not necessarily improve the career prospects of young scientists. Most of the NIH moneys went to senior scientists, who hired newly minted Ph.D.'s from the United States and overseas as postdocs in their laboratories, often on large research projects. The chances of young scientists getting their own grants fell from what it had been in the 1970s. If this happened again, it would reduce the career attractiveness of science and engineering and counteract the purposes of the "best and brightest" fellowship policy. Expanding the NSF fellows program would work best if it were accompanied by structural changes in R&D funding programs, such as special awards for young scientists and engineers and increased fellowship support for postdocs so that they are not completely dependent on principal investigators for research funding. The National Academies' report, *Rising above the Gathering Storm* (Committee on Prospering in the Global Economy

16. In 2006 the MIT physics department reported that two young researchers turned down MIT job offers to work in Europe, where they were more able to get funding. Sarah Shipley Hiles, "Young Scientists Hit the Hardest as U.S. Funding Falls," *Boston Globe*, January 23, 2006.

2005), and some of the other reports quoted in box 9-1, have made some suggestions along these lines. Ideally, the best and brightest fellowships would focus NSF and other agencies on developing research spending policies to help young investigators advance their careers.

In sum, the policy of providing additional fellowships should be seen as part of a broader set of policies that increases demand for science and engineering workers and offers greater career opportunities to young investigators.

Alternatives and Concerns

There are two other policies through which the United States can increase the employment of scientists and engineers, as either complements or substitutes for the proposed increase in fellowship support. The first is to encourage more foreign-born scientists and engineers to immigrate to this country. The second is to strengthen science and math education from kindergarten through grade twelve (K–12) so that the United States has more young people with the interests and talents to go into science and engineering. These policies are almost polar opposites. The first free rides on the interests and talents of persons born overseas and on the lower wages and limited research facilities available in their native countries; the second seeks to build up domestic supplies over the long run. I discuss each in turn.

Free Riding on Foreign Talent

At present, the United States can hire as many high-quality scientists and engineers from overseas as it wants. Some of the best international students come to the United States and choose to stay and work here. Many become citizens. The United States also attracts many foreign-trained scientists and engineers as immigrants. Why should the country spend anything to support U.S. students in science and engineering when it can exploit the brain drain and get immigrant talent?

One reason why this strategy—ignoring domestic supplies in favor of relying on a perpetual global brain drain—is undesirable is that the United States is an excellent source of talented science and engineering students, about whose abilities our universities have greater knowledge than about the talents of international students. Another reason is that the potential to free ride will not go on forever. As other countries improve their university systems and as their economies grow, competition for top students and scientists and engineers will increase, reducing the supplies of immigrant workers to the United States or raising their price. Thirty years ago, many U.S.-educated Ph.D. science and engineering graduates from Taiwan and Korea remained in the United States. Today, a larger proportion of these graduates return to their native countries. Such a pattern is a natural part of global economic progress. Currently, the United States attracts and retains large numbers of Chinese and Indian students and gains many immigrant specialists from these countries. As China and India develop, though, supplies from those countries will also diminish. The U.S.-born scientists are more likely to remain in the United States as a permanent part of the supply.

The country should try to retain the best and brightest foreign talent coming to the United States. It should end the policy of requiring prospective international students to declare that they have no intention of staying and working in the United States when in fact the country wants them to stay. It should increasingly tilt immigration visas toward more highly skilled persons. In some cases, it should grant quick citizenship to immigrant specialists. As long as immigrant scientists are as productive and trustworthy as native-born scientists in national security–related industries, the country would lose nothing by fast-tracking citizenship for certain immigrants so as to maintain the policy of having only citizens work on some national security programs.[17] The 2006 decisions by the Department of Defense and the Department of Commerce to withdraw proposed tight restrictions on immigrant researchers working on sensitive technologies shows that the security-conscious agencies recognize the contribution that even noncitizen scientists and engineers can make to national security (Brainard 2006; Field 2006). Nevertheless, we should not solely count on free riding on foreign supplies as a long-term strategy to maintain world leadership in science and technology.

It is important to recognize, however, that there is a fundamental trade-off between the supply of immigrant labor and of native-born labor in science and engineering, as in any other part of the labor market. At any given level of demand, increased immigration in any particular specialty lowers the wages and opportunities for natives in that area and thus reduces the incentives for domestic talent to invest in that specialty. Con-

17. Paula Stephan and Sharon Levin (1992) find that among individuals making exceptional contributions to science and engineering, foreign-born and foreign-educated individuals are disproportionately represented, presumably due to the selection process. Increased recruitment of foreign-born researchers is likely to reduce average productivity. I know of no evidence that naturalized American citizens are more or less likely to be security risks. The 1999 case of naturalized American Wen Ho Lee suggests that security officials may be overly suspicious of naturalized scientists and engineers.

versely, increased domestic supplies will reduce the incentives for immigrants to come to the U.S. in pursuit of a specialty. The appropriate strategy should be to seek a balance between the two sources of supply.

Strengthen K–12 Science and Math Education

The polar opposite way to expand the science and engineering workforce is to invest more in science and math education in elementary and secondary school. For example, there is much to be said for raising teacher pay overall and in science and mathematics in particular. There may be a particularly high payoff to developing special science and math magnet schools in different cities and states, similar to the Bronx High School of Science in New York, the North Carolina School of Science and Mathematics, and comparable schools in other states. But investments in K–12 will take fifteen to twenty-five years to affect supplies, and thus cannot help maintain a strong U.S. science and engineering workforce in the next twenty or so years. Because investments in K–12 will improve the science and math education for many students who are likely to never consider science and engineering careers, moreover, they will invariably be less cost-effective than the proposed fellowship program, which focuses on highly able students who are interested in science and engineering and can be enticed toward graduate studies in those areas.

Special Pleading?

Every industry and group wants the government to spend more on it. Most advocate for themselves in the name of the national interest. The organizations behind the policy papers quoted in box 9-1 represent the top U.S. research universities and high-tech firms, the science-engineering parts of the Department of Defense, and the scientific establishment. These are all groups that will benefit directly from increased federal support for science and engineering students and from increased research spending. Much of the rest of the country will benefit indirectly. The cynical and jaded observer of national politics might wonder if this is nothing more than special pleading on behalf of these groups. I disagree.

The big payoff from successful investment in science and engineering will be through greater productivity and continued comparative advantage in high-tech industries that will affect the national economy. Most analysts believe that investments in knowledge have greater social than private returns; this makes it natural to support subsidizing science and engineering students as opposed to, say, subsidizing law or business students. Although estimates of the gap between the social and private returns to basic research, which underlie these beliefs, are uncertain, virtually all estimates, including the most recent ones, indicate that the gaps remain large (Popp 2004). Yes, some will benefit more than others from the proposed expansion of science and engineering fellowships, but the odds are high that most Americans will benefit, which is more than can be said of many other government programs.

Considering the geographic distribution of the award, the benefits of having more trained specialists would flow to many states. Science and engineering doctorates are dispersed across states, and employment in high-tech establishments relative to total employment is even more widely dispersed across states. The areas with the highest concentration of science and engineering doctorates per employee are Connecticut, Delaware, the District of Columbia, Maryland, Massachusetts, New Mexico, and Virginia. Other states with high science and engineering doctorate shares relative to the national average include California, Colorado, Hawaii, New Jersey, Rhode Island, Vermont, and Washington (NSF 2006c, table 8–22). Given the mobility of Americans across state lines, the geographic distribution of doctorates and high-tech firms within the country should not be an issue of great concern.

Conclusion

The number of NSF graduate research fellowships—the most prestigious national awards—has fallen relative to the number of science and engineering baccalaureates, inadvertently signaling young people that additional studies in science and engineering are not worth pursuing. However, this message and its outcome can be reversed by a policy that increases the number and value of graduate research fellowships. This will attract more Americans into science and engineering without limiting the potential for continued flows of immigrant specialists. It will also attract women and minorities to science and engineering. And it will do all this at a relatively modest cost compared to the potential gains.

We should not forget, however, that maintaining our scientific and technological leadership will require not only increased numbers of fellowships but also increases in government spending on basic research and a shift in the locus of that spending toward young researchers.[18]

18. The American Association of Universities (2006) proposes that the federal government increase by 5,000 the number of graduate fellowships and traineeships supported by existing programs; create a 1,000-person graduate fellowship and traineeship program in the Department of Energy's Office of Science; and expand the Department of Defense National Defense Education Program, in return for student commitment to national service after their studies.

References

American Association of Universities. 2006. *National Defense Education and Innovation Initiative.* Washington.

Atkinson, Richard. 1990. *The Scientist* 4, no. 13: 11.

Atkinson, Robert D., Randolph H. Court, and Joseph M. Ward. 1999. *The State New Economy Index: Benchmarking Economic Transformation in the States.* Washington: Progressive Policy Institute.

Brainard, Jeffrey. 2006. "Defense Department Shelves Proposals to Increase Restrictions on Scientists." *Chronicle of Higher Education* (August 15).

Building Engineering and Science Talent. 2004. *The Talent Imperative: Meeting America's Challenge in Science and Engineering, ASAP.* Report. San Diego, Calif.

Business Roundtable. 2005. *Tapping America's Potential: The Education for Innovation Initiative.* Washington.

Committee on Prospering in the Global Economy of the Twenty-First Century. 2005. *Rising above the Gathering Storm: Energizing and Employing America for a Brighter Economic Future.* Washington: National Academies Press.

Council on Competitiveness. 2005. *National Summit on Competitiveness: Investing in Innovation.* Washington: National Association of Manufacturers.

Darby, Michael, and Lynne Zucker. 2006. "Movement of Star Scientists and Engineers and High Tech Firm Entry." Working Paper 12172. Cambridge, Mass.: National Bureau of Economic Research (April).

Field, Kelly. 2006. "Commerce Department Pulls Proposal to Require Broad Licensing of Foreigners in Academic Research." *Chronicle of Higher Education* (June 1).

Freeman, Richard. 2006. "Does Globalization of the Scientific/Engineering Workforce Threaten U.S. Economic Leadership?" In *Innovation Policy and the Economy,* vol. 6, edited by Adam B. Jaffe, Josh Lerner, and Scott Stern, pp. 123–58. MIT Press.

Freeman, Richard, Tanwin Chang, and Hanley Chiang. 2005. "Supporting the Best and Brightest in Science and Engineering: NSF Graduate Research Fellowships." Working Paper 11623. Cambridge, Mass.: National Bureau of Economic Research (September).

Freeman, Richard, Emily Jin, and Chia-Yu Shen. 2004. "Where Do New U.S.-Trained Science-Engineering PhDs Come From?" Working Paper 10554. Cambridge, Mass.: National Bureau of Economic Research (June).

Harvard University and National Bureau of Economic Research. 2005. "Diversifying the Science and Engineering Workforce: Women, Underrepresented Minorities, and Their S&E Careers," Science and Engineering Workforce Project, Cambridge, Mass., January 14–15.

Heylin, Michael. 2004. "Science Is Becoming Truly Worldwide." *Chemical and Engineering News* 82, no. 24: 38–42.

Jackson, Shirley Ann. 2003. *Envisioning a 21st Century Science and Engineering Workforce for the United States: Tasks for University, Industry, and Government.* Washington: National Academies Press.

Jones, Charles I., and Williams, John C. 1998. "Measuring the Social Return to R&D." *Quarterly Journal of Economics* 113, no. 4: 1119–35.

Lehming, Rolf. 1998. "What Is Happening to Academic Employment of Scientists and Engineers?" Issue Brief, NSF 98–312. Washington: National Science Foundation.

Lewis, James A. 2006. *Waiting for Sputnik: Basic Research and Strategic Competition.* Washington: Center for Strategic and International Studies.

National Science Board. 1983. *Science Indicators: 1982.* Washington: Government Printing Office.

National Science Foundation (NSF). 1965. *Scientific and Technical Manpower Resources: Summary Information on Employment, Characteristics, Supply, and Training.* NSF 64–38. Arlington, Va.

———. 1993. *Human Resources for Science and Technology: The Asian Region.* NSF 93–303. Arlington, Va.

———. 1995. *Nonacademic Scientists and Engineers: Trends from the 1980 and 1990 Censuses.* NSF 95–0306. Arlington, Va.

———. 2003. *The Science and Engineering Workforce: Realizing America's Potential.* Arlington, Va.

———. 2005. *All in a Week's Work: Workweeks of Doctoral Scientists and Engineers.* NSF 06–302. Arlington, Va.

———. 2006a. *Graduate Students and Postdoctorates in Science and Engineering: Fall 2004.* NSF 06–325. Arlington, Va.

———. 2006b. *Science and Engineering Doctorate Awards: 2004.* NSF 06–308. Arlington, Va.

———. 2006c. *Science and Engineering Indicators 2006.* Arlington, Va.

———. Division of Graduate Education (DGE). Various years. *Cumulative Index Data Set, 1952–2004.* Arlington, Va.

Office of Science and Technology Policy, Domestic Policy Council. 2006. *American Competitiveness Initiative: Leading the World in Innovation.*

Organization for Economic Cooperation and Development (OECD). 2006. *Main Science and Technology Indicators (MSTI): 2006/1.* Paris.

Pollak, Melissa. 1999. "Counting the S&E Workforce: It's Not That Easy." Issue Brief. Arlington, Va.: National Science Foundation.

Popp, David. 2004. "R&D Subsidies and Climate Policy: Is There a Free Lunch?" Working Paper 10880. Cambridge, Mass.: National Bureau of Economic Research.

Ruggles, Steven, and others. 2004. *Integrated Public Use Microdata Series: Version 3.0.* University of Minnesota, Minnesota Population Center.

Sargent, John. 2004. "An Overview of Past and Projected Employment Changes in the Professional IT Occupations." *Computing Research News* 16, no. 3: 1–21.

Shukla, Kavita. 2006. "Varsity Science: A Study in the Factors That Affect Motivation among Harvard Students and Influence Their Interest in Science, Arguing for a Science Education System Modeled on America's High School Athletic Programs." Undergraduate thesis. Harvard University.

Stephan, Paula, and Sharon Levin. 1992. *Striking the Mother Lode in Science.* Oxford University Press.

Task Force on the Future of American Innovation. 2005. *The Knowledge Economy: Is the United States Losing Its Competitive Edge?* Washington.

United Nations Educational, Scientific and Cultural Organization, Institute for Statistics. 2004. *Global Education Database.* Montreal.

U.S. Census Bureau. 1995. *Statistical Abstracts of the United States 1995.*

———. Bureau of Labor Statistics. 2006. *Employment Situation August 2006.*

U.S. Department of Defense. 2006. *Report of the Defense Science Board Task Force on Future Strategic Strike Skills.*

U.S. Senate. 2005. *National Innovation Act of 2005.* 109 Cong. 1 sess. Government Printing Office.

Creating a Better Tax System

The Simple Return

Reducing America's Tax Burden through Return-Free Filing

10

AUSTAN GOOLSBEE

The burden of an income tax can be divided into two parts, one visible and the other hidden. The first burden is obvious—it is the actual tax payment. The second, hidden burden is arises in part when taxes alter the economic decisions that people make. Another major part of that unseen burden, however, comes from the cost of complying with the system: the hours spent preparing forms, gathering documents, and reading instructions; or the money a tax filer pays someone to do the tax preparation.

This chapter proposes a program called the "Simple Return," which would make it much easier for the millions of taxpayers with a relatively simple tax status to file their taxes. As many as 40 percent of all U.S. taxpayers would be eligible to use the Simple Return, collectively saving up to 225 million hours of time and more than $2 billion a year in tax preparation fees. If one converts the time savings into a monetary value by multiplying the hours saved by the wage rates typically paid to middle- and low-income workers, the Simple Return could reduce tax compliance costs by about $44 billion over ten years. This benefit would come at a very small cost to the government. Indeed, a General Accounting Office (now known as the Government Accountability Office [GAO]) report estimated

I wish to thank Jen Paniza for research assistance and Peter Orszag, Timothy Taylor, Joshua Bendor, and the participants at the Hamilton Project authors' conference for helpful comments.

that a plan similar to the one proposed here could save the Internal Revenue Service (IRS) almost $36 million a year by reducing the number of errors in tax filings and the subsequent need for investigations (GAO 1996).

It is important to clarify what the proposal would not address. There is no doubt that some taxpayers face high compliance costs because of the way their economic situations interact with complex tax code provisions. These taxpayers might have income from a variety of sources—including an employer, self-employment, investments, and capital gains. They also might have large tax deductions, such as mortgage interest and other itemized deductions. Such taxpayers have the most complex tax positions in the country and the highest costs of compliance; they also have the highest incomes in the country. These taxpayers file the 1040 tax form, along with pages of additional information and schedules. The Simple Return would not affect or apply to them.

Most Americans, however, have a relatively straightforward tax status. About two-thirds of taxpayers take only the standard deduction and do not itemize. Frequently, all of their income comes from wages from one employer and their interest from one bank. For many people, taxes are determined by their earned income and their family status. The IRS already receives information about the sources of income for almost all of these people directly from employers, banks, and so on. The IRS then asks these people to spend time gathering documents and filling out tax forms (or paying tax preparers to do so) in order to provide the IRS with information that it already receives from other sources. Indeed, if these taxpayers do not fill out their tax forms correctly, the IRS eventually will contact them and tell them exactly how much they owe (or how much they are owed as a refund).

With the Simple Return, the IRS would take the information about income directly from the employers and banks and, if the person's tax status were simple enough, send that taxpayer a return that the IRS had prefilled with the necessary tax information. The Simple Return program would be strictly voluntary. Taxpayers who prefer to fill out their own tax forms or to pay a tax preparer to fill them out could do just that. Of course, the IRS would not be able to gather complete information on everyone, and some people's family or tax situation might change during the year, making the taxpayer ineligible for this program. But for the millions of taxpayers who could use the Simple Return—potentially 40 percent of all U.S. taxpayers—filing a tax return would entail nothing more than checking the numbers, signing the return, and then either sending a check or, more typically, receiving a refund.

The first response of many who contemplate the issue of reducing compliance costs for middle- and low-income Americans is that the benefits cannot be very large. After all, many people with a relatively simple tax status do not need to file a standard 1040 form. Instead, they file the 1040EZ, a one-page tax form for filers with less than $100,000 in income who do not need to adjust that income. Others can file the 1040A tax form, which allows a limited number of adjustments, without any need to file a sheaf of accompanying tax schedules. Yet all the forms entail gathering information, computing, and reading somewhat technical documents that include tables, worksheets, and instructions. The instruction booklet for the 1040EZ, for example, is thirty-six pages long! Doing taxes takes time and energy, and is clearly something the typical American would prefer to avoid. Anyone, especially those without a college degree or with rusty math skills, can find the forms downright maddening. This is one reason more than 30 percent of 1040EZ filers and 56 percent of 1040A filers used a paid tax preparer in 2001.[1]

For the typical U.S. taxpayer, the costs of tax compliance do not arise from a massive tax code interacting with a complex economic situation. Instead, compliance costs arise because the government is not using the information it already receives independently to calculate the taxpayer's taxes. This method of having the government tell taxpayers what it knows about their incomes and sending out a prepared tax form—known as a tax agency reconciliation (TAR) system because the tax agency does the computation—has been tested at the state and international levels. For 2004 the state of California carried out a pilot TAR program with the state income taxes of more than 50,000 taxpayers; this program was very similar to the Simple Return proposed here. The system was well received and provides a useful basis for considering the benefits and costs of a national program. TAR systems also have been used with success in several European countries (see the discussion below on the international experience).

If designed judiciously, the program would have little cost and might even save the IRS money by reducing the error rate of filers. Whatever costs might apply would be modest compared with the reductions in the costs of tax compliance. In effect, the Simple Return program proposes that the government take advantage of the extraordinary gains made in

---

1. Estimates computed from the most recent data available from the IRS *Public-Use Data File* (IRS 2001), as described later in this chapter. Tax preparers often claim that the reason easy-form filers use preparers is that they want to receive their refunds sooner. The desire for a refund, however, cannot be the full story since the share of people filing 1040EZ and 1040A who have a balance due and still hire a preparer also is high.

information technology in the past two decades to lighten the burden of tax compliance on American families. The benefit will accrue mainly to those with low and middle levels of income because they are the people who file relatively simple tax returns.

The Simple Return Program

The Simple Return program would begin early in the calendar year with taxpayers receiving a prefilled return and a letter explaining the program (see figure 10-1, a copy of the letter that went out with the California ReadyReturn pilot program). As in the California pilot program, individuals receiving a Simple Return would be free to throw it away if they were not interested in participating. Alternatively, taxpayers could use it as a starting point for doing their own tax returns. If they chose to use the enclosed Simple Return, they would confirm that the statements about their income and family status were correct and then either file the form electronically, at the IRS website, or mail it to the IRS. If a taxpayer were due a refund, the IRS could quickly process it.

The Simple Return system would phase in with three distinct waves representing different sets of taxpayers; a possible fourth wave is also discussed below.

The First Wave

The first wave would begin with the easiest cases. It would consist of automatic mailings of the Simple Return to single filers who meet the following criteria: they have no dependent children, are not dependents themselves, had only wage income on their last return, have no other credits, and did not itemize in previous tax filings. The system could start with federal workers, where the matching of incomes from the employer is particularly easy. About 9 million taxpayers might be eligible for the first wave. As table 10-1 shows, most of these taxpayers already file the 1040EZ or 1040A forms.

The IRS would prepare a Simple Return for each of these taxpayers. Then, using the address from the taxpayer's current W-2 form, the IRS would mail that individualized Simple Return and a note explaining that the recipient is eligible to participate in the Simple Return program. (The W-2 is the form that an employer must send each year to employees, the IRS, and the Social Security Administration reporting each employee's wages and the amount of taxes that the employer withheld during the previous year.)

Figure 10-1. Sample Letter for California ReadyReturn Pilot Program

California Is Changing
Filing Your Taxes Just Got Easier

www.ftb.ca.gov/ReadyReturn

Your access code is:

0000

JOE TAXPAYER
123 MAIN STREET
ANYTOWN CA 90000-0000

Have you ever thought, "There has to be an easier way to file my taxes"? We did, and we're happy to introduce **ReadyReturn**. In this voluntary pilot program, we've taken information the state already has from your W-2, done the math, and printed it all on the enclosed tax return. You may choose to **accept** the return as we presented it, **update** the return, or **ignore** this invitation and file as you normally do.

If you want to participate in the **ReadyReturn** pilot, just follow these simple steps to file your return:

Step 1: Carefully review your return

The income information was provided by:

❑ **ACME COMPANY**

Step 2: Make any needed changes

If you have other income, can claim renter's credit, want to make a voluntary contribution, or need to make other changes, you can do this at our Website: **www.ftb.ca.gov/ReadyReturn.**

❑ Your data is already there. We'll guide you through updating your return.

Step 3: File your return

Once you're ready to file your return, you must sign it to agree that it's correct and complete.

❑ Go to **www.ftb.ca.gov/ReadyReturn** and e-file. You'll get your **refund in less than a week** and confirmation that we received your return!

❑ Or, file your return on paper. Be sure to **write your social security number** on the front of the enclosed return. Your refund may take 4-6 weeks if you file on paper.

If you do not want to participate in this pilot, complete a new return yourself, use tax preparation software, or visit a tax preparer. You can use the enclosed return as a starting point for completing your new return.

If you do not use the enclosed return or have already filed, **to protect your privacy** be sure to destroy the enclosed return.

Remember to file your federal return, too. Both the federal and California returns are due **April 15, 2005**.

If you have questions about ReadyReturn or need help updating your return, please contact us:

Website:	www.ftb.ca.gov/ReadyReturn	**Toll Free:**	(800) 522-4144
Email:	readyreturn@ftb.ca.gov	**TTY/TDD:**	(800) 822-6268

STATE OF CALIFORNIA – FRANCHISE TAX BOARD – PO BOX 942840 – SACRAMENTO CA 94240-0002

FTB 966 MEO (New 01-2005)

Table 10-1. Estimating the Number of Filers Eligible for a Simple Return, 2003

Millions

Stage of implementation	All	1040	1040A	1040EZ
Number of filers overall	130.6	80.2	29.8	20.6
Wave 1				
Wages only; single; not a dependent; no children, earned income tax credit (EITC), itemization, or credits	9.1	1.4	1.3	6.4
Allow married persons, dependents, and child credits	17.5	2.9	3.1	11.5
Wave 2				
Add income from "withholdable sources"	38.6	7.0	12.4	19.2
Add capital gains distributions	39.0	7.5	12.4	19.2
Wave 3				
Add EITC	52.4	8.2	23.6	20.6
Wave 4				
Optional after alternative minimum tax (AMT) reform	57.2	13.0	23.6	20.6
Add deductions for charity, state and local taxes, and mortgage interest	. . .	. . .	. . .	. . .

Sources: Wave 1 numbers are author's calculations using shares from the IRS *Individual Public-Use Data File* (IRS 2001). The number of filers of each form in 2003 was multiplied by the share of people that would qualify, as computed using the *Individual Public-Use Data File*. Wave 2 and wave 3 numbers are author's calculations using shares from the U.S. Treasury (2003) analysis of the 1999 *Statistics of Income*. Wave 4 could only take place after reform of the AMT, as discussed in the text. The share of itemizers that would qualify comes from Gale and Holtzblatt (1997).

To participate, the taxpayer need only verify the information on the form, including income and family status. To make it easier, the taxpayer still could file the Simple Return as long as she had earned less than a threshold amount of interest income—say, $100. If there were a minor problem with the return, such as the wrong address, the taxpayer could make the changes online or on an enclosed form and file the adjusted return. If something major had changed, or if the filer had other income such as capital gains that made the Simple Return invalid, she would just do her taxes the conventional way.

The first wave also would include a second group of taxpayers: married filers, people with child credits, and people who are dependents who meet the restrictions on income and filing status noted above.[2] The IRS could put the wages of both spouses on the same Simple Return or compute the child credit. Of course, the Simple Return would be valid only if the taxpayer's personal situation had not changed in the intervening period. If a child had been born to or adopted by the filer during the year, for example,

2. The child credit reduces a family's taxes according to a schedule that is based on family income and the number of dependent children.

the filer would need to file taxes the conventional way to receive the full child credit.

With this second group included, the number of taxpayers in the first wave who would be eligible for the Simple Return could be as high as 17.5 million. Most of these taxpayers also currently fill out the 1040EZ or 1040A forms, as shown in table 10-1.

Filers in this group would not receive a Simple Return automatically but could request participation in one of two ways: by including required information on a W-4 form or by checking a box on the previous year's conventional tax return.

W-4 FORMS. The taxpayer could request participation when completing the standard W-4 form, which is filled out by every employee when starting a job or reporting a change in family status that might affect the amount of taxes withheld. Employees filling out the W-4 form would be given the opportunity to include additional information about themselves and their family status (such as child credits, spouse's Social Security number, and so on) and to request a Simple Return. Because many people only file a W-4 immediately after being hired and other people might not want their employer to have detailed personal information about them or their family status, employees could also fill out a postcard version of the information and mail it directly to the IRS, without their employer seeing it.

"SIMPLE RETURN" BOX ON CONVENTIONAL TAX RETURN. Another way taxpayers could request participation would be for the IRS to add a few lines to conventional tax returns informing taxpayers of the program. Taxpayers could check a box if they wanted the IRS to use their current year information (sources of income, whether they have children, marriage status, and so on) to predict whether they would be eligible for a Simple Return the following year. Taxpayers also could check a box indicating that they did not wish to be considered for the Simple Return. Thus any tax filer would be free either to request consideration for Simple Return status or to opt out of the Simple Return program. At every stage, the IRS would make clear that the Simple Return gives taxpayers more options without restricting existing options in any way. Checking the Simple Return box would not obligate the filer to do anything. At any time, a taxpayer who is eligible for a Simple Return could choose to file taxes the conventional way.

The Second Wave

In the second wave of the program, the Simple Return system would expand to include people with income from what are called "withholdable sources." For our purposes, this means the kinds of income the IRS would receive information on from 1099 forms and other sources than W-2s. This would include interest, dividends (though not capital gains income), pensions, Social Security benefits, unemployment insurance, and individual retirement accounts. As shown in table 10-1, the estimated number of taxpayers potentially eligible for a Simple Return under these conditions was 38.6 million in 2003. In principle, the second wave also could include capital gains distributions from mutual funds, although it could not include net capital gains from the sale of assets. In practice, however, this additional step of including capital gains distributions may not be worth the effort since it would only increase the number of taxpayers eligible for the Simple Return by about 400,000, (see table 10-1).

This second wave is especially relevant for the elderly, who tend not to have wage-paying jobs but rather live on Social Security, pension benefits, and interest income. If their income is high enough, filers pay taxes on their Social Security benefits as well as on their other income. In this second wave, where pension and interest income would be included, the majority of people on Social Security would be able to file their taxes with a Simple Return.

The Third Wave

The third wave of the Simple Return program could occur simultaneously with the second wave if the ongoing IRS modernization goes smoothly. It would use the taxpayer's tax return information from the previous year to prepare a Simple Return that would be sent out to anyone who did not itemize deductions and was otherwise eligible for a Simple Return based on the previous year's information. This would include a Simple Return for recipients of the earned income tax credit (EITC). This tax credit is available for low-income families and is adjusted according to income earned and the number of dependent children. Adding the EITC to the mix of tax provisions covered under the Simple Return would increase the number of people who were potentially eligible to more than 52 million.

It is important to note that, in most cases, the taxes calculated on the Simple Return would be the same as if the taxpayer did his own tax return or paid a tax preparer to do so. For people with situations as simple as those cited here, there are not many preferences or deductions available that they would be able to take advantage of if they filed their taxes the conventional way. However, at higher incomes there will be some borderline cases. Perhaps such filers will be close to the cutoff for itemizing their deductions rather than using the standard deduction. Some of these people would receive a Simple Return but might have a lower tax bill by filling out the conventional tax form and itemizing, perhaps with the help of a paid tax preparer, or by changing their behavior to take advantage of particular tax incentives. The Simple Return instructions would need to state clearly that the calculations are done assuming the simplest situation, using the information the IRS has available. The Simple Return is neither a tax planning service nor an attempt by the government to become involved in a line of business. Rather, it is a way for government to serve citizens better by helping those taxpayers who have simple tax situations avoid the need to fill out a return. Many of these people would likely still go to a paid tax preparer to see how much additional money they could save—and they would be free to do so under the Simple Return system.

Real-World Experience with Return-Free Filing

The California Pilot Program

In 2004 the Franchise Tax Board of California conducted a pilot program for its state income tax along the lines of the Simple Return system. Bankman (2005) provides an excellent overview of the program. The California ReadyReturn went out to over 50,000 single taxpayers who did not have any dependents and who had only wage income; it was accompanied in each case by a cover letter (figure 10-1). The returns used wage and withholding information that employers had directly reported to the state. Overall, more than 11,000 people used the ReadyReturn—more than one-fifth of those who received the ReadyReturn and letter. However, interest in using ReadyReturn was even higher: 22 percent of the people who declined participation cited as their reason that they had already filed their tax return by the time that they received the mailing. Participation among those who had not already filed was approximately 27 percent. There was no advertising of the program ahead of time; people simply received the form in the mail.

ReadyReturn users were pleased with the program. More than 90 percent of ReadyReturn users said that they saved time using the system and that it was more convenient than conventional filing (California Franchise Tax Board 2006). The Franchise Tax Board also created a control group of people who would have been eligible for the ReadyReturn but were not invited to participate. The median filing time for ReadyReturn users who filed electronically was nearly 80 percent lower than the median filing time for the control group. The ReadyReturn filers also said that they saved money using the program. The median ReadyReturn filer paid nothing to complete the state return; the median control group filer paid $30. More than 98 percent of ReadyReturn users said they were "satisfied" or "very satisfied" with the program, and more than 97 percent said that they would use it again next year. Once people experience the convenience of receiving a completed tax return, they do not want to give it up. Of the few complaints, almost all were of a technical nature (such as, "What is a PIN?") rather than about the program as a whole (Bankman 2005).

Of those who did not choose to participate, about 25 percent said they prefer to use a tax preparer, and 10 percent said they were uncomfortable receiving a prefilled return. This evidence suggests that about one-third of those who are eligible for a Simple Return might just discard it and the letter, at least for the first few years after program introduction.

California's Franchise Tax Board also observed that the ReadyReturn filers were significantly less likely to have errors than the control group's returns. Three percent of the control group received an error notice from the Franchise Tax Board, compared with 0.3 percent of filers from the ReadyReturn group. The Franchise Tax Board also noted that the rate of electronic filing rose dramatically among the ReadyReturn filers, which further reduced the board's processing costs. Indeed, the Franchise Tax Board was so confident of the cost savings that it asked the California legislature to reduce its long-term budget to reflect the savings from the program (California Franchise Tax Board 2005). There is every reason to believe that these same benefits of taxpayer satisfaction and cost savings would hold for a Simple Return applied at the federal level.

The International Experience

Tax agency reconciliation systems such as the Simple Return have been used in Europe; in some cases, they have been used more extensively than the Simple Return would be even at its maximal use in the United States. The U.S. Department of the Treasury (2003) observed that in 1999 about 87 percent of tax filers in Denmark and 74 percent of filers in Sweden had their returns prepared through a TAR system. Finland and Norway also have experimented with TAR systems. One reason that Denmark and Sweden have been able to generate such high participation rates is that their underlying tax systems are simpler than the U.S. tax system, so more people qualify. Not surprisingly, the compliance costs in these countries are substantially lower than they are in the United States. In Sweden, for example, compliance costs have been estimated at about 1 percent of revenue (U.S. Treasury 2003). Slemrod estimated the compliance costs for the individual income tax in the United States at more than 10 percent of revenue (U.S. House of Representatives 2004).

Questions and Concerns

What Share of Those Eligible for the Program Would Participate?

It is not clear how many people would accept the Simple Return offer in the near term, but the number of participants is likely to be substantial. A survey conducted by the U.S. Treasury (2003) suggested that 39 percent of people were interested in using such a system, and another 25 percent might be interested.

In the California ReadyReturn system, with no advertising and with only one mailing, about 27 percent of the people who received the return and had not already filed their taxes chose to participate. This is substantially higher than the reports in the U.S. Treasury (2003) survey, where only 17 percent of people said they would try a return-free system immediately. There is every reason to expect a substantial increase in usage over time. More than 97 percent of the people who used the California ReadyReturn said they planned to participate again, and the U.S. Treasury survey evidence suggests that initial success would likely indicate rapid future expansion. Twenty-eight percent of people said they would be comfortable trying such a system after its first year of existence, and another 27 percent said they would be comfortable trying it after its first few years. In other words, the survey evidence suggests interest could double or even triple within a few years.

With proper explanations of the program, advance media exposure, and an arrangement enabling people to opt into the system by filling out a postcard, the take-up rate among eligible participants might be as high as 50 percent in the short run and even higher in the long run. Regardless, the Simple Return does not need to achieve anywhere near complete participation to be a success. If it could reduce compliance costs for millions of people, it would obviously be a boon to U.S. taxpayers.

How Much Can Costs of Compliance Be Reduced for U.S. Taxpayers?

To estimate compliance costs, it is helpful to separate those who do not itemize into two groups: those who pay someone to prepare their tax filing and those who prepare their own tax filing.

There has been little systematic evidence on how much low- and middle-income taxpayers pay tax preparers to complete their 1040EZ or 1040A forms. The average price for paying a tax preparer to fill out a tax form that included the EITC, the provision aimed at the working poor, was around $200, although this typically included the cost of a loan made in advance of an anticipated tax refund, and a charge for e-filing and state income tax preparation (Berube and others 2002). In the instructions for tax forms for calendar year 2005, however, the IRS gave an estimated cost for paying a preparer to fill out the given form. Interestingly, the IRS also estimates that paying a preparer still requires significant time from the tax filer, but to be conservative, the estimates in this paper only include the cost of paying the preparer. The IRS estimates the average fee for a 1040EZ form to be $81, for a 1040A form to be $122 and, a bit incongruously, for the full 1040 without itemizing, without self-employment income, and without capital gains income to be $121. For 1040 itemizers, the fee on an individual basis can be predicted using the most recent IRS *Public-Use Data File* (IRS 2001). That file reports all the information on the tax returns of a nationally representative sample of more than 140,000 randomly sampled taxpayers. Because tax preparation fees in the previous year are a reported expense, the actual fees serve as predictors of the fee, depending on the situation of the itemizer.[3]

For the self-filers, the IRS estimates the filing times on its 2004 tax forms. The values for some selected forms and schedules are listed in table 10-2.

The Simple Return is more likely to be used by those with low and middle incomes. Because they tend to have fewer years of schooling, these taxpayers are estimated to take longer than average to fill out tax forms. In the performance scores of people in the National Longitudinal Survey of Youth, the response time performance for numerical calculations and for coding speed—skills used to fill out a tax return—for people at the median income level were 30–35 percent better than for people at the twenty-fifth percentile of income.[4] The median income for people filing the 1040 in 2001 was $43,850, versus $19,120 for the 1040A and $11,290 for the 1040EZ, based on the IRS *Public-Use Data File* (IRS 2001). Since these income differences would suggest that filing times for people with lower incomes might be 20–40 percent longer than estimated, the IRS values were increased by 20 percent when compliance times were computed for 1040A and 1040EZ tax forms.

The conventional economic approach for turning these times into an equivalent monetary cost of compliance is to place a reasonable monetary

3. This predicted fee comes from regressing preparer fee (for people who hired a tax preparer and reported expenses greater than $0) on adjusted gross income and dummies for each schedule A to F, and for the EITC. The average value of the predicted fee for itemizers was around $190.

4. The National Longitudinal Survey of Youth has followed a group of people, ages fourteen to twenty-one in 1979, throughout their lives.

Table 10-2. Compliance Times Estimated by the IRS for Selected Forms and Schedules, 2004

Units as indicated

Form	Time
1040EZ	3h 46m
1040A	10h 25m
Schedule 1 (interest and dividends)	0h 56m
Schedule 2 (childcare expenses)	2h 6m
Schedule 3 (credit for elderly or disabled)	1h 27m
1040	13h 35m
Schedule A (itemized deductions)	5h 37m
Schedule B (interest and dividends)	1h 26m
Schedule C-EZ (self-employment income)	1h 43m
Schedule D (capital gains)	6h 10m
Schedule E (supplemental income)	6h 14m
Schedule F—Cash method (farm income)	5h 52m
Schedule EIC (earned income credit)	0h 34m

Source: IRS 2004 tax forms.

value on the person's time and multiply that by the hours saved. To calculate the value of time for each person, the taxpayer's yearly wages are divided by total hours worked, assuming the filer worked full-time (2,000 hours a year); for anyone with an imputed value of time below the minimum wage, the estimates use $5.15 an hour.[5] It is common practice for policy analysts who work with tax data to truncate the extreme ends of the income distribution, effectively avoiding the extreme and often unrepresentative situations of people who earned at either end of the spectrum (very high or very low). Few people who earn at the high end are likely to be eligible for a Simple Return, anyway. In that spirit, the sample is restricted to people with adjusted gross income above $5,000 and below $125,000 a year—around the 10th and 95th percentiles, respectively, of filers in the sample of 2001 taxpayers.

Table 10-3 summarizes these calculations for compliance costs across income groups. Each column presents the mean adjusted gross income and tax liability for people in that group, followed by the average compliance costs in either preparer fees (for paying filers) or monetary value of time

---

5. Assuming some part-time rather than full-time work typically raises the implied hourly wage of the lower-income workers (and thus the implied compliance costs among the low-income workers). Use of only single taxpayers to avoid any issues associated with two taxpayers both working full-time gave similar results, so the listed calculation is quite robust.

Table 10-3. Summary Statistics for Compliance Costs and Tax Liability by Income Group[a]

Dollars, except as indicated

Statistics	Adjusted gross income group					
	$5,000–25,000	$25,000–45,000	$45,000–65,000	$65,000–85,000	$85,000–105,000	$105,000–125,000
Adjusted gross income (AGI)	14,526	34,057	54,264	74,181	93,801	114,334
Tax liability	622	2,893	5,794	9,092	13,426	18,323
Compliance costs for						
Self-filers (value of time)	81	210	405	636	845	1,104
Paying filers	122	138	159	182	199	212
Compliance costs as percent of AGI (median percent within group)	0.71	0.43	0.31	0.31	0.31	0.27

Source: Author's computations using the *Individual Public-Use Data File* (IRS 2001) as described in the text.
a. All values are means except those in the last row.

(for self-filers). In the last row, the table divides the compliance cost for each person by that person's adjusted gross income and gives the median share in the group.

One insight from these calculations is that the costs of compliance amount to 5–10 percent of the entire tax revenue paid by many middle- and low-income taxpayers. Many taxpayers at the bottom and lower middle of the income distribution owe little in federal income taxes (they typically owe much more in the payroll taxes that are collected to finance Social Security and Medicare). At higher income levels, the cost of compliance with the income tax rises, but the explicit income taxes owed rise much faster, so the costs of compliance for these high-income taxpayers is relatively low compared with the explicit taxes that they owe. Cutting compliance costs is similar to cutting taxes: it leaves people with more money in their pocket after tax day, or more free time they could use to make money or spend with their families. Unlike direct tax cuts, however, this reduction in the compliance burden would not reduce the revenue going to the government.

As the evidence in the bottom row of table 10-3 also makes clear, compliance costs are generally regressive across the wider span of the income distribution. They are highest at the bottom and generally fall with income; they are lowest for the top income bracket. This is why something that reduces compliance costs is likely to be progressive. If that something, such as the Simple Return, is geared toward the middle- and low-income filers, the progressivity of the reform will be even greater.

Table 10-4. Maximum Compliance Cost Savings from the Simple Return

Units as indicated

Filing category	Versus			Combined total
	1040	1040A	1040EZ	
Per person				
Time savings for self-filers	13 hours	11.2 hours	3.7 hours	. . .
Cost savings for paying filers	$121	$122	$81	. . .
Share that use paid preparer	62%	56%	32%	. . .
Nationwide totals (millions)[a]				
Wave 1 compliance burden reduction	$403	$1,016	$591	$2,009
Adding wave 2 and 3 compliance burden reduction	$430	$2,927	$1,057	$4,415

Source: Author's calculations, as described in the text, using the *Individual Public-Use Data File* (IRS 2001).

a. The nationwide totals sum the fees paid to preparers for the paying filers and the monetary value of time for the self-filers, using the implied wage rate from their tax returns. These calculations assume maximal take-up of the Simple Return as enumerated in table 10-1. Rows do not sum due to rounding.

Based on the evidence from California's ReadyReturn pilot project, the Simple Return may reduce filing and compliance times by about 80 percent for qualifying taxpayers. This would save 3.7 hours for 1040EZ filers, 11.2 hours for 1040A filers, and 13 hours for (nonitemizing) 1040 filers who do their taxes themselves. The California evidence showed that ReadyReturn filers typically no longer needed a paid tax preparer, thus presumably saving the entire fee. The top half of table 10-4 illustrates the average savings for paying filers and self-filers by form (as well as the share of people filing that form who use a paid preparer).

The bottom half of table 10-4 then sums these gains across all the people in the economy (valuing the self-filers' time at their wage rate). If everyone who was eligible to use the Simple Return actually did so, the total savings in the first wave would amount to $2 billion a year. About half of that would be reduced fees paid to preparers; the other half would be the value of saved time. After the second and third waves, the savings could be as high as $4.4 billion a year. Over a ten-year budget window, the value of time saved by the Simple Return would reach an amount as large as a $44 billion tax cut for middle- and lower-income people. Even if participation rates were only 50–75 percent of those eligible, savings from the Simple Return would be substantial.

Can the IRS Speed Up Its Processing Time to Issue Refunds More Quickly?

Currently, most businesses must submit information returns to the IRS by the end of February. These businesses include banks and other financial institutions (who submit 1099 information on financial income) and employers (who submit W-2 wage information). The W-2 information goes first to the Social Security Administration, which processes it and then turns over a master file to the IRS later in the year. The delays in processing and transfer of the files in the current system would need to be improved in order to avoid delays in refunds. (About 80 percent of taxpayers receive refunds, with the probability being about equal for itemizers and nonitemizers. See IRS 2001.)

The current system was created at a time when paper documents were the norm and lengthy processing was inevitable. It has taken some time for the government to begin incorporating the rapid advances in information technology. The IRS already has what it calls a FIRE (Filing Information Returns Electronically) system to encourage businesses to put their information returns into computer format. Any entity that files more than 250 information returns in a year is required to file electronically. Since that encompasses all of the large employers in the country, the majority of all employees in the country could easily be covered by such a system. Even if the IRS made the focus of its acceleration just those firms with more than 100 employees, the Simple Return could go out to most of the eligible population. Just 1.8 percent of employers have more than 100 employees, yet they account for around 64 percent of total employment. Indeed, only 0.3 percent of firms (17,000 individual companies) have more than 500 employees each, accounting for more than 49 percent of employees.[6] Given their size, all of them already are required to file their information returns electronically. This group of large employers should be the IRS's primary focus.

Furthermore, the state unemployment information on employees is filed quarterly in most states, so wage information, at least, would potentially be available early if the federal government were to collaborate with individual states. This information was what the state of California used for its ReadyReturn pilot, and California was able to generate the returns well before the filing deadline.

If needed, the IRS could accelerate the filing deadline for large employers who already file their information electronically and who already report their information to the states. Currently, these employers file the information with the Social Security Administration by the end of February.

---

6. U.S. Bureau of the Census, "Statistics about Business Size (including Small Business)" (www.census.gov/epcd/www/smallbus.html#EmpSize).

If they submitted the information by the end of January, it would allow the IRS to incorporate interest and dividend income into the Simple Return and to expand significantly the share of Americans who would be eligible. If the program did move up the filing date, it would certainly exempt any organization that does not already file electronically or that is below a threshold size, and would probably give a small tax credit to offset the minor inconvenience to the employers.

Even with these changes by the IRS, some small employers will turn in their information returns late, some can only do paper-based returns, and some will have other such problems. Obviously, their employees would not be eligible for a Simple Return. This poses no conceptual problem for the Simple Return, though, and does not need to delay its implementation. If it proves difficult to match information on some category of employer or some type of income in the early years of the program, the affected groups simply would not participate. Indeed, if people appreciate the Simple Return, it is entirely possible that they will pressure their employers and financial institutions to send the information in to the government earlier to make them eligible. Given the problems that the IRS has had trying to incorporate small employers and the marginal economy into their processing, these pressures would directly benefit the government by expanding coverage.

What Are the Costs to the Government of Implementing a Simple Return Program?

Previous discussions of TAR and other return-free systems (IRS 1987, GAO 1996, U.S. Treasury 2003) have grappled with how feasible it is for the IRS to use the information returns it already has to prepare tax forms in time for the April 15 deadline. Indeed, a Simple Return form would need to be sent out well before April 15 so that those who wanted to fill out their own form would have reasonable time to do so. There is no doubt that the Simple Return program would require some modernization of the processing capabilities of the IRS and its ability to match to the Social Security Administration records. The IRS already has a modernization program under way. If the IRS accelerated this modernization and implemented the Simple Return at an earlier date, it would thus offset the resultant additional costs, partially or wholly, by savings to the IRS from fewer errors in tax returns and increased electronic filing.

The entire California ReadyReturn pilot program cost less than $300,000, including the processing and mailing of the returns to 50,000 people. The California Franchise Tax Board believed it could have increased usage of ReadyReturn up to tenfold with no increase in cost had the web service been used more intensively.

Past estimates of the costs of a TAR system have varied widely. An IRS (1987) study from two decades ago estimated that such a system would increase IRS costs by $284 million. A GAO (1996) study from little over a decade ago estimated that such a system would reduce IRS costs by $36 million. The GAO report pointed out that a TAR system requires far less document matching. Processing the standard returns that taxpayers mail is more expensive and time consuming than processing the Simple Return. The GAO noted that the IRS could reduce its number of "under-reporter" cases, whereby the IRS investigates discrepancies between the return filed by an individual and the information returns filed by employers and other organizations declaring sources of income for the individual. In 1996 these underreporter cases cost an average of $17.61 for each taxpayer.

Much of the difference between the IRS estimate and the GAO estimate can be accounted for by the sharp decline in the prices of information technology and the corresponding increase in processing capabilities between the 1980s and the 1990s. Those cost trends have continued in the intervening decade. The 1996 GAO report may have been overly optimistic on the immediate cost savings at that time, but even being more realistic and assuming smaller initial cost savings, a Simple Return program implemented with modern technology would reduce the burden of tax compliance at little expense to the government.

As noted above, the modernization needed to implement the Simple Return is consistent with the IRS business vision goal of reducing the amount of paper documents it needs to process, and with the ongoing modernization program at the IRS. To date the IRS has focused most of its attention on increasing the amount of electronic filing to reduce paper forms. However, the Simple Return system also would entail a great deal less paper from the filers submitting their tax returns the conventional way. Raising the priority of modernization investments needed to accelerate the handoff of information from the Social Security Administration to the IRS will speed the date at which the Simple Return can be fully implemented and the associated cost savings realized.

What about Extending the Federal Tax Filing Deadline for the Simple Return?

The GAO (1996) report argued that the IRS could have enacted a TAR return-free system, even a decade ago, if it extended the deadline for Simple

Return filers past April 15 but that a hurdle to extending it was that many states would retain their April 15 deadlines. About two-thirds of all U.S. taxpayers live in a state where the state income tax requires some data that come from the federal tax return, such as federal adjusted gross income or federal taxable income. These people would be unlikely to take part in a delayed Simple Return system because they would need to have completed their federal tax by April 15 in order to file their state tax returns.

Extending the tax deadline seems an inferior option, though it is possible if things do not go well in the development stages of the program. Clearly, it would be preferable to process the information sooner than to delay the filing deadline. At first glance, extending the deadline might be well received by taxpayers, but because about 80 percent of the people would be receiving refunds, most would prefer to receive their money as soon as possible. If the number of eligible people exceeds the capacities of the IRS to generate a Simple Return in a timely manner, the program could be phased in. The IRS could first send Simple Returns to people in states that have no state income tax, or states in which the state income code does not rely in any direct way on the federal tax form.

How Would the Simple Return Deal with Mistakes and Corrections?

A Simple Return program would ultimately send out tens of millions of prefilled tax forms. Even if 99.99 percent of the returns were accurate, there would still be thousands of people receiving returns with mistakes. Some people might feel that they were being pressured or that they were compelled to accept the government's numbers in the Simple Return; others might worry that they would not find a mistake on the return or not be able to correct the mistake after finding it.

While it is impossible to avoid all mistakes in a Simple Return system, it is worth noting that the current system is not foolproof, either. Some employers misstate income on taxpayers' W-2 forms or send the forms to the wrong address. People make mistakes on their own tax forms, leading to entanglement in an IRS process. Paid tax preparers are not a foolproof option either. James White, GAO director of tax issues, testified before the Senate Finance Committee that 5 percent of the 71 million users of tax preparers had no confidence that they had not overpaid their taxes, and cited a nonrandom survey by *Consumer Reports* of 26,000 of its readers, in which 6 percent had discovered an error made by their tax preparers (GAO 2003). In a different study, the GAO claimed that in 1998 as many as 1 million people using a paid tax preparer (that is, up to 1 percent of total taxpayers) had overpaid their taxes (GAO 2002).

There is, therefore, little evidence that an automated system such as the Simple Return would increase the number of mistakes in the tax system. Indeed, the Simple Return would allow some mistakes to be corrected more quickly. For example, if the government has the wrong amount of income on the W-2 form from a taxpayer's employer, the taxpayer will see the error when the IRS sends him the Simple Return, before he files his taxes. This would allow the taxpayer to mail in a copy of the correct W-2 with the return and avoid any further problems. Under the current tax code, the taxpayer would not even know about this mistake until after filing the tax return, having it go through IRS processing, and then receiving a letter of inquiry from the IRS months later. The Simple Return could significantly reduce the time lag in resolving disputes and accelerate the receipt of refunds.

The Simple Return, of course, would not remove ultimate responsibility from the taxpayer. The government would turn over the information it had on income and family status, but if that information were wrong—for example, if the taxpayer actually had a large amount of capital gains income, disqualifying him from using the Simple Return, or if the taxpayer had married during the year, requiring a different tax calculation—the taxpayer still would be responsible for correcting it. Failure to do so, under current law, would be just like failing to report income or misreporting one's marital status on a conventional tax return.

There is no viable alternative to the taxpayer being responsible for filing correct tax returns. If the government were legally to absolve the taxpayer from his obligation of checking the Simple Return, it would open up the possibility of fraud and give people an incentive to convey misleading information to the government in an effort to induce the IRS to send them a faulty Simple Return that they could then sign and make official. To ease fears that a government mistake that people did not find would end up costing them a great deal of money, the IRS could set up a safe harbor level. With such a system, if the taxpayer failed to check the government's return and simply signed it and returned it, and it later became clear the taxpayer had failed to report some kind of income or change in family status, as long as the tax owed was below a certain amount (for instance, $250) there would be no additional penalty beyond the tax itself and interest. This is similar to the way a taxpayer can request an extension beyond the April 15 deadline in the current system.

An issue related to the one about mistakes is whether taxpayers would be intimidated into paying more than they should or into agreeing with something incorrect on the return because the document comes from the

IRS. It is important to remember that the program is voluntary. If any taxpayer feels intimidated or cheated or even annoyed by the Simple Return, that individual can simply discard the Simple Return and file taxes the conventional way. The evidence from the California ReadyReturn shows that most people have no problem rejecting an offer from the tax authority and doing their taxes on their own. Furthermore, most of these taxpayers do not have access to extensive deductions and credits, and so would not risk losing them by filing a Simple Return.

The point of the Simple Return is to make life easier for U.S. taxpayers, not to increase their stress level. For that reason, it would probably be better for the Taxpayer Advocate Service to send the letter offering the Simple Return. The Taxpayer Advocate Service is an independent organization within the IRS set up to protect the rights of taxpayers and advocate their interests in the event of disputes with the IRS. A letter coming from the IRS directly might make people think they were being ordered to pay a specific amount or believe that this was, in fact, the beginning of an audit.

Does the Simple Return Raise Privacy Concerns?

Some opponents of return-free filing find it invasive or inappropriate that the government would print up and mail out forms listing income and taxes. Indeed, some opponents suggest that a Simple Return would require people to divulge additional personal information to the government. Just to be clear, however, the Simple Return does not require employees to give their employers or the government any more information about themselves than they provide now, nor does the Simple Return entail the IRS receiving any more information than it receives now about wages or family status. Indeed, some privacy advocates strongly supported the California ReadyReturn pilot program because the system inherently requires the government to turn over all the information that it has on each individual—to lay all its cards on the table, in a sense.

Obviously, when tens of millions of these forms are mailed out, a small fraction may go to the wrong address. This is no different from the current system that mails W-2 information, or the Social Security Administration's mailing that lists year-by-year earnings over a lifetime. The risk that some of this information will fall into the wrong hands is not new.

Would the Simple Return Unfairly Infringe on Private Enterprise?

In California, opponents of the ReadyReturn argued that return-free filing constituted an inappropriate government intrusion on private enterprise. Bankman (2005) has pointed out that this argument implies that making the tax system more complex and more painful is desirable because doing so would increase the employment of tax preparers. In practice, the government already seeks to reduce the compliance burden of taxation in various ways. For example, the government provides people with a printed tax table indicating the tax burden for a given level of taxable income so that people do not need to calculate using the formula. Few would advocate removing the tax tables because they undermine the market for paid tax preparers. Likewise, taxpayers who do not have enough withholding at tax time and owe a penalty can ask the IRS to calculate it for them, because the rules are a bit complicated. Again, few people complain that such a service undermines free enterprise. For the government to release the information it already has and to give taxpayers an idea of what their tax situation is (which the government already does now if taxpayers make a mistake when they first file) should hardly be considered as competition with a private sector business.

Would the Simple Return Raise Taxes?

Antitax groups and some in Congress publicly oppose return-free filing.[7] For example, Grover Norquist, president of Americans for Tax Reform, testified before the President's Tax Reform Commission against any kind of automatic filing (Norquist 2005). At first, such opposition seems ironic because antitax groups have long been the most vocal critics of the compliance costs of the tax system. However, these groups seem to believe that if compliance with the tax code were to be less painful, people would be less averse to higher tax rates. These critics typically ask rhetorically, "Do you trust the government to do your taxes for you?" They argue that return-free filing is just a way for the government to raise taxes that people will not notice and a way to expand the power of the IRS over people's lives.

But the Simple Return is completely voluntary. No one needs to trust the government, share any additional information with the IRS, or pay a higher tax rate than one would without the Simple Return. Every taxpayer has the right to set aside the Simple Return and file the conventional way. In addition, the government is only doing this for people with extremely simple tax positions, so there is little room for the government to cheat people out of their deductions or to induce them to pay higher taxes.

7. Americans for Tax Reform, "Senate Conservatives Speak Out against Return Free Tax Filing Scheme," press release, October 26, 2005 (www.atr.org/content/html/2005/oct/102605pr-returnfree.htm).

People are not sharing any additional information with the IRS. Everything on the Simple Return comes from information the IRS already has about the taxpayer and information that he gives to the IRS every time he files his tax return. Indeed, if the taxpayer were accidentally to omit this information from the tax return, the IRS would contact him to tell him that he forgot to report the information.

Interaction of the Simple Return with Other Tax Policies

The Simple Return is consistent not only with current tax law but also with the major tax reform proposals that have been the subject of recent debate. In contrast, alternative proposals to achieve return-free filing (such as exact withholding) would be possible only if major changes were made to the U.S. tax code.

The Simple Return and Federal Tax Reform

The tax code is continually evolving. The Simple Return could be adapted easily to handle almost any changes in basic tax rates and standard deductions, and it even could be adapted to handle many of the more sweeping tax reforms that are sometimes contemplated.

One kind of tax reform would broaden the base and lower the rates—that is, reduce or eliminate a number of tax deductions and credits, such as the tax deductions for mortgage interest or state and local taxes—and then take the money that is saved and use it to reduce tax rates. The Tax Reform Act of 1986 proceeded along these lines, and the recent President's Advisory Panel on Federal Tax Reform produced one proposal similar to this. A second kind of proposal for tax reform would focus on switching from the current income tax to a consumption tax. Some proposals along these lines would exempt from income tax all returns from financial investment such as interest earned, dividend payments, and capital gains income. Yet another substantial reform discussed is to abolish or sharply limit the alternative minimum tax (AMT). The Advisory Panel was particularly concerned with this issue. The AMT was originally passed in the late 1960s in an attempt to ensure that all high-income taxpayers would pay at least some taxes, no matter what. Over time, though, an increasingly large share of taxpayers has been affected by the AMT, and it is slated to become an issue for even middle-income people in the near future.

The Simple Return would work well with any of these major tax reforms and, indeed, would likely be available to even more people if such reforms were enacted. The Simple Return system is not dependent on the current income tax system to function; the benefits of the policy could be sustained no matter how the income tax changed. If a tax reform eliminated a number of deductions and, as a result, reduced the number of taxpayers who itemize deductions, then the number of taxpayers who could use a Simple Return would increase. One of the major factors preventing more people from qualifying for the Simple Return is that capital gains income cannot be dealt with in the return-free setting because capital gains are not reported to the government by any third party (unlike, say, the interest earned from a financial institution). A consumption tax that exempted capital gains income would thus entitle more people to use a Simple Return.

The Fourth Wave

A reform that limited the sweep of the AMT might even allow the launch of a fourth wave of Simple Returns that would include what have been called simple itemizers. People in this group itemize deductions but only a few of them—mortgage interest, state and local taxes, and charitable contributions. Gale and Holtzblatt (1997) estimated that this group could include almost 5 million additional filers, about 10 percent of those who currently itemize deductions (see table 10-1). In a fourth wave, taxpayers would be sent both a basic Simple Return and an itemized 1040 form with all deductions filled out as zero except three blank lines for mortgage interest, state taxes, and charitable contributions. Filers would complete these three lines, add up the numbers, and compute their tax. If the Simple Return with itemized deductions yielded a smaller tax bill than the basic Simple Return, the filer could just mail in the itemized return (and keep his documentation of the itemizations).

This variation of the Simple Return to cover simple itemizers currently is impossible because of the presence of the AMT. Every taxpayer owes either the taxes calculated on her version of the 1040 form or the taxes calculated on the AMT form, whichever is greater. If a taxpayer received a Simple Return that allowed for a few itemized deductions, that taxpayer might fill in values for charitable contributions, for example, that were large enough for her to reduce the taxes owed to a level that would oblige her to pay AMT. There would be no way for her to know about this possibility, though, if she filled out the Simple Return. Such a taxpayer would, then, most certainly underpay her taxes and have to pay penalties. If the AMT were limited to those with very high incomes, this problem would disappear, and the fourth wave of the Simple Return be implemented.

The Simple Return and State Income Tax Changes

The Simple Return would likely put pressure on states to offer their own versions of a Simple Return. People clearly would not like having to do a tax return for their state income tax when the federal government has sharply reduced the cost of compliance. The California ReadyReturn case, however, suggests that many states would potentially be able to do this. In fact, state employment offices are thought to be better equipped than the Social Security Administration to convey wage information in a timely manner because the state unemployment insurance numbers often are updated throughout the year. There certainly would be a great interest among many states in a joint program with the federal government whereby states could send out a state form with the Simple Return. This is especially relevant for the majority of state income taxpayers who live in states where the federal definition of gross income or taxable income is the starting point for calculating the state income tax. Of course, in the seven states that have no state income tax—including populous states such as Texas and Florida—there would be no need for this cooperation.

Why Not Exact Withholding?

A frequently mentioned alternative to a TAR system such as the Simple Return is an exact withholding system, in which government adjusts the amount that is automatically withheld from paychecks so that the total amount withheld at the end of the year is the exact amount of taxes owed. In this way, exact withholding eliminates the need for filing a tax return. This system is used in a few countries, including Japan and the United Kingdom. Adopting this approach in the United States would require some significant changes to the tax system. Indeed, this is one of the main conclusions of the report prepared by the U.S. Treasury (2003) entitled *Return-Free Tax Systems: Tax Simplification Is a Prerequisite.*

In countries with exact withholding, there tends to be either no taxation of capital gains and interest income, or else such income is withheld at the source, similar to wage income. Furthermore, the tax structure tends to treat all filers as separate individuals filing alone rather than as married, and there is only limited allowance for special deductions or credits because everything must be clarified ahead of time in order for the firm's withholding to match exactly the tax bill. In the U.S. tax code—which taxes capital gains and interest income, does not withhold at the source on such income, changes the tax rate according to marital status and children, and has an EITC—it would be difficult to calculate withholding exactly.

Gale and Holtzblatt (1997) describe in more detail the kinds of changes one could make to the U.S. system to make it easier to establish an exact withholding system, but several hurdles seem insurmountable. First, the government would need to make significant changes to the tax code (such as not taxing capital gains and treating all taxpayers only as individuals) before it could implement exact withholding. Second, any time the government changed the tax system it would have to ensure that all employers changed their withholding rates to keep them exact. Third, exact withholding would require employers to gather significantly more information about employees than they currently do, in matters such as number of children, house payments, charitable deductions, and so on. This entails both some privacy concerns for the employees, who may not want their employers to have the additional information, and some cost concerns for the employers, who will have to do the exact withholding calculations. Fourth, in a recent survey, the public preferred a TAR system such as the Simple Return over exact withholding by a more than three to one margin—65 percent to 19 percent, with 17 percent having no preference or not answering (U.S. Treasury 2003).

The Simple Return—whereby the tax authority simply takes the information it already receives from employers and financial institutions, computes the tax, and mails out the completed form to qualifying taxpayers—requires almost no change to the tax law before implementation and is preferable.

Conclusion

The Simple Return is a straightforward idea. It requires that the tax authority take the information it already receives from employers and banks on the income and tax situation of taxpayers and use it, wherever possible, to send out a return that can spare the taxpayer the hassle of filling out a tax return or hiring a preparer. Under the current tax code, the Simple Return could eventually encompass nearly 40 percent of U.S. taxpayers. It could reduce the burden of tax compliance on Americans by about $4.4 billion a year, and most of these benefits would accrue to taxpayers with middle and low incomes. In recent decades, the tax authorities have made a substantial push toward collecting information from employers, financial institutions, and taxpayers in electronic form. As the costs of information technology and communications continue to plummet, it is time to take the next step and enact the Simple Return.

References

Bankman, Joseph. 2005. *Simplifying Tax for the Average Citizen*. PowerPoint presentation to the Meeting of the President's Advisory Panel on Federal Tax Reform. Georgetown University, May 17.

Berube, Alan, and others. 2002. "The Price of Paying Taxes: How Tax Preparation and Refund Loan Fees Erode the Benefits of the EITC." Progressive Policy Institute Survey Series. Brookings.

Burman, Leonard. 2000. "Testimony before the U.S. Senate. Appropriations Subcommittee on Treasury and General Government." LS-548. U.S. Department of the Treasury.

California Franchise Tax Board. 2005. *Budget Change Proposal: ReadyReturn*. BCP 4. Sacramento.

———. 2006. *ReadyReturn Pilot: Tax Year 2004 Study Results*. Sacramento.

Gale, William G., and Janet Holtzblatt. 1997. "On the Possibility of a No-Return Tax System." *National Tax Journal* 50 (September): 475–85.

Government Accountability Office (GAO). 1996. *Status of Tax Systems Modernization, Tax Delinquencies, and the Potential for Return-Free Filing*. GAO/T-GGD/AIMD-96-88.

———. 1997. *Taxation Policy and Administration: 1996 Annual Report on GAO's Tax-Related Work*. GAO/GGD-97-122.

———. 2002. *Tax Deductions: Further Estimates of Taxpayers Who May Have Overpaid Federal Taxes by Not Itemizing*. GAO-02-509.

———. 2003. *Paid Tax Preparers: Most Taxpayers Believe They Benefit, but Some Are Poorly Served*. Testimony of James R. White before the Senate Finance Committee. April 1, 2003. GAO-03-610T.

Internal Revenue Service. 1987. *Current Feasibility of a Return-Free Tax System*. U.S. Department of the Treasury.

———. 2001. *Individual Public-Use Microdata Files*. U.S. Department of the Treasury.

———. 2005. *Individual Income Tax Returns, Preliminary Data, 2003*. U.S. Department of the Treasury.

Norquist, Grover. 2005. "Implementing a 'Return-Free' Tax Filing Scheme." PowerPoint presentation to the Meeting of the President's Advisory Panel on Federal Tax Reform. Georgetown University, May 17.

U.S. Department of the Treasury. 2003. *Return-Free Tax Systems: Tax Simplification Is a Prerequisite*. Report to Congress.

U.S. House of Representatives. Committee on Ways and Means. Subcommittee on Oversight. 2004. "Statement of Joel Slemrod, University of Michigan, Ann Arbor." 108 Cong. 2 sess. Government Printing Office.

Reforming Corporate Taxation in a Global Economy

A Proposal to Adopt Formulary Apportionment

11

REUVEN S. AVI-YONAH AND KIMBERLY A. CLAUSING

The current system of taxing the income of multinational enterprises (MNEs) in the United States is flawed across multiple dimensions. The system provides an artificial tax incentive to earn income in low-tax countries, rewards aggressive tax planning, and is not compatible with any common metrics of efficiency. The U.S. system is also notoriously complex: observers are nearly unanimous in lamenting the heavy compliance burdens and the impracticality of coherent enforcement. Furthermore, despite a corporate tax rate 1 standard deviation above that of other members of the Organization for Economic Cooperation and Development (OECD), the U.S. corporate tax system raises relatively little revenue, due in part to the shifting of income outside the U.S. tax base.

In this proposal, we advocate moving to a system of formulary apportionment (FA) for taxing the corporate income of MNEs. Under our proposal, the U.S. tax base for MNEs would be calculated based on a fraction of their worldwide income. This fraction would simply be the share of their worldwide sales that occur in the United States. This system is similar to the current method that U.S. states use to allocate national income across

The authors acknowledge valuable feedback from Rosanne Altshuler, Mihir Desai, Jon Talisman, Michael Durst, Michael Knoll, Reed Shuldiner, Chris Sanchirico, Joann Weiner, Diane Ring, Yariv Brauner, Joseph Guttentag, Philip West, and the Hamilton Project staff, especially Peter Orszag, Jason Bordoff, and Michael Deich.

Figure 11-1. Statutory Corporate Tax Rates, OECD Countries, 1979–2004

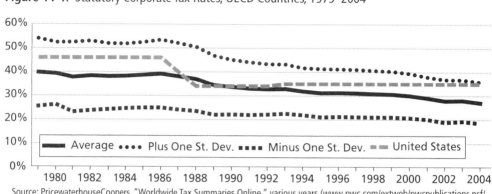

Source: PricewaterhouseCoopers, "Worldwide Tax Summaries Online," various years (www.pwc.com/extweb/pwcpublications.nsf/docid/9B2B76032544964C8525717E00606CBD).

states. The state system arose due to the widespread belief that it was impractical to account separately for what income is earned in each state when states are highly integrated economically. Similarly, in an increasingly global world economy, it is difficult to assign profits to individual countries; attempts to do so are fraught with opportunities for tax avoidance.

Under our proposed FA system, firms would no longer have an artificial tax incentive to shift income to low-tax locations. This would help protect the U.S. tax base while reducing the distortionary features of the current tax system. In addition, the complexity and administrative burden of the system would be reduced. The proposed system would be both better suited to an integrated world economy and more compatible with the tax policy goals of efficiency, equity, and simplicity.

Description of the Current U.S. System of Corporate Taxation

Under the current tax system, MNEs (both resident and nonresident) pay tax to the U.S. government based on the income that they report earning in the United States. As is typical, the United States uses a separate accounting (SA) system, where firms account for income and expenses in each country separately. The current U.S. tax rate is 35 percent. Figure 11-1 shows the evolution of corporate tax rates for OECD countries over the past quarter century. The U.S. statutory corporate tax rate has been increasing relative to other OECD countries over the previous fifteen years and is now 1 standard deviation higher than the average OECD tax rate.

The U.S. government taxes U.S. MNEs on a residence basis, so U.S. resident firms incur taxation on income earned abroad as well as income earned in the United States. This system is sometimes referred to as a credit system: U.S. firms receive a tax credit for taxes paid to foreign governments. The tax credit is limited to the U.S. tax liability, although firms may generally use excess credits from income earned in high-tax countries to offset U.S. tax due on income earned in low-tax countries, a process known as *cross-crediting*. Taxation occurs only when income is repatriated. Thus income can grow free of U.S. tax before repatriation, a process known as *deferral*.[1] Deferral and cross-crediting provide strong incentives to earn income in low-tax countries. There is also typically an incentive to avoid income in high-tax countries due to the limited tax credit.

As an example, consider a U.S.-based MNE that operates a subsidiary in Ireland. Assume that the U.S. corporate income tax rate is 35 percent, while the Irish corporate income tax rate is 12.5 percent. The Irish subsidiary earns €800 and decides to repatriate €70 of the profits to the United States. Assume, for ease of computation, a one-to-one exchange rate. First, the Irish affiliate pays €100 to the Irish government on profits of €800. It then repatriates $70 to the United States, investing the remaining profit (€630) in its Irish operations. The firm must pay U.S. tax on the repatriated income, but it is eligible for a tax credit of $100 (the taxes paid) times 70/700 (the ratio of dividends to after-tax profits), or $10. This assumes that the U.S. MNE does not have excess foreign tax credits from its operations in high-tax countries; if it does, it can use these credits to offset taxes due on the repatriated Irish profits. Due to deferral, the remaining profits (€630) can grow abroad tax-free before repatriation.

This system creates a clear incentive to earn profits in low-tax countries. Firms may respond by locating real activities (jobs, assets, production) in low-tax countries. In addition, firms may respond by shifting profits to low-tax locations, disproportionate to the scale of business activities in such locations. There are multiple ways to shift income among countries. For example, it may be advantageous for MNEs to alter the debt-to-equity ratios of affiliated firms in high- and low-tax countries in order to maximize interest deductions in high-tax countries and taxable profits in low-tax countries. Furthermore, MNEs have an incentive to distort the prices on intrafirm transactions in order to shift income to low-tax locations. For

---

1. The subpart F provisions of U.S. tax law prevent some firms from taking full advantage of deferral. Under subpart F, certain foreign income of controlled foreign corporations, including income from passive investments, is subject to immediate taxation.

example, firms can follow a strategy of underpricing (overpricing) intrafirm exports (imports) to (from) low-tax countries, following the opposite strategy with respect to high-tax countries.

In theory, firms should be limited in their ability to engage in tax-motivated transfer pricing by fear of detection. Governments generally use an arm's-length standard, requiring MNEs to price intrafirm transactions as if they were occurring at arm's length. Nonetheless, there is universal agreement that this standard leaves substantial room for tax incentives to affect pricing: arm's-length prices are difficult to establish for many intermediate goods and services. Furthermore, as argued later in this chapter, the arm's-length standard has become administratively unworkable in its complexity and as a result rarely provides useful guidance regarding economic value.

Some countries (such as Japan and the United Kingdom) use a tax-credit system similar to that used by the United States. Others (such as France and the Netherlands) exempt most foreign income from taxation, which is referred to as a territorial system of international taxation. In theory, MNEs based in these countries have an even greater incentive to incur income in low-tax countries because such income will not typically be taxed on repatriation.

Shortly before the 2004 election, the Congress passed the *American Jobs Creation Act* (2004). The international tax provisions of this law represent a subtle shift toward a territorial system of taxing international income in the United States. For example, the legislation contained a provision to allow a temporary tax holiday for dividend repatriations of 5.25 percent. This provided a substantial tax advantage to repatriating funds from low-tax countries in the year of the tax break.

On net, this holiday made investments in low-tax countries more attractive relative to the prior status quo because there is now the promise of methods for repatriating profits without incurring large tax costs. In addition, other measures of the legislation permanently lighten the taxation on foreign income, including provisions that facilitate cross-crediting as well as changes in the interest allocation rules.

Problems with the Current System

The current system of corporate taxation has both conceptual and practical weaknesses. First, the system is not suited to the global nature of international business. In particular, international production processes make the SA system of assigning profit to specific geographic destinations inherently arbitrary. Furthermore, the very nature of MNE operations generates additional profit over what would occur with strictly arm's-length transactions between unaffiliated entities. Theories of MNEs emphasize that they arise in part due to organizational and internalization advantages relative to purely domestic firms. Such advantages imply that profit is generated in part by internalizing transactions within the firm. Thus, with firms that are truly integrated across borders, holding related entities to an arm's-length standard for the pricing of intracompany transactions does not make sense, nor does allocating income and expenses on a country-by-country basis. In fact, similar logic was behind the use of FA for U.S. state governments. With an integrated U.S. economy, it does not make sense to attribute profits and expenses to individual states or to regulate transfer prices between entities of different states.

In addition, the current system is based on an artificial distinction among legal entities. For instance, companies are taxed differently based on whether they use subsidiaries or branches. As one example, deferral of taxation on unrepatriated profits is allowed for the former but not for the latter. Recently, there has been an increasingly common use of hybrid entities (treated as subsidiaries by one country and branches by another) to achieve double nontaxation.

Another related problem is that the current system is based on an increasingly artificial distinction between MNEs whose parent is incorporated in the United States and MNEs whose parent is incorporated elsewhere. The former, but not the latter, are subject to worldwide taxation with its attendant complexities. The current distinction has led to a spate of inversion transactions, in which U.S.-based MNEs formally shift the location of incorporation of their parent offshore without changing the location of their business activities. Arguably, it has also encouraged takeovers of U.S.-based MNEs by foreign-based MNEs who can benefit from territorial systems of taxation.

Second, as explained above, the current U.S. system of international taxation creates an artificial tax incentive to locate profits in low-tax countries, both by locating real economic activities in such countries and by shifting profits toward locations that are taxed more lightly. It is apparent that U.S. MNEs book disproportionate amounts of profit in low-tax locations. For example, figure 11-2 shows the top ten profit locations for U.S. MNEs in 2003, based on the share of worldwide (non-U.S.) profits earned in each location. While some of the countries have a large U.S. presence in terms of economic activity, seven of the top ten profit countries are locations with very low effective tax rates.

Figure 11-2. Where Were the Profits for U.S. MNEs in 2003?[a]

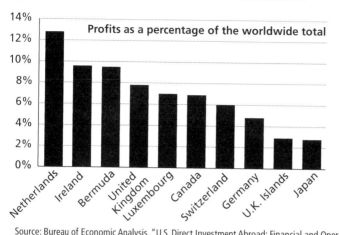

Country	Effective Tax Rate (percent)
Netherlands	5.3
Ireland	6.1
Bermuda	1.7
United Kingdom	20.1
Luxembourg	−1.8
Canada	23.5
Switzerland	4.5
Germany	8.2
U.K. Islands	1.3
Japan	36.9

Source: Bureau of Economic Analysis, "U.S. Direct Investment Abroad: Financial and Operating Data for U.S. Multinational Companies" (www.bea.gov/international/di1usdop.htm).

a. In 2003 majority-owned affiliates of U.S. MNEs earned $326 billion of net income. This figure shows percentages of the worldwide (non-U.S.) total net income occurring in each of the top ten income countries. Thus each percentage point translates into approximately $3.3 billion of net income. Effective tax rates are calculated as foreign income taxes paid relative to net (pretax) income. The year 2003 is the most recent year with revised data available. The BEA conducts annual surveys of operations of U.S. parent companies and their foreign affiliates. These data are discussed in more detail in appendix A, available online at www.brookings.edu/papers/2007/06corporatetaxes_clausing.aspx.

The literature has consistently found that MNEs are sensitive to corporate tax rate differences across countries in their financial decisions (de Mooij 2005). One recent study suggests that corporate income tax revenues in the United States in 2002 were approximately 35 percent lower due to income shifting.[2]

This problem has worsened because U.S. corporate tax rates have become increasingly out of line with those of other countries. In the past twenty years, most OECD countries have lowered their corporate income tax rates whereas U.S. rates have remained relatively constant. This growing discrepancy likely results in increasing amounts of lost revenue for the U.S. government due to the strengthening of income-shifting incentives.

Also, the literature suggests a substantial real responsiveness to tax rate differences among countries (de Mooij and Ederveen 2003). These findings imply less activity in the United States and less tax revenue for the U.S.

2. This estimate is from Clausing (2007b). For more details, see appendix A, online at www.brookings.edu/papers/2007/06corporatetaxes_clausing.aspx.

Figure 11-3. Where Were the Jobs in 2003? [a]

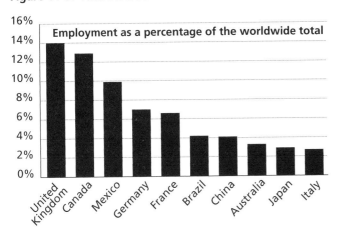

Country	Effective Tax Rate (percent)
United Kingdom	20.1
Canada	23.5
Mexico	34.8
Germany	8.2
France	25.1
Brazil	65.4
China	13.0
Australia	28.0
Japan	36.9
Italy	35.1

Source: See figure 11-2.

a. In 2003 majority-owned affiliates of U.S. MNEs employed 8.2 million employees. This figure shows percentages of the worldwide (non-U.S.) total employment occurring in each of the top ten countries. Thus each percentage point translates into approximately 82,000 jobs. Effective tax rates are calculated as foreign income taxes paid relative to net (pretax) income. The year 2003 is the most recent year with revised data available. The BEA conducts annual surveys of operations of U.S. parent companies and their foreign affiliates. These data are discussed in more detail in appendix A, available online at www.brookings.edu/papers/2007/06corporatetaxes_clausing.aspx.

government. However, the tax responsiveness of real activity is less immediately apparent in the data. For example, figure 11-3 shows the top ten employment locations for U.S. MNEs in 2003, based on the share of worldwide (non-U.S.) employment in each location. The high-employment countries are the usual suspects—large economies with close economic ties to the United States. As the accompanying table indicates, tax rates are not particularly low for these countries.

Third, the current system is absurdly complex. As Taylor notes, observers have described the system as "a cumbersome creation of stupefying complexity" with "rules that lack coherence and often work at cross purposes."[3] Altshuler (2005, p. 12) noted that observers testifying before the President's Advisory Panel on Federal Tax Reform found the system "deeply, deeply flawed," noting that "it is difficult to overstate the crisis in the administration of the international tax system of the United States."

3. Willard Taylor, "Presentation to President's Advisory Panel on Federal Tax Reform: International Provisions of the Internal Revenue Code," PowerPoint presentation, slide 9, March 31, 2005 (www.taxreformpanel.gov/meetings/docs/willard.ppt#257,1,Presentation).

Figure 11-4. Central Government Corporate Tax Revenues Relative to GDP, OECD Countries, 1979–2002

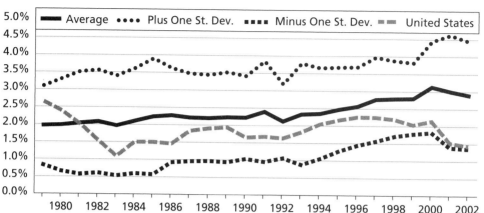

Source: GDP data from World Bank (various years); corporate tax revenue data from OECD, "Public Sector, Taxation and Market Regulation," various years (www.oecd.org/topicstatsportal/0,2647,en_2825_495698_1_1_1_1_1,00.html#500714).

Fourth, particularly given the high U.S. corporate statutory tax rates, the U.S. corporate tax system raises relatively little revenue. Figure 11-4 shows the evolution of government corporate tax revenues relative to GDP for OECD countries. For most OECD countries, revenues have increased as a share of GDP even as corporate tax rates have declined. The average OECD country receives 3 percent of GDP from corporate tax revenue by the end of the sample. Most observers attribute this trend to a broadening of the tax base for many OECD countries during this period. For the United States, revenues are lower. Although they fluctuate with the cyclical position of the economy, they tend to be closer to 2 percent of GDP. There are several plausible reasons for the lower amount of U.S. revenue, including the increasingly aggressive use of corporate tax shelters, a narrower corporate tax base, and stronger incentives for tax avoidance, which tend to increase because the U.S. tax rate is high relative to other countries.

A Proposal to Adopt Formulary Apportionment

Our proposal would address most of the aforementioned flaws with the current system of corporate taxation. Under FA, tax liabilities would reflect truly globally integrated business, and they would not be dependent on artificial distinctions among legal entities. Under FA, unlike SA, firms would have no incentive to shift income across countries. Since there would be no tax savings associated with shifting income across countries, the overall incentive to locate real activities in low-tax countries would also be reduced.

Furthermore, absent income shifting, U.S. government revenues would be higher. If the proposal offered here were implemented in a revenue-neutral fashion, it would enable a substantial cut in the corporate income tax rate. Since the proposed system could entail dramatic simplification and help finance a corporate tax rate reduction, there is justification for corporate support.

How Would Formulary Apportionment Work?

Under FA, a unitary business is defined according to whether the parent corporation exercises legal and economic control over its subsidiaries. That unitary business is treated as a single taxpayer, and its income is calculated by subtracting worldwide expenses from worldwide income, based on a global accounting system, without regard to legal distinctions among units. The resulting net income is apportioned among taxing jurisdictions based on a formula. Each jurisdiction then applies its tax rate to the income apportioned to it by the formula and collects the amount of tax resulting from this calculation.

Our proposed system would use a sales-based formula.[4] In the experience of U.S. states, income has been allocated to state jurisdictions through a variety of formulas. Historically, many U.S. states have used the so-called Massachusetts formula, which uses equal weights on property, payroll, and sales. For example, under an equal-weighted FA system, tax liability to the U.S. government would be based on the U.S. tax rate times the fraction of worldwide profits that are attributed to the United States. This fraction would be based on how much of worldwide economic activity (an average of sales, assets, and payroll shares) occurs in the United States.

Observers have noted that an FA system creates an implicit tax on the factors used in the formula, thus discouraging the location of assets and employment in high-tax locations. This formula also leaves unresolved

---

4. A similar proposal has been advocated by Durst (2007), who offers legislative language for implementing a formulary approach to corporate taxation. He notes that technical barriers to adopting FA have been overstated; defining a unitary group and establishing the destination of sales are both attainable objectives.

issues concerning the treatment of intangible property and how to value property. In part due to these concerns, we propose a simpler formula, which would consider only the fraction of sales in each location. Sales would be determined on a destination basis: that is, they would be based on the location of the customer rather than the location of production. Alternative formulas are discussed in appendix B.[5]

The key advantage of a sales-based formula is that sales are far less responsive to tax differences across markets because the customers themselves are far less mobile than firm assets or employment. Even in a high-tax country, firms still have an incentive to sell as much as possible. In addition, if some countries adopt sales-based formulas, other countries will have an incentive to adopt sales-based formulas as well, in order to avoid losing payroll or assets to countries in which these factors are not part of the formula.

The U.S. state experience reinforces the merits of this proposal. In recent years, many U.S. states have shifted to a formula that double-weights the sales factor, often based on a desire to encourage exports out of state and discourage imports into the state. State incentives to move toward a sales-based formula are well documented. For example, Edmiston (2002) generates a model with this prediction, and Omer and Shelley (2004) empirically document this trend. According to Weiner (2005), twenty-three states double-weight sales as of 2004, and eight others have an even larger weight on sales. Some states even use a sales-only formula (which was approved for Iowa by the Supreme Court).

In addition, international experience suggests that movement toward a sales-based formula is likely. Because of the widespread belief that imposing taxes on imports and exempting exports reduces trade deficits, it is possible that if some countries were to adopt a sales-based formula for apportioning corporate income, other countries would follow suit. It would also be in these countries' economic interest to avoid the implicit tax on assets and payroll that is embedded in a three-factor formula. This built-in incentive for sales-based formulas would minimize the likelihood of over- or undertaxation due to disparate formulas, which is an obstacle to adopting FA. Still, it would be ideal to have international cooperation and consensus regarding both the adoption of FA and the choice of formula. Further on, we discuss the problems that would arise if only the

5. Appendix B is available online at www.brookings.edu/papers/2007/06corporatetaxes_clausing.aspx.

United States were to adopt FA, or if different countries were to use different formulas.

Four Key Advantages of Formulary Apportionment

The first advantage associated with this proposal is that it would align the U.S. corporate tax system with the reality of a global world economy. In a world where most major corporations are MNEs, where most U.S. international trade is done by MNEs, and where many opportunities for tax avoidance have an international dimension, the current U.S. system of corporate taxation is obsolete. In particular, SA systems treat each affiliate of an MNE as a distinct entity with its own costs and income. Allocating income and expenses across countries is both complex (see discussion below) and conceptually unsatisfactory. Furthermore, such allocation generates ample opportunity for MNEs to reduce worldwide tax burdens by shifting income to more lightly taxed jurisdictions.

Furthermore, an FA system does not create an artificial legal distinction among types of MNE organization, nor does an FA system rely on an artificial distinction between MNEs whose parent is incorporated in the United States and MNEs whose parent is incorporated elsewhere.

The second advantage associated with the proposal is that it eliminates the tax incentive to shift income to low-tax countries. Because income-shifting incentives are an important part of the overall tax incentive for locating operations in low-tax countries, removing this incentive would result in fewer tax-distorted decisions regarding the location of economic activity. Under FA, firms are taxed based on their global income. Thus accounting for the income earned in each country is no longer necessary, and there is no way to lighten global tax burdens by manipulating this accounting for tax purposes. Since the share of global income that is allocated to each country under FA depends on the share of an MNE's sales that are in each country, there would be some tax incentive to distort the location of sales among markets. However, this could be combated by basing the sales definition on a destination principle. In general, firms have an incentive to encourage sales in each market in order to serve the customers there.

Thus the adoption of FA should vastly reduce tax distortions to MNE decisionmaking. Also, it is important to note that despite the emphasis on the sales of MNEs in different countries, this remains a corporate income tax, not a consumption tax. For example, tax liabilities do not arise unless an MNE is earning profits worldwide, irrespective of its sales.

Even though a unilateral move toward FA creates large incentives for other countries to adopt FA, and in particular sales-based formulas, such changes in the taxation of international income ultimately help governments set their tax policies more independently. The wishes of voters in each government influence the ideal size of government, required revenue needs, and the allocation of the tax burden among subgroups within society. Under FA, governments would be able to choose their own corporate tax rate based on their assessment of these sorts of policy goals rather than on the pressures of tax competition for an increasingly mobile capital income tax base.

The third advantage associated with the proposal is the massive increase in simplicity that it would enable for the international tax system. If FA were adopted by our major trading partners, simplification gains would be particularly large, but simplification would still exist even if FA were to be adopted unilaterally. To determine U.S. tax liability, there would be no need to allocate income or expenses among countries, resulting in far lighter compliance burdens for firms. Subpart F and the foreign tax credit would no longer be necessary since there is no deferral under this system (which is essentially territorial and treats U.S.- and foreign-based MNEs alike).

Furthermore, the likely administrative savings from abandoning the current cumbersome transfer-pricing regime are huge. The current regime consumes a disproportionate share of both public (that is, the Internal Revenue Service [IRS]) and private sector resources. For example, several recent Ernst and Young surveys of MNEs have concluded that "transfer pricing continues to be, and will remain, the most important international tax issue facing MNEs" (Ernst and Young 2006, p. 5). For the government, audit costs are three to seven times higher for federal transfer-pricing cases than for state FA audits, even in cases where the most efficient federal cases are compared to the least efficient state cases (Bucks and Mazerov 1993).

Opinions in transfer-pricing cases run to hundreds of pages each, and litigation involves billions of dollars in proposed deficiencies, such as the recently settled Glaxo case ($9 billion in proposed deficiency, settled for $3.4 billion) or the Aramco advantage case (litigated and lost by the IRS, which asserted deficiencies of more than $9 billion). There is no indication that the 1994 regulations under Internal Revenue Code (IRC) section 482 (implementing SA) have abated this trend (Avi-Yonah 2006).

By contrast, FA is relatively simple since all that it requires is determining which businesses are unitary (see following section) and establishing the destination of arm's-length sales of goods or services. Once these two elements are established, the resulting formula permits both the taxpayers and the IRS to determine the correct tax liability for each jurisdiction that uses FA. This means that there is no longer a need to apportion expenses because all a business needs is to calculate its worldwide net income. This net income is then allocated to jurisdictions based on a single formula, the tax rate of each jurisdiction is applied to the allocated income, and the tax is paid.

The fourth advantage associated with the adoption of FA for the United States is that the new system would either raise more revenue or enable a substantial rate reduction. Estimating exactly how much revenue such a change would raise is a difficult task, and the details of the implementing legislation and regulations would likely be influential in determining the ultimate effects of the proposed change. Still, previous studies and back-of-the-envelope calculations suggest that such a change is likely to generate substantial additional U.S. government revenue.

Appendix A reviews several such calculations in more detail.[6] For example, one recent study finds that tax avoidance activities reduced income earned by U.S. MNEs in the United States by more than $150 billion in 2002, lowering corporate tax revenues by about 35 percent (Clausing 2007b). Since FA would eliminate tax avoidance incentives, one would expect it to raise revenues by a similar margin. If corporate tax revenues were to increase by 35 percent, that would correspond to an increase of approximately $50 billion (annually) over the period 2001–04.

To date, the most thorough estimate of the revenue effects of FA has been done by Shackleford and Slemrod (1998), in which they use accounting data in financial reports for forty-six U.S.-based MNEs over the period 1989–93 to estimate changes in revenue under a three-factor FA system. They estimate that U.S. government revenues would increase by 38 percent. This increase is not dependent on any particular factor; a single-factor sales formula would increase revenues by 26 percent. Given the changes in the international tax environment since the time period of their data, and in particular the increasing discrepancy between the U.S. corporate tax rate and those of other countries, these estimates likely understate the current U.S. revenue gain with FA adoption.

Table 11-1 shows illustrative statistics on the operations of U.S. multinational affiliates in 2003 for all countries where the Bureau of Economic Analysis (BEA) reports data and where affiliate operations are at least 0.5 percent of worldwide totals in either sales or income. The first column

6. See www.brookings.edu/papers/2007/06corporatetaxes_clausing.aspx.

Table 11-1. U.S. MNE Operations, in Order of Excess Income Share, 2003[a]

Percent

Countries	(1) Share of sales	(2) Share of income	(3) Effective tax rate	(4) Excess income share (versus sales)
Luxembourg	0.3	7.0	−2	2,585
Bermuda	1.4	9.5	2	600
Barbados	0.1	0.6	3	324
U.K. Caribbean Islands	0.8	2.9	1	246
Portugal	0.3	0.8	6	205
Netherlands	4.4	12.8	5	194
Denmark	0.4	1.0	11	150
Ireland	3.9	9.6	6	146
Indonesia	0.4	0.8	40	71
Switzerland	4.3	6.0	5	41
Belgium	2.1	2.1	11	−3
Hong Kong	1.9	1.8	9	−6
Singapore	3.4	2.7	7	−19
Norway	0.7	0.6	66	−23
Spain	2.1	1.6	10	−24
Taiwan	0.9	0.7	19	−27
China	1.7	1.1	13	−33
Sweden	1.7	1.1	20	−33
Germany	7.6	4.8	8	−37
Korea, Republic of	0.7	0.4	28	−39
Thailand	0.7	0.4	39	−43
United Kingdom	14.0	7.8	20	−44
Malaysia	1.1	0.6	23	−48
Australia	2.6	1.3	28	−48
Japan	5.9	2.8	37	−52
Mexico	3.9	1.6	35	−58
France	5.2	2.0	25	−61
Argentina	0.6	0.2	45	−64
Italy	3.0	1.0	35	−66
Brazil	2.2	0.2	65	−92

Source: BEA, "U.S. Direct Investment Abroad: Financial and Operating Data for U.S. Multinational Companies" (www.bea.gov/international/di1usdop.htm).

a. For those economies with the largest U.S. affiliate operations. Economies are selected for inclusion in this table if either their sales share or their income share exceeds 0.5 percent of worldwide totals. The year 2003 is the most recent year with revised data available. BEA conducts annual surveys of operations of U.S. parent companies and their foreign affiliates. These data are discussed in more detail in appendix A, online at www.brookings.edu/papers/2007/06corporatetaxes_clausing.aspx.

shows the share of worldwide foreign affiliate sales that occur in each country; the second column shows the share of worldwide affiliate net income earned in each country; the third shows the effective tax rate; and the fourth shows the percentage by which the income share exceeds or falls short of the sales share. It is immediately apparent that those countries with income shares that vastly exceed their sales shares tend to be very low tax countries, and those with sales shares that exceed their income shares are typically high-tax countries. Thus it appears quite likely that a sales-based FA system would increase revenues in comparatively high-tax countries and decrease them in low-tax countries.

As one plausible conjecture, if revenues increase by 35 percent with FA, one can also calculate the tax-rate reduction that would be possible with a revenue-neutral implementation of FA. In that case, the implied new corporate tax rate would be 26 percent, 9 percentage points lower than the current corporate tax rate of 35 percent. Of course, one could also pursue an intermediate policy that allowed a smaller rate reduction and also increased revenues more modestly.[7]

Downsides of FA

There are potential drawbacks associated with this proposal. The concerns fit into three categories: first, some critics argue that FA is inherently arbitrary; second, there are a range of implementation issues; and third, the proposed FA system is likely to negatively affect some stakeholders because some domestic industries and firms would find that their tax obligations increase under the new system.

Is FA Arbitrary?

Some would consider basing the corporate income tax liability solely on the extent of sales in a particular country to be arbitrary. Indeed, this approach focuses on the demand side of the value created by the corporation. For example, the market jurisdiction would levy the entire corporate income tax in the case of an MNE that produces in one country and sells in another. Still, it is not clear that the current SA regime is less arbitrary given the incentive to shift profits to low-tax jurisdictions.

Under the current regime, it is quite possible that an MNE will not pay taxes either in the location of production (because of tax competition and production tax havens) or in the location of distribution (because it can

---

7. See appendix A online for more background.

avoid having a permanent establishment or minimize the profits attributable to the distribution function), while any taxes due to its residence jurisdiction are subject to deferral or exemption. Such a result is more arbitrary than consistently assigning profits to the market jurisdiction, especially if most countries adopt the same formula.[8]

It is true that any formula can produce arbitrary results in a given industry. For example, the oil industry has long argued that it is unfair for it to be taxed based on payroll, assets, or sales because most of its profits result from the oil reserves themselves, which are not reflected in the formula (since they are typically not assets of the company for any length of time). However, while some industries would lose under the proposed formula, others (such as major U.S. exporters) would win, and most taxpayers would gain from the increased simplicity and transparency of the FA regime.[9]

Implementation Issues

Some implementation issues arise with regard to defining a unitary business and determining the location of sales. Others are associated with interactions between countries with incongruent corporate tax systems. Furthermore, there is a potential for nontaxation or double taxation, accounting standards across countries are not uniform, tax treaties may need modification, revenues may systematically shift away from some countries, and there may be issues of compatibility with World Trade Organization (WTO) obligations.

DEFINING A UNITARY BUSINESS AND THE DESTINATION OF SALES. First, a difficult implementation issue in adopting formulary apportionment is how to define a unitary business. Current IRC section 482 (implementing SA) merely requires direct or indirect control among related parties, without even a precise definition of what control requires. However, for

8. In fact, it is likely that a high proportion of current corporate tax collections come from taxing distribution activities that rise over the permanent establishment threshold (or are conducted in a separate subsidiary) given the ubiquity of targeted tax incentives for production activities. This explains why there is so much current pressure on the definition of *permanent establishment* (Le Gall 2006). Thus, other than reducing distortions, our proposal is a less radical shift from current reality than it appears to be from a theoretical perspective.

9. It can also be argued that ignoring intangible property, which is the source of most of the value added by MNEs, is arbitrary under both our formula and the state formulas. But intangibles do not have a real location, and their value inheres in the whole MNE, which is why they cannot be adequately addressed under SA. Any formula that ignores intangibles assigns their value to the entire MNE (divided based on the other factors used in the formula), and this result more accurately reflects the nature of intangibles.

purposes of FA, mere control is not enough: in the absence of unitary business activities (that is, an integrated MNE), FA can lead to significant distortions in the way a business operates (lumping together disparate sales from different businesses). In addition, relying solely on control would violate tax treaties that require something more for a subsidiary to be an agent of the parent.

We would suggest a test of unitary business that depends on whether the subsidiary operates under the legal and economic control of the parent. Such a test would look at factors such as where overall business strategy is set, the extent to which risk is shared, and the extent to which there are transfers of goods and services among the units of an MNE. In most modern MNEs, the level of integration is sufficient to find a unitary business, as the experience of the states in administering this test has shown. Imposing a rebuttable presumption of control whenever there is a combination of legal control (that is, ownership of more than 50 percent of the stock by vote or value, with the usual attribution rules) plus some de minimis level of inter-MNE transactions should prevent tax-motivated attempts to break control.

While it is possible that taxpayers may try to avoid taxation by using independent distributing agents for their sales, it is unlikely that they would be willing to relinquish real control over their marketing and distribution activities since that is why they are organized in MNE form. In addition, we would adopt a look-through rule that would regard any sales made by an MNE to an unrelated distributor as sales made into the United States if the distributor sells the goods into the United States and does not substantially transform them before they are resold.[10] This would prevent MNEs from avoiding tax by selling their goods into the United States via unrelated straw men who would themselves have minimal profits.[11]

Second, implementing a sales-based formula depends on the ability of tax administration to determine the destination of sales of goods and services. In general, for a country such as the United States that maintains customs controls, establishing the destination of goods is not a significant problem and is already the basis of several IRC provisions.[12]

---

10. The substantial transformation test can be based on current U.S. Treasury regulation, section 1.954-3(a)(4).

11. Since we ignore intra-MNE sales, the MNE cannot engage in round-tripping transactions in which it exports goods and then reimports them into the United States.

12. See, for example, Treasury regulation 1.954-3(a)(3) (the base company sales rule), as well as the various export-related rules (IRC sections 941–943, 970–971, and 991–994), all of which rely on establishing the destination of goods sold.

The destination of services poses more difficult issues, but these problems also arise under a value added tax and have, in general, been treated successfully. For business-to-business provision of services (which covers the majority of services to unrelated parties), a rule that the destination of services is the jurisdiction in which the receiving business takes a deduction for payment to the service provider should establish the destination of the service.

INTERACTIONS BETWEEN COUNTRIES WITH DIFFERENT TAX SYSTEMS. It would be ideal for most major countries to coordinate implementation of FA and come to a joint agreement on the definition of the formula for apportioning global income. The European Union (EU) Commission is actively working on defining a common tax base and apportioning it among member states by formula.[13] If the United States and the EU both adopt FA, there is obvious potential for coordinating their efforts through the OECD. It may be possible, given current discussions of FA within the EU, to reach agreement with the EU (and possibly with other OECD members) on the adoption of FA before it is implemented. With international cooperation, the possibility of double or nontaxation would be reduced, and there would be less room for MNEs to respond strategically to variations in country formulas.

Still, while an international agreement would be ideal, we do not believe that reaching such an agreement should necessarily be a prerequisite for the United States to adopt FA unilaterally. Many significant advances in international taxation—such as the foreign tax credit and controlled foreign corporation regimes, as well as more problematic developments such as the current transfer-pricing methods—resulted from unilateral action by the United States, which was followed by most other jurisdictions and by the OECD.

Moreover, one should note that unilateral adoption by the United States of an FA system for taxing international income would create a powerful incentive for other countries that use SA to also adopt FA. In a world with both FA countries and SA countries, FA countries would immediately appear as tax havens from an SA country perspective. For example, an MNE operating in SA and FA countries would have an incentive to book

---

13. Gnaedinger and Nadal (2007) report that EU tax commissioner Laszlo Kovacs is optimistic that the common consolidated corporate tax base would move forward, despite the opposition of a minority of EU member governments. If a member country vetoes the draft legislation, the EU may turn to the enhanced cooperation procedure through which action can still proceed. According to these authors, Kovacs described a timeline through which the common tax base could be in place as soon as 2010.

all its income in FA countries: the tax liability in such countries does not depend on the income booked there but rather on the fraction of a firm's activities in that location. Such responses would likely greatly reduce the tax revenues of remaining SA countries. Thus SA countries would have a strong incentive to adopt FA.

Still, if the United States adopts FA unilaterally and other countries do not follow suit (or if they follow suit later), or if countries adopt different formulas, there is the potential for double or nontaxation. This is the largest obstacle to adoption of FA. Furthermore, even if other countries eventually adopt FA, there would likely be a transition period while governments and MNEs adapt to the new tax environment. During this transition period, there may be problematic instances of double taxation, and the firms that experience increased tax liabilities under FA may prove to be vocal critics.

Still, it is not clear that FA would produce more double taxation or double nontaxation than the current SA regime. As noted earlier, there is significant evidence that the SA regime results in undertaxation because MNEs succeed in shifting profits from high-tax to low-tax jurisdictions. However, SA can also result in double taxation to the extent that a high-tax jurisdiction successfully asserts that profits belong to it and not to another high-tax jurisdiction.

DEFINING THE TAX BASE. There are issues associated with the need for common accounting standards. Still, the unilateral adoption of FA by the United States need not require the United States and other countries to have a common tax base. However, as noted above, the ideal situation would be for most countries to adopt FA using the same (sales-based) formula. For this purpose, a common definition of the tax base is needed, as currently advocated by the EU Commission.

Such a common definition of the tax base (as opposed to harmonized tax rates, which are unlikely as well as undesirable) could be achieved: MNEs already use uniform accounting for worldwide financial reporting purposes. Thus it is possible to use financial reporting as the starting point for calculating the global profit of the MNE. While there are still differences in accounting among countries, those differences are diminishing due to the spread of international accounting standards, which have been adopted in the EU and Japan. Alternatively, it may be possible to let each MNE use its home country accounting methods for calculating the global tax base. Such changes would also have the advantage of more closely aligning book income and tax income. This could act as a damper on both the underreporting of income for tax purposes and the overstatement of income for the purpose of signaling profitability to financial markets.[14]

However, if coordination of the tax base with accounting-based measures were unachievable, FA could also be implemented unilaterally by the U.S. government, using its definition of taxable income and applying it to the entire MNE. U.S.-based MNEs already have to calculate the earnings and profits of controlled foreign corporations for purposes of subpart F and the foreign tax credit, so the additional information required for adoption would not be overly burdensome. For non-U.S.-based MNEs, financial reporting to shareholders (already required by the Securities and Exchange Commission or by home country regulators) could be used as the base for calculating worldwide income. While this would create a disparity between U.S.-based and non-U.S.-based MNEs, the result is similar to allowing MNEs to use their home state base for tax purposes, as recommended by the EU.

INTERACTION WITH TAX TREATIES. Some have argued that tax treaties will need modification with adoption of FA, but it is not clear that existing U.S. tax treaties would have to be renegotiated. Transfer pricing is currently governed by article 9 of the treaties (U.S. Treasury 2006), which assumes the SA method because it addresses the commercial or financial relations between associated enterprises. If FA were adopted, article 9 would become irrelevant in those situations to which FA applies (that is, where a unitary business is found to exist) because FA ignores the transactions between related parties and treats them instead as part of a single enterprise.

Instead, FA would be governed by article 7 (U.S. Treasury 2006), which governs the relationship between a parent company and a branch (permanent establishment) or an agent. Under article 5(7), "the fact that a company that is a resident of a Contracting State controls or is controlled by a company that is a resident of the other Contracting State . . . shall not constitute either company a permanent establishment of the other." However, it is well established that a dependent agent can be a permanent establishment (article 5(5)), and whether an agent is dependent is based on whether the principal exercises legal and economic control over the agent. "An agent that is subject to detailed instructions regarding the conduct of its operations or comprehensive control by the enterprise is not legally independent" (U.S. Treasury 2006, article 5(6)).

---

14. This is discussed in Desai (2005), where he recommends reconsideration of the dual-reporting system.

In the case of a modern, integrated MNE that operates as a unitary business, a strong argument can be made that the parent of the MNE exercises both legal and economic control over the operations of the subsidiaries, especially where the subsidiaries bear no real risk of loss and acquire goods and services exclusively or almost exclusively from the parent or other related corporations. In that case, the subsidiaries should be regarded as dependent agents of the parent. Such a finding is made with increasing frequency.[15]

If the subsidiary is an agent of the parent, article 7(2) of the treaties requires the attribution of the same profits to the subsidiary "that it might be expected to make if it were a distinct and independent enterprise engaged in the same or similar activities under the same or similar conditions"(U.S. Treasury 2006). Arguably, the application of FA, even when based on a sales-only formula, satisfies this arm's-length condition because, in the absence of precise comparables (which almost never exist), it is not possible to determine exactly what profits would have been attributable to the subsidiary under SA.

When the United States adopted the comparable profits method and profit split in the 1994 transfer-pricing regulations, some countries objected that it was violating the treaties because these methods did not rely on exact comparables to find the arm's-length price. However, these objections soon subsided, and even the OECD endorsed similar methods in its transfer-pricing guidelines. The United States always maintained that both the comparable profits method and profit split satisfy the arm's-length standard despite the lack of precise comparables. Thus, were the United States to adopt FA, it could similarly argue that the resulting allocation of profits to the subsidiary is consistent with the arm's-length standard embodied in articles 7 and 9 (U.S. Treasury 2006). Despite the OECD's traditional hostility to FA, there is no way to prove— in the absence of comparables—that any profit allocation deviates from an arm's-length result.

DISTRIBUTIONAL ISSUES. Revenues may systematically shift away from some countries under FA. The current tax-haven countries would likely experience large reductions in revenues. The key determinant of which countries would gain or lose revenue is whether countries have disproportionately large or small amounts of local corporate sales relative to corporate income.

---

15. See Le Gall's (2006) discussion of recent cases from Canada, Germany, and Italy, as well as from developing countries, and of the InverWorld case in the United States.

If one considers the operations of U.S. MNEs and their foreign affiliates as a guide, it is quickly apparent that it is difficult to make generalizations about which countries would gain and which would lose. For example, developing countries do not have systematically lower (or higher) levels of local affiliate sales relative to affiliate income in comparison with richer countries. In addition, there is no evidence in the data that this factor is related to countries' trade positions. In general, with the adoption of FA, high-tax countries would likely gain revenue at the expense of low-tax countries because high-tax countries also tend to have higher shares of local corporate sales relative to corporate income.

This conclusion assumes widespread adoption of FA. Absent that, the remaining SA countries would also lose revenue: MNEs would have a strong incentive to book income in FA countries because their tax liabilities in such countries would not be affected by this accounting. Still, despite concerns about systematic revenue losses in some countries, our proposal would help many governments by eliminating incentives for tax competition.

INTERACTION WITH WTO RULES. Finally, some scholars have argued that the use of a sales-only formula by U.S. states violates WTO rules against export subsidies because they constitute an illegal border adjustment for direct taxes. In general, the WTO rules permit border adjustability for indirect taxes but not for direct taxes.

It is not clear that the adoption of a federal sales-only formula for income taxes would be a WTO violation. It can be argued that the formula is not explicitly contingent on export performance and that it serves only as a means for allocating the income tax base among jurisdictions, as opposed to exempting transactions that would otherwise be taxable. No WTO complaint has been filed against the United States on the state formulas.

Also, if the adoption of FA by the United States occurs alongside widespread adoptions at least among OECD member countries, it would seem plausible that the WTO rules (which are widely regarded as obsolete) can be renegotiated. In general, progress in the WTO is usually impeded if the United States and other OECD members disagree but not if they agree.

Negative Effects on Some Corporate Stakeholders

Analysts have noted that adoption of FA would disproportionately affect some industries and firms negatively. For example, Shackleford and Slemrod (1998) find that FA raises tax liabilities for some industries and firms but lowers liabilities for others. They estimate that the oil and gas industry would see an increase in tax liabilities of 81 percent under FA, compared with 29 percent for all other firms in their study. The authors also estimate that some firms would experience a tax decrease.

Under our proposal, firms with a disproportionate amount of U.S. sales relative to U.S. income would see tax increases under FA, while those with relatively low U.S. sales compared to U.S. income (for example, large exporters) would see tax decreases. In addition, observers such as Durst (2007) note that intangible-intensive firms would likely be adversely affected by adoption of FA because these firms have been particularly adept at lowering their tax burdens through careful tax planning under the current system.

Still, negative impacts could be muted by several considerations. First, firms would benefit from reductions in complexity and compliance burdens. Small and medium-size businesses should be particularly appreciative of such benefits. Second, if FA is accompanied by a reduction in the corporate income tax rate, which could prove quite substantial if FA is implemented in a revenue-neutral fashion, the number of firms benefiting from the adoption of FA would increase.

Conclusion

Our proposal for the adoption of formulary apportionment for the U.S. taxation of corporate income responds to the reality of an increasingly global world. MNEs have internationally integrated operations, and they are responsive to the incentives created by discrepancies among national tax policies. A separate accounting system generates an artificial need to assign income and expenses by location, and this creates ample opportunities for tax avoidance.

An FA system would remove the complexities associated with sourcing income and expenses across locations, and it would eliminate the tax incentive to shift income to more lightly taxed locations. Absent tax incentives to shift income away from the United States, U.S. corporate tax revenues would likely increase significantly. If this proposal were implemented in a revenue-neutral fashion, on the other hand, the corporate tax rate could be cut substantially. Even a revenue-neutral implementation of FA would retain the simplicity and efficiency gains associated with the proposal.

The common objections to FA appear surmountable. We have argued that the FA system is less arbitrary than the current system and that implementation issues can be overcome. While it would be ideal to implement

FA with international cooperation, there are also natural incentives within an FA system that encourage international adoption and formula harmonization. Furthermore, it is likely that FA would be compatible with current treaty and WTO obligations.

We also maintain that U.S. adoption of FA would be preferable to the other suggested reforms. First, consider a simple base-broadening, rate-lowering reform. This would no doubt be an improvement relative to the status quo because a lower rate would reduce the tax incentive to earn income in foreign countries and other distortionary effects of the current tax system. In addition, base broadening would level the playing field among different corporate activities, reducing the deadweight loss associated with tax-induced modifications in behavior. Yet, while such a reform would be desirable relative to the status quo, it would fall short of the gains from FA in terms of compatibility with the global economy, administrative simplicity, and the efficiency gains associated with eliminating income-shifting incentives.

Second, consider the Simplified Income Tax Plan suggested by the President's Advisory Panel on Federal Tax Reform (2005, chapter 6). This plan would adopt a territorial system for U.S. MNEs, exempting foreign income of U.S. firms from taxation. Unfortunately, this proposal has a negative impact on many of the problems discussed at the beginning of this chapter. In particular, firms would have an even larger incentive to shift income to low-tax locations. Furthermore, while a territorial system could be designed to be revenue neutral, the past experience of OECD countries suggests that territorial systems raise less corporate revenue (Clausing 2007a). In addition, there would be limited simplification gains in comparison with FA because MNEs would still be responsible for sourcing income and expenses across locations, and the territorial nature of the tax system would put even greater pressure on the transfer-pricing rules. We would argue that adopting FA is the only way to achieve territoriality for U.S.-based MNEs without risking significant revenue losses, worsening income-shifting incentives, and increasing the complexity of the U.S. international tax regime.

Third, compare adoption of FA to a proposal that would simply end deferral of taxation on foreign income for U.S. MNEs. One such proposal is discussed in Altshuler and Grubert (2006) as a burden-neutral worldwide taxation plan. Under this plan, all foreign income would continue to be taxed as it is currently, there would be no required allocation of expenses to foreign income, and the U.S. corporate tax rate would be lowered to keep the overall U.S. tax burden on foreign income the same. This system would effectively end deferral for U.S. resident corporations and thus dramatically reduce income-shifting incentives. The authors estimate that a burden-neutral implementation of the proposal would entail a corporate tax-rate reduction on foreign income to 28 percent.

Still, under their plan, income-shifting incentives would not be completely eliminated: foreign-based MNEs would be largely unaffected. This consideration could create a stronger tax incentive for changing ownership patterns. For example, firms could undertake inversions, basing their parent company in a tax haven. In addition, income-shifting incentives still exist for U.S. MNEs that have excess credits.

While all of these proposals have merits, they also illustrate the difficulties associated with the taxation of MNEs in a globally integrated economy. It is nearly impossible to eliminate the tax distortions associated with the location of economic activity and profits across national boundaries without a dramatic rethinking of the nature of corporate income taxation in the world economy. We hope that this proposal contributes to that deliberation.

References

Agundez-Garcia, Ana. 2006. "The Delineation and Apportionment of an EU-Consolidated Tax Base for Multi-Jurisdictional Corporate Income Taxation: A Review of Issues and Options." Paper 9. Brussels: European Commission on Taxation (October).

Altshuler, Rosanne. 2005. "International Aspects of Recommendations from the President's Advisory Panel on Federal Tax Reform." Paper presented at the panel discussion on Tax Reform in an Open Economy. Brookings, December 2.

Altshuler, Rosanne, and Harry Grubert. 2006. "Corporate Taxes in the World Economy: Reforming the Taxation of Cross-Border Income." Working Paper. Rutgers University(December).

American Jobs Creation Act. 2004. U.S. Public Law 108-357. 108 Cong. 2 sess. (October 22).

Avi-Yonah, Reuven. 2006. "The Rise and Fall of Arm's Length: A Study in the Evolution of U.S. International Taxation." *Finance and Tax Law Review* 9, no. 19: 310.

Bucks, Dan R., and Michael Mazerov. 1993. "The State Solution to the Federal Government's International Transfer Pricing Problem." *National Tax Journal* 46, no. 3: 385–92.

Bureau of Economic Analysis (BEA). Various years. "U.S. Direct Investment Abroad. Comprehensive Financial and Operating Data." *Survey of Current Business* (bea.gov/scb/account_articles/international/iidguide.htm#USDIA1).

Clausing, Kimberly A. 2007a. "Corporate Tax Revenues in OECD Countries." *International Tax and Public Finance* 14 (April): 115–33.

———. 2007b. "Multinational Firm Tax Avoidance and U.S. Government Revenue." Working Paper. Reed College, Portland, Ore.

de Mooij, Ruud A. 2005. "Will Corporate Income Taxation Survive?" *De Economist* 153, no. 3: 277–301.

de Mooij, Ruud A., and Sjef Ederveen. 2003. "Taxation and Foreign Direct Investment: A Synthesis of Empirical Research." *International Tax and Public Finance* 10, no. 6: 673–93.

Desai, Mihir. 2005. "The Degradation of Reported Corporate Profits." *Journal of Economic Perspectives* 19, no. 4: 171–92.

Durst, Michael C. 2007. "New Statutory Language to Govern Transfer Pricing under Section 482." Working Paper. Washington: Steptoe and Johnson.

Edmiston, Kelly D. 2002. "Strategic Apportionment of the State Corporate Income Tax." *National Tax Journal* 55, no. 2: 239–62.

Eichner, Thomas, and Marco Runkel. 2006. "Why the European Union Should Adopt Formula Apportionment with a (Double) Sales Factor." Working Paper. University of Munich.

Ernst and Young. 2006. *2005–2006 Global Transfer Pricing Surveys. Tax Authority Interviews: Perspectives, Interpretations, and Regulatory Changes.* London.

Gnaedinger, Chuck, and Lisa M. Nadal. 2007. "Kovacs Optimistic on CCTB despite Opposition." *Tax Notes International* 45 (March 5): 935.

Le Gall, Jean François. 2006. "When Is a Subsidiary a Permanent Establishment of Its Parent?" Tillinghast Lecture. New York University.

Marshall, Alfred. [1890] 1997. *Principles of Economics.* Reprint. Amherst, N.Y.: Prometheus Books.

Omer, Thomas C., and Marjorie K. Shelley. 2004. "Competitive, Political, and Economic Factors Influencing State Tax Policy Changes." *Journal of the American Tax Association* 26 (s-1): 103–26.

President's Advisory Panel on Federal Tax Reform. 2005. *Simple, Fair, and Pro-Growth: Proposals to Fix America's Tax System.* Final report. Government Printing Office.

Shackleford, Douglas, and Joel Slemrod. 1998. "The Revenue Consequences of Using Formula Apportionment to Calculate U.S.- and Foreign-Source Income: A Firm-Level Analysis." *International Tax and Public Finance* 5, no. 1: 41–59.

Sorensen, Peter Birch. 2004. "Company Tax Reform in the European Union." *International Tax and Public Finance* 11, no. 1: 91–115.

U.S. Treasury. 2006. *Technical Explanation of United States Model Income Tax Convention.* Government Printing Office.

Weichenrieder, Alfons J. 2006. "What Determines the Use of Holding Companies and Ownership Chains?" Working Paper. Johann Wolfgang Goethe Universität (January).

Weiner, Joann Martens. 2005. "Formulary Apportionment and Group Taxation in the European Union: Insights from the United States and Canada." Working Paper 8/2005. Brussels: European Commission on Taxation (March).

World Bank. Various years. *World Development Indicators.* Washington.

Taxing Privilege More Effectively

Replacing the Estate Tax with an Inheritance Tax

12

LILY L. BATCHELDER

The estate tax has been a fixture of the federal tax system for more than ninety years. Together with the gift tax, it has been a fairly stable revenue source over time, generally raising between 1 and 2 percent of federal revenues, as illustrated in figure 12-1. For example, in 2007 the estate and gift taxes raised $26 billion (Office of Management and Budget 2008).

Nevertheless, in 2001 opponents of the estate tax succeeded in repealing it in a bizarre way. Currently, the estate tax is scheduled to disappear in 2010 and then return one year later. This situation is untenable, creating vast uncertainty and gruesome incentives for prospective heirs on the eve of

I owe special thanks to Surachai Khitatrakun for his work on modeling the revenue and distributional effects of the proposal. For helpful comments and discussions, I am grateful to Anne Alstott, Alan Auerbach, Jason Bordoff, Joshua Bendor, Joshua Blank, Leonard Burman, Noel Cunningham, Michael Deich, Miranda Perry Fleischer, Jason Furman, William Gale, Fred Goldberg, Michael Graetz, Richard Greenberg, Itai Grinberg, Rebecca Kahane, Joseph Kartiganer, Surachai Khitatrakun, Lewis Kornhauser, Shari Motro, Peter Orszag, Jeff Rohaly, Deborah Schenk, Leo Schmolka, Thomas Seidenstein, Daniel Shaviro, Robert Sitkoff, Timothy Taylor, David Thomas, and participants in the Hamilton Project Retreat, the Junior Tax Scholars Conference, the New York City Junior Faculty Colloquium, the New York University School of Law Faculty Workshop, the New York University School of Law Tax Policy and Public Finance Colloquium, the Stanford-Yale Junior Faculty Forum, the University of Michigan Law School Tax Policy Workshop, and the University of Toronto James Hausman Tax Law and Policy Workshop. Michelle Christenson, Laura Greenberg, David Kamin, Deanna Oswald, Ana Zampino, and Annmarie Zell provided outstanding research assistance.

Figure 12-1. Estate and Gift Taxes as a Share of Federal Revenues, 1946–2008[a]

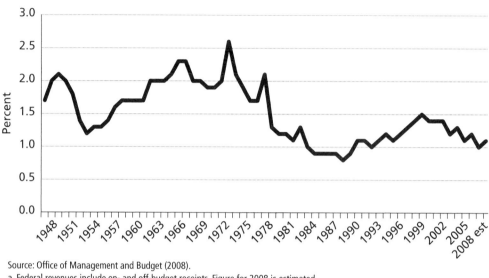

Source: Office of Management and Budget (2008).
a. Federal revenues include on- and off-budget receipts. Figure for 2008 is estimated.

2011. It does, however, create a window of opportunity to learn from the concerns voiced by repeal advocates, and to revisit the structure of the estate tax and, more generally, the taxation of gifts and bequests.

This chapter proposes seizing this political moment to transform our current system for taxing gifts and bequests into an inheritance tax.[1] Unlike the estate and gift taxes, which base tax rates on the amount a donor gives, the proposed inheritance tax would base tax rates on the amount an heir has inherited as well as his other income. Indeed, the proposal would be integrated with the income tax, and the tax would be paid by the heir. Heirs would not be taxed on lifetime inheritances of less than $1.9 million. Inheritances above this amount would be taxed at the income tax rate plus 15 percentage points. In addition, an optional feature of the proposal would replace stepped-up basis with carryover basis for bequests. If the $1.9 million exemption were adopted, the proposal is estimated to be revenue neutral relative to 2009 law.

1. Further details on the proposal, graphs of its estimated distributional effects, summaries of wealth transfer taxation in other jurisdictions, and a methodological approach are available in the longer version of this paper at www3.brookings.edu/views/papers/200706batchelder.pdf. The estimates in this version are based on an updated version of the model in which the income tax calculator and methodology for imputing spousal transfers were refined.

Transforming our current system into an inheritance tax would represent a fundamental shift in the way we tax wealth transfers: it would be more efficient and would substantially simplify wealth transfer tax planning. Most important, it would be more equitable because both the estate tax and an inheritance tax are largely borne by the recipients of wealth transfers. As a result, wealth transfer tax rates should depend on how much the donor has given. Moreover, one of the goals of taxing wealth transfers should be to ensure that heirs are taxed at least as much on the income that extraordinarily large inheritances represent as they are on earned income, and possibly at higher rates. Because an inheritance tax taxes privilege and income directly and an estate tax does not, only an inheritance tax can achieve these goals.

These theoretical differences between estate and inheritance taxes have important real-world consequences. At an aggregate level, the economic burdens of both the 2009 estate tax and the proposed inheritance tax are borne largely by the most affluent and privileged heirs in society. This is the case because both have sharply progressive rate structures, and, on average, heirs of large estates receive large inheritances and are relatively high-income themselves. But it is not always true. Some heirs of very large estates are not that well-off or receive small inheritances; some heirs of smaller estates are very privileged and affluent. As a result, the inheritance tax allocates tax burdens much more precisely based on the taxpayer's economic status, given that heirs predominantly bear the burden of both taxes. For example, the proposal burdens about 40 percent fewer heirs than the estate tax. In addition, the correlation between the average estate tax rate on inheritances under the proposal and the estate tax is only 0.33 among heirs burdened by either tax. Thus, at an individual level, the effects of the two systems differ vastly.

Large gifts and bequests should be taxed to mitigate widening economic disparities, promote equality of opportunity, and make our tax system better attuned to an individual's ability to pay. The estate tax does a good job at accomplishing all of these objectives. But an inheritance tax would do a much better job—and might be more politically sustainable as well.

Advantages of Shifting from an Estate Tax to an Inheritance Tax

There are three traditional ways of taxing wealth transfers (table 12-1). One is an estate and gift tax (collectively referred to as an estate tax) paid by the donor, where the rate depends on the amount that the donor trans-

Table 12-1. Traditional Types of Wealth Transfer Taxes

Type of tax	Payor	Amount subject to tax	Base of tax rate schedule
Estate and gift tax	Donor	Amount transferred	Amount transferred
Accessions tax	Heir	Amount inherited	Amount inherited
Inclusion tax	Heir	Amount inherited	Total amount of income including amount inherited

fers. An alternative method is an accessions tax, which taxes the recipient (referred to as the heir) and bases his tax rate solely on the amount of gifts and bequests (collectively referred to as inheritances) that he has received. Finally, wealth transfers may be taxed by requiring the heir to include inheritances in his income tax base (an inclusion tax). All three approaches have been implemented at some point within the United States and are presently in place in other jurisdictions.

There have been a variety of proposals to replace the estate tax with an accessions or inclusion tax, both of which are inheritance taxes (Alstott 2007; Duff 1993; Dodge 1978; Andrews 1967; Simons 1938; Roosevelt 1938).[2] The inheritance tax proposed here is a hybrid of the two. To my knowledge such an inheritance tax has never been proposed or enacted, but some commentators have favorably alluded to this possibility.[3] This type of inheritance tax has several fairness and efficiency advantages relative to a pure accessions or inclusion tax. Most important, there are a number of compelling reasons to shift the estate tax to this approach.

Fairness

First, such a shift would strengthen the fairness of the tax system as a whole by making the income tax better attuned to the individual circumstances that affect a taxpayer's ability to pay. Currently, the income tax covers nearly all income received, whether from work, saving, or a successful night of gambling. But a major exception is inherited income.

Intuitively, if two people have the same economic income and are similar in all respects except that one worked for the money and one inherited it, it does not seem fair to tax only the one who worked and not the heir

---

2. See also Maya MacGuineas and Ian Davidoff, "Tax Inheritance, Not 'Death,'" *Washington Post*, July 4, 2006; Gary Becker, "Should the Estate Tax Go?" *Becker-Posner Blog*, May 15, 2005 (www.becker-posner-blog.com/archives/2005/05/should_the_esta.html); Edwin R. A. Seligman, "A National Inheritance Tax," *The New Republic* March 25, 1916.

3. See Dodge (2003); Becker, "Should the Estate Tax Go?"

(Murphy and Nagel 2002). Nevertheless, that is exactly what happens under current law because recipients are allowed to exclude gifts and bequests from taxable income.

The amount at stake is large. The model used for the estimates in this paper suggests that in 2009 nonspousal heirs will inherit close to $410 billion. Even when the estate tax burden is taken into account, this inherited income will be taxed at an average rate of about 4 percent, much less than the tax rate on income from other sources, which is about 9 percent under the income tax and 17 percent under the income and payroll taxes (Congressional Budget Office [CBO] 2007).

The proposed inheritance tax can begin to rectify this inequity. While the economic burden of both estate and inheritance taxes falls largely on heirs (Batchelder and Khitatrakun 2008), an estate tax pays no attention to how much income an heir has and how much he inherits. Under the proposal, those who receive very large inheritances would be taxed under the income tax on a portion of their inheritances, just as those who do not receive inheritances are generally taxed on all of their income.

Second, replacing the estate tax with this inheritance tax would strengthen the fairness of the tax system by reducing differences in economic and political opportunity. Indeed, many of the established equity arguments for the estate tax are actually more applicable to those who receive inheritances than to those who give them.

Traditionally, estate tax supporters have argued that taxing gifts and bequests helps level the playing field between a few lucky heirs of large fortunes and all other Americans (Ascher 1990; c.f., Alstott 1996; Rudick 1950). Others have argued that the estate tax can reduce concentrations of wealth and power in family dynasties (c.f., Boskin 1977; Rudick 1950). For instance, Alexis de Tocqueville described laws regulating inheritance as part of the "moving and impalpable cloud of dust, which signals the coming of Democracy" (Tocqueville [1835] 1945). Franklin D. Roosevelt memorably maintained that "inherited economic power is as inconsistent with the ideals of this generation as inherited political power was inconsistent with the ideals of the generation which established our government" (Roosevelt 1938). But if the goal of an estate tax is to reduce inequalities of economic and political opportunity among heirs who have not personally earned their power and advantages, then it seems more appropriate to further this goal by directly taxing the receipt of large wealth transfers rather than the act of giving.

The proposed inheritance tax does just that: it taxes the receipt of large wealth transfers. Moreover, the tax rate rises with the size of the inheritance. As a result, it more effectively advances equal economic and political opportunity than does the estate tax because it directly targets extraordinarily large inheritances that, both symbolically and practically, pose the greatest threat to these democratic ideals.

Furthermore, unlike the current system, the inheritance tax creates a direct incentive to break up large concentrations of wealth. The estate tax burden on a taxable estate of $50 million is the same regardless of the number and affluence of the recipients. By contrast, under the inheritance tax proposed, if a wealthy donor gives $50 million to 1,000 regular Americans who have previously inherited an average-sized bequest, there would be no tax. Each would receive nowhere close to $1.9 million. But if the same donor gave all $50 million to one heir, the heir would be taxed, and at a higher rate than under the estate tax, because the exemption is smaller and the top marginal tax rate somewhat higher. The proposal tax would thus check the natural inclination of extraordinarily wealthy donors to give narrowly to an inner circle of heirs who typically are already affluent. An estate tax cannot directly strengthen the fairness of the tax system in these ways.

In addition to being substantively more equitable, the proposed inheritance tax is more likely to be *understood* as being equitable by the public. In 2001 advocates of the repeal of the estate tax successfully built public opposition around a stylized image of the typical taxpayer as a hard-working, frugal, generous entrepreneur who is subject to a double tax at the moment of her death (Graetz and Shapiro 2005). While there were many factual distortions in the assertions of repeal advocates, there was a kernel of truth to this image: it is the decedent who is nominally taxed, and she is subject to a separate tax based on the size of her gifts.

An inheritance tax instead focuses the spotlight—both substantively and symbolically—on the most fortunate heirs: the heir who receives a massive windfall that he has done nothing to earn and who may or may not be contributing to society in other ways. It asks him simply to contribute a portion of his economic income to the fisc, just as everyone else does. Moreover, it asks him to do so, not through a separate tax system, but via the income tax. Anecdotal evidence suggests that many people (incorrectly) believe that the income tax already is levied on gifts and bequests received. Thus, to the extent that the estate tax is indirectly effective at promoting the fairness concerns described above, an inheritance tax is still preferable because political support for it is likely to be more enduring.

Efficiency

A second set of reasons for switching from an estate tax to an inheritance tax is based on the general principle that tax policy should be designed, where possible, to minimize any negative incentives on work, saving, or giving. Some allege that an estate tax discourages all three because the potential donor knows that gifts and bequests to the next generation will face an additional tax. However, it is unclear both theoretically and empirically whether the estate tax creates meaningful net distortions to work, saving, and giving. In fact, it may reduce the distortions created by the tax system overall, given the alternatives for raising revenue.

Starting with potential heirs, the estate tax should reduce the distortions to work and saving that the tax system generates. On average, heirs tend to respond to receiving large inheritances by reducing their efforts to work and save. As a result, taxing gifts and bequests should induce more work and saving among heirs, making possible lower rates on income from these activities for everyone else.

By contrast, the efficiency effects of the estate tax are far more ambiguous with respect to potential donors. To date, there is not firm empirical evidence that potential donors tend to reduce their level of work, saving, and giving because of the potential bite of the estate tax (Kopczuk and Slemrod 2001; Joulfaian 2006b). Moreover, theoretical analysis of the estate tax suggests that the distortions it creates to the work, saving, and giving decisions of potential donors depend critically on the donor's motivation for accumulating the funds transferred. While there is considerable dispute regarding the relative prevalence of different donor wealth accumulation motives (Bernheim 1991; Hurd 1987; Altonji, Hayashi, and Kotlikoff 1992; Laitner and Juster 1996; Page 2003; Kopczuk and Lupton 2007), there is consensus that the existing pattern of gifts and bequests is due to some mix of the following three motives, each of which has different implications for efficiency (Gale and Perozek 2001; Holtz-Eakin 1996).

One motive is altruism: donors accumulate wealth because they are concerned about the heirs' welfare. For such wealth transfers, it is potentially to subsidize the transfer, especially if the heir is low income, and to have the heir include a portion of their inheritance in his or her taxable income. Doing so accounts for the probability that heirs will respond to the inheritance by relying less on government programs but also by working and saving less, thereby producing less income tax revenue (Kaplow 2001).

Another possible accumulation motive leads to "unintentional" wealth transfers. Donors with limited ability to purchase annuities or full health insurance may respond by saving funds for the possibility that they will live to a very old age or incur unusually large health care expenses. If these savings are untapped at death, they form an "accidental" bequest. Alternatively, a wealth transfer may be egoistic—the donor works and saves because he or she enjoys working or the prestige of being wealthy. Either way, the donor's wealth accumulation is not motivated by an intention to benefit the heir, and an extremely high tax rate on such wealth transfers is generally efficient (Gale and Slemrod 2001).

Finally, a large gift or bequest might be given in exchange for, say, a promise by children to take good care of their parents in old age. In such a case, the transfer is a payment for services, and distortions to the donor's work, saving, and giving decisions are minimized if the income tax applies to the transfer received by the heir.

As long as the existing pattern of wealth transfers is explained by some mix of these motives, it is most efficient for any tax on wealth transfers to take the form of the inheritance tax proposed. This is the case because the efficient tax for altruistic and exchange-motivated inheritances should apply to the amount inherited, and the tax rate should rise with the heir's income from other sources. Meanwhile, accidental and egoistic transfers should be virtually expropriated.

Put differently, the most efficient level of wealth transfer taxation turns on the relative prevalence of donor motives. But, given the consensus that current gifts and bequests evidence some mix of all three motives, the efficient form for the tax is neither a pure inclusion tax, a pure accessions tax, nor an estate tax. Instead, it is the type of inheritance tax proposed (see generally Batchelder 2008).

In addition to being the most efficient form for wealth transfer taxation, inheritance taxes also have a further potential efficiency benefit relative to the estate tax because they are nominally paid by the heir. If all taxpayers were rational and farsighted, this would not matter. A rational donor would respond to a given wealth transfer tax liability in the same manner, regardless of whether she, her estate, or her heirs pay the tax. But there is some evidence that people are not rational and tend to be influenced by salient features of a tax, such as the nominal tax rate or nominal payor, not by the actual tax rate or who bears the ultimate economic burden (Eckel and Grossman 2003; Finkelstein 2007). Because any efficiency losses from gifts and bequests arise from their impact on the behavior of potential donors, and not their impact on the behavior of potential heirs, this also argues that, all else equal, any economic distortions created by taxing wealth transfers will be smaller under an inheritance tax than under an estate tax.

Thus, because of differences in who substantively and nominally bears the tax, replacing the estate tax with the proposal should enhance economic efficiency. If anything, it should stimulate an increase in work and saving by the most productive heirs, and a slight increase in work, saving, and giving by potential donors. These effects in turn would make it possible to lower income and payroll tax rates for those who personally work for their income.

Treatment of Accrued Gains

The efficiency and fairness benefits of the proposed inheritance tax relative to our current system are magnified by an additional, optional feature, which is not included in the chapter's revenue estimates: replacing stepped-up basis with carryover basis. As an illustration, imagine someone who originally bought an asset worth $1 million, which had risen in value to $3 million at the time of her death. Under the income tax, if the asset is bequeathed, it is transferred to the heir with a stepped-up basis, which effectively means that no income tax is ever due on the $2 million capital gain even though the donor would have been taxed on the gain if she had sold the asset right before she died. If the asset instead is given as a gift while the donor is still alive, the asset is transferred with a carryover basis, which means that the recipient must eventually pay tax on the gain, but only when (if) she sells the asset.

This optional feature of the proposal would replace stepped-up basis with carryover basis so that all bequests are treated like gifts made during life. This reform could be adopted within our current system as well. The potential amount of revenue at stake could be significant. Unrealized capital gains represent 36 percent of the total expected value of all estates and 56 percent of the value of estates worth more than $10 million (Poterba and Weisbenner 2001).

An efficient tax system should distort the choice between different investments as little as possible, so that financial investments are made because of their actual risk and return characteristics and not because they offer a tax break. Replacing stepped-up basis with carryover basis should further this goal. While it increases incentives for heirs to hold on to appreciated assets, it substantially reduces incentives for donors who are near death to hold on to unproductive assets purely for tax reasons. Moreover, carryover basis is more equitable. Stepped-up basis results in higher tax burdens on donors who are not savvy about the tax law and who sell appreciated assets before they die. Thus this final element of the proposal further strengthens the fairness and efficiency benefits of the inheritance tax by ensuring that the income tax taxes all gains the same—that is, once.

Simplification

The final set of reasons to shift to the proposed inheritance tax stems from the fact that the proposed tax may substantially simplify our approach to taxing wealth transfers. Presently, the estate and gift taxes create large incentives to structure gifts and bequests in legally different but economically identical forms. For instance, gifts made during life tend to be taxed at lower effective rates than bequests. The tax rate on wealth transfers from a married couple to their children is generally lower if each parent transfers a sizable portion of their collective estate. In addition, transfers of appreciated property are taxed at lower effective rates than are transfers of nonappreciated property, in part as a result of stepped-up basis. The proposal would reduce or eliminate incentives to structure transfers in these ways and not in other ways that are economically equivalent.

In addition, an inheritance tax could simplify the taxation of wealth transfers in ways that can never be accomplished in the context of an estate and gift tax. An enormous amount of complexity in the current system results from efforts to close loopholes that would otherwise allow taxpayers to convert taxable transfers to lower-taxed or tax-exempt transfers through valuation games when the amount that potential beneficiaries will ultimately receive is unclear. To a large extent, these rules—and the tax-planning costs they create—would no longer be necessary under the proposed inheritance tax. Waiting to see who gets what would not require valuation of such split and contingent transfers up front but instead would tax heirs based on what they actually receive. An estate tax cannot adopt this wait-and-see approach. Because its tax rate is based on the amount transferred and not on the amount received, it has to be levied at the time of transfer.

Moreover, experience in other jurisdictions suggests that an inheritance tax is administratively feasible. Each component of the proposal has been implemented in various U.S. states or other countries. In fact, inheritance taxes are much more common than estate taxes are cross-nationally, and seven U.S. states have some type of inheritance tax in place.

Ultimately, the reason that opponents of the estate tax achieved their oddly temporary political success in 2001 may lie in these shortcomings of the current system relative to an inheritance tax. For example, it is hard to build political support for the estate tax on the grounds that it advances equal opportunity if it fails to encourage broad giving or to base tax burdens on the advantages the heir has received. Similarly, it is hard to make a case that the current system is simple and makes tax burdens better attuned to taxpayers' ability to pay when it takes no account directly of how advantaged and affluent heirs are, and when it imposes vastly different tax burdens depending on how sophisticated taxpayers are in structuring their affairs.

We should seize this political moment to improve the taxation of wealth transfers by replacing the estate tax with an inheritance tax. Implemented on a revenue-neutral basis, it would be fairer, simpler, and more efficient. Before turning to the specifics of the proposal, though, some basic background on our current system is necessary.

Overview of Current Law

The current method for taxing gifts and bequests has five elements: the estate tax, the gift tax, the generation-skipping transfer tax, the basic income tax treatment, and the income tax treatment of accrued gains. This section discusses each in turn.

Estate Tax

The first element, the estate tax, was enacted in 1916. At that time, Congress considered the possibility of adopting an inheritance tax and thought it would be more equitable (Ratner 1967). Indeed, the nation's second income tax, which was enacted in 1894 and struck down as unconstitutional in 1895, included inheritances in taxable income. There was also an inheritance tax in place during the periods of 1862–70 and 1898–1902, when the United States had no income tax (McDaniel, Repetti, and Caron 2003). Nevertheless, the drafters of the estate tax selected that model because they thought it would raise more revenue and balance out the state-level inheritance taxes in place at the time. They also found it convenient to model the U.S. wealth transfer tax on the British system, which was an estate tax, and thought an estate tax would be more administrable (House of Representatives 1916; Hull 1948; Ratner 1967).

As of 2007, the estate tax taxes lifetime gifts and bequests transferred in excess of $2 million at a 45 percent rate. Effectively, this means that over their lifetimes, a married couple can transfer $4 million to their children or other beneficiaries tax free. The $2 million per donor exemption is scheduled to rise to $3.5 million in 2009 (effectively $7 million per couple) before the estate

Table 12-2. Schedule Changes to Tax Treatment of Gifts and Bequests

Units as indicated

	Marginal tax rate			Exclusions		
Year	Estate and GST (percent)	Gift (percent)	Annual gift[a] (dollars)	Lifetime estate and GST (dollars)	Lifetime gift (dollars)	Basis provisions
2008	45	41–45	12,000	2,000,000	1,000,000	Gifts: carryover; bequests: stepped-up
2009	45	41–45	12,000	3,500,000	1,000,000	Same
2010	0	35	12,000	. . .	1,000,000	Gifts and bequests: carryover up to $4.3M capital gains tax-exempt
2011 and on	41–55[b]		12,000	1,000,000	1,000,000	Gifts: carryover; bequests: stepped-up

Source: See relevant federal code and Treasury Department guidelines.

a. The exclusion is inflation adjusted, so it may rise above $12,000 after 2008.

b. For estates between $1 million and $3 million, the marginal tax rate rises from 41 to 55 percent. For estates above $3 million, the marginal tax rate generally is 55 percent. However, a surtax that eliminates the lower brackets technically results in an effective marginal tax rate of 60 percent on taxable estates between $10 million and $17.184 million.

tax disappears in 2010. The estate tax then reappears in 2011 with a $1 million exemption and a top marginal tax rate of 55 percent (see table 12-2).

Gift Tax

The second component is the gift tax. It has been a stable fixture of the U.S. tax system since its enactment in 1932. The gift tax prevents donors from avoiding the estate tax by making transfers to their heirs during life. As of 2007, gifts exceeding $1 million over the donor's lifetime are subject to a 41 percent tax rate, with the tax rate rising to 45 percent for the portion of gifts in excess of $1.5 million. In addition, each year a donor can disregard $12,000 of gifts to a given heir (effectively $24,000 for a married couple), meaning that these gifts do not count toward the lifetime exemption. Unlike the estate tax, the gift tax is scheduled to stay fairly constant in the coming years, although the top marginal rate is scheduled to rise to 55 percent in 2011.

Generation-Skipping Transfer Tax

The final wealth transfer tax is the generation-skipping transfer (GST) tax, which Congress enacted in 1976 in response to concern that transfers directly to a donor's grandchildren were taxed only once under the estate and gift taxes, while transfers to a donor's grandchildren through her children were taxed twice. The GST tax imposes a second (but only a second) layer of tax on transfers to recipients who are two or more generations younger than the donor. Its exemptions and rates mirror those of the estate tax.

Under all three wealth transfer taxes, a large portion of gifts and bequests are tax exempt. For example, transfers to spouses and charities are not taxed. Similarly, amounts paid during life for education and medical expenses, and for basic support expenses for minors, are tax exempt. There are also special provisions for transfers of certain closely held businesses to address concerns that the tax might otherwise force the sale of the business. For example, any tax due on the transfer of a closely held business can be paid in installments over a period as long as fifteen years.

Basic Income Tax Treatment

In addition to these three separate taxes on wealth transfer, a fourth piece of the current system is the basic income tax treatment of gifts and bequests. Donors do not receive an income tax deduction for gifts and bequests (other than those to charitable organizations), and recipients of gifts and bequests do not have to include the amount received in taxable income. While a great deal of attention is typically paid to wealth transfer taxes and the estate tax specifically, public debate generally focuses much less on how gifts and bequests are treated under the income tax, even though the effects are often equally or more important.

Income Tax Treatment of Accrued Gains

Finally, accrued gains on assets gifted during life receive carryover basis while bequests receive stepped-up basis. Like the estate tax, stepped-up basis is scheduled to disappear in 2010 and then return in 2011. During the bizarre year of 2010, recipients of bequests are scheduled to receive a carryover basis, but the tax due on up to $4.3 million in accrued gains on inherited property will be forgiven. As with the general income tax treatment of inheritances, the public is generally not aware of how important and costly stepped-up basis is. Under some estimates and exemption levels, replacing stepped-up basis with carryover basis for bequests would over time raise about 12 percent of wealth transfer tax revenue, and taxing estates on the capital gains of all the assets in the estate at the time of transfer would raise about 25 percent (Office of Management and Budget 2000; CBO 2000).

The Proposal

The inheritance tax system proposed here represents a fundamental shift in the approach to taxing wealth transfers. There would no longer be any separate wealth transfer tax system, and the focal point of taxation would no longer be the amount transferred. Instead, taxation of inheritances would be integrated into the income tax, and the focus would be the amount received. The proposal is designed to raise approximately the same amount of revenue as the 2009 estate tax by varying the exemption level. It has five main components:

First, if a taxpayer inherits more than $1.9 million over the course of his lifetime, he would be required to include amounts inherited above this threshold in his taxable income under the income tax. The portion above this $1.9 million threshold would also be subject to a 15 percent surtax to account for the extraordinary privilege of the heir and his avoidance of payroll tax burdens on this income. To state the obvious, $1.9 million is a lot of money. An individual who inherits $1.9 million at age eighteen can live off his inheritance for the rest of his life without him or his spouse ever working, and his annual household income will still be higher than that of nine out of ten American families.[4]

Bequests that were included in income could be spread out over the current year and the previous four years to smooth out the income spike and the corresponding tax burden, while minimizing work disincentives. In addition, each year $12,000 in gifts and $60,000 in bequests could be disregarded entirely, meaning that they would not count toward the $1.9 million exemption. If a taxpayer received gifts from a given donor over the course of the year that totaled less than $2,000, that donor's gifts would not count toward the annual exclusion even if the annual sum of such gifts from multiple donors exceeded $12,000. All of these thresholds and the amount of prior inheritances would be adjusted for inflation.

The existing rules governing when a transfer has occurred, how it is valued, and what transfers are taxable would remain unchanged. Similar to current law, the proposal would not tax a large portion of wealth transfers. Transfers from spouses would continue to be disregarded entirely. To the extent that the current wealth transfer tax exemptions for charitable contributions and for gifts made during life for education, medical expenses, and basic support expenses are considered desirable, these exemptions

---

4. Author's calculations based on U.S. Census Bureau, "Table A-3. Selected Measures of Household Income Dispersion" (www.census.gov/hhes/www/income/histinc/p60no231_tablea3.pdf), and a 7 percent interest rate.

could be maintained. The income tax treatment of donors would remain unaltered. Donors would not receive an income tax deduction for gifts and bequests made unless the transfer was to a charitable organization. There would generally be no equivalent to the GST tax in order to ensure that people are only taxed on income over which they have control, but unborn heirs would be treated differently in certain circumstances.

To understand how the proposal works, imagine a person receives a bequest of $3 million above the annual exemption and has not received inheritances exceeding the annual exemptions in any prior year. This person would have to include only $1.1 million of the bequest in his taxable income. The $1.1 million would be taxed under the same rate structure as his other ordinary income plus 15 percentage points. Because the income tax brackets rise with income, this might mean that the taxable portion of his bequest would fall within a higher tax bracket than, for example, his income from working, because he received it all at once. To limit this effect, the taxpayer could also elect to file as if he received only $220,000 of taxable inheritance in the current year and the previous four years.

From an administrative perspective, the heir would be responsible for filing an annual return reporting cumulative gifts and bequests exceeding the annual exemptions. Because third party reporting is essential for maximizing compliance, donors or their estates would also have to report information on transfers above these annual exemptions and remit a withholding tax. The heir would be responsible for claiming any excess tax withheld and paying any excess tax due if his lifetime reportable inheritances exceeded $1.9 million.

If it is deemed politically necessary, the second element of the proposal would address the politically explosive issue of family-owned businesses through a special provision for illiquid assets, such as family farms. Specifically, to the extent that the tax due on such assets exceeds the liquid assets that an heir inherits, he could elect to defer the tax due with interest at a market rate until he sold the illiquid assets. This feature would eliminate the possibility that an heir would need to sell an inherited family business immediately to pay the associated tax liability. It would also eliminate the possibility that he would ever need to sell the asset if, over time, he and the other owners earn on average at least a market rate of return. At the same time, this approach would minimize incentives or disincentives to hold wealth in illiquid forms.

For example, suppose an heir who is in the highest income tax bracket receives a bequest of $10 million and has no prior inheritances. Three quarters of the bequest is a closely held business and one quarter is liquid assets, such as publicly traded stock. In this case, the heir's total tax liability would be $4.05 million. However, he could choose to defer $1.55 million of the taxes due (plus, perhaps, a small cushion) until the business was sold. Thus he would face no pressure to sell the business if he was operating it profitably, but he also would face no incentive to hold on to it.

A third feature of the proposal, which also could be included or not depending on political realities, would be to repeal stepped-up basis for bequests so that both gifts and bequests would receive a carryover basis. This would mean that if a donor had not paid the capital gains tax due on a transferred asset, the heir would eventually have to pay tax on the gain when he sold the asset. However, in order to minimize compliance costs, a bequeathed asset would still receive stepped-up basis if its value was less than $10,000 and it was not held for the production of income. This component would ensure that all capital income is taxed once, regardless of how sophisticated the donor is. It would also reduce incentives for investors to hold on to underperforming assets purely for tax reasons as they near the end of life.

Fourth, moving to an inheritance tax would permit a different and simpler method for taxing split or contingent transfers made, for instance, through trusts. The proposal would wait to see who gets what before taxing transfers for which the taxable status of the beneficiary is unclear. In the meantime, it would impose a withholding tax. When an heir eventually received his inheritance, he would receive a refund if the amount withheld on his share of the funds was more in present-value terms than the tax he actually owed (using an interest rate equal to the rate of return earned on the transferred assets). Essentially, this approach is economically equivalent to the tax system having perfect foresight regarding which potential beneficiaries will receive what. As a result, the proposal would eliminate many of the tax planning incentives and complicated valuation rules that exist under current law.

Finally, the proposed inheritance tax would not be phased in but rather would become fully effective on a date before enactment, such as the date the bill was introduced. Both inheritances received and estate and gift taxes paid before this date would not be taken into account. The only exception would be for inheritances received after the effective date on which estate or gift taxes had been paid; such inheritances would be tax exempt.

These transition rules would limit gaming and evasion by preventing donors from making transfers up to the lifetime gift tax exemption once enactment appears likely, thereby obtaining two lifetime exemptions. They would also be reasonably precise because most individuals only receive one

Table 12-3. Comparison of Current Law and Proposal

Item	Current law	Proposal
Tax on bequests	45 percent to extent lifetime gifts and bequests made exceed $2 million	Income tax rate plus 15 percentage points to extent lifetime gifts and bequests received exceed $1.9 million
Tax on gifts	45 percent to extent lifetime gifts made exceed $1 million	Same as above
Annual exclusion	$12,000 of gifts made per donee	$12,000 of gifts received; $60,000 of bequests received
Capital gains treatment for gifts	Carryover basis, taxed at time of sale	Carryover basis, taxed at time of sale
Capital gains treatment for bequests	Stepped-up basis, accrued gains never taxed	Carryover basis, taxed at time of sale
Liquidity provisions	Tax on certain closely held businesses can be paid in installments over fifteen years with below-market interest rate; also special valuation provisions	Tax on illiquid assets can be deferred at market interest rate until sale, regardless of how far in future, to extent that tax exceeds liquid assets received
Generation-skipping provisions	GST tax	Generally none

substantial inheritance over their lifetime. For example, the Survey of Consumer Finances suggests that among children who receive a bequest greater than $1.7 million, the bequest on average represents 94 percent of their lifetime inheritances to date.[5] Ireland applied these transition rules and is the only jurisdiction identified that transitioned directly from an estate tax to an inheritance tax. Table 12-3 summarizes the main differences between the proposal and current law.

The Proposal's Likely Effects

Shifting from the current system to the proposed inheritance tax would have a number of important effects. It would change the economic burden of taxes on gifts and bequests. It would alter the incentives faced by donors and heirs, and the nature and level of tax complexity. Finally, it could affect the states' wealth transfer tax systems. This section discusses the proposal's likely effects.

Revenue and Distributional Effects

The Urban Institute–Brookings Institution Tax Policy Center (TPC) estimated the revenue and distributional effects of the proposal relative to

---

5. Based on raw data from the Survey of Consumer Finances, Federal Reserve.

current law. To our knowledge, this is the first time these effects of a U.S. inheritance tax have been estimated. The estimates are based on the TPC estate tax microsimulation model, which was adapted to estimate the amount that individual heirs inherit and each heir's other income. The estimates are very rough because of data limitations that require multiple levels of imputation, and because they rely in part on data from 1992. They are also restricted to the core proposal to change the rate structure applying to gifts and bequests. No attempt is made to model the provisions regarding trusts, illiquid assets, or carryover basis.[6]

According to the TPC model, the proposal raises roughly the same amount of revenue as 2009 law if the lifetime exemption for the inheritance tax is $1.9 million. The total amount both taxes raise in 2009 is approximately $17.5 billion. Under 2009 law, the estate and GST tax exemptions are $3.5 million, the gift tax exemption is $1 million, and the tax rate for all three is 45 percent.

One variant to the proposal that was considered is applying a 10 percent surtax rate instead of the proposed 15 percent surtax. In this scenario, the lifetime exemption that raises the same amount of revenue as 2009 law is $1.6 million.

Given that the incidence of all wealth transfer taxes appears to fall much more heavily on heirs than donors (Batchelder and Khitatrakun 2008), the distributional effects of the proposal generally should be examined from the heir perspective by considering whether it alters which heirs are burdened by wealth transfer taxes, and the tax rate that applies to their inheritances. As a result, this section focuses on the proposal's effects by measures of the heir's economic status.

Theoretically, the distributional incidence of an estate tax and an inheritance tax would be identical if both systems applied a flat rate to all inherited income, including the first dollar received, or if the inheritance tax rate was unrelated to the heir's other income and all estates had only one heir. In practice, however, the two have quite different distributional effects. Donors typically give to multiple heirs, and neither the estate tax nor the proposal exhibits flat tax rates due to their lifetime exemptions and the proposal's link between the tax rate on inheritances and the heir's income tax schedule. While both are highly progressive in aggregate, they are

6. Details on the methodology can be found in the appendix to the online version at www3.brookings.edu/views/papers/200706batchelder.pdf. See also Jeffrey Rohaly, Adam Carasso, and Mohammed Adeel Saleem, "The Urban-Brookings Tax Policy Center Microsimulation Model: Documentation and Methodology for Version 0304," January 10, 2005 (www.urban.org/uploadedpdf/411136_documentation.pdf).

Figure 12-2. Average Tax Rate on All Inheritances, by Inheritance Size

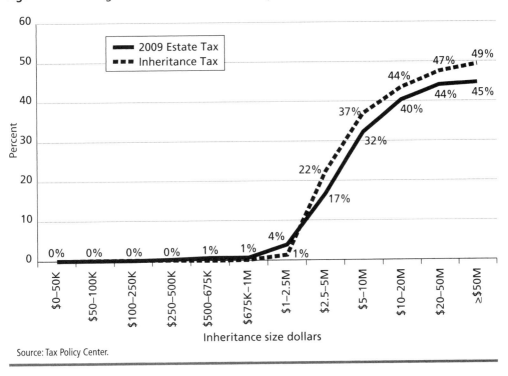

Source: Tax Policy Center.

progressive in different ways. Moreover, at an individual level, their distributional effects differ to a much greater degree.

In aggregate, the distributional effects of the proposal relative to the estate tax depend on what measure of ability to pay is applied. As illustrated by figure 12-2, the proposal is more progressive by inheritance size. The average tax rate on all inheritances received is higher under the estate tax for inheritances below $2.5 million, while for inheritances above $2.5 million it is higher under the inheritance tax. (Lower tax rates on some inheritances must be counterbalanced by higher taxes on others because the proposal is revenue neutral.)

The proposal is also more progressive by a comprehensive measure of heir income, which is referred to as *heir economic income* and includes the heir's cash income plus one-fifth of his inheritance.[7] We used this measure

7. For the definition of cash income, see Tax Policy Center, "The Numbers" (taxpolicy center.org/TaxModel/tmdb/TMTemplate.cfm?DocID=574).

Figure 12-3. Average Tax Rate on All Inheritances, by Heir Economic Income

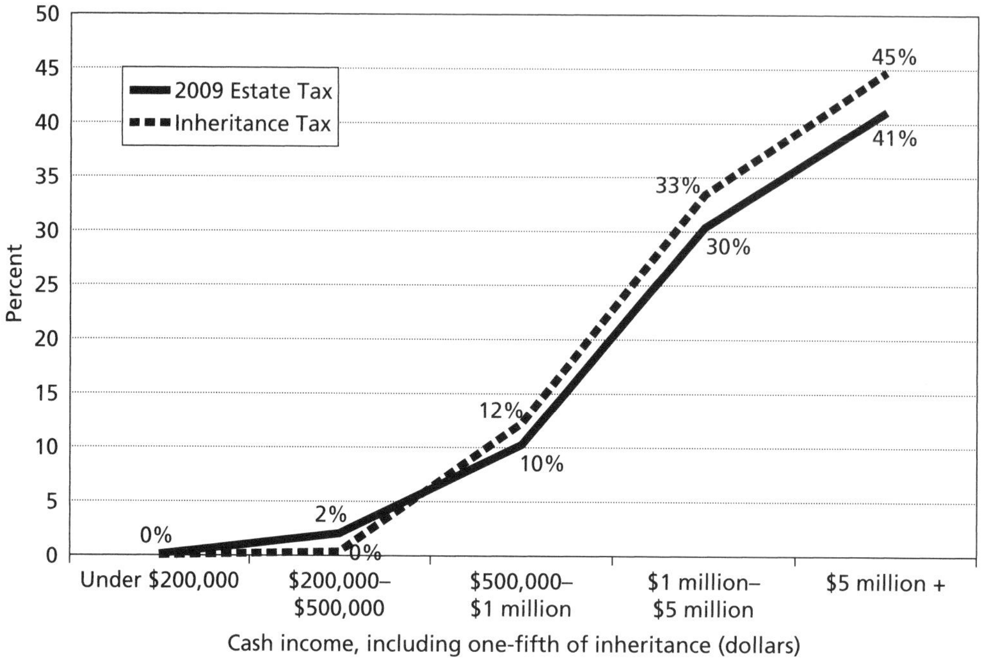

Cash income, including one-fifth of inheritance (dollars)

Source: Tax Policy Center.

because focusing solely on an heir's cash income (analogous to adjusted gross income) would not include any of his inherited income. However, including all inheritances received in the current year in an heir's income measure for the current year does not provide an accurate picture of an heir's long-term economic status either because, on average, people appear to smooth their income over several years (Landsberger 1971) and bequests are unusually lumpy. As seen in figure 12-3, the proposal is also more progressive by this measure of heir economic income, although both taxes are highly progressive. Heirs with economic income of less than $500,000 pay higher average tax rates on their inherited income under the estate tax. Heirs with $500,000 or more of economic income pay more tax under the inheritance tax.

By contrast, the proposal is generally less progressive if the average tax rate on inheritances is compared by the estate size. Estates of less than $5 million face a higher average tax rate under the inheritance tax, and estates of more than $5 million generally face a higher tax rate under the estate tax. An exception is the largest estates (more than $50 million) for which the inheritance tax rate is higher. It is not clear, though, why one should care about this type of progressivity. Greater progressivity along this dimension implies that heirs inheriting from larger estates generally pay more tax under the proposal, and heirs inheriting from smaller estates pay less, even if the latter group has inherited more and has more non-inherited income than the former.

In practice, the proposal would likely be even more progressive than the current system along all three of these dimensions. The simulations do not include replacing stepped-up basis with carryover basis. Since the percentage of the value of bequests that accrued capital gains represent rises with the size of the estate, which is positively correlated with heir economic income and inheritance size, this feature of the proposal should magnify its progressivity. More important, to the extent that donors respond to the incentives to give more widely and to those with less preinheritance income, pretax gifts and bequests might be more progressive by inheritance size and heir economic income if the proposal were adopted. This potential behavioral response is not included in the TPC estimates either.

Despite these improvements in the aggregate allocation of wealth transfer tax burdens, one might reasonably ask whether the differences between these two systems are really worth the effort. In figure 12-3, the two lines certainly follow each other quite closely. One might interpret this as implying that there is not a significant difference in the incidence of the estate tax and the proposal, and in how much each enhances the precision of the income tax in measuring ability to pay. This is an understandable reaction, but figures 12-2 and 12-3 paint an incomplete picture. By focusing on aggregate statistics, they mask crucial differences between the two systems at a microlevel. When one focuses on individual heirs instead, it becomes apparent that the two systems affect very different people, often in radically different ways.

One way to understand the individual-level differences between the two systems is by considering the correlation between the two tax rates represented in the lines in figures 12-2 and 12-3. The correlation is only 0.33 (or 0.71 when weighted by inheritance size). Correlation is a measure of the tendency of two variables to increase or decrease together, and 0.33 is quite low. Its square (the R^2) suggests that only 11 percent of the inheritance tax rate of individual heirs is directly accounted for by the heir's estate tax rate, and vice versa, if the burden of both taxes is assumed to fall on heirs.

This weak correlation can be seen graphically in figure 12-4, which shows the average estate and inheritance tax rates for heirs who pay some tax under at least one system, weighted by inheritance size. Each point

Figure 12-4. Relationship between Average Tax Rate on Inheritances under the Proposal and Current Estate Tax for Individual Heirs[a]

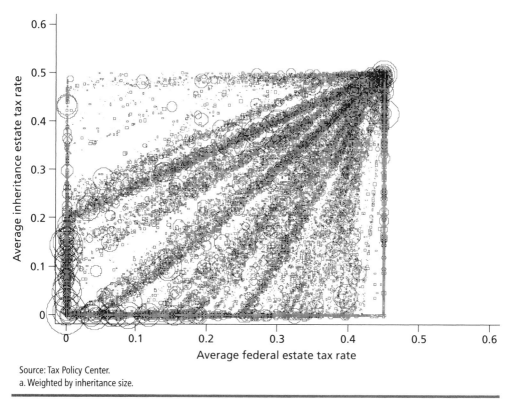

Average inheritance estate tax rate

Average federal estate tax rate

Source: Tax Policy Center.
a. Weighted by inheritance size.

represents an heir weighted by inheritance, and each circle represents multiple heirs or especially large inheritances. While on average the estate tax rate rises with the inheritance tax rate, many inheritances are subject to a much larger estate tax rate than inheritance tax rate, or vice versa. A full 37 percent of heirs burdened by the estate tax inherit less than $1 million in the year examined, but no heir burdened by the inheritance tax has cumulative inheritances of less than $1.9 million. In fact, 10 percent of the revenue raised from the estate tax is raised from heirs who are represented by the points along the graph's x-axis—heirs facing zero tax burden under the proposal.

These individual-level differences between the two systems can be understood still further by considering the winners and losers from the proposal. Our estimates suggest that, overall, each year there are more

Figure 12-5. Average Change in Tax Liability for Winners and Losers among Those Receiving Inheritances, by Inheritance Size

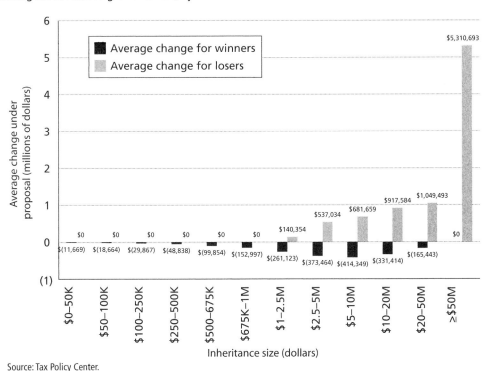

Source: Tax Policy Center.

than twice as many heirs who are winners (18,000) under the proposal as there are losers (8,000). The vast majority of these winners are people inheriting less than $2.5 million. Moreover, as illustrated by figures 12-5 and 12-6, the amounts won and lost are substantial. Heirs who are extraordinarily privileged and inherit more than $50 million owe about $5.3 million more in taxes, on average. Similarly, those with economic income of more than $5 million who lose under the proposal pay about $2.2 million more, on average. Conversely, roughly 95 percent of heirs have economic income in the current year of less than $200,000. While very few of such heirs are burdened by the estate tax, those who are would all be better off under the proposal, saving $62,000 on average.

The final issue modeled was the number of taxpayers affected. These estimates suggest that almost 65 percent more heirs are burdened by the estate tax (21,500) than by the inheritance tax (13,000). The reverse is true

Figure 12-6. Average Change in Tax Liability for Winners and Losers among Those Receiving Inheritances, by Heir Economic Income

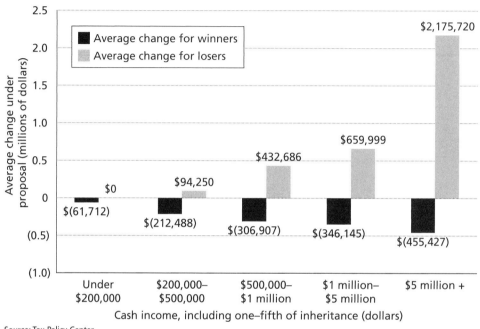

Source: Tax Policy Center.

if one assumes the burden falls entirely on estates. Then about 38 percent more estates are burdened by the inheritance tax (9,400) than the estate tax (6,800). This implies that the number of taxable returns should roughly double under the proposal because more heirs are responsible for paying the inheritance tax (13,000) than estates are responsible for paying the estate tax (6,800).

Despite these differences, the percentage of all heirs and estates burdened by either tax is tiny. Only an estimated 0.5 percent of heirs bear some estate tax burden annually, and only 0.3 percent would bear any inheritance tax burden. Thus, while the proposal would often substantially change the tax burden on heirs, it would not dramatically change the number of taxpayers affected.

Level of Work, Saving, and Giving

The previous revenue and distributional estimates assume that there is no behavioral response to the proposal in the form of changes in the level of work, saving, and giving. This section considers this assumption. The behavioral response could go either way, but it is limited by the fact that the proposal is revenue neutral.

Previous empirical work suggests that wealth transfer taxes induce an increase in work by heirs (Brown, Coile, and Weisbenner 2006; Joulfaian 2006a; Holtz-Eakin, Joulfaian, and Rosen 1993). However, it is unclear whether the proposal would increase or decrease heir labor supply because it is estimated to raise the same amount of revenue. Tax burdens under the proposal are more calibrated to inheritance size and heir income, but there is little evidence of how the labor supply response of heirs varies by inheritance size or income. Nevertheless, the proposal may generate somewhat more income tax revenues than the estate tax because it taxes heirs in higher income tax brackets more heavily and thus may induce relatively more work by such heirs.

The effect of the proposal on heirs' saving is also unclear because there is little evidence of what effect receiving an inheritance has on an heir's savings rate (Gale and Slemrod 2001).

With regard to potential donors, studies have also found the size of estates—and thus donors' work, saving, and giving decisions—are responsive to the estate tax rate (Kopczuk and Slemrod 2001; Joulfaian 2006b; McGarry 2000). This may be the product of greater tax evasion; but because the proposal is revenue neutral, it should not reduce the level of donor work, saving, and giving. Instead, if anything, it could induce a slight increase in such behavior to the extent that potential donors irrationally tend to respond more to a tax that they nominally pay rather than to one nominally paid by their heirs.

Recipients of Gifts and Bequests

While the proposal should not have a large effect on the magnitude of giving, it could affect giving patterns in a number of ways that would alter the estimated revenue and distributional effects. In particular, it could change the identity of individuals receiving inheritances and the amount of charitable contributions.

The proposal should induce donors to give slightly more broadly, especially to lower-income heirs and grandchildren, although the effect could be quite small. It creates incentives to do so because the tax rate turns in part on the heir's income tax rate, and also because transfers to additional heirs are tax exempt if the heir remains below the $1.9 million lifetime exemption. Neither of these incentives exists under current law. A wealthy donor can give to 100 heirs or 1, to Paris Hilton or a foster child, and the tax rate remains unaltered.

How much donors would actually respond to these changed incentives is uncertain. Donors do seem to be willing to give beyond their children; presently about one-third of taxable transfers go to nonchildren (Joulfaian 1994).[8] The proposal would also eliminate existing disincentives to give to grandchildren. But most current transfers to non-children are by childless adults, and there is little existing evidence regarding the price elasticity of wealth transfers to nonspousal heirs.

Donors may also alter their individual giving by allocating more outright to surviving spouses. Current law discourages a decedent from transferring her entire estate to her surviving spouse because doing so results in wasting her lifetime exemption. Well-advised donors appear to respond to this incentive. Thus, by eliminating this bias, the proposal should result in more spousal transfers.

Turning to charitable contributions, presently about 11 percent of the value of estates filing estate tax returns is distributed to charitable organizations.[9] While the effect of the estate tax on charitable giving has been an important part of the debate about estate tax repeal, once again, the likely effects of the proposal are unclear.

In some respects, the proposal strengthens incentives for charitable giving. It expands the incentive to give appreciated property to charities because of the repeal of stepped-up basis. There is also a new incentive to give to tax-exempt nonprofits, such as 501(c)(4)s, that are currently ineligible for the charitable deduction under the income and estate taxes. (Such tax-exempt entities, by definition, are not subject to the inheritance tax.)

However, in other ways the proposal weakens incentives to make charitable contributions. It creates the possibility of tax-free transfers to individuals, such as grandchildren, siblings, or good friends, who would otherwise be subject to the estate tax. Which effect will dominate—and whether the proposal will increase or decrease charitable contributions—will depend on how donors respond to these cross-cutting incentives. Again, on this front, the evidence is mixed (Joulfaian 2000; Schervish and Havens 2003).

---

8. See also Lutz Hendricks, "Bequests and Retirement Wealth in the United States," 2001 (www.lhendricks.org/Research/bequdata_paper.pdf).

9. Internal Revenue Service, "Statistics of Income Division, Estate Tax Returns Filed in 2005 with Total Gross Estate Greater than $1.5 Million," November 2005 (www.irs.gov/pub/irs-soi/05es01fym.xls).

Tax Planning, Compliance Burdens, and Administrative Burdens

One of the most subtle but important advantages of the proposal is its potential for simplification. In this area, it helps to distinguish two types of costs that taxpayers bear. A tax system can impose direct compliance costs on taxpayers, for example, by requiring them to spend multiple hours reading instructions and filing returns. It also may impose indirect compliance burdens—which are typically more costly—by creating incentives to structure transactions in ways that are economically identical but taxed more lightly.

The proposal could slightly increase direct compliance costs because more tax units will have to file returns. As summarized above, there would be about twice as many taxable returns. While this is a substantial increase in percentage terms, both taxes burden a tiny fraction of the population. Instead, the more important source of new compliance costs will be information reporting and withholding requirements as heirs and donors have to report gifts and bequests falling above the annual exclusions but below the lifetime exemption.

There are also some areas in which the proposal could alter tax planning incentives. For example, it could, on the margin, induce more transfers to grandchildren through restricted trusts because there is no GST tax. This might, however, result in donors' transfers being closer to their pretax preferences because of the current tax disincentive to transfer wealth to grandchildren.

Despite these potential increases in complexity, on net the proposal is likely to reduce tax planning and compliance burdens for three general reasons. First, the proposal would eliminate the need for careful planning of spousal transfers. Currently spouses can reduce their joint tax liability by making sure that each transfers an amount equal to the lifetime exemption to their heirs, for example, through a credit shelter trust. Some well-advised wealthy donors take advantage of this opportunity; others do not. But under the proposal, it would not matter. Any tax would be based on the amount the heir receives, regardless of whether it was from the mother or father.

Second, the proposal would significantly narrow the current substantial differences in how gifts and bequests are taxed. Unlike the current estate and gift taxes, the same lifetime exemption would apply, the tax rate would apply to the pretax inheritance, and all accrued gains on appreciated property would eventually be taxed. Indexing the lifetime exemptions to inflation would also reduce the incentive to transfer (or appear to transfer) wealth earlier in time, when the present value of the exemption is higher.

Finally, the proposal should reduce tax incentives to engage in valuation games. While it does create more valuation points, it reduces the incentive to try to shift value to tax-exempt spouses and charities when the ultimate beneficiary is unclear, by waiting to see how much is received by whom. As a result, a wide swath of current rules could be eliminated. Indeed, the current rules to address valuation games—including those governing marital trusts, charitable trusts, grantor trusts, Crummey trusts, and the GST tax—compose one-fourth of a leading casebook (McDaniel, Repetti, and Caron 2003).

Overall, the proposal should reduce taxpayer compliance burdens because the existing tax planning incentives that would be reduced or eliminated likely impose much larger burdens on taxpayers than any new information reporting and filing costs. Moreover, this reduction should be mirrored at the governmental level. With fewer rules to enforce and fewer tax planning strategies to address, administrative burdens should decline.

Finally, the proposal would be administrable. Each component of the proposal has been successfully implemented at the state or federal level in the United States or in other countries. Indeed, the United States had an inheritance tax during parts of the late nineteenth and early twentieth centuries. Moreover, seven U.S. states and twenty-three countries currently impose some kind of inheritance tax, and at least five countries currently apply a carryover basis for bequests, including Germany, Australia, and Japan.

State Wealth Transfer Taxes

The existence of state inheritance taxes raises the last question about the likely effects of the proposal: how it would affect the states. Historically, the federal estate tax offered a dollar-for-dollar credit for state wealth transfer taxes up to a limit, which allowed states to receive part of the revenue from federal wealth transfer taxes without actually imposing any new economic burden on their residents. Although this credit was in place for more than eighty years, it was replaced with a deduction for state wealth transfer taxes in 2005. (The credit is scheduled to reappear in 2011.) Because the credit was worth more than the deduction, the economic effect was to cut back on federal revenue sharing with the states. Eliminating the credit also created an incentive for elderly residents to move to a state without any wealth transfer tax. In response, the number of states with a wealth transfer tax had declined from all fifty in 2001 to twenty-eight by late 2005, although state wealth transfer taxes have proven more resilient than some observers expected (Yablon 2006).

Under the proposal, any desired level of federal revenue sharing could be achieved. For example, a credit or deduction could be offered for state inheritance taxes and an heir's share of state estate taxes. If full federal revenue sharing were not reinstated, the proposal could also leave states freer to retain wealth transfer taxes if they so wish. States would likely act to conform their wealth transfer tax to the inheritance tax model in order to piggyback on the new federal reporting requirements, as they did under the federal estate tax credit (even the states that had an inheritance tax). Because it is generally easier for a retired individual to move to a state with no estate tax than it is for all of her heirs to move to states without inheritance taxes, such a shift could reduce the pressure on states to eliminate wealth transfer taxes when competing for wealthy residents.

Questions and Concerns

Because an inheritance tax represents a fundamental change to our current system, it is likely to generate a number of questions and concerns. This section considers three.

Doesn't the Proposal Give an Unfair Advantage to Bigger Families?

One common reaction to the proposal is to point out that it will impose lower tax burdens on donors with larger families. While true, whether this is unfair depends on the incidence of wealth transfer taxes and one's views of why gifts and bequests should be taxed in the first place. The view taken in this chapter is that wealth transfers should be taxed because they are like other income, and if someone inherits an extraordinary sum, that transfer confers a special advantage that should be taxed at somewhat higher rates. The chapter also argues that wealth transfer tax rates should turn on the amount inherited and the economic status of the heir because heirs largely bear the burden of wealth transfer taxes. In this view, it is privilege and ability to pay that matters, and heirs from larger families should indeed be taxed more lightly. If one child and his nine siblings each inherit $1 million from their parents, this child is less privileged and has less ability to pay than any only child who inherits $10 million from his mother and father.

Why Not Tax Inheritances from Relatives at a Lower Rate?

Another common objection is to point out that most jurisdictions with inheritance taxes impose lower tax rates on inheritances from relatives and to ask why the proposal does not follow this practice. This is also factually correct. Every U.S. state and nineteen of the twenty-three countries with an inheritance tax impose higher taxes on gifts and bequests received by non-relatives. Often, the tax rates rise as the relationship to the donor becomes more attenuated, with inheritances from parents bearing lower tax rates than, for example, those from aunts.

The rationale for this practice is unclear. Most likely it results from a natural sympathy toward the idea of giving to one's children and relatives.[10] While understandable, it misses the point of taxing inheritances. An inheritance tax does not seek to encourage giving more to nonrelatives than to one's children. It simply seeks to tax all people on all of their income. While the practical effect of doing so may be to encourage broader and more equal giving because inheritance tax rates are typically progressive, this is not a drawback. It is more equitable. Such broader and more equal giving breaks up wealth dynasties, softens inequalities of opportunity, and can narrow economic disparities. This ordinary practice in other jurisdictions with inheritance taxes should not be followed.

Shouldn't the Proposal Go Further?

The final question sometimes raised is whether the proposal goes far enough. If it already proposes a fundamental change to wealth transfer taxation, why not take on a variety of related issues? Two related reforms are worth consideration but, as a matter of political economy, probably are not advisable.

APPRECIATED ASSETS. The first possibility is to tax gains on inherited assets at the time of transfer and not when the heir sells the asset. This could be accomplished by taxing donors or their estates on all such accrued gains. Alternatively, the receipt of gifts and bequests above the $1.9 million lifetime exemption could be treated as a realization event for the heir, meaning that the heir pays the capital gains tax due on the appreciated assets when he inherits them.

Both of these options have advantages. Each would reduce lock-in incentives further than replacing stepped-up basis with carryover basis.

---

10. The lower exemptions for inheritances from more distant relatives or nonrelatives may also stem from a presumption that the heir has or will inherit much more from his parents. Since most jurisdictions use annual and not lifetime exemptions, bequests from nonrelatives generally do not affect the tax rate on bequests from one's parents.

The first would do so more fully. The second would enhance the progressivity of wealth transfer taxation because appreciated assets tend to make up an increasing share of estates as estate value rises. Moreover, contrary to public perception, both reforms would be administrable. Five countries successfully treat gifts or bequests as realization events, including Canada. Instead, the main downside of both options is political. The Canadian experience suggests that estate and inheritance taxes are unlikely to survive if coupled with taxing accrued gains at the time of transfer (Bird 1978, citing Benson 1971).

TAX INCENTIVES. The second possibility is to reform certain tax incentives related to the estate tax, including the estate tax charitable deduction, the gift tax exclusion for amounts paid for education and medical expenses, and income tax exclusion for life insurance payments paid upon death. The proposal presents no barriers to replicating these tax incentives, but whether it should do so is another matter. For example, the exclusion for education expenses undercuts the ability of the proposal to promote equal opportunity in light of the vast sums that wealthy parents spend on private schools, colleges, and graduate schools, and the significant share of wealth embedded in human capital (Kaplow 2001, citing Davies and Whalley 1991 and Jorgenson and Fraumeni 1989). Likewise, the ideal tax treatment of charitable contributions may be quite similar to the ideal taxation of gifts and bequests—which, as argued, is not a deduction for the donor.

More generally, there are a variety of ways in which the current set of tax incentives in the tax code as a whole is far from ideal (Batchelder, Goldberg, and Orszag 2006; Furman 2006; Edlin 2005; Halperin 2002; Bittker and Rahdert 1976). Most tax incentives operate through deductions, exclusions, and, more rarely, nonrefundable credits. As Fred Goldberg, Peter Orszag, and I have argued elsewhere, if tax incentives are desirable at all, a fairer and more efficient default mechanism for delivering them is through uniform refundable credits. Nevertheless, reforming existing tax incentives related to wealth transfers is a vast undertaking and probably should be pursued separately.

Conclusion: Why Tax Wealth Transfers at All?

Ultimately, the most fundamental question that might be asked of the proposal is why we should continue to tax wealth transfers at all. Estate tax repeal advocates were fairly successful in their efforts to create some doubts about whether the estate tax should exist. Polling data suggest that 47 percent of the public believes the estate tax should be repealed, even after it is explained to them who actually pays the tax (Graetz and Shapiro 2005, citing Greenberg Research). Those who are convinced of the merits of estate tax repeal may believe that this chapter has focused on a straw man by comparing an inheritance tax to the current system because neither is desirable. This conclusion, therefore, presents a number of compelling reasons why we should continue to tax wealth transfers, regardless of the method. An inheritance tax is simply the better approach.

To begin, economic disparities in the United States are extensive and rising. While median household income has stagnated over the past decade, the top 1 percent of Americans received about 20 percent of all pretax income in 2004, which was their highest share since 1929 with the exception of the stock market bubble in 1999 and 2000.[11] Wealth disparities are even more extensive: the wealthiest 1 percent of individuals own more than one-third of total wealth.[12] While estimates vary widely, all the evidence suggests that inheritance is a significant driver of these gaps. Inherited wealth represents 35 to 45 percent of all household wealth (Kopczuk and Lupton 2007).

Many view reducing economic disparities as an important goal of the tax system. This is an important reason why there are rising marginal rates. If one views economic income as the best measure of ability to pay and well-being, this implies taxing gifts and bequests. Gifts and bequests should come out of the after-tax income of the donors because they are choosing how to spend the money and could just as easily choose to spend it on goods that would be taxed. As a result, a donor is generally economically better off than someone who spent the same amount on taxable goods but did not have the option of spending more on market consumption or gifts. Inheritances should also be included in the heir's income—or subject to a separate wealth transfer tax as a proxy—because they are just as much income for the heir as are wages or lottery winnings.[13]

11. See U.S. Census Bureau, "Historical Income Tables: Income Equality," May 13, 2005 (www.census.gov/hhes/www/income/histinc/ie4.html); Thomas Piketty and Emmanuel Saez, "Top Fractiles Income Shares (Including Capital Gains) in the U.S., 1913–2004," table A3 (elsa.berkeley.edu/~saez/tabfig2004prel.xls).

12. Lutz Hendricks, "Bequests and Retirement Wealth in the United States," 2001 (www.lhendricks.org/Research/bequdata_paper.pdf).

13. If one's primary concern is inequality of all consumption, the analysis is quite similar. The ideal approach is then to have an inheritance tax by taxing gifts and bequests as consumption by the donor and taxing heirs on consumption from inherited income (c.f., McCaffery 1994). But if one's concern is inequality of private market consumption, that may imply a different approach (Stiglitz 1978).

Moreover, many believe that the tax system should seek to promote more broad-based economic and political opportunity and the breakup of dynastic wealth. In this view, we have a social obligation not only to mitigate economic disparities between the rich and poor but also to help ensure that all children have very roughly the same opportunities in life. This is a hard goal to accomplish. But one of the most obvious ways to begin is by taxing gifts and bequests slightly more heavily than other income because of the advantages they provide, and using the revenue to fully fund programs promoting greater opportunity for the least advantaged.

At the same time that fairness considerations push in favor of maintaining or expanding wealth transfer taxes, there is no consensus about whether doing so results in efficiency losses and, if so, how large. The most efficient level of tax on gifts and bequests depends to a large extent on the donor's motivation for accumulating the wealth transferred and how much heirs increase their work and saving in response to the tax. It could be higher or lower than current law. But it is plausibly higher, especially if, as appears to be the case, most transfers are not motivated by pure altruism.

Finally, there is no consensus that our current wealth transfer taxes are more complicated than a correspondingly progressive tax on noninherited income (Gale and Slemrod 2001), and the proposal should be simpler. For all of these reasons, wealth transfer taxes should be maintained.

If anything, the above considerations and others suggest that we may want to expand wealth transfer taxes in the future. Fiscal shortfalls are projected to increase dramatically in the coming years, and the estate tax is a small but important source of revenue. According to estimates by the Joint Committee on Taxation, the cost of making estate tax repeal permanent after 2010 over the 2007–2016 period is $386 billion (Friedman and Aron-Dine 2006). It would be significantly higher if the estate tax were repealed for the entire period. Taxing wealth transfers more heavily could also increase economic growth. There is emerging evidence that countries grow faster if large inheritances and firms managed by heirs are a smaller share of GDP (Bloom and Van Reenan 2006; Morck, Strangeland, and Yeung 2000). In addition, according to the estimates prepared for this chapter, the average tax rate on inheritances under the proposal (and 2009 estate tax law) is only about 4 percent. Relative to the average income and payroll tax rate on noninherited income of almost 17 percent (CBO 2006), this seems unduly low.

More revenue could be raised if the exemption levels were lowered, the surtax was increased, or accrued gains on bequeathed assets were taxed. The revenue increase could be substantial: if inheritances were simply subject to the same average income and payroll tax rate as labor income, the inheritance tax would raise roughly $68 billion in 2009 alone.

But regardless of whether wealth transfer taxes are or should be expanded, the proposed inheritance tax is a better way to tax gifts and bequests than the estate tax. It focuses directly on allocating tax burdens fairly between those who have received inheritances and those who have not, rather than between those who do and do not make large wealth transfers. Given that both taxes are borne largely by heirs, the inheritance tax more equitably bases the tax rate on the economic status of the heir. Furthermore, this chapter has shown that the incidence of the two taxes is quite different, with each burdening many heirs who are not burdened at all by the other. Under the estate tax, the heir's tax rate turns on the success and generosity of his donors. Under the inheritance tax, it turns on his privilege and affluence.

The proposed inheritance tax would thus strengthen the ability of our current system to achieve its underlying goals. It would be more effective at reducing economic disparities and inequality of opportunity. It would make the income tax more equitable by basing tax burdens on a more accurate measure of the taxpayer's economic status. It could enhance efficiency and result in significant simplification benefits. And ultimately, by better aligning wealth transfer taxes with our ideals, the proposed inheritance tax could reinvigorate public support for taxing inheritances in the first place.

References

Alstott, Anne L. 1996. "The Uneasy Liberal Case against Income and Wealth Transfer Taxation: A Response to Professor McCaffery." *Tax Law Review* 51: 363–402.

———. 2007. "Equal Opportunity and Inheritance Taxation." *Harvard Law Review* 121: 469–542.

Altonji, Joseph G., Fumio Hayashi, and Laurence J. Kotlikoff. 1992. "Is the Extended Family Altruistically Linked? Direct Tests Using Micro Data." *American Economic Review* 82, no. 5: 1177–98.

Andrews, William D. 1967. "The Accessions Tax Proposal." *Tax Law Review* 22: 589–633.

Ascher, Mark L. 1990. "Curtailing Inherited Wealth." *Michigan Law Review* 89: 69–151.

Batchelder, Lily L. 2008. "How Should an Ideal Consumption Tax or Income Tax Treat Wealth Transfers?" Colloquium Series on Tax Policy and Public Finance, New York University, January 17.

Batchelder, Lily L., Fred T. Goldberg Jr., and Peter R. Orszag. 2006. "Efficiency and Tax Incentives: The Case for Refundable Tax Credits." *Stanford Law Review* 59, no. 1: 23–76.

Batchelder, Lily L., and Surachai Khitatrakun. 2008. "Dead or Alive: An Investigation of the Incidence of Estate versus Inheritance Taxes." Annual meeting of American Law and Economics Association, May 16.

Benson, E. J. 1971. *Summary of 1971 Tax Reform Legislation 31*. Ottawa, Canada: Department of Finance.

Bernheim, B. Douglas. 1991. "How Strong Are Bequest Motives? Evidence Based on Estimates of the Demand for Life Insurance and Annuities." *Journal of Political Economy* 99, no. 5: 899–927.

Bird, Richard M. 1978. "Canada's Vanishing Death Taxes." *Osgoode Hall Law Journal* 16, no. 1: 133–45.

Bittker, Boris, and George K. Rahdert. 1976. "The Exemption of Nonprofit Organizations from Federal Income Taxation." *Yale Law Journal* 85, no. 3: 299–358.

Bloom, Nick, and John Van Reenen. 2006. "Measuring and Explaining Management Practices across Firms and Countries." Working Paper 12216. Cambridge, Mass.: National Bureau of Economic Research (May).

Boskin, Michael J. 1977. "An Economist's Perspective on Estate Taxation." In *Death, Taxes and Family Property,* edited by Edward C. Halbach, p. 56. St. Paul, Minn.: West Publishing.

Brown, Jeffrey R., Courtney Coile, and Scott J. Weisbenner. 2006. "The Effect of Inheritance Receipt on Retirement." Working Paper 12386. Cambridge, Mass.: National Bureau of Economic Research (July).

Congressional Budget Office. 2000. *Budget Options 2000.*

———. 2007. *Historical Effective Federal Tax Rates: 1979 to 2005.*

Davies, James B., and John Whalley. 1991. "Taxes and Capital Formation: How Important Is Human Capital?" In *National Saving and Economic Performance,* edited by B. Douglas Bernheim and John B. Shoven, pp. 163–200. University of Chicago Press.

Dodge, Joseph M. 1978. "Beyond Estate and Gift Tax Reform: Including Gifts and Bequests in Income." *Harvard Law Review* 91: 1177–1211.

———. 2003. "Comparing a Reformed Estate Tax with an Accessions Tax and an Income Inclusion System and Abandoning the GST." *Southern Methodist University Law Review* 56: 551.

Duff, David G. 1993. "Taxing Inherited Wealth: A Philosophical Argument." *Canadian Journal of Law and Jurisprudence* 6, no. 1: 3–62.

Eckel, Catherine C., and Philip J. Grossman. 2003. "Rebate versus Matching: Does How We Subsidize Charitable Contributions Matter?" *Journal of Public Economics* 87, no. 3–4: 681–701.

Edlin, Aaron S. 2005. "The Choose-Your-Charity Tax: A Way to Incentivize Greater Giving." *Economists' Voice* 2, no. 3: article 3 (works.bepress.com/cgi/viewcontent.cgi?article=1045&context=aaron_edlin).

Finkelstein, Amy. 2007. "E-ZTax: Tax Salience and Tax Rates." Working Paper 12924. Cambridge, Mass.: National Bureau of Economic Research (February).

Friedman, Joel, and Aviva Aron-Dine. 2006. "New Joint Tax Committee Estimates Show Modified Kyl Proposal Still Very Costly." Washington: Center on Budget and Policy Priorities (June 13).

Furman, Jason. 2006. "Two Wrongs Do Not Make a Right." *National Tax Journal* 59 (September): 491–508.

Gale, William G., and Maria G. Perozek. 2001. "Do Estate Taxes Reduce Saving?" In *Rethinking Estate and Gift Taxation*, edited by William G. Gale, James R. Hines Jr., and Joel Slemrod, pp. 216–247. Brookings.

Gale, William G., and Joel Slemrod. 2001. "Overview." In *Rethinking Estate and Gift Taxation*, edited by William G. Gale, James R. Hines Jr., and Joel Slemrod, pp. 1–64. Brookings.

Graetz, Michael J., and Ian Shapiro. 2005. *Death by a Thousand Cuts: The Fight over Taxing Inherited Wealth*. Princeton University Press.

Halperin, Daniel. 2002. "A Charitable Contribution of Appreciated Property and the Realization of Built-in Gains." *Tax Law Review* 56: 1.

Holtz-Eakin, Douglas. 1996. "The Uneasy Empirical Case for Abolishing the Estate Tax." *Tax Law Review* 51: 495, 511.

Holtz-Eakin, Douglas, David Joulfaian, and Harvey S. Rosen. 1993. "The Carnegie Conjecture: Some Empirical Evidence." *Quarterly Journal of Economics* 108 (May): 413–35.

Hull, Cordell. *Memoirs of Cordell Hull*. 1948. New York: Macmillan.

Hurd, Michael D. 1987. "Savings of the Elderly and Desired Bequests." *American Economic Review* 77, no. 3: 298–312.

Hurd, Michael D., and James P. Smith. 2002. "Expected Bequests and Their Distribution." Working Paper 9142. Cambridge, Mass.: National Bureau of Economic Research (September).

Jorgenson, Dale W., and Barbara M. Fraumeni. 1989. "The Accumulation of Human and Nonhuman Capital, 1948–84." In *The Measurement of Saving, Investment, and Wealth*, edited by Robert E. Lipsey and Helen Stone Tice, pp. 227–82. University of Chicago Press.

Joulfaian, David. 1994. "The Distribution and Division of Bequests: Evidence from the Collation Study." Paper 71. U.S. Treasury Department, Office of Tax Analysis (August).

———. 2000. "Estate Taxes and Charitable Bequests by the Wealthy." *National Tax Journal* 53 (September): 743–63.

———. 2006a. "Inheritance and Saving." Working Paper 12569. Cambridge, Mass.: National Bureau of Economic Research (October).

———. 2006b. "The Behavioral Response of Wealth Accumulation to Estate Taxation: Time Series Evidence." *National Tax Journal* 59 (June): 253–68.

Kaplow, Louis. 2001. "A Framework for Assessing Estate and Gift Taxation." In *Rethinking Estate and Gift Taxation*, edited by William G. Gale, James R. Hines, and Joel Slemrod, pp. 164–204. Brookings.

Kopczuk, Wojciech, and Joseph P. Lupton. 2007. "To Leave or Not to Leave: The Distribution of Bequest Motives." *Review of Economic Studies* 74, no. 1: 207–35.

Kopczuk, Wojciech, and Joel Slemrod. 2001. "The Impact of the Estate Tax on Wealth Accumulation and Avoidance Behavior." In *Rethinking Estate and Gift Taxation*, edited by William G. Gale, James R. Hines Jr., and Joel Slemrod, pp. 299–343. Brookings.

Laitner, John, and F. Thomas Juster. 1996. "New Evidence on Altruism: A Study of TIAA-CREF Retirees." *American Economic Review* 86, no. 4: 893–908.

Landsberger, Michael. 1971. "Consumer Discount Rate and the Horizon: New Evidence." *Journal of Political Economy* 79, no. 6: 1346–59.

McCaffery, Edward J. 1994. "The Uneasy Case for Wealth Transfer Taxation." *Yale Law Journal* 104, no. 2: 283–365.

McDaniel, Paul R., James R. Repetti, and Paul R. Caron. 2003. *Federal Wealth Transfer Taxation*. 5th ed. New York: Foundation Press.

McGarry, Kathleen. 2000. "Inter Vivos Transfers or Bequests? Estate Taxes and the Timing of Parental Giving." *Tax Policy and the Economy* 14: 93–121.

Morck, Randall K., David A. Strangeland, and Bernard Yeung. 2000. "Inherited Wealth, Corporate Control, and Economic Growth: The Canadian Disease?" In *Concentrated Corporate Ownership*, edited by Randall K. Morck, pp. 319–69. University of Chicago Press.

Murphy, Liam, and Thomas Nagel. 2002. *The Myth of Ownership: Taxes and Justice*. New York: Oxford University Press.

Office of Management and Budget. 2000. *Historical Tables, Budget of the United States Government, FY 2001*. Government Printing Office.

———. 2008. *Historical Tables, Budget of the United States Government, FY2009* Government Printing Office.

Page, Benjamin R. 2003. "Bequest Taxes, Inter Vivos Gifts, and the Bequest Motive." *Journal of Public Economics* 87 (May): 1219–29.

Poterba, James, and Scott Weisbenner. 2001. "The Distributional Burden of Taxing Estates and Unrealized Capital Gains at Death." In *Rethinking Estate and Gift Taxation*, edited by William G. Gale, James R. Hines Jr., and Joel Slemrod, pp. 422–49. Brookings.

Ratner, Sidney. 1967. *Taxation and Democracy in the United States*. New York: Wiley.

Roosevelt, Franklin D. 1938. "Message to the Congress on Tax Revision (June 19, 1935)." *Public Papers and Addresses of Franklin D. Roosevelt*. Vol. 4. New York: Random House.

Rudick, Harry J. 1950. "What Alternative to the Estate and Gift Taxes?" *California Law Review* 38: 150.

Schervish, Paul, and John Havens. 2003. "Gifts and Bequests: Family or Philanthropic Organizations?" In *Death and Dollars: The Role of Gifts and Bequests in America*, edited by Alicia H. Munnell and Annika Sundén, pp. 130–58. Brookings.

Simons, Henry C. 1938. *Personal Income Taxation*. University of Chicago Press.

Stiglitz, Joseph E. 1978. "Notes on Estate Taxes, Redistribution, and the Concept of Balanced Growth Path Incidence." *Journal of Political Economy* 86 (April): S137–50.

Tocqueville, Alexis de. [1835] 1945. *Democracy in America [De la démocratie en Amérique]*. Translated by Henry Reeve. New York: Alfred Knopf.

U.S. House of Representatives. Committee on Ways and Means. 1916. *To Increase the Revenue, and for Other Purposes*. Report 64-922. 64 Cong. 1 sess.

Yablon, Robert. 2006. "Defying Expectations: Assessing the Surprising Resilience of State Death Taxes." *Tax Lawyer* 59 (Fall): 241.

Contributors

ROGER C. ALTMAN has served since 1996 as chairman and co–chief executive officer of Evercore Partners, currently the most active investment banking boutique in the world. Altman served two tours of duty in the U.S. Treasury Department, initially under President Carter as assistant secretary for domestic finance and later under President Clinton as deputy secretary. Previously he was vice chairman of the Blackstone Group and responsible for its investment banking business. Altman is a trustee of New York–Presbyterian Hospital, serving on its Investment Committee, and also is vice chairman of the board of the American Museum of Natural History. He is a trustee of New Visions for Public Schools and is a member of the Council on Foreign Relations. He received an A.B. from Georgetown University and an M.B.A. from the University of Chicago.

REUVEN S. AVI-YONAH is the Irwin I. Cohn professor of law at the University of Michigan Law School and director of the International Tax LL.M. program. He specializes in international taxation and international law, and is widely published in these subject areas. Avi-Yonah has been a visiting professor of law at the University of Michigan, New York University, and the University of Pennsylvania, and has also served as an assistant professor of law at Harvard and as an assistant professor of history at Boston College. In addition, he has practiced law with Milbank, Tweed, Hadley and McCloy, New York; Wachtell, Lipton, Rosen, and Katz, New

York; and Ropes and Gray, Boston. Avi-Yonah earned his B.A., summa cum laude, from Hebrew University and then earned three degrees from Harvard: an A.M. in history, a Ph.D. in history, and a J.D., magna cum laude, from Harvard Law School.

LILY L. BATCHELDER is associate professor of law and public policy at the New York University School of Law. Her research focuses on income taxation, wealth transfer taxation, income volatility, and social insurance. Before joining the NYU faculty, Batchelder practiced at Skadden, Arps, Slate, Meagher, and Flom, where her practice focused on transactional and tax policy matters. In addition, she previously served as a fellow at the Wiener Center on Social Policy at the John F. Kennedy School of Government, and as a client advocate for a small social services agency in Brooklyn, New York. Batchelder is a member of the National Academy of Social Insurance. She received her J.D. from Yale Law School, her master's of public policy from the John F. Kennedy School of Government, and her A.B. from Stanford University.

JASON E. BORDOFF is policy director of The Hamilton Project and has written on a broad range of topics concerning economic growth and economic security. He is also a term member of the Council on Foreign Relations. Bordoff previously served as special assistant to Deputy Secretary Stuart E. Eizenstat at the U.S. Treasury Department and worked as a consultant for McKinsey and Company in New York. He graduated with honors from Harvard Law School, where he was treasurer and an editor of the *Harvard Law Review*, and clerked on the U.S. Court of Appeals for the D.C. Circuit. He also holds an MLitt degree from Oxford University, where he studied as a Marshall scholar, and a B.A., magna cum laude and Phi Beta Kappa, from Brown University.

KIMBERLY A. CLAUSING is a professor of economics at Reed College. Her research focuses on the taxation of multinational firms, exploring how international tax incentives affect international trade, government revenues, and the location of economic activity. Recently she has worked on related policy research with the Brookings Institution and the Tax Policy Center. During 2006–07 she was an associate professor of economics at Wellesley College. From 1999 to 2000 Clausing was a Fulbright research scholar in Brussels, Belgium. During 1994–95 she worked at the Council of Economic Advisers as a staff economist specializing in international economic policy. She received her B.A. from Carleton College in 1991 and her Ph.D. from Harvard University.

SUSAN M. DYNARSKI, associate professor of public policy at Harvard University, studies and teaches the economics of education and tax policy. She has been a faculty research fellow at the National Bureau of Economic Research since 1999 and a visiting fellow at Princeton University. Dynarski has a special interest in the interaction of inequality and education, and has studied the impact of grants and loans on college attendance, the impact of state policy on college completion rates, and the distributional aspects of college saving incentives. She has testified on her research to the U.S. Senate and the President's Commission on Tax Reform. Her research has been published in academic and policy journals, as well as featured in the popular media. Dynarski holds an A.B. in social studies from Harvard College, a master's in public policy from the Kennedy School of Government at Harvard University, and a Ph.D. in economics from the Massachusetts Institute of Technology.

RICHARD B. FREEMAN is the Ascherman professor of economics at Harvard University, codirector of the Labor and Worklife program at Harvard Law School, and director of the Labor Studies program at the National Bureau of Economic Research. Freeman is a member of the American Academy of Arts and Sciences and is an affiliated scholar of the Center for the Advancement of Scholarship on Engineering Education at the National Academy of Engineering. Freeman served on the Committee on Policy Implications of International Graduate Students and Postdoctoral Scholars in the United States. He has published over 400 articles dealing with a wide range of research topics including the job market for scientists and engineers, and income distribution and equity in the marketplace. He is currently directing (with Daniel Goroff) the National Bureau of Economic Research–Sloan Science Engineering Workforce project and a London School of Economics research program on the effects of the Internet on labor markets, social behavior, and the economy.

JASON FURMAN is a senior fellow in the Economic Studies program (currently on leave) and was formerly director of The Hamilton Project at the Brookings Institution. Furman previously served in the Clinton administration as special assistant to the president for economic policy. Earlier in the administration, Furman served as staff economist at the Council of

Economic Advisers and as a senior director at the National Economic Council. He also served as senior economic adviser to the chief economist at the World Bank. Furman has been a visiting lecturer at Columbia and Yale Universities and was a visiting scholar at New York University's Wagner School of Graduate Public Service. He received his Ph.D. in economics from Harvard University.

WILLIAM G. GALE is vice president and director, Economic Studies program, and the Arjay and Frances Fearing Miller chair in federal economic policy at the Brookings Institution. He is the director of the Retirement Security project, a joint venture of Brookings and Georgetown University's Public Policy Institute. He is also codirector of the Tax Policy Center, a joint venture of the Urban Institute and Brookings. His areas of expertise include tax policy, budget and fiscal policy, public and private pensions, and saving behavior. Gale has written extensively in academic journals and popular outlets and is coeditor of *Rethinking Estate and Gift Taxation*; *Economic Effects of Fundamental Tax Reform*; *Private Pensions and Public Policies*; and *The Evolving Pension System: Trends, Effects, and Proposals for Reform*. He is coauthor of the forthcoming book *Taxing the Future: Fiscal Policy in the Bush Administration*. Before joining Brookings in 1992, Gale was an assistant professor in the department of economics at the University of California at Los Angeles and senior economist for the Council of Economic Advisers.

AUSTAN GOOLSBEE is the Robert P. Gwinn professor of economics at the University of Chicago Graduate School of Business. He is also a senior research fellow at the American Bar Foundation and a research associate at the National Bureau of Economic Research. His areas of expertise include tax policy, budget and fiscal policies, public and antitrust law, and the information economy. He is a Sloan research fellow and a Fulbright scholar, and has been named one of the 100 global leaders for tomorrow by the World Economic Forum in Switzerland. Previously Goolsbee served as a special consultant for Internet policy, Department of Justice, Antitrust Division, 2000–01; was lead editor of the *Journal of Law and Economics*, 2001–04; and was associate editor of *Law and Social Inquiry*, 1997–2001.

ROBERT GORDON is a senior vice president for economic policy at the Center for American Progress. He was the domestic policy director for the Kerry-Edwards campaign and the policy director for John Edwards when he was senator and during Edwards's presidential primary campaign. Gordon was previously a law clerk for Justice Ruth Bader Ginsburg, a Skadden fellow at the Juvenile Rights Division of the Legal Aid Society, and an aide at the National Economic Council during the Clinton administration. Gordon is a graduate of Yale Law School and Harvard College.

JONATHAN GRUBER is a professor of economics at the Massachusetts Institute of Technology, where he has taught since 1992. He is also the director of the Program on Children at the National Bureau of Economic Research, where he is a research associate. He is a coeditor of the *Journal of Public Economics* and an associate editor of the *Journal of Health Economics*. Gruber's research focuses on the areas of public finance and health economics. His recent areas of particular interest include the economics of employer-provided health insurance, the efficiency of the current system in delivering health care to the indigent, the effect of the Social Security program on retirement behavior, and the economics of smoking.

THOMAS J. KANE is professor of education and economics at the Harvard Graduate School of Education, and faculty director of a new research center partnering with school districts and states to analyze innovative policies. His work has had an impact on thinking about a range of education policies: test score volatility and the design of school accountability systems, teacher recruitment and retention, financial aid for college, race-conscious college admissions, and the economic payoff to a community college. From 1995 to 1996, Kane served as the senior staff economist for labor, education, and welfare policy issues within President Clinton's Council of Economic Advisers. From 1991 through 2000, he was a faculty member at the Kennedy School of Government. Kane has also been a professor of public policy at the University of California, Los Angeles, and has held visiting fellowships at the Brookings Institution and the Hoover Institution at Stanford University.

LORI G. KLETZER is professor of economics at the University of California, Santa Cruz, and a senior fellow at the Peterson Institute for International Economics. She has held teaching and research appointments at Williams College, the University of Washington, the Brookings Institution, and the Institute for International Economics. Her research focuses on the effects of globalization on the domestic labor market as well as on the causes and consequences of job displacement, job training, racial differences in the incidence of job loss, and the microeconomics of college choice, careers, and wages. Her publications appear in a number of professional journals, and she is the author of two books: *Job Loss from Imports: Measuring the Costs*, a study of the costs to workers of trade-related job loss; and *Imports, Exports, and Jobs: What Does Trade Mean for Employment and Job Loss?* She received her Ph.D. in economics from the University of California, Berkeley, and her B.A. from Vassar College.

JEFFREY R. KLING is deputy director and senior fellow in the Economic Studies program at the Brookings Institution, where he also serves as director of the Policy Evaluation project. Over the past ten years, he has led interdisciplinary teams of researchers in studies of housing vouchers and the effects of moving out of high-poverty neighborhoods, based on extensive data collection about experiences of families in HUD's Moving to Opportunity randomized voucher experiment. Kling has previously served as assistant professor of economics and public affairs in the department of economics and the Woodrow Wilson School at Princeton University, special assistant to the secretary at the U.S. Department of Labor, and assistant to the chief economist at the World Bank. He is a graduate of Harvard University, where he was elected Phi Beta Kappa with a B.A. in economics, and he holds a Ph.D. in economics from the Massachusetts Institute of Technology.

ALAN B. KRUEGER is the Bendheim professor of economics and public affairs at Princeton University. He has published widely on the economics of education, labor demand, income distribution, social insurance, labor market regulation, and environmental economics. Since 1987 he has held a joint appointment in the economics department and Woodrow Wilson School at Princeton. He is director of the Princeton University Survey Research Center and a research associate of the National Bureau of Economic Research. He is a member of the board of trustees of the Russell Sage Foundation and is on the board of directors of the American Institutes for Research. He was editor of the *Journal of Economic Perspectives* from 1996 to 2002. In 1994–95 he served as chief economist at the U.S. Department of Labor. He received a B.S. degree with honors from Cornell University, an A.M. in economics from Harvard University in 1985, and a Ph.D. in economics from Harvard University in 1987.

JENS LUDWIG is professor of public policy at Georgetown University; faculty research fellow at the National Bureau of Economic Research; and nonresident senior fellow at the Brookings Institution. Ludwig is a member of the editorial boards of *Criminology*, the *Journal of Quantitative Crimi-*

nology, and the *Journal of Policy Analysis and Management*. He has served as the Andrew Mellon visiting fellow in economic studies at the Brookings Institution, as a visiting scholar to the Northwestern University–University of Chicago Joint Center for Poverty Research, and as a visiting professor at the University of Chicago Law School. His coauthored paper on race, peer norms, and education was awarded the Vernon Prize for best article by the Association for Public Policy Analysis and Management (APPAM). In 2006 he was awarded APPAM's David Kershaw Prize for distinguished contributions to public policy by the age of forty. He received his Ph.D. in economics from Duke University.

MOLLY F. MCINTOSH is a Ph.D. candidate in the economics department at Princeton University. Her research fields are labor economics and public finance. Before coming to Princeton University, McIntosh worked for two years as a research assistant for Isabel Sawhill and Gary Burtless at the Brookings Institution. She earned her bachelor's degree in economics from the University of California–Berkeley in May of 2001.

PETER R. ORSZAG is the seventh director of the Congressional Budget Office (CBO). His four-year term began on January 18, 2007. Before joining the CBO, Orszag was the Joseph A. Pechman senior fellow and deputy director of the Economic Studies program at the Brookings Institution. While at Brookings, he also served as director of The Hamilton Project. In previous government service during 1997 and 1998, Orszag served as special assistant to the president for economic policy and as senior economic adviser at the National Economic Council. His main areas of research have been pensions, Social Security, budget policy, higher education policy, homeland security, macroeconomics, and tax policy—topics on which he has published widely in academic journals. Orszag graduated summa cum laude in economics from Princeton University and obtained an M.Sc. and a Ph.D. in economics from the London School of Economics, which he attended as a Marshall scholar.

HOWARD ROSEN is executive director of the Trade Adjustment Assistance Coalition, which advocates on behalf of workers and communities experiencing dislocations due to changes in international trade and investment. In 2001 he helped draft provisions included in the Trade Act of 2002 that significantly expanded the Trade Adjustment Assistance program. He is also currently a visiting fellow at the Peterson Institute for International Economics. Rosen served as minority staff director of the Joint Economic

Committee of Congress, executive director of the Competitiveness Policy Council, research associate and later assistant director of the Institute for International Economics, and economist at the U.S. Department of Labor. Rosen has written extensively on issues relating to international trade, macroeconomic policies, and labor market adjustment. He received his B.A. and M.A. in economics from George Washington University, where he concentrated on international economics.

ROBERT E. RUBIN joined the Clinton administration on 1993, serving in the White House as assistant to the president for economic policy and as the first director of the National Economic Council. He served as the seventieth secretary of the treasury from January 10, 1995, until July 2, 1999. He joined Citigroup on October 26, 1999, as director and chairman of the Executive Committee, and also serves as chairman of the board of the Local Initiatives Support Corporation, the nation's leading community development support organization. He also serves on the board of trustees of Mount Sinai–NYU Health and is a member of the Harvard Corporation. In June 2007 he was named cochairman of the Council on Foreign Relations.

ISABEL SAWHILL is Cabot Family chair and senior fellow in the Economic Studies program at the Brookings Institution, where she also serves as codirector of the Center on Children and Families. Sawhill was vice president and director of the Economic Studies program from 2003 to 2006. She is the author and editor of numerous books and articles, including two volumes of *Restoring Fiscal Sanity*, with Alice Rivlin; *One Percent for the Kids: New Policies, Brighter Futures for America's Children*; *Welfare Reform and Beyond: The Future of the Safety Net*, with R. Kent Weaver, Andrea Kane, and Ron Haskins; *Updating the Social Contract: Growth and Opportunity in the New Century*, with Rudolph Penner and Timothy Taylor; and *Getting Ahead: Economic and Social Mobility in America*, with Daniel P. McMurrer. Sawhill serves on various boards and was an associate director of the Office of Management and Budget from 1993 to 1995. She currently serves as president of the National Campaign to Prevent Teen Pregnancy.

JUDITH E. SCOTT-CLAYTON is a doctoral candidate in public policy at Harvard University's Kennedy School of Government, where her primary research fields are labor economics and public finance. Her current research focuses on the economics of higher education and its role in addressing or exacerbating inequalities in educational attainment and labor market outcomes. With Susan Dynarski she has examined the equity and efficiency costs of complexity in the federal system for student financial aid, and has proposed strategies for simplification. Her other research examines the causes and consequences of a large increase over the past thirty years in the amount of time college students spend working while still enrolled in school. Her academic study is funded by a National Science Foundation graduate research fellowship. Judith graduated summa cum laude from Wellesley College in 2000.

DOUGLAS O. STAIGER is a professor of economics at Dartmouth College and a research associate of the National Bureau of Economic Research. Staiger's work focuses on school accountability, the quality of medical care, and the labor market for nurses.

Index